China Now

China Now

An introductory survey with readings

Edited by

D. J. Dwyer BA, PhD (London)

Professor of Geography and Head of the Department of Geography and Geology, University of Hong Kong

Longman
1724-1974

LONGMAN GROUP LIMITED
Burnt Mill
Harlow
Essex CM20 2JE

Distributed in the United States of America
by Longman Inc., New York

*Associated companies, branches and representatives
throughout the world*

© Longman Group Limited, 1974

First published 1974

ISBN 0 582 48076 0   Paper
ISBN 0 582 48075 2   Cased
Library of Congress Catalog Card Number: 73—87225

Printed in Great Britain by
Whitstable Litho Ltd, Kent.

Acknowledgements

We are grateful to the following for permission to reproduce copyright material:
George Allen & Unwin Ltd, Beacon Press and Farrar, Straus & Giroux, Inc. for an extract from 'The Old Industrial Order' from *Land and Labour in China (1932)* by R. H. Tawney. Reproduced by permission of the Publishers; American Geographical Society for an extract from 'The Fenghsien Landscape: A Fragment of the Yangtse Delta' by George B. Cressey from *Geographical Review*, Vol. 26, No. 3, July 1936, pp. 396–413, an extract from 'Shanghai' by John E. Orchard from *Geographical Review*, Vol. 26, No. 1, January 1936, pp. 1–29 and an extract from 'The Changing Railroad Pattern in Mainland China' by Kuei-Sheng Chang from *Geographical Review*, Vol. 51, No. 4, October 1961, pp. 534–48; Association of American Geographers for an extract from 'The City as a centre of change' by Rhoads Murphey from *Annals of the Association of American Geographers*, Vol. 44, 1954, and an extract from 'The historical and geographical role of Urumchi, capital of Chinese Central Asia' from *Annals of the Association of American Geographers*, Vol. 53, 1963. Reproduced by permission; the author for the article 'The million city of mainland China' by Sen Dou Chang from *Pacific Viewpoint*, No. 9, 1968; United States Central Intelligence Agency for a table prepared by the Agency from *People's Republic of China Atlas 1971*, p. 69; the author and University of California Press for an extract from 'Economic Aftermath of the Great Leap in Communist China' by Kang Chao from *Asian Survey*, Vol. 4, No. 5, May 1964. © 1964 by The Regents of the University of California. Reprinted by permission of The Regents; The Clarendon Press for an extract from *China: The Land and the People* by L. H. Dudley Buxton, 1929, pp. 61–5; Congress of the United States Joint Economic Committee for an extract from 'Population Policy and Demographic Prospects in the People's Republic of China' by John S. Aird from *People's Republic of China: An Economic Assessment*; Current Scene for an extract from 'China as a trading nation' by Audrey Donnithorne from *Current Scene*, Vol. 10, No. 2, 1972, and extract from 'Mao Tse Tung's Goals and China's Economic Performance' by Dwight H. Perkins from *Current Scene*, Vol. 9, No. 1, 1971, an extract from 'The Maoist Revolutionary Model in Asia' by John J.

v

Acknowledgements

Taylor from *Current Scene*, Vol. 9, No. 3, 1971 and an extract from 'The Changing Pattern of U.S. — China Relations' by A. Doak Barnett from *Current Scene*, Vol. 10, No. 4, 1972; Geographical Association for an extract from 'China's Natural Calamities and their Consequences' by D. J. Dwyer from *Geography*, Vol. 47, 1962, and the article 'Sinjao: A Chinese Commune' by John Rose from *Geography*, Vol. 51, 1966; China Quarterly for an extract from 'Eyewitness of the Cultural Revolution' from *China Quarterly*, No. 27, October/December 1966, and the article 'A Review of China's Economy in 1970' by W. Klatt from *China Quarterly*, No. 43, July/September 1970; McGraw-Hill Book Company for a table modified from *Land of the 500 Million* by G. B. Cressey. Copyright © 1955 by McGraw-Hill, Inc. Used with permission of McGraw-Hill Book Company; Methuen & Company Ltd and Current Scene for a table based on a table by M. Freeberne in 'The Changing Map of Asia' from *The Changing Map of Asia* edited by W. G. East *et al* and a table by S. Washenko in 'Agriculture in China' from *Current Scene*, Vol. 9, 1971; Alfred A. Knopf, Inc., and Oxford University Press for figures compiled from *China: New Age and New Outlook*, by Ping-chia Kuo and *The Economic Development of Communist China* by T. J. Hughes and D. E. T. Luard. Published by Oxford University Press under the auspices of the Royal Institute of International Affairs. Reprinted by permission of the publishers; the Authors and Royal Geographical Society for an extract from 'The Coal Industry in Mainland China since 1949' by D. J. Dwyer from *Geographical Journal*, Vol. 129, 1963, and an extract from 'Containing China?' by C. A. Fisher from *Geographical Journal*, Vol. 137, 1971, and The University of Chicago Press for extracts from 'Luts'un: A Yünnan Village' by Hsiao Tung Fei and Chih I Chang from *Earthbound China*, 1945, published by The University of Chicago Press. Reproduced by permission of the Publisher.

We are also grateful to the following for permission to reproduce maps and figures:
The Controller of Her Majesty's Stationery Office for Figure 6 from *China Proper* (published by the Naval Intelligence Division of the Admiralty), Vol. 1, 1944, p. 19; the Aldine Publishing Company for Maps I and II from *An Historical Atlas of China*, A. Hermann, 1966, pp. 2 and 3; the Royal Geographical Society and the author for Figure 2 from 'Containing China?' by C. A. Fisher, *Geographical Journal*, Vol. 137, 1971, p. 288; Universe Books for a figure from *The Limits of Growth*, by D. H. and D. L. Meadows, J. Randers and W. W. Behrens III. A Potomac Associates book published by Universe Books, New York, 1972; Current Scene for five figures from *Current Scene*, Vol. 8, No. 17, September 1969.

Contents

Contents

Contents

Contents

Introduction

The aim of *China Now* is to review the basic aspects of the development of modern China in a simplified manner, for introductory courses on China itself, the Far East or Asia generally, in colleges and universities. It is hoped that the volume may also prove suitable as a general introduction to modern China for the intelligent layman.

The Survey covers in an integrated fashion selected geographical, historical, socio-economic and political character-istics important to the understanding of presentday China; it also serves to introduce the Readings, which are inter-disciplinary in selection and broadly consecutive in arrange-ment. The Readings include selections from the work of many of the best-known students of China's development. Emphasis has been placed in them upon (*a*) the geographical, historical and socio-economic background to the Communist period, (*b*) Communist policies and the dimensions of pro-gress in socio-economic development since 1949, and (*c*) China's foreign relations, including the recent *détente* with the United States. A list of recommended further reading concludes the volume.

A word is perhaps necessary about the rendering of Chinese place names in the text. In the Readings I have left these as they appeared in the original, while in my own Survey I have adopted current English usage for the sake of simplicity rather than followed any one of the more scientific systems of transliteration.

D. J. DWYER

Hong Kong
May 1973

Survey

The rise of the Communists to power is no isolated event. Certainly it is not merely the work of a group of revolutionary extremists. Its roots reach far back into the structure of the old society, the abuses of government, the inequalities and miseries suffered by the people, and a widespread demand for change.

PING CHIA KUO*

China is a country of immense size, both in area and in population. Stretching from latitude 18°N to latitude 54°N and from longitude 74°E to 135°E, and covering 9.3 m sq km (3.6 m sq miles), China is the third largest country in the world, after the USSR 22.5 m sq km (8.7 m sq miles) and Canada 9.8 m sq km (3.8 m sq miles). China is slightly larger in area than the USA. Unfortunately much of China's vast territory is agriculturally useless, for in the west especially it consists of high mountains, deserts and barren, windswept plateaux. The fact that relatively little of China can be cultivated — agriculture and population are intensely concentrated into basins and plains occupying less than one-fifth of the entire area — and that the major cultivable areas are found in the east rather than in the west (Fig. 0.1), has shaped the spatial pattern of China's development. This has especially been the case since the early eighteenth century, when China's population began to increase rapidly after a lengthy period of stability and to concentrate alarmingly in certain restricted areas capable of intensive cultivation (Fig. 0.2), and when China also came under the influence of expansionist colonial powers whose major avenue of advance was from the eastern seaboard.

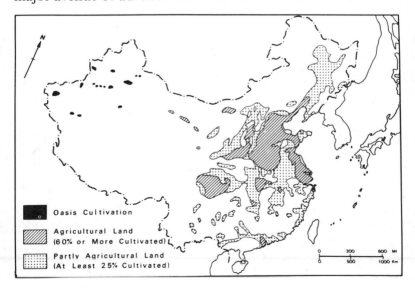

Fig. 0.1 China's agricultural land

3

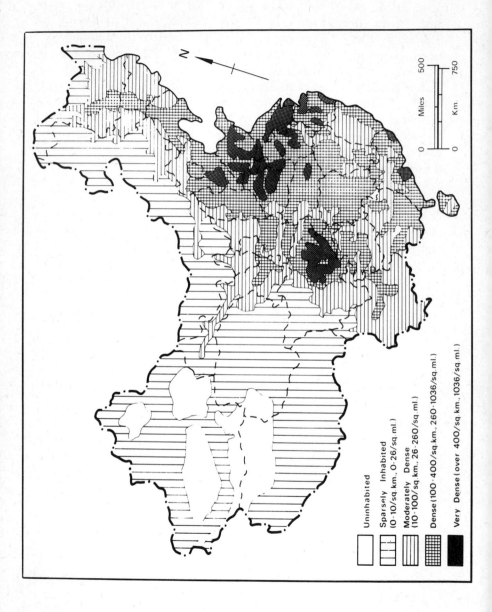

Fig. 0.2 Distribution of population

The land surface

In general, the physique of China is elevated in the west and falls gradually towards the Pacific Ocean (Fig. 0.3). Physically, China descends eastwards from the high interior of Tibet and Mongolia by means of a discontinuous series of steps; but a major exception in the west is the important basin of Szechuan.* This densely peopled area, with the city of Chungking its regional focus, is an old lake basin lying between the high mountains of western China to the north and the elevated Yunan plateau to the south. Its principal connection with the other densely populated parts of China, from which it is relatively isolated, is eastwards through a series of spectacular gorges cut by the Yangtse river. The lofty highlands in the west of China are relatively recent in the geological sense; it is the hilly coastal belt which comprises southeast China and the Shantung peninsula which represents the oldest geological remnants. These now worn-down areas are thought to have once been part of an ancient continent called Cathaysia, which occupied much of the area between presentday China and Japan. Immediately to the west of the Cathaysian remnants, before the mountains of the west are reached, is a great structural trough or series of depressions running from northeast to southwest. This includes the Manchurian and the North China Plains, the central basin of the Yangtse and the wide valley of the Siang river further to the south.

The simplest physical division of China is into three major segments bounded by three west—east fold zones which are continuations of the intensely folded mountain chains of Tibet. The most important of these fold zones is that of the Tsinling Shan, which has been called 'the most impressive and decisive divide in all China' [1]. Generally over 2 440 metres (8 000 ft) and at least 160 km (100 miles) in width, the Tsinling Shan constitutes a very real barrier between north and south as far east as the headwaters of the relatively short Hwai river. It is China's most important climatic and vegetational divide, the area to the north of it being a subhumid environment, while to the south rainfall is usually adequate.

* The use of a good atlas map of China in conjunction with this survey is recommended.

5

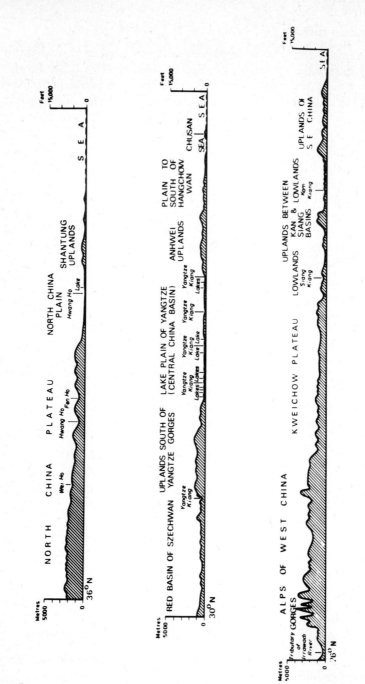

Fig. 0.3 Sections across China from west to east

Although lower and easier to cross, in some senses the Hwai-yang Shan, south of the Hwai, can be looked upon as a continuation of the Tsinling Shan. The Tsinling–Hwaiyang line forms the divide between the great northern plain of China and the central Yangtse basin. It is the fundamental agricultural divide between the north and the south which Dudley Buxton describes in the second of the readings (p. 67).

Stretching east from the high tableland of southwest China is the Nanling, a belt of hilly country between the Yangtse and the Si Kiang. Again, this west–east fold zone is an important climatic divide, for to the south of it is the only part of China that has virtually tropical conditions all year. The third of the major west–east divides is the In Shan, though this fold belt is known by a variety of names in its different parts. The eastern extension of the In Shan helps to define the northern narrowing of the North China Plain and to separate it from the Manchurian plains to the northeast. Further west, as a border chain, it separates the North China Plain from the Mongolian plateau, and it also clearly dictates the alignment of the west–east section of the famous northern 'big bend' or loop of the Hwang Ho around the Ordos plateau. In general, it may be said to demarcate China proper from Manchuria and Mongolia.

The great rivers

These three major fold axes have had marked effects upon the courses of China's three great rivers, the Hwang, the Yangtse and the Si, which together gather all but a very small proportion of the internal drainage of the country. The Hwang Ho shows this relationship most clearly, especially in its great loop between the northern barrier of the In Shan and the southern one of the Tsinling Shan after it leaves the Tibetan highlands.

From its source at the Tsaring lake in Tibet to the sea, the Hwang Ho covers nearly 4 850 km (3 000 miles). It runs through tremendous ravines in the western mountains and then cuts into relatively lower country by means of the Liuchia gorge above the city of Lanchow. At Lanchow, the big northward bend begins around the arid Ordos plateau, an ancient geological block. The Hwang Ho runs north for 805 km (500 miles), then east under the rim of the In Shan for another 325 km (200 miles). The valley is broad and mature, with many deserted meanders, some over 100 km away from its present course, and in parts there is rich, irrigated agriculture.

When the river bends south its character changes abruptly. It falls swiftly, with many rapids, in a narrow, immature trough between the provinces of Shansi and Shensi. Here, and in the southern half of its great bend generally, the river is flowing through a region of loess deposits which have given a characteristic stamp both to the landscape and to the settlement and economy of this part of China. The loess, or yellow earth, is a superficial, windblown deposit of great depth, originally derived from Mongolia during the Pleistocene period. It sustains only a rather bare treeless landscape, though it is a fertile soil wherever water can be supplied in sufficient quantities. It is also highly susceptible to erosion and for this reason the loessland is one of China's major problem agricultural areas. It is also, perhaps, China's most unique landscape. As one observer has put it,

> The world . . . seems to be made of one material — loess: the soil is loess; houses are made of pounded loess bricks or dug out of loess; roads are tracks sunken in loess; vegetation is coated with loess, and the blueness of the sky itself is compromised by yellow veils of loess [2].

At Tungkwan, the Hwang Ho is diverted abruptly to the east by the barrier of the Tsinling Shan and it takes on the direction of the Wei Ho, a major tributary which joins it from the west. The valley widens and the river emerges on to the North China Plain at Kaifeng. It is because of disastrous flooding in this lower section, plus the various channels it has shifted to in crossing the plain, that the Hwang Ho has become known as 'China's sorrow'. In its wanderings across the plain, from mouths well to the north of Tientsin to ones as far south as the present mouth of the Hwai river, historically the Hwang Ho has posed an unanswered challenge to the orderly development of agriculture in the North China Plain.

Chinese civilization is thought to have originated in an area

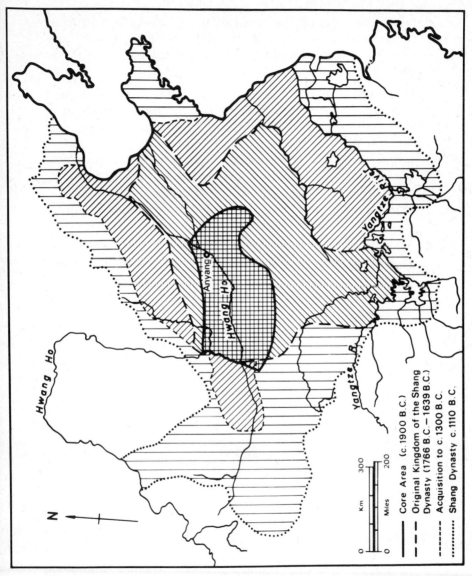

Fig. 0.4 The cradle area of the Chinese state

around the lower-middle course of the Hwang Ho immediately to the west of Kaifeng (Fig. 0.4). Penetration south by the Han Chinese followed, towards the Yangtse. Later, Han colonization reached the basin of the Si Kiang; but in more modern times the most decisive role in the growth and unity of the state has undoubtedly been played by the Yangtse basin:

> It would be hard to imagine for any country a more magnificent arterial highway than the main stream of the Yangtse provides for China from the borders of Tibet to the eastern sea, and its great navigable tributaries, themselves comparable in size to the largest of European rivers, provide a wonderful network of waterways linking north and south to the central corridor. It is this, more than any other single geographical factor, which has made possible the growth and consolidation of so vast a cultural and political entity as China [3].

The Yangtse rises in Tibet at a height of some 4 900 metres (16 000 ft) and flows 5 150 km (3 200 miles) to the sea. A characteristic feature of its upper course is the series of deep gorges in which it flows south parallel and close to the upper reaches of several of the major rivers of southeast Asia, notably the Mekong, the Salween and the Irrawaddy. This is in conformity with the north—south trend of the relief in this part of the Tibetan borderland. At Shihku, however, the Yangtse makes an abrupt bend to the northeast. It then turns east and after some distance enters the famous Red Basin of Szechuan, which is so called from the characteristic colour of its fertile soils. This is a densely peopled and intensively cultivated area, and the Yangtse flows through it as a broad navigable stream which receives many important tributaries, themselves navigable. It is thus both a major source of water for irrigation and the most important artery of an indispensable system of local water communications. Chungking itself, the basin's principal city, is not only a marketing, administrative, and more lately an industrial centre, but also an important river port for connections along the river eastwards to Shanghai.

The Yangtse leaves the Red Basin by means of series of gorges between Wanhsien and Ichang. Below Ichang it enters its huge central basin, which is an alluvial lowland studded with thousands of lakes large and small. In many senses this is the heart of China. Not only is it densely peopled and highly important agriculturally but it also contains the large Wuhan industrial node, which is composed of three important cities, Hankow, Wuchang and Hanyang.

The largest of the lakes is the Tungting lake. The lakes are important not only for water supply for the intensive agriculture which characterizes the basin but also because they act as regulating reservoirs in times of flood, though, like the Hwang Ho, the Yangtse has regularly brought sorrow in the form of extensive flooding both to this basin and to the lower parts of its course. South of Tungting lake, there is an easy natural corridor to Canton via the valley of the Siang river, while the centrality of this vital part of China is further enhanced by the fact that at Hankow the Yangtse is joined from the north by another important tributary, the Han, which is a major route from central China to the northwest.

After leaving the central basin, the Yangtse flows through hilly country until it reaches Nanking, the former capital of China under the Kuomintang government, which marks the apex of its delta. The delta is a great bay filled with the vast load of sediment brought down by the river over the years. It has been calculated that the Yangtse delta grows 1 mile seawards every seventy years [4], and certainly in the delta there are now some of the most densely peopled areas of China which were little more than sandbanks in the bay about 1 000 years ago. The whole area is crisscrossed with the maze of channels and irrigation ditches, vital for the dense farming population of the area, which is described by Cressey in his paper in this book on population and agriculture in the Yangtse delta. At the edge of the delta, commanding the whole basin of this great river, stands Shanghai, China's largest city.

The Si Kiang originates in the high plateaux of Yunnan and Kweichow and, though its basin is much more restricted in area than those of the Yangtse and the Hwang Ho, it is of an agricultural importance greater than its size would indicate because its lower parts enjoy a tropical climate and thus a year-long growing season. The valleys of the main river and its principal tributaries are relatively narrow, and there are

11

only minor inland basins such as the one around Tsangwu; but its delta is by far the largest focus of population in south China. This densely peopled delta is the work of two other streams besides the Si Kiang, the Si Kiang itself keeping to the western margin. A branch of the Si Kiang in the delta forms the well-known Pearl river, and it is on this distributary that the city of Canton is situated.

(Climate)

China's vast size is mirrored by the great variety of its climates but within this variety there are two major controlling elements. The first is that China is situated on the eastern fringe of the largest land mass in the world. Thus continental influences are almost everywhere much stronger than maritime ones. This is particularly apparent in temperature patterns (Fig. 0.5). Secondly, all China's many climatic types show some degree of monsoonal influence. This implies the reversal of winds between summer and winter.

The winter monsoon is characterized by largely dry, cold weather, with northerly or northwesterly winds blowing over China from the cold heart of Asia in Siberia and Mongolia. In summer, however, there is a general air flow into China from the south which, coming across adjacent seas, brings rainfall which diminishes in amount towards the north and the interior of the country (Fig. 0.6). Both the winter and the summer monsoons weaken markedly at the line of the Tsinling Shan and the Hwai river, and because of moisture deficiency further to the north, this is the limit of irrigated rice growing.

Basically, the monsoonal rhythm in China's climate results from the great contrast in thermal properties between the vast Asian land mass and its adjacent seas to the south. In winter the land cools relatively more quickly than the sea and becomes intensely cold; pressure over the land is therefore relatively high. At this season cool air moves outwards from the interior of the land mass. The situation is reversed during the summer months. The land mass heats up relatively quickly and pressure becomes low relative to that over the seas to the south. At this season relatively warm and moist air moves into China.

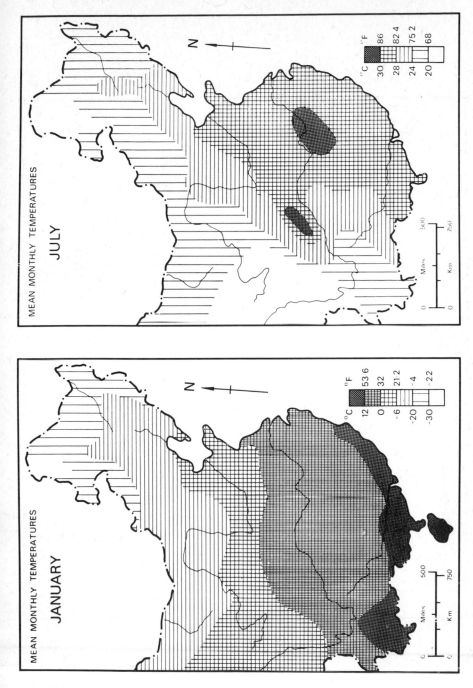

Fig. 0.5 Temperature patterns, January and July

13

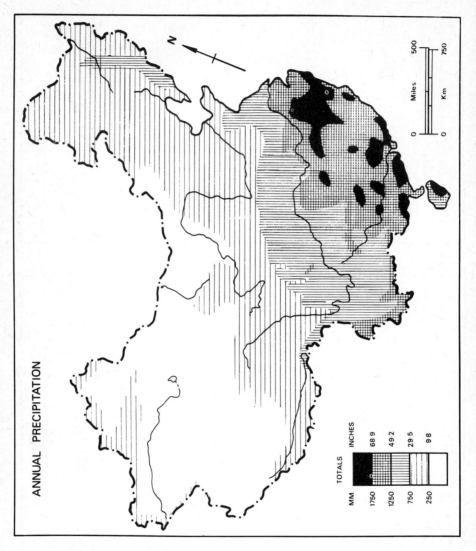

Fig. 0.6 Annual rainfall

This characterization of the monsoon is a very generalized one [5]. In reality, its mechanism is complex and there are many variations of type, some caused by non-monsoonal influences. In particular, depressions moving to the east are an irregular feature in some areas of central China during the winter. They bring much needed rain to parts of the Yangtse valley at this season, for example. Again, the heaviest rainfall is often associated with summer typhoons rather than with the monsoon itself. These violent storms usually arise in the Pacific near the Philippines, though a lesser number originate in the South China Sea. They are small but intense low pressure areas and more than half develop winds of hurricane force. If they move on to the south or east China coast, as some do almost every year, they may cause heavy damage and loss of life. Fortunately, as they move inland they quickly lose force and peter out.

Temperatures are extreme only in the far north and west of China. There is a rather small annual range of temperature in south China but in the north, in Manchuria, the range may be between five and six times as large as in the south. The climate of Manchuria is markedly continental. At the city of Pinkiang (formerly Harbin), in the heart of the great Manchurian plains, the temperature falls to an average of $-18°C$ $(-2°F)$ in the month of January but reaches an average of $22°C$ $(72°F)$ in July. Pinkiang's rainfall is 660 mm (26 in) a year, almost all of it concentrated into the summer months, as is common in China.

In the important North China Plain, at the northern end of which stands Peking, the range of temperature between summer and winter remains considerable. Peking's average monthly temperature for January is $-5°C$ $(23°F)$, and for July $26°C$ $(79°F)$, a range of $31°C$ $(56°F)$. Average temperatures are below freezing for three months. Peking's rainfall is 635 mm (25 in), again with a marked summer maximum, but as elsewhere in the Plain this modest total is highly variable from year to year, and as a result agricultural prospects are frequently uncertain.

Further south again, in the Yangtse valley, climatic conditions are less extreme, though there is a well-marked cool season from December to March. The coolest temperatures are recorded in the lower parts of the valley, especially in the delta, where dry continental winds sweeping from the north-west across the North China Plain may bring marked cold spells. Here there is no natural protection by mountains from northerly winds, whereas the central Yangtse basin is pro-tected to some extent by the Tsinling Shan and the Tapa Shan. Average January temperatures for Shanghai and Hankow reflect this, Shanghai's being slightly cooler at 3°C (38°F). The more inland position of Hankow results in higher summer temperatures, 26°C (80°F) as against Shanghai's 23°C (73°F) July mean. Both stations record similar annual rainfalls (Shanghai 1 143 mm (45 in); Hankow 1 220 mm (50 in)), again with summer maxima.

Within the Yangtse valley, indeed within China as a whole, the Red Basin of Szechuan is climatically unique. In the heart of China, climatic extremes are to be expected but here, if anything, the reverse is the case. Chungking's winter is rather warmer than that of Hankow, while its summer temperatures are very similar. This is because the hills surrounding the basin prevent the incursion of cold waves in winter. In addi-tion, the rainfall of the basin is better distributed throughout the year than that of other parts of the Yangtse valley. The combined result is a growing period of eleven months and a greater variety of agricultural products than any other part of China.

South of the Nan Shan, China may be characterized as subtropical and, further south, tropical. Canton has a January mean temperature of 13°C (56°F) and a July mean of 28°C (83°F). Rainfall is much heavier everywhere in this area (1 616 mm (64 in) at Canton), with nine-tenths of it coming in the summer. Frost is experienced only on the highlands, whereas ice may form in winter on the Yangtse and the Grand Canal. Here crop growth is continuous. Two crops of rice a year may be obtained, with perhaps a catch crop of vegetables in between if there is sufficient water. The major contrast between the south and the north is, of course, in winter:

> North China is almost wholly the colour of yellow earth. The few poplars, elms and willows are leafless; the arable lands lie fallow or carry in them seedlings of winter crops. Dust storms are common and taint every-

thing, even the sky, a pale yellow. South China and the Ssu-ch'uan [Szechuan] basin, in contrast, remain green; the green of vegetation on the hillslopes and of growing winter crops in the valleys [6].

The south is a land of bamboo, bananas, pineapples, lichees, sugar cane and, in its most tropical parts, coconut palms and rubber.

Western China is very different at all seasons. If a line is drawn along the course of the Great Wall from Wanchuan (Kalgan) towards Lanchow and then continued farther to the southwest into the Tibetan plateau, that very large area of China which would lie to the northwest of it is characterized by excessive dryness, though the actual boundary of cultivation is a constantly fluctuating one. This is the agricultural frontier — the margin along which settled cultivation peters out, except in oases, and scattered livestock rearing becomes predominant — and this was one of the major reasons for the building of the Great Wall. Large areas receive less than 130 mm (5 in) of rain a year and, at best, are semidesert. In the far west, in Sinkiang province, is the huge Takla Makan desert, the driest part of Asia. Here too is the Turfan Depression, well below sea level, where the highest temperatures in China have been recorded. 'No place on earth is so far from the ocean in miles or so inaccessible to maritime moisture' [7]. Urumchi, the principal city of Sinkiang, receives less than 100 mm (4 in) of rainfall annually and has mean monthly temperatures ranging between −15°C (5°F) in January and 23°C (73°F) in July.

Chinese origins and population growth

Until relatively recent times, the history of population movement and the development of the Chinese state has been predominantly one of movement towards the south; the colonization of Manchuria by Han Chinese is much more recent, in fact largely twentieth century [8]. Chinese civilization is almost interminably ancient. 'No other country in the modern world has inherited a cultural tradition so long, distinctive and unbroken' [9]; and it is perhaps even more

Table 0.1 *China's dynasties*

Dynasty	Year	Event	Capital
Ching (Manchu)	1911	Sun Yat-sen Sino—Japanese War (1895) Treaty ports and other concessions	
	1644	Taiping rebellion (1850—65)	Peking
	1644		
Ming		Portuguese reached Canton (1516)	Peking
	1368		Nanking
Yuan (Mongol)	1368	Marco Polo (1275—92)	Peking
	1260		
Sung	1279		Hangchow
Five Dynasties	960		Kaifeng
	906	First printed book	
Tang		Brilliant culture	Loyang
		Expansion to Canton	Sian
	618		
Southern and Northern Dynasties			Nanking Tatung
		Grand Canal constructed	Sian
	420	Fa Hsien reached India	Nanking
Tsin		Arab vessels reached Canton	Loyang
	265		

Three Kingdoms			{ Loyang
			  Chengtu
			  Nanking

	220		
		Expansion to west	
		Paper invented (AD 105)	Loyang
Han	AD 0 — BC		
		Chang Chien crossed Pamirs	Sian
	206		
Chin	256	Great Wall completed	Sian
	250	Mencius (372—288 BC)	
		First use of iron	
		Confucius (551—479 BC)	Loyang
Chou		Expansion to Yangtse valley	
		Salt monopoly	Sian
		Copper coins	
	1027		
	1027		
		Use of bronze	
Shang		Central Hwang Valley focus	Anyang
		Oracle bones	
	1523		

Source: Based on G. B. Cressey, *Land of the 500 Million: a geography of China*, New York, McGraw-Hill, 1955, p. 23.

pertinent to add that possibly no people in the world today is as aware of its cultural inheritence as the Chinese. Further, another fact widely realized within China is that, as Table 0.1 shows, only since the Industrial Revolution has the West outpaced China in technical development.

So far as is known, China has always been inhabited by people of mongoloid characteristics. There is no evidence that the Chinese migrated from other areas into their present realm. The continuous archaeological record begins in the later neolithic period (though there are even older traces) and there are abundant sites of this date in the north. Authentic Chinese history has been said by early Chinese writers to begin with the Emperor Hwang Ti, whose traditional date of accession is 2697 BC. As Buchanan has put it, however:

> The real history of China is not so much the history of the rise and fall of great dynasties as the history of the gradual occupation of the Chinese earth by untold generations of farming folk spreading out southwards, westwards and northwards from an original 'cradle area' in the middle reaches of the Yellow River valley. And the real actors in the drama of Chinese history have not been the great emperors, nor the great generals, nor even the celebrated beauties, the 'flower-shadows behind the silken curtain' of imperial China, but rather the nameless peasants who set forth and carved out for themselves homes and tiny plots of beans or rice or sweet potatoes far from the villages where they were born [10].

The landscape of the 'cradle area' consisted of loess, either *in situ* or transported by water and redeposited. It was open, easily worked country and thus attractive to early man with his primitive farming tools. Popular legend has the Hsia dynasty following somewhat after Emperor Hwang Ti and being founded in 2205 BC by Emperor Yu, who became famous for his efforts to control the waters of the Hwang Ho. There are no factual records of Emperor Yu's activities, but during the 1930s excavations did uncover extensive evidence of the late Shang dynasty (Table 0.1) preserved at Anyang its capital city (Fig. 0.4). They revealed an advanced Bronze Age culture in which the cultivation of wheat and millet and the keeping of animals was important. Urban life was well developed even at this early date, and written records date back to 1200 BC. Large collections of inscribed bones of even earlier dates were also found. These are the so-called oracle bones and were used for religious purposes.

Later assimilation of contrasting environments into the Chinese state through the expansion of the Chinese, or Han, people was gradual but constant (Fig. 0.7). The Yangtse valley, then a region of dense forest and marsh, occupied by scattered aboriginal tribes was gradually colonized. Beyond the Yangtse, as Schafer vividly puts it,

> [The Chinese] . . . moved into the rich valleys of the south in 'pools' — dense aggregations of hopeful humanity, supported by troops who killed those natives bold enough to resist, leaving the survivors to be indoctrinated, exploited or enslaved by Chinese agents and their aboriginal collaborators [11].

To a degree, this infiltration is still going on, notably in the remote hill country of the southwest where live some of China's largest non-Han minorities, and also in the far west, in Sinkiang province.

The south had been organized into Chinese provinces well before the birth of Christ. To the north and northwest, it was a very different story. Increasing aridity eventually forbade agriculture and thus a critical distinction arose between two mutually hostile ways of life: that of the Han Chinese, who gradually became more and more completely sedentary agriculturalists, and that of the nomadic mongols, whose relatively harsh environment allowed only the herding of sheep, goats, camels and horses. As a result, 'between the true agriculturalist (Chinese) and the true pastoralist (Mongol) has lain a transitional zone, which throughout history has been contended for and which is marked geographically by the 15 in isohyet and historically by the Great Wall' [12].

By the time of the birth of Christ the broad outlines of today's agriculturally settled area of China had been established, though with populations very small by today's standards. Probably for a lengthy period the south was occupied by little more than scattered, almost garrison, communities of Han Chinese, but it is equally true that very early,

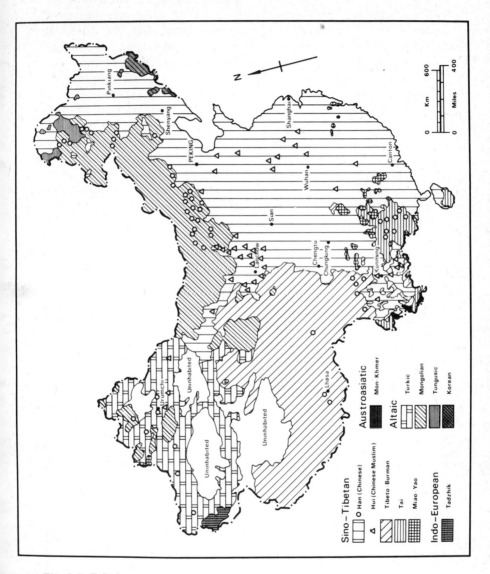

Fig. 0.7 Ethnic groups

because of the agricultural richness of the Yangtse valley especially, the north had become parasitic on the south for food supplies. This was accentuated by the construction of the Grand Canal during the sixth century AD, the principal motivation for which was the transport of grain to the north.

A remarkable feature of much of the period of recorded Chinese history is the apparent stability of population numbers (though the reliability of the early estimates must, of course, be open to conjecture). It appears that at best there was only very slight expansion in population between the first century AD and the end of the sixteenth century (Fig. 0.8). A count taken under the Han dynasty in AD 2 put the population at 59 million, though presumably, as with later counts and official estimates, this would include only the Han Chinese and not the other peoples. As late as 1578, a Ming dynasty count gave 61 million; but between 1700 and 1850 the population of China increased threefold, from about 150 million to 430 million.

This was in large part due to the introduction of crops

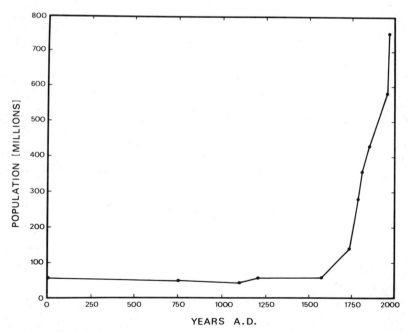

Fig. 0.8 Population growth

from the New World — maize, sweet potatoes, Irish potatoes and peanuts — which made food production possible from hillslopes unsuited to wet rice cultivation. Unfortunately, all too often slopes were cleared for planting that could not support continuous cultivation, and serious erosion soon set in. Widespread land abandonment followed in the uplands, with the result that the increased population become even more dense in the flat plains and river valley bottoms. As Tuan has pointed out for south China:

> The hills and mountains . . . support fewer people in the twentieth century than they did in the first part of the nineteenth. . . . The stratified pattern of land use — wet rice on the narrow valley floors and dry crops on the hillslopes — had largely given way to a pattern in which the hillslopes (after about 1820) reverted increasingly to secondary forests, coarse grasses, and tea and tree plantations [13].

As a result of this agricultural contraction, already the mid-nineteenth century, 'the Chinese people with the technological means at their disposal had probably approached a maximum in land utilization in China Proper' [14]. In spite of this, for almost the whole of the next century there was to be still greater population pressure on the available agricultural resources and ever-deepening misery for the mass of peasant families (Reading No. 1).

Pre-Communist China

The condition of China in the immediate pre-Communist period can, nevertheless, only very partially be explained by increasing population pressure. While it is true that agriculture reached a general intensity unknown anywhere else in the world, so that a cultivated area about two-thirds that of the United States became worked by fifteen times as many farm households and supported a population over three times as large [15], there were other important factors which also contributed to the state of collapse and chaos China had reached before 1949. The system of land tenure was a potent cause of peasant discontent. While it is difficult to generalize (the average cultivated area per farm was 1 hectare (2.5 acres)

23

but there were major variations both in size of holdings and in systems of tenure) in China as a whole the distribution of land ownership was extremely unequal. As indicated by the classic study of Luts'un village by Fei and Chang, parts of which appear in the Readings (No. 4), this kind of situation could not always automatically be equated with oppression of the landless and the extraction of extortionate rents. But in general, 'the universal landlord domination of the country-side was oppressive economically, politically and socially, and perpetuated a general backwardness from which no escape was possible without a decisive break with the old forms of land tenure' [16].

In many senses, the very *ethos* of the state for long was antidevelopmental. As has already been pointed out, Chinese history testifies to lengthy periods before the European Industrial Revolution during which scientifically and technically China far outpaced the West. The use of iron was much earlier, more extensive and more sophisticated in China. Wells were being drilled into the Szechuan brine fields to depths of 600 metres (2 000 ft) even before the birth of Christ [17]. The Chinese invented gunpowder and movable block-type printing. Nevertheless, these and other notable technical advances did not produce an industrial state.

Basically, as the paper by Murphey (Reading No. 8) explains, the reason was the unchanging structure of society, particularly the grip which the scholar—administrator class was able to take upon the highest seats of power from early times and maintain well into the twentieth century. They saw to it, as Needham has put it with regard to the impact of iron technology, that 'like the legendary ostrich, China could digest cast-iron and remain unperturbed thereby' [18]. The merchant and industrial entrepreneurial class remained lowly and scorned and the peak of ambition became success in the examinations for the civil service.

Possessing only the extensive local handicraft industries which are described by R. H. Tawney (Reading No. 6), China remained self-contained, militarily primitive and pre-industrial, and thus became easy prey for the intruding West. Even in 1926 Mao Tse-tung estimated China's modern industrial proletariat at only 2 million, and this was probably a generous figure. Another, slightly later, estimate gave a figure

of only 1 million workers in modern-style production, compared with some 10 million engaged in traditional handicrafts. The latter, it was estimated, produced three-quarters
of China's total industrial output (excluding Manchuria) even
as late as the 1930s.

Although there were early travellers to China such as
Marco Polo, and the Portuguese had established a permanent
base at Macao at the entrance to the Si Kiang as early as the
mid-sixteenth century, the full impact of the West was not
felt until the nineteenth century. Even as late as 1793 an
official British proposal for closer trade relations carried to
China by Lord Macartney could be summarily dismissed by
the Emperor with the grandiose words: 'Our Celestial Empire
possesses all things in prolific abundance and lacks no product within its own borders; there is therefore no need to
import the manufactures of outside barbarians' [20]. China
thereafter tried to pursue a policy of exclusion, but with
rapidly diminishing success. Foreign trade was officially confined to Canton, and then only during certain months of the
year. 'Factories', or trading posts, were allowed there, but
only outside the city walls and with stringent restrictions
upon contact between the Western merchants and the local
people. All these efforts collapsed because of the growth of
the opium trade.

This infamous trade grew up because there was little China
needed from the West in return for her tea, silks and other
exotic products. The Western merchants had to pay in silver,
that is until the Chinese desire for opium from India was
discovered and encouraged by them. Soon the opium trade
grew to such proportions that the balance of trade was
reversed in favour of the West and, more important, opium
addiction had become a national problem in China.

The Chinese attempt to suppress the drug traffic led eventually to war with Britain, a humiliating defeat, the secession
of Hong Kong Island and the opening of Shanghai and other
ports to international trade. By the end of the century several
more of the so-called treaty ports had been forcibly opened
(Fig. 0.9). Foreign nationals were living in them under their
own laws. France, Germany and Japan, in addition to Britain,
had taken Chinese territory and 'the intrusion of Westerners
into China, the vice-like grip over industry and the privileged

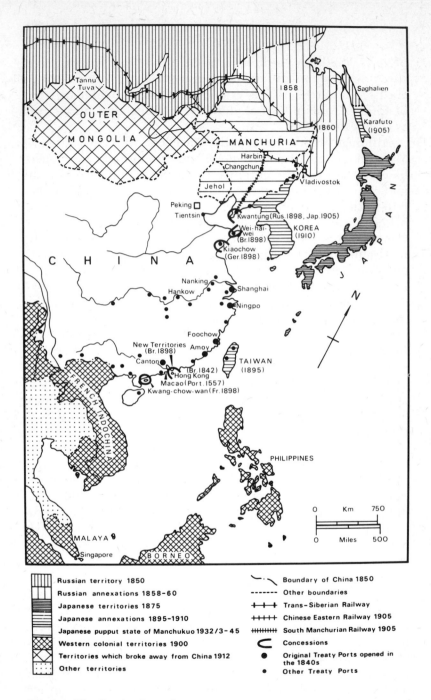

Fig. 0.9 The foreign intrusions

position which foreigners enjoyed, was a constant and growing offence to all Chinese' [21]. Shanghai with its International Settlement and French Concession, as described by Orchard (Reading No. 7) perhaps more than any other part of China epitomized the system of foreign dominance.

Some Chinese were not unaware of the need for modernization, and especially for industrialization, but their efforts were largely stifled by the inefficiency, corruption and general introspectiveness of the administrative system. One such was Sheng Hsuan-huai (1844—1916), who initiated several manufacturing enterprises; but by and large, far from encouraging indigenous enterprise, the Manchu government, in its final degenerated phase and under constant intrusive pressure from outside powers, loaded the industrial dice heavily in favour of foreigners.

Huge indemnities imposed on China following the Sino—Japanese War (1894) and the antiforeign Boxer Rebellion (1902) were met in part by levies on indigenous industry. The treaty which ended the Sino—Japanese War allowed all foreigners to establish industries in China. A transit tax, the *likin*, was imposed on all goods passing from one province to another but the goods of foreign merchants were exempt. Meanwhile, as general internal administration fell further and further into corruption and disarray, local transport facilities, health services and water control schemes all deteriorated. The population, nevertheless, was increasing relentlessly. 'In a relatively peaceful year for China, when the influx of poverty-stricken refugees to the safety of the city was small, the Shanghai Municipal Council collected 5 590 exposed corpses from the streets of the International Settlement alone' [22]. As the reading from Mallory (No. 5) indicates, soon China was to become known internationally as the Land of Famine.

Such industry as developed grew up mainly at the Treaty Ports under the stimulus of investment from Europe, the United States and, later, Japan. The spatial distribution of advanced economic activities thus became very distorted in this respect. Factory industry was, geographically, 'a modern fringe . . . stitched along the hem of the ancient garment', to use R. H. Tawney's telling phrase [23]. The only exception was Manchuria, which was first deeply penetrated by Russian and Japanese capitalism for the development of mining, heavy industries and the construction of railways and later forcibly taken over by the Japanese from 1931 onwards.

The first person to give real hope was Sun Yat-sen. After graduating from Hong Kong with a medical degree in 1892, he devoted the rest of his life to China's problems. Eventually his revolutionary leadership was widely recognized, and when the Manchu dynasty was overthrown by a popular uprising in 1911 he became the first President of the Chinese Republic. This new form of government solved no real problems, however, despite the initial high hopes with which Sun Yat-sen had been inaugurated. Warlordism became rife, and until the middle 1920s local wars, banditry and armed oppression characterized China. Then Sun Yat-sen set about forming a mass party with popular support and its own army. This was the Kuomintang.

Sun Yat-sen died in 1925 but the next year General Chiang Kai-shek led a victorious expedition from Canton to the north against the warlords. At this time there was cooperation with the growing Chinese Communist Party, which had been founded in Shanghai in 1921, and Russian advisers actually accompanied the northern expedition. But as soon as the northern expedition accomplished its objectives the alliance between the Kuomintang and the Communist Party foundered, and thereafter Chiang Kai-shek made the elimination of the Communists his principal goal. About the same time, the Communist Party, under the influence of Mao Tse-tung, one of its original founders, began to abandon its ideas of revolution via the urban proletariat, which had been the Russian model, and to concentrate on the organization of the largest but most disadvantaged segment of Chinese society, the peasants in the countryside. If ten points were to be given for the accomplishment of the revolution, Mao was to state later, seven would have to be given to the peasants, compared with only three to the army and the urban proletariat.

The Chinese civil war between the Kuomintang and the Communist Party can be said to date from 1927. Because of the need for unity in the war against Japan, it was not finally to be resolved until 1949. At first Chiang Kai-shek's grip on the country was strong and the Communists were forced to retreat into the mountains, particularly in Hunan and Kiangsi in central China, where, in areas inaccessible to Chiang's forces, peasant soviets were established and armed forces gradually trained. Finally, the Communists were dislodged and in October 1934 began their famous Long March, a retreat which carried the remnants of their forces deep into China's western mountains and eventually to a safe base in the northwest, at Yenan in Shensi province. It was during the Long March that the leadership of Mao Tse-tung became indisputably established.

A united front against Japan between the Kuomintang and the Communist Party was agreed just before the outbreak of the Sino—Japanese War in 1937 and this led to a crucial revival in Communist fortunes. Chiang's pressure on the Yenan base was released and, in fighting the Japanese, Communist troops were able to bring greater areas under their control. By the time Japan surrendered in 1945 the Chinese Communists occupied considerable areas of northern China. In addition, the Russians were in control of Manchuria.

Very soon the civil war was resumed but this time the Communists were much stronger territorially and materially than ever before. As part of Mao's strategy towards the peasants, their forces had gained a deserved reputation for treating the ordinary people well in the areas they occupied. In contrast, rampant corruption and widespread indiscipline existed in the Kuomintang ranks. The general economic situation also deteriorated rapidly, and Kuomintang rule appeared more and more oppressive. Hyperinflation became endemic. Despite massive support from the United States, the Kuomintang regime collapsed as much from its own inadequacies as from external Communist pressure. By the end of 1949 Chiang Kai-shek, his leading officials and the rump of his forces had retreated to Taiwan.

Rehabilitation, 1949—52

With the inauguration of their new regime in the autumn of 1949, the Communists were at last able formally to extend their control from the western, and poorer, third of the country to embrace the major two-thirds, including the great river basins with their teeming agricultural populations, cosmopolitan coastal cities and important industries. As a result of the bitter civil war against the Kuomintang, preceded by the Sino—Japanese war and before that by over two decades of famine, warlordism and virtual non-existent control by central governments, China was indeed in a sorry state. Manufacturing industry was virtually at a standstill; railway and road communications were extensively disrupted. There was widespread hoarding of food and other commodities, for not only were there severe food shortages, caused largely by serious flooding because of the wartime neglect of water control systems, but also inflation was so rampant that paper money was becoming virtually worthless almost as soon as it was printed.

Industrial output in 1949 was only half that of its previous peak, while food production was perhaps 25 per cent below its previous best [24]. Peking's answer to this great challenge quickly took form in a positive and specific programme, aimed at evolving a strong central government in order to carry out a programme of socialist transformation:

> Discarding both the old Confucian principles and the pseudodemocracy of the Kuomintang as relics of a bankrupt past, they upheld an authoritarian, socialist state, patterned after the experience of Soviet Russia but modified to fit the conditions of China as the most appropriate form of government. This alone, they felt, would create the vital conditions for a strong central government [25].

Part of the early years was devoted to eliminating 'counter-revolutionaries'; in 1951, for example, scores of thousands were put to death. The screw was also turned on certain private businesses and they were forced to close on one pretext or another. But most of the rehabilitation period up to the launching of the First Five-Year Plan in 1953 was concerned with more positive policies. The initial land reform (to be discussed below), and with it the physical elimination of many landlords, assured the Party of even more widespread peasant support.

As the paper by Chang (Reading No. 10), demonstrates, communication facilities were rapidly restored, especially on the railways, troops being used for many tasks. Effective food distribution was organized and thus the threat of regional famines averted. Perhaps the greatest achievement of all, however, was the control of inflation. In 1949 a unified currency was introduced. The use of foreign currencies for everyday purposes was banned and dealing in foreign exchange was made a state monopoly. Large official trading companies were formed which gave the government of virtual monopoly of the wholesale trade and prevented exploitation of shortages by speculators. Retail selling agencies were also set up, thus keeping private retailers' prices down. It was announced in 1950 that the budget had been balanced, 'a refreshing contrast to most of the budgets of the previous thirty years' [26].

The First Five-Year Plan, 1953—57

Some elementary forms of centralized planning had been initiated as early as the first months of 1950 but it was not until the autumn of 1952 that a First Five-Year Plan (1953—57) was announced. A State Planning Committee was established to administer the Plan and later this Committee became the State Planning Commission, directly under the State Council, or cabinet. As Hughes and Luard point out [27], this economic planning followed patterns already established in broad outline by the Soviet Union, but there were some significant differences, due mainly to circumstances in China in the early 1950s being different from those in Russia in 1928, when the Soviet Union's First Five-Year Plan was launched.

Most important, nationalization had proceeded much further in Russia before its First Five-Year Plan. In China much of the economy was still in private hands. 'In 1952 the private sector of the economy, according to official estimates, controlled over a third of the total output of modern industries, nearly two-thirds of the total trade turnover, and practically the entire output of agriculture' [28]. The Chinese First Five-Year Plan therefore had to be designed both to elicit response from countless small, privately owned enterprises and also to pave the way for the eventual incorporation of such enterprises into a centralized state system. The ultimate objective was not merely to raise levels of production, but, of even greater importance to the new regime,

31

as the original Plan document stated, 'to convert China step by step from a backward agricultural country into an advanced, socialist industrial state' [29].

As initially announced, the Plan did not contain a fully worked out programme of development. No overall rationale for development was published; planning proceeded rather on the basis of annual targets for individual items. As Premier Chou En-lai later stated, the Plan was not even completed in draft form until early 1955, more than two years after it had been said to have become operative [30]. There must therefore be grave doubt as to whether the authorities were in any position to begin a comprehensive Plan in 1953, despite their brave pronouncements.

Notwithstanding its shaky foundations, however, the principles of the Plan were announced in September 1953. They were:

1. There should be a rapid growth of heavy industry through the development of the capital goods industries.
2. In the growth of industry, the consumer goods industries should take second place.
3. New industrial centres should be established close to raw material supplies; in other words, attention should be paid to lessening the concentration of industry in the coastal cities.
4. Agricultural development should be directed towards ensuring adequate supplies both of food and of raw materials for industry.
5. The agricultural surplus should be increased, and general productivity both in agriculture and industry should rise, in order to provide more capital for industrialization.

Stress was also laid on the maximum use of Russian aid. In 1954 a Russian loan of £400 million was received to cover the cost of 156 enterprises, including complete factories, imported from Russia [31]. Soviet technicians and instructors arrived in large numbers and were put to work throughout China in helping to implement the targets of the Plan (Table 0.2). Its core was the construction of 694 industrial enterprises said to be 'particularly vital'.

The total value of the enterprises financed by the Soviet

Table 0.2 *Industrial production, 1952–57*

	Unit	Pre-Communist production peak (incl. Manchuria)	Planned target 1957	Production 1952	Production 1957
Steel	million tonnes	0.9	4.1	1.3	5.2
Coal	million tonnes	61.9	113.0	63.5	123.9
Electricity	billion kWh	6	15.9	7.3	19
Crude oil	million tonnes	0.3	2.0	0.4	1.4
Cement	million tonnes	2.3	6.0	2.9	6.7
Cotton cloth	million bolts	41.0	164.0	111.6	156.2

Source: Based on Kuo, p. 153; Hughes and Luard, p. 42.

Union was equivalent to about 6 per cent of Chinese investment in capital construction during the Plan. Russia had first
agreed in 1950 to help China in constructing fifty industrial
projects and obtained in return China's agreement to the
establishment of four joint-stock companies: to operate a
civil airline between the two countries; to develop mineral
deposits in Sinkiang; to extract oil in Sinkiang; and to build
ships at Dairen. However Russia was dilatory in pursuing
these advantages, largely because of Stalin's cautious attitude
towards aid to China. It was only after the death of Stalin in
1953 that a warmer tone in Russian policy emerged. In
October 1954 Khrushchev and Bulganin themselves went to
Peking to confirm the better relationship. One result was that
the four joint-stock companies were dissolved. As Kuo has
pointed out, it is possible that Russia came to aid China only
because by then it had become evident that China knew how
to help herself [32].

The overall aim of the First Five-Year Plan was quite
explicit: the maximum possible development of heavy
industry, with light (consumer goods) industries coming a
bad second and agriculture an even worse third. Fifty-eight
per cent of total investment during the Plan period went into
industry compared with only 8 per cent into agriculture,
forestry and water conservancy. Within its stated aims, and
considering the general circumstances of China at the time,
the First Five-Year Plan has since been held by most outside
observers to have been generally successful. Some notable
individual advances in industrial development were achieved:
in the coal industry for example, as the paper in the Readings
by the present editor indicates. The first Chinese-made
lorries, aeroplanes and oil tankers were turned out, and by
the end of the Plan general industrial production had risen to
a level double that of 1952 (Table 0.2). But within China
there were some who at the time regarded concentration on
heavy industry as excessive. Even in May 1957, what was
very widely publicized later outside China was being freely
admitted by Li Fu-chun, the Chairman of the State Planning
Commission: that too much attention had been paid to
large-scale industry and not enough to local industry, agriculture and commerce.

However, there was much on the credit side, not the least

the open admission of mistakes and deficiencies in planning. More important, for virtually the first time in Chinese history there was real, internally controlled growth in the economy resulting from central direction by an effective national government.

By the middle of 1956 virtually all private industrial enterprise had been brought under at least joint state—private ownership. At the end of the Second World War, the Ministry of Economic Affairs of the Kuomintang government had estimated that a $10 000 million loan from international sources would be necessary to finance postwar industrialization plans. But the method by which China managed to acquire capital for the new industries was not through massive foreign aid but rather by means of increased production based on hard work at all levels of society coupled with a considerable amount of austerity. This is a lesson yet to be learned by many other developing countries. As Kuo puts it:

> The people were told that they must be prepared for a shortage of consumer goods. But in exchange for such sacrifices and 'bitter struggle' they would have guns and tanks, factories and power plants, trucks and mechanised equipment, all of which would provide the sinews a modern world power [33].

Nevertheless, despite the initial objective of industrial dispersal stated in the Plan, and a degree of success in developing cities in the interior (see, for example, Reading No. 15 by Wiens on Urumchi), the emphasis on large-scale industry did tend to lead to the continuation of concentration in a relatively limited number of cities, though a major expansion in steel making was undertaken at Paotow in Inner Mongolia and also at the middle Yangtse industrial complex centred on Wuhan. Accentuated industrial concentration was particularly noticeable in the already well-established Manchurian heavy industry complex: the great integrated iron and steel works at Anshan, the major coal-mines at Fushun, Fuhsin and Hokang, and the machine building complex at Shenyang. Perhaps most important of all, because agricultural development during the period of the Plan was allowed to lag so badly, a bitter harvest in the form of widespread food shortages was to be reaped in later years.

⟮ The collectivization of agriculture ⟯

Although in terms both of output of crops and of such vital inputs as irrigation extension, water conservancy and fertilizer production, agriculture developed only very modestly during the First Five-Year Plan, fundamental changes in agricultural organization that have shaped the economic and social pattern of presentday China were occurring during this period. These had their roots in the reforms instituted in the Shansi–Shensi area 'liberated' by the Communists as early as 1946 and they were to culminate in the mass formation of full-scale people's communes in the autumn and winter of 1958.

The Communists had stated from their beginnings as a revolutionary party in China that the collective organization of agriculture was one of their major goals in economic reform. As is well known, the Chinese revolution differed from the Russian revolution in that it depended largely on success in the countryside on a basis of peasant support rather than revolutionary action in the towns through the urban proletariat. Agricultural reform was therefore vital not only for economic considerations but also because of its political implications. In another sense, collectivization was seen as the principal means of forming socialist men from a previously highly individualistic peasantry.

The new regime distinguished five classes of society in the countryside: landlords, rich peasants, middle peasants, poor peasants and landless workers. Its first efforts, between 1949 and 1952, were directed towards land reform, that is the elimination of landlordism and fulfilling an earlier promise to give land to the tiller. Such a programme had been advocated by Sun Yat-sen long before the Communists came to power, but the Kuomintang government had proved incapable of effectively accomplishing it. Now the process was rapid, thorough and frequently violent — large numbers of landlords were killed, often after village 'trials' by cadre-led peasant 'courts' — and the process was eventually extended even to what was designated the 'surplus property' of rich peasants.

Peasant pressure on the land was already such, however, that few of the middle and poor peasants gained substantial land holdings from the reform. This was especially true in south China, where before the reform, as the study of Luts'un village (Reading No. 4) shows, even the holdings of the landlords had tended to be small. Such a policy could at best have been only a very partial solution to China's agrarian problems because, besides the continuing fragmentation of land into tiny holdings, a new situation had arisen as a result of the reform in which because of their continuing poverty those who now possessed land might still lack farm animals or even relatively simple tools [34].

The next stage in collectivization therefore quickly followed. This was the formation of mutual aid teams in which up to fifteen households were grouped together in order to pool their labour, animals and farm tools, though the ownership of the animals and the tools, as well as the land, still remained with the individual families. The mutual aid teams were obviously designed to increase the scale of rural work units but one problem they could not solve was the natural desire of each family to give its best attention to its own land. By 1954, 58 per cent of all peasant households were said to be members of such teams. In the following year the initial steps in a further stage of collectivization were taken with the formation of the first agricultural producers' cooperatives. By the end of 1956, 96 per cent of all peasant households had been formed into these groups. Though the size of the cooperative varied, the average was between thirty and forty households.

At first, individual landownership was retained in the co-operatives, and at least in theory the members were free to withdraw from participation. After payments for taxes, welfare and state savings had been met, the profits of each group were shared on the basis of the labour and land provided by the members. But this system of organization contained contradictions just as serious as those of the original land reform [35]. In many cases expansion of production depended on irrigation facilities built by collective effort but sited on land which was still individually owned. In some instances, mechanization was becoming feasible but the boundaries of the individual plots presented problems. Further, the land contribution was apparently weighted relatively heavily in the calculation of the dividends payable to the individual families: to many of the peasants this seemed an undesirable retention of a repugnant feature of the old pre-land-reform system.

It was at this stage that individual peasant landownership, only so recently extended in the initial land reform, was virtually wiped out. A new system of 'advanced cooperatives' was instituted in which all land was pooled. All boundaries were removed and all record of separate ownership disappeared. A tiny plot only was allowed for family use, though individual marketing of vegetables, fruit or livestock from this plot was permitted. The transition to the advanced cooperatives occurred mainly in 1956 with the grouping of (usually) five of the original cooperatives into the new larger units. By 1957 the greater part of China's rural population had been reorganized in this fashion and was being paid purely on the basis of labour input.

Labour was divided into production brigades averaging twenty households. Each cooperative was run by a management committee elected by the farmers. Sometimes there were production teams of seven or eight households working below the brigade level. The cooperatives were typically between 140 and 160 hectares (350 and 400 acres) in size. Writing of the whole collectivization process, from the original land reform to the reabsorption of land into the advanced cooperatives, Buchanan, a sympathetic observer, has claimed that 'as a result of this step-by-step process of change, with each advance followed by a period of consolidation and preparation for the next stage, the Chinese peasant, so conservative and individualistic according to some writers, "became socialist without knowing"' [36]. While this must be considered very doubtful (there was undoubtedly local peasant resistance, though its scale is not clear, and agriculture stagnated in 1957 perhaps as a result not only of active resistance but also of widespread passive resentment), what this major change did reveal was the uniqueness of the grip the new regime had taken upon China's vast rural population during less than ten years. It also revealed the extent of the authority, as well as the personal magnetism, of Mao Tse-tung himself as a national leader. In July 1955 he called for complete collectivization by 1960. In fact, collectivization was achieved by his cadres as early as 1957.

The communes

The biggest change of all was still to come. This was the formation of the people's communes. In June 1958 it was announced that 9 200 of the cooperatives in Liaoning province had been merged into 1 500 larger units, each having an average membership of 2 000 households. This enlargement of scale, the announcement said, would enable manpower, materials and financial resources to be used more efficiently and also allow capital construction work, particularly in water conservancy projects, to be better carried out. Almost immediately counterpart action in the cities, the beginnings of the first urban communes, was also made public. It was announced that in Peking, Tientsin and other cities housewives had been setting up crèches, communal kitchens, laundries and other services in order to enable more women to undertake directly productive work. The first fully developed agricultural communes appeared in Honan, where, it later transpired, in April some twenty to thirty cooperatives comprising about 20 000 members in all had been merged. In August Chairman Mao inspected the Honan experiment and immediately gave the signal for wholesale movement to this new plane of even more extensive collectivization. Within a year all the cooperatives had been reorganized into the new people's communes.

There can be no doubt that the rural communes represent 'perhaps the most sweeping and far-reaching measure of social transformation the world has seen, in which the way of living of about a fifth of the earth's population has been radically changed' [37]. In the first place, their advent removed the administrative functions from the *hsiang*, which had formerly been the lowest level of local government. Many communes were roughly coincident in area with the *hsiang* they replaced; they averaged about 5 000 households each. They assumed responsibility for the development of all resources of their areas, both agricultural and industrial, and they were also given an important role in national defence, each training a local militia from among the peasantry.

Within each commune, payments of wages are made several times a year and are determined by work performance supplemented by bonuses for those workers who contribute more than the 'norm'. Not only has the concept of private ownership of land been almost completely submerged but, at least in theory, private housing too is at the disposal of the commune. In the early years, even the minimal private plots allowed in the advanced cooperatives were abolished. The private plots were later restored, however, as a result of the disastrous experience of the 'three bitter years' (1959–61) to be outlined below. As the paper by Rose (Reading No. 12) indicates, communal kitchens and dining rooms, credit facilities, central nurseries, hospitals and even old people's homes have been organized by many communes. As Freeberne has pointed out, in essence each commune has become formally responsible for 'seven guarantees', concerning food, clothing, medical care and childbirth, education, housing, marriages and funerals [38].

The pattern of organization of the communes involves production brigades and production teams at the intermediate and lower levels. These have been increasingly emphasized in recent years as a result of costly previous experience of trying to organize agriculture on too large a scale, that is at commune level, which frequently implied ignoring variations in local conditions within each commune. Some observers have contended that in their original form the communes failed as agricultural units largely for this reason, and the position now seems to be that the commune itself handles all external relations both with other communes and with higher authorities (such as forwarding production plans to the national planning organization for approval), decides in which projects it might invest its resources, and runs local industrial enterprises. It is also responsible for the sale of all products as well as for capital accumulation. The production brigade arranges the cropping programme, draught, animals and farm tools in the part of the commune for which it is responsible. Each production team actually carries out the farming work in its own particular area in accordance with agreed production targets. The commune council is composed of members elected by the production brigades. Each brigade might consist of about 100 families and each team of about twenty to thirty families.

It is difficult, even almost a decade and a half since they were first announced to assess the contribution of the communes to China's development. As Hughes and Luard have pointed out, the organization of the agricultural labour force into these still larger collective units has undoubtedly facilitated local work on irrigation improvement, flood control and other forms of capital development [39]. With regard to crop output, however, before the communes were instituted the government had already admitted that many of the upper-middle peasants who remained outside the cooperative farms in fact produced higher yields. This kind of comparison is no longer possible since peasant farmers are not now allowed to maintain an independent existence. Nevertheless, it is known that morale on the communes was greatly lifted by the reintroduction of the peasants' private plots and that the output of such items as vegetables, eggs and pigs has since seemed to present few problems, presumably because of the greater individual effort put into the private plots.

Collectivization on a commune scale has undoubtedly made easier the collection of taxation and compulsory crop deliveries, not to mention the physical control of possible recalcitrants. It has also contributed to more efficient transfers of food between the various parts of China with the result that today China is no longer the land of famine it was even as late as the 1930s, though this is probably not to say that hunger and malnutrition have yet been completely eliminated. Finally, it is undoubtedly misleading solely to stress the economic aspects of the commune. The final end in view, as Buchanan states [40], is not only to increase individual peasant wellbeing but also to secure the transition to a new type of socialist man:

> Only if we keep clearly in mind the fact that it integrates the totality of elements making up peasant life — production, welfare, education, administration and defence — can we understand the scale of the changes which transformed an almost atomistic structure of isolated peasant communities into the tightly knit interdependent complex of 'cells' which is Chinese rural society today [41].

On the other hand, writers with less sympathy for the regime have questioned whether the commune system can, in the long run, provide the extraordinary human incentives necessary if the growth of the economy is to exceed that of China's vast population.

The Great Leap Forward and the three bitter years

Kang Chao's paper (Reading No. 13), analyses a major shift in national economic policy which was taking place concurrently with the formation of the communes and was to end with disastrous results. This was the drive for tremendously accelerated production, both agricultural and industrial, which became known as the Great Leap Forward. One of the first signs of the new policy came in December 1957 when the All-China Trade Union Congress announced long-term production targets for steel which included a forecast of the production of 40 million tons of crude steel by 1972, which was to be the last year of a Fourth Five-Year Plan [42]. In 1957 steel production had been only just over 5 million tons (Table 0.2). Early in 1958, the slogan 'Overtake Britain in fifteen years' was promulgated nationally; the *People's Daily* claimed in an editorial in the March that 'A spring of great leaping progress is now at hand'; and Mao Tse-tung himself assured the nation in a speech that, 'the great liberation of the productive force of the labouring people has the same effect as the smashing of the nucleus of an atom' [43].

The Great Leap, it was made clear, was to be accomplished through a policy of 'walking on two legs'. As is illustrated in Reading No. 11, on the development of the coal industry, this meant the promotion of mass methods of simple, small-scale production to supplement the output of large factory units and the decentralization of certain aspects of industrial control from the Peking ministries to local administrations. In coal and other forms of mining, hundreds of thousands of shallow pits were dug by hand by commune members in a frantic search for new deposits and increased local production. But perhaps the most startling manifestation of the Leap were what became known in the West as the backyard steel furnaces. An increased target of 10.7 million tons of crude steel for the end of 1958 had been announced in the August of that year, and it was made clear that 'the battle for steel' was to be one of the most crucial aspects of the Leap Forward. By mid-1958 it was believed that the grain harvest would be a mammoth one and commune members were ordered to concentrate even more upon small-scale industries. Backyard steel furnaces were built all over China. Shipyard workers in Shanghai, for example, were reported to be using old oil drums lined with firebricks as small blast furnaces, and by the autumn it was being claimed that such methods were accounting for as much as two-fifths of total steel production. 'In the busiest centre of Peking . . . after the neon lights go out, molten steel begins to flow from furnaces operated by workers in barbers' shops, photo studios, the children's store', reported the New China News Agency [44].

All too soon the backyard steel furnace movement collapsed and China was plunged into three lean years of severe food shortages as a result of the unrealistic policies of the Great Leap Forward. The reasons were not hard to find. As Emerson has pointed out [45], almost overnight an originally cautious economic plan for 1958 had been abandoned and an atmosphere of unbounded but ill-founded enthusiasm generated in which Party workers and commune cadres promised to double, triple and even quadruple production regardless of methods, quality or real cost. The principal means of expanding industry became through vast additions of unskilled labour operating primitive, small-scale enterprises. As with much of the steel production, the output of many of these plants soon proved to be virtually useless. In addition, because of the volume of low quality goods being moved, the national transport system was soon reduced to near chaos.

Perhaps even more important was the fact that the unprecedented enthusiasm for industrial production which swept the nation until the early months of 1960 diverted both attention and large quantities of manpower from agricultural production, and in the midst of the severe statistical breakdown that characterized the height of the Leap it was discovered that grain production had been grossly overestimated. Incredible claims issued from time to time throughout 1958, finally culminated in April 1959 in an announcement by Premier Chou En-lai of an increase of more than 100 per cent in the output of food grains and cotton from 1957 to 1958. The plan for 1959, he stated, called for still further expansion, in food grain output by 40 per cent and in raw cotton by 50 per cent. Within four months, however, the government formally admitted Chou's statement to be exaggerated. The 1958 output claims for food grains and cotton were reduced by one-third and the 1959 targets by a half [46]. Output data for several other important crops was also revised severely downward. In industry, too, more sober reassessments eventually prevailed. It was announced that the published 1958 output for steel, for example, was being reduced from 11 to 8 million tons and that the product of the backyard furnaces was not really steel at all. At the same time, the 1959 steel target was lowered from 18 to 12 million tons and the coal target from 380 to 335 million tons [47]. Even these drastically reduced figures, agricultural and industrial, were probably exaggerations (see Table 0.3).

There seems no doubt that the excesses of the Great Leap Forward contributed very significantly to a general deteriora-

Table 0.3   *Food grain production*

Year	Millions of tonnes
pre-1949 peak	139
1952	154
1957	185
1958	250
1960	150—160*
1962	170—180*
1964	180—200*

* Unofficial estimates

Notes

(a) Figures include potatoes converted to grain equivalent on a basis of 4 tons of potatoes equal 1 ton of grain.

(b) The 1958 figure, even though officially reduced from an initial claim of 375 million tons, has been seriously disputed by non-Chinese observers. Actual production may have been within the range of 195—205 million tons. There appears to have been little expansion in production from 1964 until 1969, when perhaps the harvest somewhat exceeded 200 million tons. In March 1971 Premier Chou En-lai claimed in an interview that the 1970 harvest had reached 240 million tons but some Western observers are currently using lower estimates, within the range 210—220 million tons.

Source: Based on Freeberne, 1971, p. 382 and Steve Washenko, 'Agriculture in China: priorities and prospects', *Current Scene*, Vol. 9, No. 10, 1971, pp. 1—6.

tion in agricultural organization and production during the period 1959—61 and that severe repercussions were also felt for some years in the industrial and other sectors of the economy, although even today the relative importance of the factors contributing to China's disastrous harvests and the 'three bitter years' of this period is not clear. Serious food shortages appeared in the spring of 1959. New restrictions were placed on the distribution of flour and certain vegetables; supplementary foods became hard to obtain; and the percentage of wheat flour in the basic ration was cut to the lowest level since the beginning of rationing in 1954 [48]. These measures became even more austere in the summer, and later the regime was forced to import substantial quantities of food grains, mainly wheat from Canada and Australia.

As the note on the three bitter years in the Readings illustrates, the official Chinese explanation for the food problem was inclement weather conditions. An official report for 1960 cited 'natural calamities of an order unknown for the last century' and stated that the agricultural area so affected amounted to 900 million *mow** out of a total cultivated area of 1 600 million *mow*. Floods, drought and typhoons were said to have been widespread. Though there is a certain amount of evidence of unusually bad weather between 1959 and 1961, it is not generally accepted by non-Chinese observers that this is anything like a complete explanation of the widespread shortages of the period [49]. To make matters worse, as a result of the development of ideological disputes, Russian advisers and technicians were withdrawn from China in the middle of 1960 and all Russian aid suspended. As a result, the Chinese were unable to operate some important industrial installations, at least for a time. Reduced to confusion by the excesses of the Great Leap Forward and hampered by a lack of technical expertise, industrial production declined substantially (Table 0.4).

The Cultural Revolution

Since the collapse of the Great Leap Forward, official statements concerning economic progress have been few and

* The Chinese government in 1915 adopted the standard 6.59 *mow* to 0.4 ha (1 acre).

Table 0.4   *Industrial production, 1958–70*

	Unit	Highest Leap Forward output (1958–60)	Lowest output (1961–62)	1966	Lowest Cultural Revolution output (1967–68)	1970
Steel	million tonnes	13	8	13	10	17
Coal	million tonnes	300	170	240	190	300
Crude oil	million tonnes	4.6	4.5	10	10	18
Electricity	billion kWh	47	30	47	41	60
Cement	million tonnes	10.6	5.5	12	10.2	13
Machine tools	thousand units	38	25	48	40	50
Trucks	thousand units	19.4	1.0	47	31	75
Tractors	thousand units	10.8	6.7	17.6	15.3	21
Locomotives	units	600	25	140	200	280
Chemical fertilizer	million tonnes	2.5	1.4	5.5	4.0	7.0

Source: United States Central Intelligence Agency, *People's Republic of China Atlas*, Washington, 1971, p. 69.

lacking in statistical detail. It seems clear, however, that during the nadir of the three bitter years the commune system all but broke down, and as a result, when the 1960 harvest turned out to be much worse than expected, a mass movement of 'all people to agriculture and food grains' had to be begun, completely reversing the cry of 'all people to iron and steel', which had been the mass line in 1958 [50]. At the same time, the attention of planning at the national level was firmly refocused upon agricultural problems and it was stated that 'the whole nation must concentrate on strengthening the agricultural front and must carry out the policy of taking agriculture as the foundation of the national economy. . . . In heavy industry the scope of capital construction in 1961 should be appropriately reduced.' Significant changes followed within the communes themselves. The often unwieldy nature of such large units of production was recognized and production brigades, subordinate groups within the general commune, were made the basis of agricultural organization. Later, the production brigades were reduced in importance in favour of still smaller production teams which were often, it seems, villages or hamlets. As the *People's Daily* put it:

> The small labour brigade should have, under the general plan laid down by the large brigade, the right of sowing what the soil demands, the right of determining technique and the number of the labour force, the right of managing animals and implements, the right of handling part of the funds. The masses must daringly be trusted [51].

Additionally, in what was perhaps an even more significant change in policy, small private plots amounting to about 5 per cent of the total area of each commune were restored to the peasants in order to boost morale, and private trading in pigs, poultry and vegetables from them was allowed.

The first five years of the 1960s were a period of slow recovery, both agricultural and industrial. Agricultural recovery began in the late summer of 1962, whilst by 1965 industrial production had probably reached a level slightly higher than that of 1958 (Tables 0.3 and 0.4). In 1966, however, as 'Foreign Expert' describes (Reading No. 17), the country was once again thrown into turmoil, this time by the onset of the Cultural Revolution. This essentially concerned ideological matters and marked the vigorous reappearance of Mao Tse-tung himself on the national scene after being out of touch with day-to-day affairs for a lengthy period following his resignation as Chairman of the People's Republic in December 1958. Essentially,

> Mao appeared to be trying to return his people and the communist party to the revolutionary womb so that they might be reborn unsullied by the stain of 'original sin' inherited from the old regimes through the weakness or 'sabotage' of the leadership which had come to power with the creation of the People's Republic [52].

Mao abhorred the factionalism which he observed developing in China, between technocrats and peasants for example, as well as between those motivated by material and those by ideological incentives, the less and the better educated, the city and the rural dwellers and, not the least, the Left and Right wings of the Party led by Lin Piao and Liu Shao-chi respectively. He determined to cleanse the state by eliminating such differences, reimposing his own ideological thinking upon both the Party and the Chinese people, disposing of diehard revisionists and those who were unreformable, and imbuing the new generation, which had not experienced the pre-1949 years of struggle, with his own revolutionary ideals.

Early in 1966, therefore, a Mao-inspired struggle was begun within the Party against a so-called anti-Party group led, among others, by the Mayor of Peking. This group was alleged to be constituting a covert opposition to the ideology of Mao and his chief lieutenant Lin Piao, and in a new departure Mao showed he was no longer willing wholly to trust even the Party: he appealed over its head to the whole nation. It was this tactic which threw China into two years of turmoil which included street fighting, mass executions, intervention by the army and sabotage in many areas. It also led to the formation of the Red Guards, large loosely organized bands of youthful pro-Mao activists (especially discontented students and unskilled workers) who roamed the country for many months, interfering with administration at all levels and coercing people into the pro-Maoist ideological line.

The first great parade of the Red Guards took place in mid-1966. It was followed in the winter months and early in 1967 by a greatly stepped-up struggle against 'persons in authority in the Party taking the capitalist road', allegedly headed by President Liu Shao-chi [53] (who was disgraced and eventually expelled from the Communist Party). Thereafter, in 1967 and 1968, some form of disturbance — open fighting, sabotage or strikes — was reported in every province and autonomous region in China [54]. Some local party organizations said to be tainted by 'old ideology' were overthrown, and revolutionary committees approved by Mao's group seized their power. Elsewhere, established provincial leaderships strongly opposed the new movement, often by force. There was even a mutiny at Wuhan. In the midst of this violent chaos, Mao's wife, Chiang Ching, leapt into prominence as a sponsor of Red Guard activities. Besides Liu Shao-chi, the head of state, Teng Hsiao-ping, the Party general secretary and Lo Jui-ching, the vice-minister of defence, fell from office. Antiforeign feeling was whipped into hysteria by the Red Guards and in the summer of 1967 the British mission in Peking was burnt down and its staff assaulted.

'As the People's Republic was celebrating its eighteenth birthday in October 1967, China was split from east to west, and from north to south; and the Party was riven from top to bottom' [55]. A struggle to install pro-Mao revolutionary committees was in full swing throughout the country, and it was only towards the end of 1968 that the most recalcitrant areas, Sinkiang and Tibet, finally capitulated. Subsequently, at the Ninth National Congress of the Party in April 1969, Mao Tse-tung's thought was officially raised to parity with Marxism—Leninism and Lin Piao (who was himself denounced in 1971 and said to have been killed fleeing to Russia) was confirmed as Mao's successor.

In terms of orderly economic development, the Cultural Revolution cost China dearly. As Perkins makes clear in his paper in the Readings (No. 20), Mao saw to it that 'when it became clear . . . that the opponents of the Cultural Revolution were using fear of economic disruption to undermine the movement, it was economic growth that was jettisoned, at least for the time being, not the revolution' [54]. The economic issues facing the country were virtually ignored in the Chinese literature between 1966 and 1969, except for vague appeals to promote production [57]. In terms of industrial output, Western estimates pointed to a drop of between 15 and 20 per cent in 1967 compared with the previous year, and speaking before a gathering of 10 000 activists in Peking in April 1968 Chou En-lai admitted that 'planned targets had not been realized' [58]. Very little capital construction was undertaken during the Cultural Revolution and only late in 1968 was it possible to detect some upturn. Agriculture, it seems, suffered less, presumably because the ideological struggles were fought out more in the towns and cities than in the villages. Commune control probably weakened somewhat, resulting in some rise in 'economism' or private enterprise by the peasants. Although no firm figures are available, it is likely that there was neither any significant increase nor any marked shortfall in food grain production between 1965 and 1969, output remaining roughly at the level of that of 1957 during these years [59].

Since 1970 the economy appears to have gained momentum once again under the general line that 'agriculture is the foundation of economy' and 'grain is the key link'. The 1970 and 1971 harvests were said by official Chinese sources to have been excellent (though China is continuing to import substantial quantities of grain), while industrial output is now comfortably exceeding that of the immediate pre-Cultural Revolution period (Tables 0.3 and 0.4). The most recent official Chinese claim for steel production, for example, is for an output of 23 million tons in 1972, an increase of 2 million tons over the figure for the previous year [60]. As Klatt's paper in the Readings (No. 18) points out, assuming the continuing normalization of economic life, China can probably expect encouraging, if modest, rates of industrial and agricultural development during the remainder of the present decade.

Though remaining, on a world scale, very much an underdeveloped nation for the foreseeable future (Fig. 0.9), and continuing to be very much self-contained (see Donnithorne on China's trade, Reading No. 19), China could become a considerable industrial nation in terms of the total output of her industries before the end of the present century. Now not only are her known industrial resources larger than in the pre-Communist period but the means of mobilizing them effectively have been created and the economy is more balanced than in the past both structurally and spatially. Much of the actual realization of improved living standards by the masses will depend, however, upon the future rate of growth of the population *vis à vis* that of the economy, and on the vital question of population limitation China's policy over the last two decades has been equivocal, as Aird's paper (Reading No. 9) demonstrates. In its most recent phase, 'After some initial confusion on the part of the Red Guards as to whether birth control was "revisionist", it was finally resolved to be a Maoist idea and family planning activities initiated in the countryside during previous years were not disturbed' [61]. Since then, China's 'barefoot doctors' working in the rural areas have been reported as being active in distributing pills and other contraceptives.

External relations

Communist China's emergence on to the world stage could hardly have been more dramatic for, as Fisher points out in the extract from his lengthy two-part paper 'Containing China?' (Reading No. 21), it is likely that the United States would have soon followed the British action of January 1950 in recognizing the new government but for the development of hostilities in Korea in the summer of the same year. Taking the lead in supporting the United Nations intervention on the side of South Korea, the United States first diplomatically and later militarily came face to face with the new China, which in October 1950 extended massive support to North Korea in the form of 'volunteer' troops, largely to prevent the possible development of an external threat to its own Manchurian heavy industrial region posed by General MacArthur's forces in Korea. Lines were drawn between the United States and China at this time which persisted until China's remarkable development of 'ping pong diplomacy' in April 1971 (when, quite unexpectedly, a United States table tennis team playing in Japan was invited to undertake a goodwill visit to the People's Republic) and the subsequent visit of

President Nixon to China in February 1972. These lines included massive United States military and economic support for the Chiang Kai-shek regime in Taiwan, the stationing of the Seventh Fleet in the Taiwan Straits, the secession of United States trade with China and, later, the formation of the SEATO defence alliance in 1954.

During its early years, the new Chinese government clung very closely to the Soviet Union. Its early economic planning, as has been shown, was influenced strongly by the Soviet experience. The Russians withdrew their forces from Manchuria on schedule, concluded a formal Sino—Soviet Alliance effective for thirty years and gave substantial aid to China's industrialization. The foreign policy statements of the two nations mirrored each other very closely, those of Peking, in particular, being extremely militant. In general, however, the new regime was too preoccupied with the serious internal economic problems involved in preparing for and working through the First Five-Year Plan to do very much that was active to support its numerous exhortations to people's revolution, aimed in particular at its Asian neighbours, and its virulent anti-Americanism. The major exception was the war against the French in Indo—China, for China was quite heavily involved indirectly through supporting the Vietminh with war supplies. About 1 000 Chinese supply trucks took part in the siege of Dien Bien Phu, for example [62]. In the event, China was accorded a major role at the Geneva conference of 1954 which resulted in the partition of Vietnam at the seventeenth parallel and, in terms of ambitions to great power status, was able to restore much of the prestige lost through reverses in Korea.

By the middle 1950s China had adopted a more outward-looking stance in foreign relations, one designed to generate and coordinate international opposition to the 'imperialist aggression' of the United States, especially among the developing nations. To this end, China played a leading role in convening a major conference of Afro—Asian nations in the Indonesian city of Bandung in April 1955, but the results were somewhat disappointing, for Chou En-lai found at Bandung that, far from being united in their opposition to the United States, a sizeable section of the twenty-nine nations represented revealed not only marked pro-American tendencies but, perhaps more important, grave suspicion of China in terms of its declared encouragement of Communist expansion and subversion. Ceylon, for example, formerly non-aligned, sharply attacked what it termed the 'new colonialism' of Russia and China, and echoed the general view that the nations attending were opposed to power blocs of any sort [63]. The Chinese response was one of conciliation, even to the point of inviting Thailand and Cambodia to send representatives to south China to assure themselves that no preparations were being made for the invasion of their borders. Together with the other nations at Bandung, China espoused the principle of peaceful coexistence, publicly at least.

The Sino—Soviet power bloc which had become so widely feared was not to last very much longer. As Taylor explains in his paper (Reading No. 22), ideological strains were beginning to develop between Russia and China as early as 1956, not least in terms of the strategy to be adopted towards potential revolutionary movements in the developing countries. In Russia, Khrushchev confirmed the possibility of peaceful transition to socialism, that is, that Marxist—Leninist forces could come to power through a non-violent or even a parliamentary transition, and this important ideological departure was formalized in the 1957 Moscow Declaration of Communist Parties.

There was basic disagreement between China and Russia on this point. In Moscow the Chinese delegation to the meeting, headed by Mao Tse-tung, privately circulated a memorandum insisting that 'what is most important is to proceed with the hard work of accumulating revolutionary strength'. Further friction was generated by the generally more liberal Soviet policies that were being propagated by Khrushchev at this time, especially after his bitter public denouncement of the legacy of Stalinism. As Russia relaxed somewhat under Khrushchev's leadership, the question of the purity of Marxist—Leninist doctrine as against current Russian practice began to arise in the minds of the Chinese. To Mao, such liberalizing trends were both potentially dangerous at home, where strict control was still required if China was to become economically strong, and internationally anathema if they were to divert attention from the ultimate attainment of the world socialist situation through revolution. Very soon after the 1957 Moscow Declaration, China moved to a position first of serious internal criticism and then of open manoeuvring against Russia, for example in pressing for the exclusion of the USSR from various Afro–Asian organizations. Finally, after an attempt to resolve the ideological issue failed at the Moscow Conference of 1960, which was attended by eighty-one Communist parties, the split became open, and all Russian aid to China was withdrawn.

While, in Chinese eyes, Russia proceeded if not down a capitalist at least down a 'revisionist' road in terms of Marxist–Leninist ideology during the 1960s, China continued to be uncompromising towards the United States and fervent in both advocacy and, where possible, financial and material support for Communist revolutionary movements in the developing countries. As Lin Piao put it in 1965, the Chinese viewed North America and Western Europe as the 'cities' of the world surrounded by potentially revolutionary 'rural areas' in terms of the developing nations of Asia, Africa and Latin America. In time, given Maoist purity of purpose, the revolution would surely be accomplished in the 'country-side' (as it had been in China itself), and then the 'cities' would inevitably fall.

In Africa some important footholds were opened up, particularly in Tanzania, which after 1967 received substantial Chinese financial aid for its agricultural development and also became the base for the building by China of a major railway from Dar es Salaam into landlocked Zambia. Of the Asian nations, Indonesia, on the point of collapse under the Sukarno regime, at first seemed to offer the greatest prospects. The Peking-backed Indonesian Communist Party had almost achieved power by mid-1965, when its premature *coup* action (in which China was probably involved) resulted in decisive retaliation by the Indonesian army and its elimination as a political force. Both Russia and China continued to be active in materially supporting North Vietnam against the South but, characteristically, at loggerheads with each other over the coordination of such support.

The revolutionary furrow that China ploughed during the 1960s was, in general, a lonely one and by no means an unqualified success as Taylor's paper (Reading No. 22) shows. This period was also characterized by growing Chinese reaction to border problems and the ultimate realization that despite the successful production of first an atomic bomb (in 1964) and later a hydrogen bomb (in 1967), China could hardly withstand the military might of Russia if the Soviet government chose to embark upon a policy of direct action to settle the ideological confrontation. Relations with India deteriorated sharply as a result of a serious anti-Chinese uprising in Tibet in 1959, as a consequence of which India gave sanctuary to the Dalai Lama. Thereafter, the situation along the Himalayan frontier gradually reached breaking point and direct hostilities between the two countries erupted in 1962. Later, friction along the border with Russia increased substantially, and in 1969 there were serious clashes between the two countries in the Sinkiang and Ussuri river border sectors. China's attitude, as expressed by Mao Tse-tung, was that during former periods of Chinese weakness Russia had seized sections of Chinese territory and 'we have not yet presented our account for this list'. By early 1972 Russia had reportedly moved forty-four divisions to the border with China compared with the thirty-one divisions that were facing Western Europe.

As Doak Barnett indicates in his paper (Reading No. 23), the context of the worsening of the Sino—Soviet dispute is one of the most important background factors in the present Chinese attitude of *détente* towards the United States. Another is the Chinese realization of the growing power of Japan. As he points out, American attitudes towards China had already been changing substantially for a number of years. Moderate influences were prevailing and the last three American presidents had all been working gradually towards the normalization of relations with Peking. Notwithstanding this revaluation, the public change in Chinese attitudes towards the United States which occurred during the spring of 1971 took the Nixon administration by surprise. The change in China's external relations since then has been immense and, in complete contrast to the days of the Cultural Revolution when China almost withdrew completely from the world stage and recalled every ambassador overseas except one, today all the world seems to be making for China's door. In August 1971 the United States announced its support for China's admission to the United Nations. This was formally accomplished the following October, though it involved the failure of a United States attempt to allow the Taiwan regime to retain its seat also. By early 1973 a cease-fire had been arranged in Vietnam. It is as yet too early to assess the consequences of China's massive *volte face* in external relations, though clearly much will depend not only on the future conduct of China's own diplomacy but also on the attitude Russia decides to adopt towards these dramatic developments.

A balance sheet

Because of the paucity of official statistics for more than a decade, and the impossibility of carrying out independent field investigations for an even longer period, published assessments of China's socio-economic development during the Communist period tend to contain a good deal of opinion rather than substantiated fact, opinion which, moreover, is often highly coloured by the political stance of the writer. 'I believe that today academic objectivity is impossible', Buchanan has written concerning his own work on China [64], and some flavour of this basically unsatisfying aspect of modern Chinese studies is conveyed by the Readings, which differ markedly in the degree of sympathy they display towards the Communist regime.

Through whichever political spectacles one looks at modern China, it is undeniable that, as Dernberger has aptly put it, even today 'by any standards of common sense or economic analysis, China is an underdeveloped country faced with the major economic realities of too many people who live on limited fertile land and whose average productivity is too low' [65]. As he states, the rate of growth of China's huge population is perhaps the problem which is most basic, in the sense that it conditions almost all others, for even if the Chinese were able to reduce their birth rate to 1.5 per cent by 1973, about 16 million people would still be added to the total population each year. A country in this position is forced, in a sense, to run harder and harder in the economic race all the time in order to remain in roughly the same position in terms of *per capita* benefits.

Yet, despite Dernberger's assessment, it is equally true that

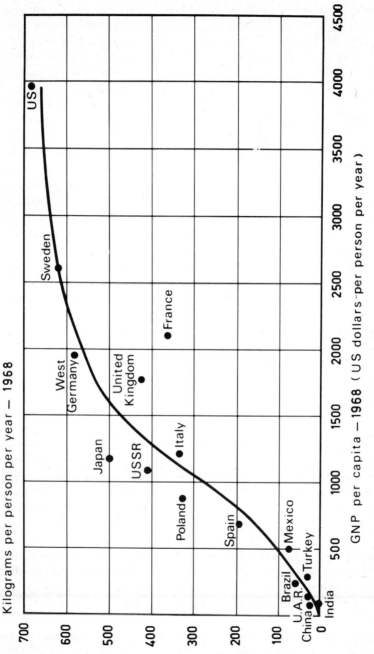

Fig. 0.10 World steel consumption and GNP per capita

during the period since 1949 the Communist regime has
brought about a very substantial improvement in general
living conditions in China and that, trimming away the
various mistakes and excesses of the period, a solid core of
real progress in economic development still stands revealed.
The development of the agricultural sector will probably
remain for many years the principal determinant of the pace
of China's future economic growth for, as has been the
experience of Russia and several other Communist countries,
relatively rapid industrial expansion has proved much easier
to stimulate than sustained increases in agricultural output.
In 1965 the output of China's heavy industries may have
been double that of 1957 and total industrial output in the
former year half as much again as in the latter (the progress
of light industry being affected by shortages of agricultural
raw materials) [66]. In addition, as Reading No. 15 indicates,
during the period since 1949, a rigorous industrial decentralization policy had been undertaken, involving the rapid
development of such cities as Sian, Paotow and Lanchow,
both for strategic reasons and to develop the industrial
resources of the interior provinces [67]. Furthermore, the
communications network had been extended on a scale
generally sufficient to meet these changes both in the volume
of industrial output and in industrial location.

In agriculture the record is much less encouraging. Despite
a good deal of publicity from Peking concerning the extension of farming into formerly marginal areas including, in the
early years of the regime, claims to have 'conquered nature',
the basic fact remains that although greater in total area than
the United States, China possesses a very much smaller proportion of cultivable land (and of course a very much larger
population). Only 11 per cent of China's total area is
cropped, and within this proportion the amount of new land
gained for agriculture during the period since 1949 is likely
to have been relatively small, perhaps little, if any, more than
the amount of cultivable land lost to urban expansion and
other construction projects during the same period. Because
of the abundance of labour in the countryside, crop yields
are high per unit of land, but nevertheless very low per unit
of labour. The regime, from several possible alternatives,
chose the reorganization of the peasantry as the principal

means of increasing agricultural production, hence the basic commune system which was attained during the late 1950s. The communes have not yet solved China's agricultural production problem, however, though on the other hand the production of food grains has broadly kept pace with population growth which, in the circumstances, and comparing the disappointing Indian experience of the last two decades, is possibly an achievement in itself.

As has been demonstrated already, within the general commune system smaller production groups have now been given a good deal of responsibility as a result of earlier failures to organize agricultural production successfully at the level of the communes themselves. A little private land has also had to be given back to the peasants in the communes as an incentive. In addition, other agricultural solutions beside peasant organization have received greater attention in recent years. Little is heard nowadays about reclaiming vast areas of virgin land for farming; the emphasis has shifted rather towards still further developing existing high-yield areas with the objective of eventually producing a consolidated area of advanced farming in which high yields will be virtually guaranteed, and then gradually extending this area into those of lower yields.

In respect of the planned area of guaranteed yields, a great deal of attention is being given to the further development of irrigation facilities, often in the form of numerous small improvements carried out by local communes, and also to the increased application of chemical fertilizers. The use of chemical fertilizers in China is still low both on a world scale and by the standards of such leaders in Asian agriculture as Japan and Taiwan. Given the accumulation of sufficient capital on a national level to invest in significantly increasing present fertilizer production (or else financing greater imports of fertilizer), the potential for improving yields by fertilizer application is significant. If, for example, China could attain only Japan's pre-Second World War rice yields, this would increase output by 90 per cent [68]. But for the present, and possibly even for the next decade, China's food grain and general agriculture production is so low in relation to population size, that luck with the weather, through the critical agricultural sector, will continue to play an important part in determining the rate of expansion of the economy.

Having said this, there is a good deal on the credit side of what has been called 'the Chinese experiment' which should also be recorded in final summary. Geographically, as Buchanan stresses, there is for instance 'the tremendous re-appraisal of the Chinese earth which followed the coming to power of the People's government in 1949' [69]. This has revolutionized ideas about China's resource endowment and has emphasized the potential importance of the interior in terms of industrial resources. It has led to concerted efforts to tame wandering and eroding rivers, often again on the basis of huge labour inputs mobilized by the communes (which, it must be stressed, must not be viewed only in their agricultural role). It has also involved a significant develop-ment of hydroelectric resources. Again, the vigorous develop-ment of local, small-scale industrial and handicraft enterprises must be mentioned. Although these were undoubtedly over-emphasized during the Great Leap Forward, there can be no doubt of the general importance of such enterprises in China's economy both in terms of the development of de-centralized production facilities and as a means of dealing with the classic problems of Asian rural manpower absorp-tion: seasonal unemployment and general underemployment. J. K. Galbraith's assessment, after a recent visit to China, is that 'No other country has attacked the problem of recurrent and disguised unemployement . . . with the energy and im-agination of the Chinese' [70], although he also goes on to add that 'one senses, also, that their effort still falls well short of solving the problem'. How, one wonders, could it be other-wise in such a short time, considering the vast numbers of people in the Chinese countryside?

Lastly, a word of caution must be given against using only Western concepts of economic development and the good life to assess the Chinese model. Mao once characterized the Chinese people as 'poor and blank' and wrote that 'on a blank sheet of paper free from any mark, the freshest and most beautiful characters can be written, the freshest and most beautiful pictures can be painted' [71]. During his period of power, he has been concerned very largely with transforming the Chinese people ideologically, in imprinting his own vision of the socialist future for mankind upon their blankness, rather than with leading them in an overt quest for plenty. The ultimate objective in China is socialist man not necessarily spectacular increases in gross national product — this is yet another aspect in which the role of the communes must be viewed — and two impressions seem to strike most visitors. The first is the atmosphere of hard work, dedication and diligent effort in the country. The second is the spartan nature of the leadership of the regime. As Galbraith puts it: 'As to whom the production is for, there is a quick and easy answer: it is for everyone in about the same amount. Somewhere in the recesses of the Chinese policy there may be a privileged party and official hierarchy. If so it is the least visible ruling class in history' [72]. This is a refreshing contrast from the undisguised opulence of the ruling élites of most other developing countries, as is the virtual absence of corruption at all levels in the society. China is materially poor, but also dignified, internally strong and self-reliant.

Readings

On what basis should our policy rest? It should rest on our own strength, and that means regeneration through one's own effort.

MAO TSE-TUNG

**Earthbound China
the pre-Communist period**

1 The Chinese peasantry

Never before have such impressive pictures of country life been unfolded before me as on this journey through inner China. Every inch of soil is in cultivation, carefully manured, well and professionally tilled, right up to the highest tops of the hills, which, like the pyramids of Egypt, slope down in artificial terraces. The villages, built of clay and surrounded by clay walls, have the effect of natural forms in this landscape: they hardly stand out against the brown background. And wherever I cast my eyes, I see the peasants at work, methodically, thoughtfully, contentedly. It is they who everywhere give life to the wide plain. The blue of their jerkins is as much part of the picture as the green of the tilled fields and the bright yellow of the dried-up riverbeds. One cannot even imagine this flat land devoid of the enlivening presence of these yellow human beings. And it represents at the same time one great cemetery of immeasurable vastness. There is hardly a plot of ground which does not carry numerous grave mounds; again and again the plough must piously wend its way between the tombstones. There is no other peasantry in the world which gives such an impression of absolute genuineness and of belonging so much to the soil. Here the whole of life and the whole of death takes place on the inherited ground. Man belongs to the soil, not the soil to man; it will never let its children go. However much they may increase in number, they remain upon it, wringing from Nature her scanty gifts by ever more assiduous labour; and when they are dead, they return in childlike confidence to what is to them the real womb of their mother. And there they continue to live for evermore. The Chinese peasant, like the prehistoric Greek, believes in the life of what seems dead to us.

The soil exhales the spirit of his ancestors, it is they who repay his labour and who punish him for his omissions. Thus, the inherited fields are at the same time his history, his memory, his reminiscences; he can deny it as little as he can deny himself; for he is only a part of it.

2 Agriculture: the north and the south

A list of the agricultural products of any country is necessarily somewhat bewildering, especially when the country is of such a size as to include almost all the different food plants commonly cultivated. The traveller who is accustomed to a farm in western Europe or in America may wonder what a farm in China really looks like and what are the main differences between it and those to which he is accustomed. In the first place, while there are many differences in China, we may in very general terms describe two types of farms, those of the north and those of the south; but of course by thus limiting ourselves we shall necessarily miss some of the most characteristic features of Chinese farming.

A visitor to the north of China who had been correctly told that wheat was the principal crop might well expect to find the type of farm to which he was accustomed. He would probably look first, in order to estimate the sort of man the farmer was, at the fences and gates, or even wonder vaguely if there were any hedges. He would find none. In some cases, according to the nature of the soil, he might find stone walls, or in the plain mud walls, but never a wooden or iron fence, and certainly no hedgerows. The road along which he travelled, if it were in the loess country, would probably be a deep sunken lane like those of northern France but much deeper. If it were an old Imperial highway he would still see the paving stones in places; in others they would be broken, and cart tracks, unless the roads were all sunken, would lead out and run alongside all the roads. No roads and no fences would strike the eye first. Secondly, the small size of the holdings would be noticed; this would be easily seen, though in some regions in the summer time there is mile after mile of green wheat. Perhaps the most striking feature would be the almost entire absence of wild vegetation and no neglected coppices or spinneys. The yellow landscape has a utilitarian aspect, and there are none of the odd corners of semiwild vegetation untilled and neglected which add such a charm to some British landscapes. What would strike the stranger perhaps more, especially if he were accustomed to our mixed farming, would be the fact that all the land is arable; there is no pasture, and such places as are untilled are the sandy or stony wastes of a riverbed, where the river has flooded, or where owing to the summer drought it has ceased to flow. A closer inspection would also show him that the land was cultivated with the greatest care, as intensively as parts of Belgium are cultivated. Outside a village or town there may be little gardens, like our allotments, but unless they are frozen hard they are sure to be cultivated, and are probably bearing two or three crops side by side. There are no flower gardens, and only such flowers as are incidental to a crop. Most of the crops have a familar look — wheat and beans we are all accustomed to — but, especially in the north, there will very likely be fields with a tall unfamiliar grain 8 feet high with great purple panicles, quite unlike our grains; this is the *kaoliang*, a millet.

Another most marked difference between the familiar fields and those of China is the absence of horses. There may be a few, but along the road most of the freight will be in wheelbarrows, or on the backs of donkeys. There is no trace of dairying, nor is the farmer proud of his animals; they are there for work, not as thoroughbreds. Pigs there will be about the place, especially in the villages, but no sties; the pigs will be routing about in the village streets or in the midden. A close examination, or several days spent on a farm in north China, will reveal further features; first the meticulous care with which everything is used — they do not make any bonfires in China — secondly the abundance of labour and the low standard of living which makes it cheaper to employ human labour instead of beasts. At dawn in the pleasant cool air when the morning is still fresh, before the sun gets up — for it is very hot even in northern China in the summer — the stranger will see the oxen being led out to graze on the wayside, in case there is any green thing about, and further on the low grave mounds in the middle of the fields, which must never be ploughed. On this scanty nourishment they will do their day's work. The beasts will probably be in the charge of a small boy, and are never allowed to wander free. This explains why gates and hedges, which are principally directed against wandering domestic animals, are so unnecessary. The women of the household will collect all the dry sticks and any odd inflammable material which we should let lie or put on the rubbish heap, and will make their fires with them. Except on the grave mounds and in the precincts of a temple there will be no trees, and if any shrubs manage to escape attention for a short time they are sure to be grubbed up for firewood.

But if in northern China fields of wheat are to be seen which recall familiar things, in southern China everything is entirely strange. The ricefields, great shallow swamps with the green spears sticking from them, the fierce-looking ungainly water buffaloes, the tea plants on the hillside, possibly the fields of the forbidden poppy, all are entirely unfamilar and are so far from resembling any farm which we know at home that it is hardly profitable to compare them. But the most striking difference both between northern and southern China, and also between northern China and lands which we know, is the great boundless stretch of yellow loess in the north which blankets every natural feature and which penetrates everything; it forms the soil from which everything grows, it is used to build houses and walls, and when the wind is blowing from the north it fills the air with a yellow fog so dense that one can hardly see.

Although China is essentially an agricultural country, somewhat paradoxically it cannot feed itself. Under the conditions which prevailed at the beginning of the nineteenth century and still to a certain extent exist today, the failure of a crop meant starvation. Efforts were made by the emperors to store up grain against bad times, the old grain being sold annually and replaced by new. But these measures failed in a country where a journey might be of many months' duration, and even intelligence, much more supplies, would necessarily be long on the road. As she has not been a country of industrial development, today still confining herself mainly to domestic industries, it would appear as though, in the absence of superfluous food, China could do little trade. This has never been the case. It is remarkable that without to any extent exploiting what are called normal natural resources China has for many years been able to export a large amount of agricultural products which were not of food value. At the beginning of the nineteenth century, when western trade was limited to the factories at Canton and one or two other places, China was exporting an enormous quantity of tea. The East India Company took nearly £2 million worth even in 1814 and lesser amounts of silk. In exchange China received woollen and cotton goods (especially woollen), opium, and some manufactured metal, and a certain amount of tropical products, which she had been buying from native traders for hundreds of years. In the last 100 years an extraordinary change has come over Chinese agricultural products. Tea, which once represented three-quarters of her trade, fell in the middle of the nineteenth century to only just over half, while today it is almost a negligible quantity, a serious matter as I have already shown, as many of the tea gardens were not fit for other uses and have now gone out of cultivation. Silk, on the whole, has held its own, but there has been no increase commensurate with the demand or with the increase in population. India, better suited to grow tea, has destroyed that trade, while the industrialization of Japan has proved a serious rival to a country which still produces silk by primitive methods. In the last forty years China has begun to export a variety of materials, and in the last twenty the trade in oils has enormously increased, so that today she exports more of them than she does of any other single article, even including silk. This is all the more remarkable in a land where the only animal fat in use is bacon and where therefore vegetable oils are of particular value.

3   Population and agriculture in the Yangtse delta

Twenty miles south of Shanghai, near the edge of the growing Yangtse delta, lies the crowded county of Fenghsien. On one side is the ocean, from which the land has persistently been snatched. On the other is the exotic metropolis of Shanghai [1], singularly out of harmony with this ancient agricultural countryside.

Above Fenghsien fly the planes of the air service from Shanghai to Canton. As viewed from the air, the most striking features of the flat, green landscape are the micropattern of the fields and the net of closely spaced canals. Other areas may have an equal intensity of agriculture, but in few parts of the world is there a similar development of canals and ponds. In one measured square mile there are no less than 27.8 linear miles of these waterways (44.5 km in 2.5 sq km), and the average spacing is only 116 metres (380 ft) [2]. It is these that give the area its distinctive stamp and make the *geo*graphy essentially *hydro*graphy.

From the air one may see the lines of maritime dikes bordering the silt-laden sea, which protect the land from high tides. These barriers enclose successively reclaimed areas similar to the Dutch polders. Within the newer dikes the canals are laid out in rectilinear plan, in contrast with the irregular pattern in the older land, west of the innermost, and older, dikes. Scattered clusters of broadleaf trees and bamboo surround groups of farmhouses, and one is seldom out of sight of a market town.

Flagstone trails take the place of roads, for there are no carts and few wheelbarrows. Passenger and freight boats move slowly along the larger waterways; smaller farm boats carry fertilizer or produce over the smaller canals. Outside the dikes, along the shore, are numerous salterns, where thousands of evaporating trays are spread out.

But the full intensity of land use is not to be understood from the air. One must descend, perforce by parachute, for there are no fields large enough to set down a plane. Grave mounds, rising to 2.5—3 metres (8—10 ft), provide the best vantage points. Tall reeds hide many of the canals; but on all sides there are gardenlike fields, covered in summer with cotton and rice and in winter with wheat and broad beans. There are no fences, and field boundaries are mere ridges among the flooded fields. Farmsteads and canals cover as much as a quarter of the area; grave mounds occupy from 5 to 10 per cent of the arable land.

Even from the highest graves there are few broad vistas because of the trees and bamboo which half hide the scattered farmsteads. Along the canals are thatched shelters for the irrigation pumps. The innumerable grave mounds betray the long past; the numberless cheerful children suggest problems for the future. With a rural population of 800 to a sq km (2 000 a sq mile) there can be little idle land and but infrequent cessation in man's supreme occupation — the quest for food.

The fundament

If we could sweep aside the cover of vegetation and the structures of man, the vicinity of Fenghsien would present a monotonously flat sky line. No part of the area is now more than 3.5 metres (12 ft) above sea level (Woosung Horizontal Zero) [3]. But for the intervention of man, the delta would be crisscrossed by random drainage ways, most of them tidal thoroughfares. The mean tidal range at Gutzlaff outside the Yangtse estuary is 3 metres (10 ft), and in the narrow part of Hangchow Bay the range exceeds 6 metres (20 ft). During high spring tides and onshore typhoon winds all the region would be inundated. After each of these occasional invasions of muddy Yangtse water an increment of silt would veneer the area. Well borings at Shanghai have penetrated 280 metres (920 ft) without reaching the bottom of the delta [4]. The Yangtse today carries an annual burden of silt and clay amounting to 494 million tons, which is spread out over the

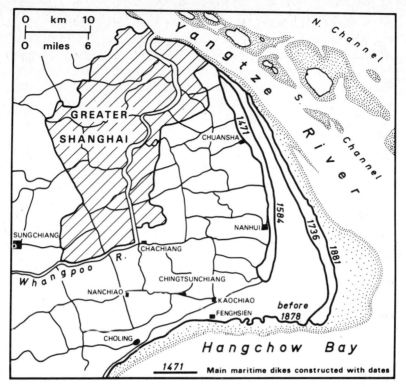

Fig. 3.1   Situation of Fenghsien in the Yangtse delta and in relation to Shanghai

floor of the East China Sea. Measurements in Hangchow Bay by the Whangpoo Conservancy Board show an average silt content of 1 000 parts in a million, by weight. Changing shore currents influence the areas and rate of accretion, so that the boundary between land and sea varies with the size and slope of the submarine delta. Von Heidenstam [5] estimates a shoreline advance of 1 mile in sixty years, but it is clear that the distribution of land and sea has been and is influenced by both erosion and deposition. This is the foundation that man has reclaimed so completely that there are no longer natural drainage ways.

Fenghsien is a humid subtropical land with monsoonal tendencies (Köppen's Cfa), somewhat similar to the southeastern United States. The winter brings occasional freezing temperatures and a flurry of snow, but the ponds rarely have more than a paperthin coating of ice. Most of the rain falls during the summer, but every month has at least 50.8 mm (2 in) of precipitation; the yearly average is 1 096 mm (45 in). The growing season is more than 300 days. Summer temperatures are high, and there is much humidity. Statistics for nearby Shanghai from 1873 to 1930 show that during July the mean temperature is 36.7°C (98°F) and the relative humidity is 84 per cent; in January the mean temperature is −6°C (21°F), and in December the relative humidity is 76 per cent. During the summer of 1934 Shanghai experienced twenty-one consecutive days during which the daily maximum was more than 37.8°C (100°F), and for sixty days the daily maximum averaged 36°C (97°F).

No trace remains of undisturbed natural vegetation. Many temple courtyards and ancestral burial plots contain large specimens of pine (*Pinus Massoniana* and others), cypress (*Cupressus funebris*), ginkgo, elm, and oak. Farmsteads are invariably shaded by fir (*Cunninghamia lanceolata*), pine (*Cryptomeria japonica*), cinnamon (*Cinnamomum japonicum*), and broadleaved forms such as camphor and candleberry; and scattered trees are found along the canals and in the fields. Groves of bamboo are common. Wood is rarely used for fuel, and the local supply of lumber is inadequate for house, furniture, and boat construction. Reeds on the canal banks and grasses on the grave mounds furnish fuel and forage; straw is used for fuel, rope, sandals, and thatch.

The soils of Fenghsien reflect their alluvial origin and the centuries of exploitation. Mechanically the soil is a silt loam, fine enough to permit flooded rice fields to retain their water for several days, according to the weather. From the ocean inland to the Whangpoo there is a steady gradation from coarse to fine and from light to dark. In the newer soils of the polders there is little humus, and the salinity is high enough for a white efflorescence to form on all ridges. No mature soil profiles were found anywhere in the region. During the centuries of utilization, several thousand crops have been taken from the fields. As agricultural practices involve using the straw and sometimes even the roots for fuel or other purposes, there is a large drain on the resources of the soil. Were it not for repeated and painstaking application of canal muds, compost, and human wastes, crop yields would be low.

Dikes and canals

In this ancient and intensely human land the present land-scape patterns are unintelligible without an appreciation of the succession of past cultures. Fortunately the major outline of the record is available. Fenghsien, in common with most other counties of China, has an official gazetteer containing information on geography, political changes, famous people, and economic conditions — a valuable aid in reconstructing the succession of landscape changes [6]. Twenty miles southwest of Fenghsien city a large river formerly emptied into Hangchow Bay, possibly a mouth of the Yangtse or at least a continuation of the upper Whangpoo River. Before 1050 the discharge of fresh water was so great that the bay was also fresh. After this date the flow lessened and the bay became brackish, so that locks were constructed at the mouth of the river to prevent inflow. By 1471 the passage was completely closed and the flow reversed to the present Whangpoo.

The official construction of sea dikes seems to have been begun in AD 721. Little is known about the location of earlier dikes, but the records indicate that in 1171 the dikes southwest of Fenghsien city were constantly being shifted in-land. It is not possible in this paper to trace the long record of construction and erosion, but it may be mentioned that the main dike, which passes near the wall of the city of Fenghsien, apparently dates from 1471. It is made entirely of earth and has a height on the inner side of 2.5–3 metres (8–10 ft) and a width on top of some 4.5 metres (15 ft). The land on its seaward side continued to receive flood silts after its construction, so that the land level outside the dike is commonly 0.5–1 metre (2–4 ft) above that inside. In front of this main dike are four other dikes in a distance of 5.6 km (3½ miles). The outermost, a mud wall 1.5 metres (5 ft) high, is being undercut by storm waves and is in disrepair. This foreshore has been reclaimed as rapidly as deposition has taken place, but its agricultural utilization is handicapped by the salinity of the soil. In 1633 the land was reported to extend from 1.5–6.5 km (1–4 miles), widening eastward, and was classed as the dry, the medium, the wet, and the alluvium. By 1878 the foreshore east of Yangtse Cape had grown out 9.5 additional km (6 miles).

Several lateral dikes connect those parallel to the shore and divide the reclaimed areas into polders. In the outer polders ground water is still too saline for drinking, and farmers must carry fresh water a mile or more. The water problem in the polders is primarily one of drainage. Rice is not grown, partly because the soil in the paddy fields is too sandy to hold water and irrigation pumps are lacking. The newness of the area is betrayed by the planned pattern of parallel drainage ditches and right-angled laterals. Since the surveys of the Whangpoo Conservancy Board in 1920 a large additional polder has been ditched. Residents in this new area report that there has been some cultivation since 1915 but that all houses have been built since 1920 or 1925.

Along the sea there now extends a continuous series of maritime dikes from Hangchow around the mouth of the Yangtse and up the Whangpoo River. All drainage inside the main dike thus reaches the sea by way of Shanghai. Surplus water in the outer polders drains directly to the sea through sluice gates at low tide.

The tidal movement through the canals varies considerably in height and velocity from place to place. Near the Whangpoo there is a range of 1—2 metres (4—6 ft), and the current in the main canals makes it necessary for boats bound in the opposite direction to tie up along the bank. The discharge of fresh water by the Yangtse is so great that the incoming tide is never brackish. That there is some dependence on ground water was demonstrated during the protracted drought in the summer of 1934, when many of the smaller canals were nearly dry and the depth of water in others was so reduced as to hinder navigation.

From the main dike pronounced contrasts are to be seen. Trees are abundant in the inner, or older, areas but are scattered outside. In the polders house groups are smaller and more commonly of woven reeds rather than bricks. There is no navigation on the canals outside the dike, and there are few old landmarks such as temples. In contrast to the planned rectangularity of the outer canal net, the older system is disorganized. No trace remains of original rivers, except possibly in the canals linking the larger rivers.

Two thousand people to the square mile

People are inescapable in Fenghsien — old scholars giving their birds an airing, children tending the buffaloes, women weeding the crops, boatmen punting their shallow skiffs, groups of men and boys operating an irrigation pump. From dawn till dusk people are busy in the fields, and one can rarely find a secluded spot out of sight of humanity.

The average population density of the Yangtse Plain, which includes all the level land below Ichang, is 1 277 to a square mile (472 per sq km). In many parts of the delta this figure is doubled, as in the island of Tsungming in the Yangtse estuary, where there are 2 873 people for each sq mile (1 104 per sq km). A recent estimate credits Fenghsien with a population of 304 480 and gives the area as 1 238.5 sq km [7]. A census in 1865 reported 140 215 people. Across the canal from Chachiang a partial house-to-house census was taken of 1 sq mile of farm land. This incomplete enumeration indicates a density of about 2 050 to a sq mile (800 per sq km) in a purely agricultural area. Individual house groups, sometimes of a clan, reported two to thirty families and 8 to 120 people. There are no resident foreigners in the area, and the only mission station is a Jesuit church and orphanage at Chingtsunchiang. The Southern Methodist Mission at Sunkiang has had several outstations in the county.

Except for the few urban centres, the population inside the main dike is evenly distributed. The surveys of the Whangpoo Conservancy Board locate practically all farm-houses and show no localization or systematic pattern of distribution. Canal junctions and trail intersections have not produced concentrated settlements. Roadside teahouses, isolated stores, and country temples are uncommon and have not resulted in settlement nucleuses. Almost without exception houses are on waterways, but the waterways are so closely spaced that there is no linear arrangement. Access to water is not needed so much for transportation as for domestic use.

There is little circulation on the part of the farm population. Each family group lives a practically self-contained life in the midst of the fields it cultivates. Only a few times a year is it necessary to visit the city for supplies or for temple festivals. There are few wants that call for frequent purchases at nearby shops, nor is there the ready money with which to satisfy such wants if they did exist. The few needs and the low rate of circulation probably account for the absence of focuses of rural settlement. In Fenghsien near neighbours are unavoidable, and there is no necessity to group farmhouses for sociability, as there would be in a more sparsely populated land.

Most buildings are made either of poorly burned grey brick, pounded earth, or woven reeds. There may be a veneer of plaster, usually whitewashed. The better buildings are roofed with tile; the others are thatched. The floor is made of brick or pounded earth. Farm buildings invariably are one-storeyed; only in parts of the larger towns are two-storeyed buildings to be seen. There are neither cellars nor attics. Windows, sometimes made of translucent sea shells, are few and small. Wood is expensive, and its use is restricted to doors, windows, and roof beams.

Every farmhouse has its courtyard for threshing grain and domestic uses. Unlike those of north China, these courtyards are unwalled except for a possible hedge. The houses have from two to ten rooms, arranged in a row, not more than three being connected. The usual arrangement is a combined kitchen and living room with a bedroom on each side. Simple chairs and tables, bedframes of woven fibre supported on stools, and chests for extra clothing make up the furniture. Instead of a barn, an extra room houses tools and supplies. The water buffaloes and yellow cows may have a shed to protect them from the rain, but pigs, chickens, and dogs find shelter for themselves. Each farm has a privy, where all human wastes are collected in large jars until needed on the fields. Threshing is done either with a flail or by driving the farm animals over the grain. In each courtyard are large piles of straw, to be used for fuel or perhaps for weaving cheap rope or making straw sandals.

The most elaborate structures are the temples, but most of the buildings are in need of repairs. Their roofs are made of uncoloured tile. There is a nunnery at the north gate of the city of Fenghsien and another east of Kaochiao. The more pretentious grave plots may have an encircling wall and an ancestral hall for family tablets. Despite the antiquity of the area, there are surprisingly few material souvenirs of the past.

There are no pagodas and only a few dilapidated pailous, or stone archways. Even the more important family graves are usually without stone markers. The stone bridges are probably among the oldest structures.

Farmers and fishers

Three primary occupations furnish a livelihood to these people: agriculture, fishing, and salt production. The agricultural harvest consists of cotton and rice in the summer and wheat and broad beans in the winter. During the winter there is some fallow land, but in summer the whole countryside is under cultivation. Few fields exceed 90 metres (300 ft) in length; many are only 30 metres long by 15 metres wide (100 ft by 50 ft). A crop such as soybeans may be planted in two or three rows along a path, and much corn is grown in odd patches less than 3 metres (10 ft) in diameter. Where an entire area is in the same crop, it is often impossible to determine field boundaries. There are no fences and few stone corner markers. Muddy ridges a foot high and a foot wide separate flooded fields but are invisible amidst the standing crops. Maps of land utilization thus fail to show the tiny size of farm units, which through successive inheritance subdivisions have been reduced to small fractions of an acre.

Water buffaloes, yellow cows, and a few oxen are available for ploughing, but a large amount of work must be done by hand. To ensure better drainage, sweet potatoes, beans, and, often, winter wheat are planted in ridges some 250 mm (10 in) high, which are spaded up by hand. Planting, weeding, and harvesting bring all members of the family into the fields.

Cotton has been raised around the sandy margins of the Yangtse delta for centuries. Today it is the dominant cash crop, and the development of modern mills in Shanghai has made the area the most important cotton-producing region in China. A small amount of cloth and braid is made in the homes, but most of the cotton is exported through hong merchants in the towns, where it is usually ginned before shipment. The cotton seeds are planted before the Ch'ing Ming festival in April, in the fields in which winter wheat has been raised, as soon as, or even before, the wheat is harvested. During dry summers the crop may be irrigated two or three times, but this is not always necessary. The harvest comes in late August and September. The staple is short and the yield low. Farmers report a yield of 70–100 *chin* of unginned cotton to a *mow*.* In many parts of Fenghsien cotton occupies two-thirds of the cropland, and almost everywhere it occupies half of it. On the sandy and saline soil of the polders it is more widespread than inside the main dike.

The yield of rice is inadequate to supply the local needs and must be supplemented by imports from Shanghai. It is reported to be from 100–180 *chin* of unhulled rice to a *mow* (18–32 bushels an acre†). Rice requires more labour than any of the other staple crops. It is sown in seedbeds in April and transplanted in May to the fields in which broad beans have been grown during the winter. For three months the plants must be in standing water. Every ricefield borders a canal or pond, and chain pumps are in operation every few days. About three-quarters of the pumps are worked by animal power. Along the main canals a few farmers have contracted for watering with a company that has an engine-operated pump, mounted on a boat so that it may be moved from field to field as needed.

Each farmstead has a small plot for vegetables and melons, carefully guarded by a watchman toward the harvest season. Corn, sweet potatoes, and soybeans locally cover as much as 10 per cent of the crop area each. A little kaoliang is raised for wine. Interplanting of corn and melons or sweet potatoes is common.

Wheat and broad beans are the winter staples. Wheat is planted in September, and broad beans are planted in October; both are harvested in April. They are reported to yield about 150 *chin* to a *mow*. Wheat, the more extensive crop, is shipped in part to Shanghai, and both wheat and rice straw is shipped to Shanghai for fuel.

Rotation is practised rather generally, two years of cotton and wheat being followed by one of rice and beans. Some fields are kept almost continuously in cotton because of its cash return. In the newer polders, especially those that are saline, cotton covers as much as 80 per cent of the arable land. The rest of the area is in corn and soybeans but not

* 1 *chin* = 0.5 kg (1.3 lb); 6.59 *mow* = 0.4 ha (1 acre).
† 1 bushel = 0.04 cu m.

rice. There is considerable winter fallow, along with some soybeans, but no wheat. No mulberry is grown, though silk is an important industry some tens of miles to the south and west.

About a quarter of the farmers are owners; the rest are tenants. Farm land is valued at $40.00 to $70.00 (Chinese currency) a *mow*. The annual rent is $8.00 to $12.00 when paid in cash, but more often it is a share of the crop. Taxes amount to $0.30 a *mow* every six months.

Fish largely replaces meat in the Fenghsien diet. There is some fishing in Hangchow Bay, but there are no harbours along the Fenghsien shore in which to land a catch. The fishing of Fenghsien is done in canals and ponds. Where there is a noticeable tidal movement, bamboo weirs with bottleneck enclosures have been built across the canals to trap the fish; elsewhere large, square nets, 2.5 metres (8 ft) and more on a side, are let down from a bamboo framework. Trained cormorants also are commonly used, and fishermen usually have about a dozen of these birds to a boat. Most of the fishing is only a part-time occupation.

The ever-industrious farmer harvests aquatic plants and bottom mud to fertilize the fields. With scythes attached to long poles he cuts the vegetation growing in the ponds and with a long-handled scoop shovel drags up the rich mud from the canal bottom.

Salt production and other occupations

The production of salt from sea water along the Fenghsien foreshore dates back many centuries. The hsien records refer to salt boilers, but all the production today is by solar evaporation. Directly east of the city of Fenghsien dikes have been built out to the highwater mark, but further south is a large unreclaimed area, which is covered with salterns. Twice monthly, on the first and the fifteenth of the Chinese month, this area is flooded at high tide. The tide leaves behind a veneer of salt-impregnated silt. As needed, the top 6 mm (¼ in) of this silt is scraped from an area 30 metres (100 ft) or more in radius and is heaped into pyramids 3 metres (10 ft) high.

In front of each pyramid are two percolating basins. A few

bushels of silt is placed in these basins, and water from near-by ponds or tidal thoroughfares is poured over them. This water dissolves the salt and slowly seeps into a cistern. Workers carry the brine from the cistern to wooden trays, into which it is poured 1 cm (½ in) deep and allowed to evaporate. Each day or two, as a layer of crystal salt accumulates, it is scraped up and is ready to be sold. The process continues throughout the year, but with lessened activity during the winter. Each tray is taxed eight coppers a year, and the salt is marketed under the supervision of the Salt Gabelle [8].

Secondary production in Fenghsien is small. There are a few mills, engine operated, for hulling and polishing rice; cotton gins have already been mentioned; oilseeds are pressed into cakes in at least one factory; and there are blacksmiths, coffinmakers, tailors, and the like. On the banks of the Whangpoo at Chachiang are two establishments where coal dust from Shanghai is converted into coke for reshipment to that city. Other industry is confined to the home.

Trade and transport take the time of many, trade in the towns, transport over the canals. Most of the shops are small, open directly to the street, with a frontage of some 6 metres (20 ft); but despite its small size a shop may have a dozen apprentices. Regular boat service operates over the main canals. Company, or hong, boats, 9 metres (30 ft) long and sculled by three or four men, carry freight and passengers at low rates. Freight is mainly agricultural produce and moves by boats of various sizes. Where there is a towpath or when the wind or tide is adverse, trackers pull from the bank, but ordinarily boats are sculled by means of a large oar in the stern or are punted with bamboo poles.

The influence of Shanghai is increasingly felt. A steam-launch service from the Shanghai Bund, along the Whangpoo, operates three times a day, stopping at Chachiang. From Chachiang there is supplementary motorboat service once a day through the canals to Fenghsien city. Chachiang is reached from Shanghai in two and a quarter hours. Several dozen people a day make the trip, most of them small merchants or coolies looking for work in Shanghai. Most of the metropolitan contacts are indirect and reflect the increased market for cotton and the availability of imported rice.

An old walled city: Fenghsien

Two of the urban centres may be considered for their contrasts — the city of Fenghsien, the old, walled county seat,
and Chingtsunchiang, a newer, unwalled commercial centre
along one of the main canals. These two towns are type
examples for much of south China.

Fenghsien is laid out as a typical administrative centre, in
which capacity it served until recently when the county seat
was transferred to Nanchiao. Encircling the city is the brick
wall, originally built in 1386, nearly square, some 7.5 metres
high and about 710 metres long on each side (25 ft and
2 300 ft), with a low parapet and bastions at short intervals.
Outside the wall is a moat, originally 73 metres wide and
2 metres deep (240 ft and 7 ft), but now about 25.5 metres
(75 ft) wide. There are four gates, one at the middle of each
side; each gate formerly had a gate tower and a screening extension wall, but the towers are now in ruins. Within the wall
two principal streets connect the four gates, and their inter-
section locates the business focus. The present built-up part is
a rough square, the corners of which touch the gates, so that
a triangular area is left in each corner of the city; these areas
are now devoted to agriculture. Even within this built-up part
there are numerous ruins, which reflect the decadent political
status of the town.

The streets are from 3—7.5 metres (10→25 ft) wide and
have been paved with stone since 1832. There are no two-
wheeled vehicles and few wheelbarrows. The shops are small
and are limited to domestic needs. The largest buildings are
the former magistrate's headquarters or yamen, a large Confucianist hall, and several temples. As the hsien capital,
Fenghsien was once provided with four granaries, which had
a capacity of 110 000 *catties* (roughly 55 000 kg). Near the
Confucianist temple are a new-style school and a small
reading room and public library. The city has one telephone
but no electric lights.

Small suburbs cluster about each of the gates: the most
important is that at the west, where the launch service starts
for the Whangpoo.

A new city: Chingtsunchiang

Chingtsunchiang is 16 km (10 miles) southwest of Fenghsien

city on the main canal leading to Nanchiao, the present capital. It is the most important city of the region studied. The urban area extends 1 140 metres (3 700 ft) along the canal and has a maximum width, including the canal, of 180 metres (600 ft). The population in 1933 was 4 533. These people, almost all of them living in one-storey houses, occupy a built-up area of roughly 0.25 sq km (one-tenth of a sq mile). The main street follows the west bank of the canal, alongside it except in the central district, where shops are crowded in between. Across the canal is another, shorter street, of much less importance. Side streets are mere entryways from the countryside. Chingtsunchiang is unwalled, but the urban area is sharply defined. Fields extend directly to the almost continuous line of city buildings, usually without outward-facing buildings.

There is no pagoda, but there is a pawnshop with a fortresslike tower, from which one may view the pattern of the city. More than half of the area is under roofs. Residences and their tiny courtyards are directly connected with the family shop and seldom have a separate entrance. No boundary can be drawn between business and residential areas; in fact, apprentices often sleep on benches in the shops. Except in the central district, one-storey structures prevail.

Chingtsunchiang is a typical example of the teeming south China cities — tremendously congested, dirty, smelly, with innumerable diseased dogs, without conception of sanitation. Yet for all that there are signs of progress. Electricity, used in the larger shops only, is brought from Nanchiao. A new school has 300 children in six grades and kindergarten; the tuition is $6.00 (Chinese currency) a year. The former temple is now largely given over to a public tearoom and education hall, the only visible evidence of civic interest in recreation. Catholic influence is strong in this part of south China, and Chingtsunchiang has a Jesuit church and orphanage.

Four main lines of business distinguish the city: cotton, with three wholesale firms; wood, with two; beans, with one; and rice, with three shops. Cotton and beans go to Shanghai, from which the rice comes. The largest of the cotton firms has ninety small ginning machines, with a capacity of 14 500 kg (32 000 lb) a day. The only weaving is done in the homes, where there are many small looms operated by women; their output is about 6 metres (20 ft) a day of a strip a little more than 60 cm (2 ft) wide. The trade in wood is extensive — poles from Foochow, bamboo from Hangchow, and other lumber from Hankow. The two firms, one at each end of the town, keep a considerable part of their stock afloat on the canal. An inventory disclosed a diversity of small enterprises: fourty-four were engaged in selling food and twenty-one in selling clothing; thirty-nine in manufacturing and merchandising, including sale of new-style goods (flashlights, paraffin, cigarettes, soap, enamelled washbasins, etc.); and seventeen in services ranging from 'spirit money' and native medicine to a native and a 'foreign-style' hospital.

The uniqueness of Fenghsien

The distinctive quality of Fenghsien lies in its intimate relation to water, the integrator of the landscape. Canals are the arteries of this composite organism. They provide circulation, nourishment, and elimination and determine the quality of the life that makes this land unique.

These artificial rivers carry off surplus rainfall and at the same time provide a rarely failing source of water for irrigation: thus they largely free Fenghsien from flood and drought. Few fields are more than 45 metres (150 ft) from either a rainwater pond or a canal. The canals are from 1.5—15 metres (5—50 ft) wide, and most of them are navigable for farm skiffs, though the smaller ones are partly obstructed by reeds. Their banks are from 2.5—3.5 metres (8—12 ft) high, according to the height of the land above sea level. Most transportation is by boat. Slower freight boats move about 2 miles an hour; the faster sculled boats travel 4—6 miles an hour. A daily flow of vegetables and a seasonal tide of wheat or cotton move toward the cities, and out from them, in turn, comes the parade of gaily decorated 'flower boats' carrying night soil to replenish the fields.

Many fine stone bridges cross the canals, some of them arched, others made from long, flat slabs of Soochow granite. They furnish excellent vantage points from which to observe the manifold functions of a canal. Near the edge of the typical village one may look countryward and see water buffaloes submerged to their nostrils for their daily soaking. Further on, a fisherman paddles along in a boat while his cormorants dive for fish. Across the canal girls nearly as submerged as the buffaloes are gathering clams. Small boys float about in tubs collecting water chestnuts. A dozen geese swim silently along in search of food.

Towards the village, passing boats crowd the canal, here constricted by the accumulation of refuse; for in the absence of arrangements for the disposal of garbage or waste the canals form a convenient place to toss broken dishes and debris. Most villages have a common drain under the flagstones down the centre of the street, and this too empties into the canal. Where the tidal range is adequate, the daily ebb and flow carries out refuse; elsewhere, especially during a protracted dry spell, the water becomes more or less stagnant.

Adjoining each house along the canal is a flight of stone steps, at the foot of which one may observe women doing the family laundry by pounding the clothes on a stone, or washing the daily rice and vegetables in a wicker basket sloshed in the water. To complete the picture, the canals are the sole source of water for domestic use and water carriers at the foot of other steps dip up buckets of muddy water, which they peddle from house to house. Small wonder that the Chinese have learned to drink hot tea rather than unboiled water!

Without the protection of the maritime dikes this thronging life of the canals would not exist, but without industrious people there would be no dikes! It is thus man that is the most impressive element of the landscape.

4 Luts'un: a Yunnan village

Luts'un is located in a fertile valley, about 100 km (62 miles) west of Kunming, close to the Burma Road. We started our study with this village because we found here a simple form of economy in which neither commerce nor industry plays an important part. The main occupation of the people is the management and cultivation of farms, and the villagers are either petty landowners or landless labourers. Landlords with large holdings are lacking, and absentee owners are few and insignificant. It seems to us that this village represents a basic type of farming community in interior China. The life of the peasants is characterized by the use of traditional farming techniques on rather fertile land and under a strong pressure of population. In these fundamental ways Luts'un represents, in miniature, traditional China. It is also logically a prototype of the types of villages described later, where the development of handicraft industries and the commercial influence of the town complicate the structure.

Luts'un is a village of 122 households, with 611 individuals — about the average size for the region. The total area of farms owned by the villagers, privately or collectively, is about 920 *mow*, or about 56 ha (140 acres). Owing to the fertility of the soil, the yield from a unit of farmland is higher even than that of the area around Lake Tai, the well-known rice-producing area in eastern China. However, the distribution of land among the villagers is unequal. Most of them either have no land or have too little land for their maintenance. These must seek employment on the land of others, since there is little opportunity for gaining a livelihood in occupations other than agriculture, and they form a large supply of hired labour. The petty owners, on the other hand, are able to manage their small estates by employing cheap labour to work for them and themselves to enjoy leisure. The dichotomy of work and leisure among the villagers is characteristic of this type of village economy.

The average size of a holding is small — less than 0.4 ha (1 acre). It tends to diminish gradually under the increasing pressure of population, because, according to custom, brothers have equal rights of succession to land. Since there is no open and easy source of income other than in agriculture, most of the small landowners must eventually become landless labourers. Some of them will remain single all their lives and then die out completely. Occasionally rural families may, through hazardous ventures in the outside world, suddenly rise to wealth; but such families are soon levelled down by the merciless pressure of population. One or two generations is quite enough to reduce the holdings of a rich family to petty units. The movement upward on the economic ladder is slow, but the movement downward is rapid. The supply of landless labourers is maintained by a constant increase in the population and a constant decrease in the size of landholdings. The traditional structure of the village is thus dependent upon the existence of two groups of people: the petty owners, who form a leisure class; and the landless labourers. This is the type of rural economy that we shall analyse in the following pages. . . .

Crops and climate

Only two crops, rice and broad beans . . . serve as the basis of the agricultural economy of the village. From the surrounding higher lands the valley appears to be covered by a solid carpet of green, furnished in early summer by the rice plants and in late fall by the beans. A walk through the fields, however, reveals the presence of additional crops. Corn grows on the sandy land bordering the stream, various vegetables are raised in the gardens back of most of the houses, wheat is planted in scattered squares among the fields of broad beans, and the trailing vines of green beans impede the walker as he traverses the paths between the rice paddies. There are many secondary crops in addition to these, but they are produced in relatively small quantities. Since all of these secondary crops are raised in small quantities and almost exclusively for consumption by the farmers themselves, they do not constitute an important part of the economy and are therefore omitted from the calendar.

Although rice and broad beans are often grown alternately on the same plots of land, the acreage devoted to rice is much greater than that sown with beans. In the absence of actual statistics, our estimate that the bean acreage is approximately 70 per cent of the rice acreage is probably not greatly in error. The explanation for this fact lies in two factors: soil and terrain. Owing to the narrowness of the valley and the rocky deforested nature of the mountains surrounding it, the small tributary streams carry a considerable load of sand. The flooding of these streams results in small areas with sandy soil, which are not suitable for rice cultivation but must be devoted to corn and other crops. The land farther away from the streams is of two types, both of which are suitable for rice. On the higher slopes at the east side of the village, the loose, well-drained soil is excellent for broad beans, though it does not produce abundant crops of rice. Farms in this area are invariably double-cropped. On the lower slopes, nearer the main stream, on the other hand, since the sticky, poorly drained soil is ideal for rice but unsatisfactory for beans, the fields usually lie idle during the autumn and winter. . . .

The leisure class

We first arrived in Luts'un on 16 November 1938, during the period of winter inactivity. Walking from the district town, we were impressed by the absence of workers in the fields of luxuriant broad-bean plants. As we entered the village, we observed many men idling about, some talking in groups, others squatting at the door of their houses, puffing their pipes. Catching sight of strangers in city garb, they immediately gathered around to ask questions. They welcomed us cordially when it was learned we were from the university, and the master of the primary school immediately invited us to lunch. Their hospitality and the warm, leisurely atmosphere of the village brought to my mind the old Chinese poem:

> The harvest's wealth this plenteous year
> Has gladdened us, for we may share
> With welcome guests who travel from afar.

But this mood was quickly dispelled when we saw, stumbling along the roughly paved paths of the village, lines of heavily laden coolies with lean, hungry faces and in worn, ragged clothing. On their backs they carried huge blocks of salt, burdens beneath which their bodies were bent almost double. Inquiries directed to our new friends elicited the information that these people were salt-carriers, whose job it was to transport salt on their backs from the well to the district town — more than a full day's walk. For this they were paid a wage of 20 cents a day. So, almost at the moment of entering the village, we were introduced to the startling contrast between the two classes who inhabit it: those who do not need to work during the slack agricultural period and those who must work continuously.

It was not long, however, before we learned that those who talk and smoke during the period when there is no farm work to be done spend their time in the same way during the busy periods on the farm. The salt-carriers, on the other hand, transfer their energies to the farm when the work is ready there. The individuals who enjoy their leisure are idle, not because they are not able-bodied or cannot find employment, but simply because they are landowners. As such, they receive the greater part of the produce of the land. The landless, on the contrary, must labour on the land, whether or not they are really able to work. The line of demarcation between the leisure class and the worker class coincides roughly with the line separating the haves and the havenots. This situation is rather shocking, in the light of the avowed national policy that 'those who work on the land shall possess the land'.

The cases which follow serve to illustrate the characteristics and attitudes of individuals belonging to the leisure class.

Wang the Christian, our landlord, during our first visit to

the village, was about forty years of age and able-bodied, although, because of a former addiction to opium, not strong. He spent fully half of his time in bed; rarely retiring later than 9 o'clock in the evening and rising shortly before breakfast, at 9 o'clock in the morning. He attended church regularly; and on market days he spent all his time in the teashop, where he sometimes painted pictures for his admiring friends. He was the owner of 35 *kung** of land but rarely performed any farm work himself. During the winter of 1938 the labourer he employed to plough his single-cropped farm left the village, after being accused of theft, leaving his task uncompleted. Wang answered our suggestion, that he himself finish the work, with the statement that it would not be necessary because other labourers would be available. The result was that the rest of the farm was not ploughed until the next year, but my landlord was not much perturbed. Despite this fact, he is regarded by the villagers as an industrious man, and this judgement is probably deserved; for when the labour supply proved insufficient during the 1,939 harvest, he did join the crew on the farm. But this was an exceptional case, as proved by his statement that he had not touched agricultural tools for many years.

Others, with equivalent amounts of land, are even less industrious. Sze, the schoolmaster, and the former officials Wang and Chang, all opium-smokers, were usually in bed when we called on them. When we asked them bluntly why they did not work on their land, they were amused by our ignorance of the tradition that manual work was not for men like them. . . .

Many similar instances could be cited to illustrate the lives of members of the leisure class who are able to live in idleness owing to special economic conditions in the village. Since agriculture is the only industry, there are practically no opportunities for employment other than in farming. Therefore, the landless and those with little land constitute an abundant and, consequently, a cheap labour supply which permits the landowners to free themselves from toil on the land. The latter are thus forced up into a distinct social class by the army of labourers beneath them. . . .

* 1 *kung* equals 0.38 *mow* or 0.057 acres.

Family holdings

Table 4.1 gives the distribution of family ownership of land in Luts'un. The *kung*, instead of the *mow* (in terms of which the land survey records appear), is used as the unit, because, as we have demonstrated, it alone is significant in the lives of the owners.

Table 4.1   *Size of farms in Luts'un*

Size of farm (in kung)	No. of households
0	38
1— 5	14
6—10	21
11—15	8
16—20	5
21—25	3
26—30	15
31—35	1
36—40	7
41—45	0
46—50	6
51—55	0
56—60	3
61—65	1

The total land owned by individual families comprises about 1 800 *kung*, or 690 *mow*, which is an average of 5.7 *mow*, or 0.3 ha (0.87 acres), per family. Thirty-one per cent of the households in the village, however, are landless. The 1 800 *kung* are owned as follows: 446 (25 per cent) by 35 per cent of the households with less than 16 *kung* each; 614 (34 per cent) by 19 per cent with 16—30 *kung* each; and 740 (41 per cent) by 15 per cent with 31—65 *kung* each. In other words, a minority of the population holds most of the land, and the majority is landless or has insufficient land for its support. But it is noteworthy that there are only petty owners here, for the largest estate comprises only 65 *kung*, about 25 *mow* or about 1.6 ha (4 acres).

Collective holdings

A substantial amount of land is owned by social groups, such as clans, clubs, and temples. It comprises, in fact, 27 per cent of all the land owned by members of the village. The largest such holding comprises 135 *kung*, or more than 52 *mow*, which is more than double the largest private holding. Table 4.2 presents a complete list of the groups, together with an inventory of their respective properties.

The largest property-holder of the village is the Temple of the Lord of the Earth, an institution which is found in almost every village in the region. Possessed of all the appurtenances of a place of worship, it is yet more than that; it is, in fact, the material embodiment of the community organization. Its

Table 4.2   *Collective holdings*

Type of land	No. of mow
1. Land owned by groups in Luts'un:	
Temple to the Lord of Earth	52.671
Wei clan	28.407
Family shrine of Wang Wen Yi Kong	27.268
Pine Garden of Wang clan	26.748
Another branch of Wang clan	23.732
Tien Sen dam	15.608
Taoist Music Society	14.109
Fraternity of Honesty and Righteousness	12.756
Imperial Teaching Society	9.803
Older Fraternity	7.004
Confucius Club	6.749
Temple (Hong Chiao Kong)	5.084
Chang clan	3.085
Chou clan	2.201
Dam for the new ditch	2.085
Total	237.310
2. Land within the village owned by groups outside the village:	
Temple of the God of Literature	7.067
White-Robe Nunnery	5.950
Chia No. 1 of the district town	4.285
Congregation of God of the Military	3.118
Educational bureau of the district	2.784
Total	23.204
Grand total	260.514

property, acquired mainly by the reversion of the land of many villagers who perished during the Muslim rebellion of 1855–73, is considered the possession of all the inhabitants of the village, for whose benefit the income is disbursed. Specifically, its funds are spent for (1) the maintenance of the village temple; (2) part of the maintenance of the village school; (3) emergency restoration of the dam; (4) entertainment of soldiers passing through the village; (5) gifts at the marriages and burials of villagers; and (6) partial subsidization of the village government.

Although the resources of the temple are supposed to be administered for the welfare of the population as a whole, their management is not subject to the will of all the people. The treasurer is not a part of the formal administrative system of the village but is charged with the duty of representing the people in bargaining with the headman. He is theoretically selected by common consent; in practice, the position is held in rotation by the influential men of the village by their common consent. The invariable practice of ignoring the poor in questions of administration is justified by the statement that their poverty disqualifies them, since they could not reimburse the public coffers were they to make mistakes. It is impossible to say how much profit accrues to the treasurer, for, since the only concern of the people is that the traditional functions be performed, there is no system of auditing or making public his accounts.

There are a number of landowning clubs, differing widely in their purposes and activities. The Confucius Club is now inactive, and the rent from its properties is assigned to the school. The Taoist Music Club, with a voluntary membership, performs ceremonies in honour of various gods on the first and fifteenth days of each month and is also invited to participate in village funeral ceremonies. Its income, derived both from its property and from fees paid by individuals for whom it performs services, is used to defray the expenses of its meetings. The Imperial Teaching Society, which is supposed to have been organized during the Ching Dynasty for the purpose of reading and interpreting the book of moral teachings promulgated by the imperial palace, holds meetings on the first and fifteenth of each month. It still fulfils its original function of teaching morality; but it is, in addition, a charitable organization which assists the poor in meeting burial expenses.

Ownership of land by the clan may arise through agreement by a group of brothers to leave a portion of their inheritance in a common pool to avoid the necessity of constant sharing of their own produce for the general clan welfare or through donation of land by wealthy members for the care of needy ones. The gift of Wang Wen Yi Kong, a well-known official, was an example of the latter sort. The income from the clan lands is used to finance sacrifices to the ancestors and clan feasts and to provide scholarships for the college education of its members and general assistance to poor members. The treasurer who manages the clan land is selected on the basis of ability and prestige, factors which also determine his tenure. Since the office may be profitable, there is keen competition for it, and all the aspirants watch the incumbent closely, at the same time seeking to reduce his personal profit by making constant demands for expenditures of the funds. The treasurer of Wang's clan told me that there was never a peaceful clan feast and that many ended in violent disputes. At the feast of the Pine Garden branch in 1939, after solemn sacrifice to the ancestors, someone demanded that the treasurer open his accounts to inspection. The latter refused but was forced to give another feast to pacify his fellow-clansmen.

Other owner groups are the monks of the Temple of the God of the Military and of the Temple of the God of Literature; the irrigation organization, which devotes its income to the maintenance of the irrigation dams and ditches; and the educational bureau, whose land provides the revenue to pay part of the expenses of the village school.

Landless households

Of the thirty-eight landless households in the village, only four are able to make a living from non-agricultural occupations; all the rest are dependent for at least part of their livelihood on farm employment and constitute a large proportion of the total labour supply. The members of nineteen of these households are called 'new settlers' by the villagers. . . . Of these nineteen families, one operates a farm which it possesses temporarily on the basis of a loan; seven rent land;

and the remaining eleven work only as labourers on the farms of others.

This labelling of certain of the villagers as 'new settlers' piqued our curiosity, especially since we knew that at least some of them had been inhabitants of Luts'un for many years and since we were aware of the fact that the village it-self did not have a long history. The old residents declared that the village had grown up during their lifetimes, asserting that in their youth only a few houses marked the site. Until the war, immigration had been an important factor in the growth of the population, for the fertile land and the system of hiring workers for the cultivation of the land had con-stantly attracted labour from outside. Our inquiries first elicited the statement that new settlers are those who have come to the village in recent years, but it was obvious that the factor of recency alone was not actually very important. The labourer Kon Wen, for example, though the son of an immigrant, had been born in the village; but he was still con-sidered a 'new settler'. It soon became evident that the real criterion was the possession of land. Those immigrants who acquire land are then, and not until then, accepted as members of the community, while those who remain landless continue to be regarded as outsiders. In this agricultural village, as in other similar sections of China [1], ownership of land is a necessary qualification for complete integration into the community.

The acquisition of land by immigrants is, however, not generally easy. The individual who moves into an area whose land is already fully utilized must, if the economy is strictly agricultural, support himself as an employee or as a tenant unless he has the power to deprive the earlier residents of their land. The latter usually have a potent advantage in such a struggle because they are entrenched in their holdings by law and custom, both of which militate against the landless intruder, who has to work against well-organized resistance in his struggle for land of his own. In a later section we shall describe the restrictions imposed on the disposition of land in Luts'un, where clan members always have a prior right to acquire land which is being sold [2].

Even in the absence of restrictive laws or customs, the acquisition of land by newcomers in a community is unusual, inasmuch as individuals with the capital required for purchase of property rarely emigrate. It seems to be pretty generally true here that most immigrants who leave their homes do so under the pressure of poverty and that they cannot hope to save enough from their wages to buy farms. . . .

Tenancy

Unlike the hired labourer, who is paid solely on the basis of time or of production, a tenant has an interest in the productivity of the land. With his payment of annual rent, he takes over from the owner all responsibility for the exploitation of the farm, and it is he who must accept the risk and provide the working capital. He may work the farm himself or hire labourers instead, whichever he chooses, for all income in excess of the sum he pays the landlord is his to dispose of in any way he sees fit.

The nominal rental is approximately 60 per cent of the rice yield. In practice, however, this rate rarely prevails. A typical example of the deviations from the theoretical standard is the case of Chen, who leased one farm, of 10 *kung*, for half the yield of rice; another, of 5 *kung*, from the Wang clan for 10 *piculs* (33 per cent of the 30-*picul* production); and a third, of 25 *kung*, of the common land of a neighbouring village, which yielded 180 *piculs* and for which he paid 100 *piculs*, or 55 per cent. The high rental of 60 per cent (15 *piculs* out of a yield of 25 *piculs*) paid by Kang Wen in 1937 on a farm of 4 *kung* rented from Chou was the result of an increase demanded of him because of an exceptional harvest the preceding year; for ten years he had been paying only 12 *piculs*. Brother Wang, on the other hand, rented a piece of land from the son of his father's brother for only 4 of the 10 *piculs* it produced. These instances show that, under ordinary circumstances, the nominal rate is 60 per cent is in reality the maximum and is seldom in effect. Even at this high rate, an owner of high-grade land would receive a rent of only $4.80 a *kung*, which is approximately $1.00 less than the income he could enjoy by retaining the management of his farm and employing others to work it. Land rented at the more usual figure of 50 per cent would bring $1.50 less. These figures confirm the villagers' observation that an owner will find managing his farm much more profitable than renting it out. In the light of these financial considerations, a scrutiny of the circumstances under which a proprietor would be willing to rent his land seems pertinent.

As might be anticipated, a very limited number of 1 800 *kung* owned by the individual households of Luts'un are rented, and there are special reasons to account for the few exceptions to the general rule. Most of the 140 rented *kung* are located so far from the village that the owners are not able to manage them. A few others belong to widows, as in the case of a sister-in-law of Chao, the village headman, who has no adult males in her house and rents her farm to her nephews. Still other land is leased at low rates by wealthier families to their poorer relatives as a form of assistance. The case of Wang, mentioned previously, is of this nature.

Although the households of Luts'un rent out very little of the land they own, they do rent, for their own use, a considerable quantity from others, as indicated by the discrepancy of 1 000 *kung* between the 1 800 they own and the 2 800 they manage. The ownership of the about 1 000 *kung* rented by the villagers may be analysed as follows: 624 *kung* owned by groups in Luts'un, 60 *kung* located within the

Table 4.3 *Size of farm managed by the villagers*

Size of farm (in kung)	No. of households	Percentage
0	18	15
1– 5	6	
6–10	8	16
11–15	6	
16–20	14	
21–25	19	48
26–30	25	
31–35	7	
36–40	9	
41–45	2	
46–50	5	21
51–55	0	
56–60	1	
61–65	2	

village but owned by outside groups, 100 *kung* in the village owned by outside individuals, and 200 *kung* lying outside the village and belonging to individuals and groups of other villages.

The distribution of the land managed by the households of Luts'un, regardless of ownership, is presented in Table 4.3. A comparison of these figures with those in Table 4.1 will disclose that management of land is much more evenly distributed among the villagers than is ownership. Although there are thirty-eight households which hold title to no land, there are only eighteen with none under their management. Forty-three households (35 per cent) own, but only twenty (16 per cent) manage, less than 16 *kung*, while almost half of them farm from 16—30 *kung* of their own or rented land, in contrast to the 19 per cent who are the actual proprietors of such estates. Again, the number of farmers managing large amounts of land is greater than the number of owners of large farms.

These figures demonstrate that the holders of relatively large properties, as well as the landless and the small owners, tend to expand the amount of land under their management through renting rather than through purchasing land. Table 4.4 gives the distribution of ownership by those households which cultivate rented farms. This table shows clearly that those who rent land are not necessarily landless or even poor people; the rich rent land too. This is because tenants

Table 4.4 *Size of unit owned by tenants*

Size of unit (in Kung)	No. of households
0	19
1— 5	13
6—10	17
11—15	7
16—20	1
21—25	1
26—30	2
31—35	1
Total	61

can enjoy a profit even if they operate their rented land by hired labour. Moreover, the rent on the collectively owned land is usually much lower than the normal rate. To be tenants of the collective owners is, in fact, a privilege. Those who are able to rent a piece of land from their clan are not far from acquiring a piece of land of their own. Since the largest owners who rent out land are collective owners, it is easy to see why the tenants are not limited to the poor. This fact should be borne in mind when we come to the discussion of the problems of tenancy in interior China — problems which should be understood as different from those in coastal China, which have been studied heretofore. In coastal China, tenancy is inevitably a system of exploitation of the peasants, while in the interior this is not necessarily true. . . .

Samples of family budgets

By accepting a lowered standard of living, approximately 30 per cent of the Luts'un landowners are able to free themselves from physical labour. . . . We may now attempt to define roughly the standard which represents the line below or above which work is considered the lesser or the greater evil. This will necessitate an examination of the standards of living of village families of both the leisure and the working classes. If our generalization is valid, then those who work will be found to have a living standard below the line of satisfaction and those who do not work will have a standard above that line.

The measurement of a family's consumption of goods and services is not an easy task, especially in a community such as Luts'un, where virtually no one maintains written records and where the economy is, to a large extent, self-sufficient. In a society where all commodities were purchased, the expenditures of a family would reflect its living standards. Although this situation may be approximated among city-dwellers, it does not exist in rural areas, where labour and important goods are provided by the family itself and seldom appear in cash transactions. Hence a complete budget will include, in addition to those items for which payment is made, an evaluation of this self-sufficient portion of the household economy. Since the villagers do not maintain records and the maintenance of daily records by the investigator was impossible, it was necessary to select as informants a few families representing different economic levels. They were asked to give in detail their consumption for the past year, and the resultant quantities were translated into monetary terms. . . .

Households A and B represent the landowning class. Household A owns 40 *kung*, of which it cultivates 36 *kung*, yielding 350 *piculs* of unhusked rice, and rents 4 *kung* to a clan brother for 16 *piculs* of rice. Approximately 130 *piculs* of polished rice are available for use or sale after refining (which reduces the husked rice to 146 *piculs*) and the deduction of 10 per cent for spoilage and shrinkage. This represents a surplus of roughly 100 *piculs* over the 28 *piculs* needed in the family's diet, with a cash value of $250 at the price level of October 1938. The income from rice alone would thus more than cover the family's normal living expenses, which, excluding the cost of a son's education, wholly paid for by the clan, amount to $120. Other income (e.g. the income from beans alone amounts to one-quarter that of rice, or about $80) increases the amount available for extraordinary expenses to more than $100.

Household B owns a farm of 14 *kung* and holds an additional plot of 13 *kung* through temporary transference. Its farm of 27 *kung* yields 240 *piculs* of unhusked rice or, after refining, 96 *piculs* of polished rice. After the reduction of 40 *piculs* for home consumption and allowing for storage losses, 50 *piculs* will be available for sale and will bring $125. This sum added to $60 for the bean crop, little more than covers the family's annual cash expenditures of $160. The head of this family, however, supplements his income by buying and selling in the markets. In 1939, for example, he made a profit of $100 by purchasing oxen and transporting them to Kunming for sale and a profit of $50 through the sale in Luts'un of paper which he purchased in the distant village where it was manufactured.

Although neither of these households is considered to be the wealthiest in the village, the standards of living of both are representative of the upper stratum. Each owns a two-storey house with three rooms on the ground floor and a large porch extending the length of the front wall. The porch is the locus for eating and most other domestic activities, while a central room, containing the best furniture and the ancestral tablets, is reserved for more formal occasions. The remaining two rooms are partitioned to make three or four sleeping compartments, one of which we occupied in Household A during our first visit in the village. It proved to be very light, airy, and comfortable. The second storey does not serve for living quarters but is used entirely as a storeroom. At one side of the front yard is a kitchen, at the other a pig pen — both separate from the house. There is a vegetable garden at the side of the house, with a privy in one corner. The arrangement of buildings and grounds outlined here is representative of the homes of the higher-income groups in the village. These houses are appreciably superior in quality and cleanliness to those we have observed in coastal China. This high standard of housing seems to be characteristic of the province of Yunnan, where even in the small villages exceptionally fine houses are not at all uncommon.

The members of Households A and B wear excellent clothing. The heads of the families have long robes for formal occasions, as well as hip-length jackets for ordinary wear, some made of silk or other expensive materials. The women likewise are provided with good wardrobes, which include silver ear-rings and hair ornaments. In Household A the boy wore a student uniform with leather shoes and European shirts, and the three-year-old child wore knitted jackets and caps of foreign style. Since the best clothing of these families is purchased for special occasions, such as marriages or funerals, its cost does not appear as part of the normal living expenses.

These families also maintain a high standard for the food they consume. The household's average daily consumption of meat, which is obtained both from the pigs they slaughter and by purchase in the market, is more than 227 g (½ lb). Their diet includes an abundance of vegetables, raised in their own garden, and wine, which they make themselves; and every evening a dessert of wheat or rice-flour cakes and honey is served. During the time we boarded with Household A, the wife, an excellent cook, whose skill is abetted by the quality of the ingredients she uses (e.g. she is able to afford lard instead of vegetable oils), never failed to produce a delectable meal. Similarly, the food we frequently shared with Household B was always very good, even when special dishes were not prepared for us. It is otherwise in the poorer homes. The food in the house in which we boarded during our second visit was so inadequate that we were compelled to supplement it by travelling to the district town for additional meals.

It is commonly conceded that these two families (Households A and B) enjoy the highest standard of housing cloth-ing, and food in the village. While their budgets show that the food they purchase constitutes only 14 per cent of their total cash expenditures, the inclusion of the items they produce themselves shows that food makes up about 31 per cent of the total living cost for Household A and about 53 per cent for Household B. But these figures present a distorted picture because that for Household A is computed on the basis of a total which includes an educational item which actually is not paid by the family. If this item is excluded from the com-putation, food comprises 47 per cent of the real living cost. Household B spends less for housing than does Household A because its newer house requires fewer repairs and less fuel. On the whole, however, the scale of living of these two families is almost identical.

Household C belongs in the owner-tenant class. It is closely similar to Household A in the amount of land cultivated and in the size of the family; but it differs greatly in its income, by virtue of the necessity for paying rent. The payment of 150 *piculs* of grain for rent and polishing and the deduction of 10 per cent for spoilage reduce the amount of refined rice available for use or sale to 65 *piculs*. After the family's requirement of 42 *piculs* for food has been satisfied, there remain only 23 *piculs*, which can be sold for $55. To this amount may be added $80, the income from the broad-bean crop. The cash income will thus barely cover the cash expenditures of $120. Because of the lack of a reserve, it is often necessary to sell the rice intended for the table to meet unusual expenditures and then to buy rice when it is needed for food. This is a financial handicap, since it is frequently necessary to sell at low prices and to buy at high prices.

Expenditures for food occupy a prominent place in

Household C's budget, accounting for approximately 71 per cent of the total living costs. Of the total cost of food, meat comprises only 3 per cent, in contrast to 25 and 34 per cent for Households A and B, respectively. The poverty of this family is manifested most conspicuously in the clothing of its members. Their garments are worn and patched, and even the head of the family lacks socks and is often without shoes.

Since its original house was torn down, to make the materials available for sale, and replaced by a small, two-storey building with no windows in the second floor and with only two rooms on the ground floor, the family has suffered from overcrowding. All the members slept in one room until the marriage of the son, when the living-room was converted into a bedroom. As a result of this overcrowding, the whole family was suffering from malaria at the time of our second visit to the village. The family head was so changed by the ravages of the disease that I failed to recognize him in the pale, feeble old man who came tottering toward me with the aid of a stick. He attributed his misfortunes — the death of his wife a few months earlier and the illness of his two daughters and son — to the unlucky influence of his son's new wife, who was also ill. He bitterly lamented the marriage of his son to this girl, who was, he insisted 'a vehicle of ill fortune'. The small expenditure for medicine by a family so stricken by disease is attributable to the fact that prayer is substituted for more material remedies. It is said that the daughter-in-law had died but was restored to life by the prayers of a Christian. So the Christian God, who, according to their belief, demands no pecuniary reward, is relied upon for the physical wellbeing of the family.

Households D and E are representative of the landless families. They do not own their own homes but rent ramshackle, one-room huts outside the gates of the village. While we were visiting Household E one day, following a period of rainy weather, part of the saturated earth walls of the dark, windowless house suddenly collapsed, letting in a flood of unaccustomed light. We were appalled by this catastrophe; but the family accepted it calmly, for, as we learned, it was a frequent occurrence. The wife simply remarked that once more they would have a poor night's sleep. Then we discovered that the water was still trickling through the poor thatching of the roof into the attic where the family slept. The building in which Household D lived was equally unsatisfactory. Because the floor is lower than the garden at the back, it was flooded whenever there was rain, until at the suggestion of a neighbour a ditch was dug through the house to carry off the water. Both houses are almost constantly filled with smoke, since, by reason of the inadequate clothing of the occupants, a fire is essential for warmth in chilly weather and since poverty necessitates the burning of grass and wood rather than charcoal. The smoke was so heavy that we, unaccustomed to it, were unable to open our eyes and were convinced that the equipment of an investigator should include a gas mask. Inasmuch as the activities of almost all the occupants are carried on within the walls of these wet, smoky hovels, it is not surprising that, although each family had produced six or seven children, only one was alive at the time we were in the village. The last death had occurred during the year before our visit. The living members all suffer from trachoma, and the head of Household D is nearly blind.

Both of these families depend entirely upon wages for their livelihood. Even though they are employed most of the time, with food provided by their employers, their food costs are as much as 60 or 70 per cent of their total budgets, or up to 80 per cent of their cash expenditures. If the amount provided by employers is taken into account, food will be found to constitute a much larger proportion of their total living requirements.

Mr Chang, co-author of this book, became a close friend of the members of Household E and so was able to secure accurate information as to their income. The husband was employed for about 350 days during the year and earned approximately $35. The wife worked 10 days a month in December and January, 30 days a month in August and September, and 15 days a month during the rest of the year; her wages for the 200 days she worked during the year were $10. In addition, the man carried salt six times for $6.00, and there was some subsidiary income from other activities, such as dealing in the market. The total cash income was thus only slightly greater than the cash expenditures for current needs.

Food consumption varies widely among the villagers; the poorer people eat only two meals a day except during the ume they work on the farm, while the more prosperous are distinguished by the fact that they always eat three times daily. Yet it is apparent that food consumption is the least elastic of all the categories, for, according to our figures, its percentage in the budget drops rapidly with increase of income. The clothing percentage, on the contrary, rises with income, suggesting that the poorer peasants are very inadequately clothed. Our findings in this respect correspond with observations made in India, among Shanghai workers, and among the peasants of Wuhsing, Chekiang [3]. Although actual expenditures for housing by the wealthier families, who own their own homes, represent a smaller proportion of the living expenses than do the rents paid by the poorer families, the assignment of rental values to these structures would reverse the situation. This again reflects the extremely low standard of the housing facilities for the poorer villagers. With the exception of taxes, which fall proportionately more heavily upon the poor, the percentage of the expenditures for other, more flexible, goods and services increase with the income. . . .

Ceremonial expenses

Our discussion thus far has been confined to items of current expense — those necessary for day-to-day living. Another important category of expense is that connected with the ceremonies which are necessary at life-crises, such as birth, marriage, and death. We shall not discuss the importance of the ceremonies in meeting the crises or the justification of the expenditures, for we are concerned here only with the economic aspects of the social structure as it exists. This section will be devoted to expenses involved in five types of ceremonial occasions — namely, marriage, funeral, and birth ceremonies, the ceremony for general good fortune, and the ceremony in celebration of long life.

The funeral ceremony for the father of the schoolteacher took place while we were in the village. During the six days it lasted, a feast was provided twice a day. On the first day, twenty-one tables of six guests each were served. On the succeeding days the guests were much more numerous: on the second day, thirty-eight tables were served; on the third day, forty-five tables; on the fourth day, seventy tables; on the fifth day, ninety-eight tables in the morning and 105 in the evening; on the sixth day, sixty tables. These figures represent a total of 4 026 individual meals; the entire village was fed by the family for several days and, in addition, there were visitors from other villages. The number of guests would have been still larger except for the fact that the magistrate of the district was giving a funeral feast for his father on these same days. Yet the schoolteacher was apologetic about the limited number of guests, explaining, 'I did not send out announcements, because I did not want to bother people. So only those who have wanted voluntarily to console me have come.' With my statement that the cost of such a lengthy ceremony must be a heavy burden, he disagreed vehemently: 'Only by spending as much as I am able to can I pay honour to my deceased father. That is my obligation. I would feel only shame if I could not spend the money in his honour.'

The tenant-farmer of Household C was arranging a marriage ceremony for his son while we were in the village. When we offered to shop for him on a visit we were about to make to Kunming, he gave us, after consulting with his wife, a long list of merchandise, which included three types of cloth and a woollen blanket. The old woman in our landlord's house reprimanded him for his extravagance, admonishing him against the spending of so much money during these hard times and urging that some native cloth would be quite sufficient for the son. After conferring again with his wife, the man eliminated the blanket from the list, but the remaining items still cost him well in excess of $10. When we were about to make a second trip to the city, he asked us to buy him a quantity of a certain tea which I had served him, replying to my protest that it was very expensive with the simple statement that he must have only the best. On another occasion he asked that I obtain for him a special type of red card for invitations. I was repeatedly amazed by his insistence on obtaining nothing but the best for the ceremony and his utter disregard of the cost, since I knew . . . that he is normally extremely thrifty and has a low standard of living. He works on the farm himself, does not smoke or drink, is usually barefooted, and wears patched clothing. Ordinarily, he buys nothing which is not essential, but in the case of this ceremony he threw all financial discretion to the winds and seemed to acquire a completely different personality. Despite the fact that, as a consequence of the marriage of his son, he was in debt for several tens of dollars and his store of rice had been sold, the smile on his worn face revealed an inner peace which made us feel that his life's goal had been attained. The old women in our landlord's household explained: 'We don't experience real happiness in our own marriage, we achieve it when we accomplish our son's marriage.' On the other hand, there are those for whom it is impossible to raise money for marriage ceremonies and who are thus doomed to lifelong bachelorhood.

The conventional expenditure for funeral ceremonies is more variable than that for marriages, since a marriage can be delayed and planned and accumulated for, while the time for a funeral is determined by death alone. During our second stay in the village a man who lived across the street from us died. The family was so poor that it was necessary to borrow money even for a coffin; and on the day of burial there was but one table of guests, those who had come in to assist with the funeral. In cases of extreme poverty the corpse may even be left at the side of the road for days until it is buried by some philanthropic organization. . . .

Opium smoking

In 1938, according to the estimates given me by the villagers, the monthly consumption of opium for the village was 5.5 kg (200 oz). At the price of $4.00 an oz, then current, the annual expenditure for this drug would be $10 000. Because this figure seemed incredibly high, we recorded the names of all the addicts, i.e., those who had to smoke daily, during our second visit in 1939. Despite the fact that the number was said to have been much reduced, owing to the price increase and the effectiveness of the government's prohibition, our census revealed thirty-eight addicts. Since the minimum per capita daily consumption would be 0.03 oz, which in September, 1939, cost $0.50, the annual minimum cost of opium for these thirty-eight individuals would be $7 000.

Since the government now prohibits the raising of the poppy plant, all these smokers, except those wealthy ones

who have opium left from previous years, must rely on outside sources. Although governmental regulations specify that
addicts must register and that they shall be given a supply for
a tapering-off period, only eight of the villagers have com-
plied; the rest depend on smuggled supplies and are responsible for the heavy drainage of money out of the village. We
were told that, if this situation continues, all the rice in
excess of that actually consumed by the villagers will be
required to pay the opium bill. This statement is not far from
the truth, for, on the basis of 1939 prices, $5 000 spent for
opium would require the export of 8 750 *piculs* of rice grain.
The significance of this figure will be apparent when we recall
that the total yield of the village, according to our estimate,
is only about 21 000 *piculs*, of which about 9 000 are needed
locally for food. It is obvious that such a large proportion of
income cannot be dissipated without seriously curtailing
other consumption and depressing the standard of living.

It is true that the number of addicts has decreased during
recent years, for the middle-aged man who has not at some
time smoked opium is extremely rare. Yet, despite severe
regulation by the government, about half of the addicts have
not completely rid themselves of the habit. Since Luts'un
produced opium of an exceptionally good quality before its
cultivation was made illegal, the use of the drug required no
expenditure of money. At one time, even the women and the
children smoked, and at the present time almost anyone who
feels unwell will resort to a pipe for relief.

The elimination of poppy raising was relatively easy, and
not a flower is to be seen in Luts'un; but the eradication of
the opium habit is another matter. Without medical assistance the termination of smoking is accompanied by almost
intolerable torture. Moreover, although the price increase will
exert a pressure which must inevitably reduce still more the
amount of opium consumed and the number of addicts,
failure to take positive action on the problem will result in
serious economic consequences. There is no doubt that the
price factor will be effective only after many families have
been financially ruined. It is evident that, unless the prohibition on smoking is accompanied by a sound medical policy,
impetus will be given to the collapse of the village economy
and to administrative corruption.

When the villagers, in accordance with the traditional economic attitude, have attained an adequate standard of living and have renounced the painful experience of work, they are faced with the problem of whiling away their many leisure hours. For my landlord who neither works nor uses opium, this is a burdensome problem, which he can solve only by sleeping long hours and by loitering about the church and the teashops. To the smokers, however, there is no such problem. We have always felt that the spread of opium over China in the last 100 years was not accidental but that there must have been some factor in the social environment which gave it its impetus. We are now inclined to believe that the existence of this leisure class must have been in some degree responsible, for lying contentedly on an opium bed, gossiping with one's fellow-addicts, would seem to be an adequate solution to the problem of passing that time for which there is no constructive use. Smoking has become integrated into the social system and is a link in a vicious circle: the man who has leisure smokes; the man who smokes will have a profound distaste for work.

5 China: land of famine

Food is the most urgent problem of the Chinese. This fact is reflected even in the speech of the people. In China the polite salutation on meeting a friend is 'Have you eaten?' instead of the customary inquiry as to one's health or wellbeing usually employed in other tongues. This form of greeting is a creation of the rural community, and the implication is that if the person so saluted has not eaten the inquirer will see that his needs are quickly met. Foreigners who study the language with a Chinese teacher find that almost the first words and phrases given to them have to do with food, eating, and money (with which to buy food). 'The rich man has food to eat, the poor man has none', forms the basis of one of the first lessons. Beggars are referred to in the colloquial idiom as 'food wanters'; and they all provide themselves with pails or bowls in which they can receive the refuse from the tables of the well-to-do.

The food problem is an ancient one in China: from the earliest times famines have been an ever recurring scourge. A study recently completed by the Student Agricultural Society of the University of Nanking brought to light the surprising and significant fact that between the years 108 BC and AD 1911 there were 1 828 famines, or one nearly every year in at least one of the provinces. Untold millions have died of starvation. In fact the normal death rate may be said to contain a constant famine factor. Depleted vitality following years of want also tends to increase the death rate. Chinese history is filled with the details of past disasters and not only recounts at great length the nature of the calamity and its causes but names the officials under whom relief work was administered and describes the methods pursued in bringing succour to the unfortunate victims.

The Emperor Yü, who lived 4 000 years ago, achieved great renown and is still regarded by the Chinese people as a national sage, for the wisdom displayed in his flood prevention work on the Yellow River. Since his time officials have repeatedly endeavoured to follow his example, and fame has been more readily achieved by devising methods to relieve and prevent famine emergencies than in almost any other way.

The great drought that occurred in north China in 1920–21, during which, according to the best obtainable information, 500 000 of the natives perished, is still fresh in the minds of the public. Mr Dwight W. Edwards, in his comprehensive report [1], estimates that at the height of the distress nearly 20 million people were destitute. In some of the worst affected districts not only was the entire reserve of food consumed but also all other vegetation. A house-to-house canvas revealed the following bill of fare: k'ang, mixed with wheat blades, flour made of ground leaves, fuller's earth, flower seed, poplar buds, corncobs, hung ching tsai (steamed balls of some wild herb), sawdust, thistles, leaf dust, poisonous tree bean, kaoliang husks, cotton seed, elm bark, bean cakes (very unpalatable), peanut hulls, sweet potato vines ground (considered a great delicacy), roots, stone ground up into flour to piece out the ground leaves. Some of the food was so unpalatable that the children starved, refusing to eat it.

Everything of any intrinsic value was sold by the poorer people, even including the roof timbers; and interest rates rose until even 100 per cent was considered not unreasonable in some places. There was extensive migration of the people from the dry regions, in some localities whole villages moving out. The sale of women and children, particularly young girls, reached such proportions that a special committee was organized for the protection of children. Prices ranged from $3.00 to $150.00, Chinese currency ($1 in United States currency equals approximately $2 in Chinese), and thus the sacrifice of one or two of the younger members of the family served to provide the wherewithal to purchase food for the rest. Parents were not ready to give up their children but did so rather than see them starve.

Mr Edwards estimates that more than $37 million, Chinese

currency, was made available to meet the needs of the sufferers. Of this more than half was administered under international auspices; and this included large sums from abroad, particularly America. At the height of their operations the international committees alone were feeding more than 7 700 000 individuals.

A notable work was accomplished. But what of the future? Has a starving population today been saved simply to die during the next famine a few years hence unless further aid is forthcoming? Is there no means by which these great disasters can be prevented?

Wellwishers of China who have studied her famine problem have brought forward many schemes for improving conditions. They reflect the particular interest with which their authors are identified, ranging all the way from the fundamentalist missionary's faith that if the Chinese masses will become Christians 'the Lord will provide' to the machinery salesman's idea that China's only hope is the early adoption of industrialism.

Conservancy engineers tell us that the most urgent need is the control of China's rivers to prevent devastating floods, the carrying-out of irrigation, land reclamation, and similar projects to increase the cultivable land. Economists propose the introduction of better banking methods which will lower the interest rates and make possible the application of the surplus capital in the cities to the rural sections of the country. Or, again, they advance the proposal to relieve the pressure of population in the thickly settled regions by colonization of the vast areas of Manchuria and Mongolia. Provision of better transportation facilities is also urged so that the abundant crops of a prosperous district may be quickly and cheaply moved to a section where flood or drought may have created a condition of want.

The educator advocates the teaching of agriculture in the schools and colleges and the advanced training of foresters. He traces China's ills, particularly of the northern provinces of the country, to deforestation – a process which has been under way for centuries.

Many of those who give their thought to the social aspects of the situation point to the phenomenally high birth rate and insist, quite justly in the author's opinion, that no permanent solution of the problem of famines in China is possible until the people are content to regulate the size of their families according to their resources.

All agree that the present unusually bad conditions are in a measure traceable to the political disorganization of the country. However, there is no more appropriate time than the present to consider by what means better conditions can be brought about; and indeed there are many remedial measures that can be initiated even in these disordered days.

The question is one of such magnitude that, if any appreciable progress is to be made, all of the plans mentioned above must be followed. But there are certain types of work that will yield results more quickly than others, and it is the author's purpose not only to present plans but to examine them in some detail and endeavour to point out the relative importance of each.

Economic causes of famine

The struggle for existence in China is indescribably hard. The meagre statistics available show a condition among the great mass of the people which Westerners are at first inclined to doubt and which, when proved to their satisfaction to be true, they are never able to understand. One often hears statements about the 'margin of livelihood' in China, but facts show that there is no margin at all if the population be regarded as a whole. The bare food requirements for a normal year are greater than the present production and importation of edibles, and this leads to the undernourishment of a part of the people and the eating of unwholesome food substitutes by the poorer classes.

Lack of statistics

The lack of reliable statistics regarding conditions in rural China has made the study of famines and the adoption of methods of relief and prevention a difficult matter. Without any standards of comparison it is even difficult to determine what constitutes a state of famine. Apart from these purely statistical difficulties, foreign investigators, even those long resident in China and conversant with the language, often bring back conflicting reports from the same district. A man of a sympathetic and impressionable nature will pronounce the whole countryside in the grip of the most abject want, while the inquirer with the more practical viewpoint reports normal conditions.

Recognizing the need for more detailed and accurate information the China International Famine Relief Commission in the summer of 1922 made a survey of rural conditions. It was carried out by students from nine universities who spent their summer vacation in the country collecting data on the basis of carefully prepared questionnaires and under the supervision of professors of economics of known standing. This was probably the first scientific attempt of any importance to secure dependable facts concerning the social and economic conditions under which the country people live; and some of the results of this inquiry will be utilized in these pages [2].

The cost of living

Various estimates have been made of the cost of living in interior China. On account of poor transportation this cost is greatly affected by the size of the last harvest in the particular district examined; and, since these estimates always refer to restricted areas, allowance must be made if the figures are to be applied to the country as a whole.

Professor C. G. Dittmer after a detailed examination of the budgets of about 200 families near Peking reaches the conclusion that a family of five can live in comparative comfort, according to local standards, on an income of $100 a year, Chinese currency [3]. This would provide sufficient simple food, a house that would at least afford shelter from the elements, two suits of clothing for each person, enough fuel for cooking, and a surplus of $5.00 for miscellaneous expenses. However, he goes on to say that the Chinese families examined by him all lived within their incomes, even though they received no more than $50.00 a year, and that those earning $70.00 a year were able to save money. The Manchu families included in the survey all showed a deficit if their income was less than $90.00.

In Professor Dittmer's analysis of family expenses, the cost

of food ranged from 68—83 per cent, the regular diet being
two meals a day of corn bread and salt turnips. Rent averaged
5—15 per cent, the best house costing but $15.00 a year. Fuel
and light required on the average 6—7 per cent of the yearly expenditure, and clothing 3.4—8.5 per cent. Miscellaneous
expenditures (including books, recreation, savings, etc.)
ranged from 1.3—6.6 per cent, and for the families with the
largest incomes the average annual amount was only $8.90.
This last item is a real measure of the family's standard of
living. In the United States even the poorer classes have at
least 20 per cent of their income remaining after the bare
necessities of life are assured — more than three times the
proportion enjoyed by the most fortunate Chinese families
included in this survey.

The figures arrived at by Professor J. B. Tayler are somewhat higher: he gives the total annual income requirement
for a family of five roughly as $150.00 [4]. The higher esti-
mate may be due in part to the fact that the investigation on
which he bases his opinion was made several years after that
of Professor Dittmer, and living costs had risen considerably
in the meantime. It should be pointed out that his estimates
are based on the requirements for the adequate sustenance of
a poor family rather than on an average of what is actually
spent by them. The figures obtained from rural investigation
have shown that a large proportion of the incomes are below
the poverty line; and to give the actual expenditure on which
a family is known to have survived does not necessarily mean
that its members have received sufficient food or clothing to
keep them in health.

Professor Tayler's appraisal of the food requirements is
founded on a model diet for a poor Chinese farming population prepared by Dr G. Douglas Gray of the British Legation,
Peking, and Professor Bernard E. Read of the Peking Union
Medical College. According to this diet 2 985 g (104 oz) of
grain, 900 g (32 oz) wheat, 675 g (24 oz) millet, and 1 350 g
(48 oz) kaoliang, 425 g (15 oz) of vegetables, 283 g (10 oz)
of oil, and in winter 450 g (16 oz) of cabbage are needed
daily for a family of five. This diet is for a northern family
since no rice is included. It contains no luxuries: there is no
meat nor fish nor eggs. It is only about one-third of the value
of the diet required in England to yield an equal protein

content and an equal number of calories, the English diet containing a large proportion of animal products. Professor Tayler puts the clothing requirement at $20.00 a year, housing at $5.00, light at $5.00, and allows $7.00 for miscellaneous expenses. The $113.00 left from the budget of $150.00 is not enough to purchase the food requisite for the diet given above but, allowing for the period of inaction during the winter when the people are able to reduce their food allowance, is sufficient to maintain life. The cost of living in eastern and southern China is higher than in the north, because rice is more expensive than the northern grains; but the greater clothing and fuel needs in the north tend to reduce the difference.

Taking the more liberal allowance of $150.00 estimated by Professor Tayler as the poverty line, let us examine the China International Famine Relief Commission's survey, which covered 240 villages in Chihli, Kiangsu, Shantung, Anhwei, and Chekiang, with a total of 7 097 families, or 37 191 individuals. We find that more than half the population of the eastern villages and more than four-fifths of that of the northern villages had an income below the poverty line. No less than 17.6 per cent of the families of the eastern villages and 62.2 per cent of those of the northern villages had incomes of less than $50.00. This represents not only the actual cash income but also the value of crops raised and earnings from village industry. Professor Tayler says:

> The pressure of population is evidently a grim reality, and a considerable percentage of the families seem to go to pieces under this pressure. In the case of Chihli the figures are almost unbelievable. It is not contended that they are exact. In a certain number of cases the income given may have been very far from the truth, in many cases it may have been appreciably below, perhaps as much as 20 or even 30 per cent; but when allowance has been made for the utmost that can be conceded in this direction, the results still have a comparative value and they are certainly sufficiently startling.

It is interesting to note, for the sake of comparison, that the Peking police estimate of the income necessary for independence, as given in *Peking: a social survey*, is $66.00 a year for a family of two and $93.00 a year for a family of four [5]. This would nearly coincide with Professor Dittmer's calculation.

Somewhat similar surveys have been made recently (1925) by the Chinese Government Bureau of Economic Information, and the results arrived at are not sufficiently different to alter these conclusions. For instance, an investigation of the current wages in Shansi, one of the most prosperous and well governed provinces today, shows that the rate varies from $2.00 to $7.00 a month, including board, according to the line of work. The average for all trades is $4.50 a month, or $54.00 a year, Chinese currency. Farm hands are generally engaged by the year, their remuneration with board and lodging being $15.00 to $20.00 annually. The Bureau states that wages have increased from 100—200 per cent during the past decade [6].

Another investigation, the results of which were published by the same Bureau [7], was conducted by Dr Ta Chen, Professor of Sociology of Tsing Hua College, Peking. An examination was made of two villages, Chenfu, which is 6 miles from Peking and which may be considered as representing conditions in the north, and Huichow, Anhwei, in the rice-growing belt of central China. The following estimate of the cost of living was arrived at:

Table 5.1   *Cost of living in Chenfu and Huichow, 1925*

	Chenfu	Huichow
Food	$84.00	$106.60
Clothing	40.00	40.00
Rent	6.00	5.50
Miscellaneous (fuel, light)	5.00	5.00
Total expenses	$135.00	$157.10
Occupational earnings	93.12	88.80
Deficit	$41.88	$68.30

It will be seen that the cost of living is greater in the south, a result which bears out the Famine Commission figures. Also it appears that the people in neither village had sufficient income to meet the requirements of this standard of living, many of them being entirely dependent on occupational earnings. The average size of the families was 4.9 in Chenfu, and 4.4 in Huichow. These figures are slightly smaller than the findings of the Famine Commission but they cover only 147 families, while the latter survey included 7 097.

Food requirements not met

As has been said above, normal annual food requirements are greater than the entire domestic production plus the imports. In accordance with the diet which has been accepted as necessary to preserve health, the grain needed for a family of five is 1 075 kg (2 372 lb) a year. Mr D. K. Lieu of the Chinese Government Bureau of Economic Information estimates that the average yield of wheat, the staple food in the northern provinces, is about 544 kg/0.4 ha (1 200 lb/acre) which, after deducting loss in husking and milling, would leave 227 kg (500 lb) of flour [8]. It would, therefore, take 1.6 ha (4.7 acres) to provide for a family of five. But 33 per cent of the holdings are less than 0.4 ha (1 acre), and 55 per cent are 0.6 ha (1.5 acres) or less, while the number of large farms is very small indeed. The average size of the families who have as much as 0.6 ha (1.5 acres) is 5.7, and the number in the families increases with the size of the holdings. The same land in good years is capable of producing, besides the winter wheat, a crop of beans or millet which is harvested in the fall; but even assuming two crops a year which, because of frequent floods and droughts, is possible only a part of the time, it will be seen that the yield does not meet the needs.

The staple food in central and southern China is rice. Probably two-thirds of the entire population of China make it their chief diet. Mr Lieu estimates the average yield of clean rice at 975 kg/0.4 ha (2 150 lb/acre) in the richest rice-growing region. The average yield for all rice-growing provinces is probably about 635 kg/0.4 ha (1 400 lb/acre). At this rate it would take 0.68 ha (1.7 acres) to provide the 1 076 kg (2 372 lb) necessary for an average family. But, as has been said, 55 per cent of the families have holdings of less than 0.6 ha (1.5 acres). During the last three years for which statistics of the Maritime Customs are available the excess of imports of rice over exports averages about 17 million *piculs*, or

119

1 024 million kg (2 260 million lb) a year. If we place the number of rice eaters at 300 million this quantity divided among them would mean 3 400 g (7.5 lb) apiece. In addition, much of the land is capable of producing two crops, which helps to bring the yield up to requirements. The picture, however, is blacker when it is borne in mind that, although there is an embargo on the export of rice and of some other cereals, much smuggling is practised and the embargo is often raised by the military dictators in times of provincial warfare in return for large contributions from interested merchants to the war chests. Chinese rice is always in demand and brings a good price in Japan; and no doubt much rice finds its way thither without being recorded by the Customs authorities.

It will be recognized that these figures are quite general in nature and most unsatisfactory to the exact. As was re-marked at the beginning of this chapter adequate statistics are lacking. One must talk in terms of specific localities, and here the figures are eloquent enough. Personal experience would corroborate the truth of the observations derived here-from over a much wider area and in much more touching terms of human misery.

It is this lack of any margin of livelihood that is one of the fundamental causes of famine. It will be readily seen that the destruction or failure of even one crop results in severe dis-tress and, in many cases, in actual famine. Analogous condi-tions in Western countries result only in a period of hard times, for the population has an economic reserve on which to call.

Natural causes of famine

While the fundamental causes of famine are traceable to the economic circumstances in which the people live, the im-mediate cause is usually the result of some natural phenomenon. We are prone to associate the idea of serious food shortage with protracted droughts, swarms of locusts, widespread floods, or other visitations of nature's wrath, perhaps even to the extent of minimizing the part played by social, political, and economic factors. This is to be expected, since it is the spectacular or bizarre that is considered by the Press to be of the greatest human interest and since it is through the newspapers that we learn of the world's affairs.

Thus the appalling situation of the millions of Chinese who live along the Yellow River, a situation which assures actual starvation for great numbers upon the loss of even one crop, will receive scant mention in the world's news until a flood pushes them over the edge into the abyss of famine.

But there are some famines that are due almost solely to natural causes, and there are scarcely any to which natural phenomena do not contribute. Probably in no other country — certainly in no other country of its size or of anything like its population — are the natural features less favourable to the inhabitants than in China. The mass of the people live on the great alluvial plains traversed by meandering rivers, very few of which have well defined channels. The rainfall is very irregular, especially in the north. Long periods of drought are frequent when the crops are a total failure; severe floods occur when the rivers break their dikes and inundate thousands of square kilometres of farm lands, destroying the growing foodstuffs in addition to causing loss of life and doing great damage to property.

Deforestation

Scientists ascribe these conditions or their augmentation to the depletion of China's forests by successive generations of inhabitants. It is believed that the area now constituting China proper was once heavily wooded, and there seems to be ample historical and geological proofs of this theory.

The contrast between present and former conditions in Shansi has been recently described by Professor Lowdermilk [9] of Nanking University, who studied on the spot the processes of converting a forest cover to denuded slopes. Nine-tenths of Shansi is mountainous, and over most of the slope area a gradient of 25 per cent obtains. Under the torrential thunderstorm type of rainfall the unprotected surface is rapidly destroyed. In northern Shansi the soil layer is removed in three to ten years. Referring to the former extent of forest, Professor Lowdermilk says: 'Perhaps the most trustworthy indications are the existing temple forests. To include all areas of similar altitude, or higher, with the existing temple forests would in itself indicate an extensive forest cover for Shansi.'

We are not concerned here with the reasons for the destruction of this great resource. It is enough to know that the actions of former generations have resulted in a deforestation more complete than that of any other great nation. Not only has deforestation had much to do in bringing about present conditions, but it is generally believed that a gradual drying up of the areas in the north and west is taking place and that more and more of the present fertile country will become like the regions of central Asia, and for the same reason.

Drought: historical data

Without doubt the worst famines in China have been caused by a lack of sufficient rainfall for a long period. Lack of rain occurs most often in northern and central China. While most other natural disasters result in only a partial destruction of the crops, a drought makes of a normally flourishing countryside a barren waste. When it is remembered that in China almost the entire population exists by agriculture, it can be imagined what effect a dry period has, especially if it continues for two or three years, as sometimes happens. In time of drought it is only in those districts where irrigation is practised that any crop at all can be harvested, and unfortunately these districts are too few in number and small in extent.

In 1878 Alexander Hosie, of the British Consular Service in China, compiled from the mass of historical and statistical data contained in the great Chinese compendium known as the T'u Shu Tsih Ch'eng a record of the droughts which occurred in China from the commencement of the T'ang Dynasty in AD 620 to the end of the Ming Dynasty in 1643 [10]. More recently a compilation from the beginning of the Christian era up to the end of the last century has been made by Dr Co-Ching Chu, of the National Southeastern University, Nanking [11]. While these two compilations are not in entire harmony — for the records, themselves obviously neither complete nor exact, are open to different interpretations — they give the best available information on the history of droughts.

Mr Hosie finds that in the millennium from 620 to 1619 there were recorded 610 years when one or more of the provinces had insufficient rain, and in 203 years great or very severe drought is specified. Probably in those years the distress was sufficient to cause famines of some magnitude, and that extremely severe food shortage was experienced during at least fifteen of the worst years is indicated by an allusion to cannibalism in the Chinese records. It is interesting to note that cannibalism is mentioned as having occurred most often in Shensi, less frequently in Honan, Shansi, and Shantung, and only once or twice in provinces further south. The great famines occurred when the droughts were of long duration or when the area affected was large. The province of Chekiang is recorded as having suffered for the six successive years 1170—75 and the four successive years 1180—83. Instances when two or more provinces were simultaneously affected for several successive years, though uncommon, are not rare. For example Chihli and Honan were both affected during the period 1296—98 and in the five consecutive years 1324—28. For the three years 990—92 the three provinces of Chihli, Honan, and Shensi are recorded as having suffered simultaneously. Chihli, Honan, Shansi, and Shantung have most frequently had droughts simultaneously or in successive years. This fact, coupled with the more frequent mention of cannibalism in the northern provinces and with the fact that of the 216 great droughts 100 were in the provinces of Chihli, Honan, Shansi, Shantung, and Shensi, leads indisputably to the conclusion that it is this part of China north of the Yangtse valley and extending to the boundary of Mongolia where a chronic drought condition exists. . . .

Rainfall of China

The northern provinces, where droughts are most frequent and most severe depend upon the summer monsoons for their rainfall. In normal years there is ample precipitation in June, July, and August, a slight snowfall occasionally during the winter, and showers in April and May. Perhaps it would be better to say that this is the ideal year rather than the normal, for it is not often that the showers occur at the planting season in April and May, and many times the winter wheat is not favoured with snowfall. The total annual rainfall is not large. Hann gives 533 mm (21 in) as an average for northern China, 70 per cent of which falls in the three months of June, July and August. The principal crops in the north are wheat, which is harvested in June, and millet and kaoliang, which are gathered in September. If the snows and early spring showers fail, there is a small wheat crop; and if the summer rains likewise do not occur, there is no harvest for the entire year.

Although the northern and central parts of the country are more susceptible to drought, it occasionally occurs in the more southern provinces; but usually it does not affect so great an area. In the central and southern provinces the principal crop, rice, requires a great deal of moisture.

Breaking a drought

The ancient Chinese methods of breaking a drought are interesting, and they are probably as effective as any discovered in the West. When matters really become serious the governors of the provinces concerned issue mandates forbidding the slaughter of livestock, and the population goes without meat for three days. If this does not bring the desired rain, processions are formed, and a sort of holiday is declared in order to invoke the heavens. In Hantan, Chihli Province, there is an iron tablet which has most wonderful properties for bringing rain. In 1924 there was a very dry spring, and the summer monsoon did not arrive in June as it should. Matters finally reached such a pass that the Central Government in desperation decided to bring the iron tablet to Peking from the country. This was done in July, and lo, the heavens opened, and China had one of the worst floods of several decades.

Before the overthrow of the monarchy the responsibility for breaking protracted droughts rested with the Emperor, since it was his duty to importune the heavens on behalf of the people. The prayer of Tao Kwang for rain which was made in 1832 is a splendid example of a memorial on this subject of drought. The following translation is taken from *The Middle Kingdom* by S. Wells Williams.

Oh, alas! imperial Heaven, were not the world afflicted by extraordinary changes, I would not dare to present extraordinary services. But this year the drought is most unusual. Summer is past, and no rain has fallen. Not only do agriculture and human beings feel the dire calamity, but also beasts and insects, herbs and trees, almost cease to live. I, the minister of Heaven, am placed over mankind, and am responsible for keeping the world in order and tranquillizing the people. Although it is now impossible for me to sleep or eat with composure, although I am scorched with grief and tremble with anxiety, still, after all, no genial and copious showers have been obtained.

Some days ago I fasted, and offered rich sacrifices on the altars of the gods of the land and the grain, and had to be thankful for gathering clouds and slight showers; but not enough to cause gladness. Looking up, I consider that Heaven's heart is benevolence and love. The sole cause is the daily deeper atrocity of my sins; but little sincerity and little devotion. Hence I have been unable to move Heaven's heart, and bring down abundant blessings. . . .

Prostrate I beg imperial Heaven (*Hwang Tien*) to pardon my ignorance and stupidity, and to grant me self-renovation; for myriads and of innocent people are involved by me, the One man. My sins are so numerous it is difficult to escape from them. Summer is past and autumn arrived; to wait longer will really be impossible. Knocking head, I pray imperial Heaven to hasten and confer gracious deliverance — a speedy and divinely beneficial rain, to save the people's lives and in some degree redeem my iniquities. Oh, alas! imperial Heaven, observe these things. Oh, alas! imperial Heaven, be gracious to them. I am inexpressibly grieved, alarmed, and frightened. Reverently this memorial is presented [12].

Flood occurrence

Floods occur in all sections of the country but in some parts more frequently and seriously. The greatest number of floods occur in the provinces of Chihli, Shantung, Honan, Kiangsu, Anhwei, and Chekiang. Parts of all these provinces lie in the great eastern plain, which has been built up of recent river deposits. The great plain is practically level for immense distances, and the streams are held in their courses by means of earthen dikes, most of which were built hundreds of years ago. The country is so flat that when the dikes give way a tremendous area is flooded, and unfortunately this is almost always the district that is the most thickly settled and under the most intensive cultivation.

Most of the rivers carry a great quantity of silt which slowly builds up the stream bed, necessitating the constant raising of the dikes. Eventually a point is reached where even the bed of the river is above the land outside the dikes. As L. H. Dudley Buxton has well put it, the rivers are *on* the plain, not *in* it [13]. This is the reason why the heavy silt-laden rivers have changed their courses so often, for when the dikes fail the entire stream abandons its old bed for the lower country, and the task of forcing the flow back into its original channel presents too great a problem for the crude methods of the people.

It is the frequent inundation of the plains that has made them so level, for the immense quantity of silt, which but for the floods would have been carried by the streams to the sea, has been deposited over the country. This process, repeated many times during thousands of years, has tended to fill the depressions and slowly to build up new land. As the process has gone on the gradient of the streams has been constantly decreased, with corresponding lessening of their ability to carry their load of mud to the sea. One beneficial effect can be credited to the frequent floods in the plains. The new earth deposited is extremely rich, and this constant acquisition of virgin soil has helped to keep up the productivity of the country.

Slow drainage of flood waters

The immediate loss of life and property is not the only terrible aspect of a flood, but also the wholesale destruction of the growing crops and the slow drainage which often prevents the next planting. In some regions it takes as much as two or three years for the waters of a severe inundation to find their way to the sea. This slow drainage, while due in part to the level nature of the country, is probably influenced to a greater extent by the network of dikes built along the streams and canals. These hold back the flood waters until their volume overtops the dikes, or the latter are breached by wave action, and then the water rushes on until it reaches the next obstruction. Naturally every effort is made by the natives, who are protected by these dikes, to postpone the evil day when their own fields will be covered with water, and they carefully patrol them to prevent the inhabitants of inundated districts from making breaches to hasten the draining of their own land.

The lack of forest cover on the hills results in an extremely rapid run-off; and this, coupled with the torrential rains liable to occur in almost any part of the country, transforms even dry stream beds into raging torrents within a very brief time. Although these conditions are prevalent in nearly all the provinces, there are certain districts where the configuration of the land and the nature of the rivers cause disasters of especial severity and frequency.

The Hwai River

The first in importance, from the point of view of crop losses and resultant famine distress, is in the valley of the Hwai in the provinces of Anhwei and Kiangsu. The Hwai River, which rises in Honan and flows through Anhwei into Kiangsu, has no regular channel to the sea but has emptied into Hungtse Lake since the Yellow River in 1191 burst its banks and usurped the original channel of the Hwai. In normal years when the rainfall is not too great and is sufficiently distributed the result of the summer rains is simply to raise the water level in the lake and perhaps to inundate a stretch of country contiguous to its boundary, the flood waters finding their way to the sea through the Grand Canal and the Yangtse River. But when the rainfall is unusually heavy, as happens every few years, the capacity of the lake is not sufficient as a ponding basin. Mr John R. Freeman, the eminent American hydraulic engineer, after a brief examination of this problem reported as follows:

> ... Although much of this area is flat and absorptive, floods sometimes run off this large area into the vast,

shallow Hungtse Lake at a rate of more than 200 000 cubic feet per second, as estimated from flood marks established by the American Red Cross engineers in 1914, and even reached the rate of 440 000 cubic feet per second in the exceptionally high flood of 1916, as measured by the engineers of the Kiang-Hwai Board.

Neither the St Lawrence River at Montreal, nor the Mississippi River above the entrance of the Missouri, at its greatest flood period carries so high a rate of discharge.

The Hungtse Lake acts as a great natural equalizer and its outflow is somewhat controlled by sluiceways; but the flood trying to escape therefrom is pent in on the north by a broad ridge of sediment and dikes pertaining to the abandoned Yellow River channel and is held back on the east by the embankments on the Grand Canal, which to the limit of its capacity strives to lead the flood south to the Yangtse River, in which it is somewhat aided by the flow to the Yangtse through a chain of lakes.

These great floods give more than the channels can accommodate and they rupture the Grand Canal dikes, but even when the flood breaks over and sweeps away this barrier, its free escape seaward over the vast, low-lying area of more than 80 km (50 miles) wide by 160 km (100 miles) long, is barred by the great Maritime Dike, known as the Fan Kung Dike, which was built about 900 years ago to protect this lowlying region from the sea.

The vast network of large and small canals within this area and the sluiceways through the Maritime Dike, all in combination, are utterly insufficient to safely or promptly discharge such a flood [14].

After the flood of 1911 with its resulting immense loss of life and property, the American Red Cross, under an arrangement with the Chinese government, sent a Board of Engineers headed by Colonel William L. Sibert to investigate the Hwai River Conservancy Project. In its report this Board stated that the last flood had inundated 27 100 sq km (10 470 sq miles) in Anhwei and 5 960 sq km (2 300 sq miles) in Kiangsu and that these provinces are subject to a disaster of equal severity on the average once every six or seven years and a disaster of minor importance every three or four years. This area, larger than Belgium, comprises some of the best farming land in all China.

Assuming that the normal yield of rice is 907 kg/0.4 ha (2 000 lb/acre), the loss due to one of these serious floods is more than 7 250 million kg (16 000 million lb); and, counting the less severe inundations, probably 1 359 million kg (3 000 million lb) of China's principal food is destroyed annually as a result of these catastrophes. This is sufficient to feed more than 6 million adults. Allowing for the children, more than 7 million of the population could be supported from this annual wastage.

Coupled with the damage occasioned by the years of high water is the loss that results from the lack of drainage of Hungtse Lake and the other lowlying regions. It is estimated that more than 242 000 ha (600 000 acres) could be reclaimed if the proper conservancy scheme were carried out. This would mean an increase of more than 544 million kg (1 200 million lb) of rice annually — sufficient to feed a population of nearly 3 million. In other words the total annual loss to the country from this uncontrolled river is sufficient to provide food for approximately 10 million people.

The Yellow River

The Hwang Ho, or Yellow River, 'China's Sorrow', seems to have been a problem since the dawn of history. The earliest annals give accounts of great inundations and of efforts to control the ravages of this menace. It is difficult to present an idea of the extent of the damage caused by the Yellow River floods. They occur at present less often than along the Hwai, and the area affected varies in extent from a few to many thousands of square kilometres. The river has been meandering back and forth for thousands of years, as can be seen from the extent of the delta built up. It is not possible to trace all the courses of the river even in historic time from a study of the most authentic material available it seems clear that the Yellow River has flowed into the sea as far north as

Tientsin, and its most southerly outlet was probably through the Yangtse River at Shanghai.

While floods of relatively minor importance occur as often as once or twice in every decade, there have been but three great migrations of the river in the past 1 000 years. On several occasions, however, there have been extremely severe floods when the river has left its course but later returned to its old bed. Such an instance is the flood of 1887—89 when a break occurred in the southern dike in the province of Honan. According to Chinese official records more than 2 million people lost their lives either from drowning or from starvation during the resulting famine, and nearly the whole province of Honan south of the river was inundated.

It is not only in times of unusually high water that there is danger of flood along the Yellow River. The distance between the dikes is great, and this permits of considerable meandering so that the current is constantly shifting from side to side. Hence when the river is rising the current may suddenly swing in towards a dike in an unprotected stretch, which, unless rapid and adequate measures are taken, soon crumbles away. This is what happened in Shantung Province in the summer and fall of 1925 when the southern dike was breached and an area of about 2 071 sq km (800 sq miles) was flooded. The loss in crops alone was estimated at $20 million, and yet the river was not at an unusually high stage when the disaster occurred.

The rivers of Chihli Province

There are eight principal rivers entering the Chihli plain. In ancient times these streams reached the sea through many channels. But when the Grand Canal was extended from the Yellow River to Tientsin in the thirteenth century no crossings were provided, or if provided were not maintained, and the waters were all led into the Hai Ho, which flows through Tientsin. This was already the outlet for the Pei Ho and the Yung Ting Ho, and its capacity has not been sufficient to carry off the flood waters in years when the rainfall has been heavy. Since 1891 there have been seven serious inundations of the central Chihli plain. It would therefore appear that this district is subject to floods on the average once every six or seven years. The total catchment area is more than 227 000 sq km (88 000 sq miles); and when it is considered that all but a very small part of this water must reach the sea through the Hai Ho, a small stream, it can be understood why these disasters occur. The last serious Chihli flood was in the summer of 1924. During the severe storms in July it was estimated that the inflow into the river system was twenty-five times as great as the outflow through the Hai Ho. The difficulty of obtaining accurate reports simultaneously from various sections of the province makes it impossible to state exactly what extent of country was inundated at any one time; but it has been reliably established that an area of no less than 12 945 sq km (5 000 sq miles) was covered with water long enough to destroy completely the growing crop which should have been harvested in September and October and that a large portion of this area was still inundated during the autumn, thus preventing the planting of the winter wheat. The lower section of the plain is but a little above sea level, and it usually takes two or three years for all the flood waters to reach the ocean.

If the value of the crop be put at only $30 per 0.4 ha (1 acre), the loss to the province was nearly $100 million Chinese currency, simply from the destruction of growing foodstuffs. When to this are added the losses due to failure to plant the winter wheat and subsequent crops the sum will exceed $125 million. As such a catastrophe happens on the average every six or seven years, it may be estimated that the annual loss from these floods is not less than $18 million. This sum is sufficient to provide a livelihood for 120 000 families, or more than 600 000 people, according to the standard of living now prevailing in northern China. Nor must one overlook the loss from demolition of buildings and the drowning of livestock and of human beings. In 1917 the dikes which protect Tientsin gave way, and damage to the extent of many millions of dollars was done in the city itself. In 1924 a similar catastrophe was narrowly averted: the principal seaport of northern China stands in constant danger of inundation with each successive flood.

In the Kan River delta region of Kiangsi Province large areas between the various mouths of the river and around the Poyang Lake have been diked in and produce a good yield of rice annually. In the 1924 floods most of these dikes were breached, and hundreds of square kilometres of good farming land were covered with water.

It is not intended to discuss here all the areas of China subject to floods; in fact, there is not sufficient dependable information concerning many of them to make it possible to give more than a general indication of the damage wrought by inundations. The specific examples given have been selected because in their case more reliable data are available and because they are the most frequently or most severely affected. If a thorough tabulation of the annual loss due to this cause could be made, the sum arrived at would reach a staggering total. In 1922–23 there was a severe flood of the Tsao Ngo River in Chekiang. In 1924 central China was visited by the worst inundation recorded in many years, and large areas in Hunan, Hupeh, and Kiangsi were covered with water by an overflow of the Siang, the Kan, and the Yangtse Rivers. The same year saw a serious flood of the West River in Kwangsi and of the Min River in Fukien, as well as the flood in Chihli already mentioned. Other areas where floods occur include the basins of the following rivers: the Fen (Shansi), the Han (Hupeh), the Pearl (Kwangtung), the Liao (Manchuria), and the Min (Fukien).

Mention has already been made of the terraces on the hillsides, built by the labour of centuries. In the torrential rains that occur every few years these hillside fields are sometimes destroyed over wide areas. In the hilly region of southwestern Chihli during the storms of 1924, 584 mm (23 in) of rain fell in 33 hours at one place, and other places registered 457 mm (18 in) in 32 hours and 228 mm (9 in) in 9 hours. No wonder that the fields are washed away. In some districts the destruction from this cause is so complete that whole villages are forced to seek new homes.

Then again, rich farming country near the foothills is often destroyed by the flooding of the streams which carry with them not only coarse sand and pebbles but also small boulders. There are places where such a heavy deposit of sand and stones is left on the fields after a flood season that they have to be abandoned. The loss from this source in Chekiang Province during the 1922 floods was very large.

The locust pest

Locusts are one of the three principal natural causes of famine. This pest, which consumes the growing crops, leaves the countryside as barren as a protracted drought. While these insects are essentially herbivorous, they are known to attack and absolutely ruin even the trees; in this respect they are more damaging than a lack of rain.

Many stories are told of the countless numbers of locusts composing a migration. They always move in the daytime, and sometimes the swarms are so dense as to shut out completely the light of the sun. One invasion in Russia is said to have occupied an area 32 km (20 miles) both in length and in breadth. In addition to the distress which follows the destruction of their crops, the people of a locust-infected district are often subjected to epidemics caused by the decayed insects getting into wells, cisterns, and reservoirs and clogging the drains, thus poisoning the drinking water.

There is no continent and almost no part of the world that has not been visited at one time or another by this scourge: only the arctic regions appear to be immune. But it is especially the territories between latitude 20° and 45°N and between 15° and 45°S that suffer most from locusts [15].

In his paper on calamities M. Raoul Montandon, President of the Geographical Society of Geneva, lists the major disasters that have followed invasions of locusts, beginning from the year 125 BC. In this list China appears but three times, namely in the years 1835, 1878, and 1892. The failure to include catastrophes which occurred prior to the nineteenth century was probably due to the lack of intercourse between China and the West in former times which made reliable data difficult to obtain. The 162 famines recorded in the Chinese historical records for Shensi Province include twenty which were caused in whole or in part, by locusts.

Alexander Hosie in his studies of the Chinese histories already referred to mentions visitations of locusts in the following provinces and years between AD 620 and 1643: 840 (Fukien); 869; 953; 991 (Shantung); 1016 (Chihli and Honan); 1027 (Shensi and Honan); 1033; 1053; 1176 (north China); 1215 (central China); 1240 (Kiangsi); 1298 (Kiangsu); 1310 (north China); 1326 (Kwangsi); 1330

(Hunan); 1334 (central China); 1541 (Chihli); 1581 (Chekiang); 1605 and 1640 (Chekiang).

It would seem from the above list that while locusts have visited nearly all parts of the country it is the central and northern provinces that have been most often attacked by the scourge.

The available information would indicate that locusts have not caused such serious disasters in China as in other countries subject to their depredations. Rather they have served to aggravate bad conditions due to other causes. This is notably the case in the visitation of 1878, which followed two years of drought in northern China. It must also be remembered that the northern Chinese are accustomed to eating locusts a practice which would in some degree recompense the farmers for the losses sustained by the action of the insects on the crops.

Earthquakes

Although China lies outside the great earthquake zones of the world (the Pacific girdle and the Mediterranean—Himalayan belt) the country is not exempt from seismic disasters. A list compiled from the historical records mentions 3 394 earthquakes for the 3 693 years between 1767 BC and AD 1896 [17]. The greatest catastrophe of this nature occurred in 1556 in the Wei Ho Valley when 800 000 people of Shensi, Shansi, and Honan are said to have lost their lives. Among the regions most subject to seismic disturbances particular interest attaches to the Kansu—Shensi area because of the geological nature of the terrain. This area is in the loess, the peculiar yellow-coloured silt or loam that covers vast areas of northern China. Owing to the vertical cleavage of the loess the deeply eroded hills rise almost perpendicularly from the valleys, and a severe earthquake shock easily displaces this loose earth and causes it to slide down into the valleys in tremendous quantities. Seismic disturbances do not usually destroy sufficient foodstuffs to cause shortage, although the victims of such a cataclysm may suffer want for a few days until broken communications can be re-established. In the loess country, however, a severe quake may destroy both grain reserves and growing crops.

The Kansu earthquake of 1920

In the great earthquake which occurred in eastern Kansu on 16 December 1920, there are several points of particular interest which are worthy of comment here. The severity of the distress following a quake is usually dependent upon the density of population and number of buildings in the affected district. For instance, the earthquake which took place in Vernyi, Turkestan, in 1911 resulted in but 400 deaths, although from a seismic point of view it was a severe shock; while more than 100 000 people are said to have perished in the Japan disaster of 1 September 1923, which demolished the populous cities of Yokohama and Tokyo. China is indeed a land of contrasts where almost every rule is broken. Here in Kansu it was the country population that suffered the most. This is easily explainable. Scarcity of wood has forced the farmers to make their homes in caves which they excavate in the hillsides [18]. Very few of the cave dwellers in the affected district escaped, for the first shock occurred at 7 pm, and since, it was wintertime and dark, the people were all in their earthen retreats and were buried under many feet of loose earth before they realized what was taking place. The city of Kuyüan with a population of about 70 000 reported only 400 deaths, while 40 000 perished in the surrounding country districts.

Since this disaster occurred in the early part of the winter the crops had all been harvested, the threshing was done, and the supply of grain needed to support the family until the next harvest was stored in the cliff dwellings. It thus happened that the grain reserves in the area worst affected were practically all destroyed.

The change effected in the topography by this earthquake was very great. Landslides blocked the rivers, in many cases changing their courses. Some of the dams were as much as 1 mile thick and many feet in height; and, though every effort was made by the people and relief committees to open them before the high-water season, in some places it was impossible to do anything, and much distress was caused by floods.

The Yunnan earthquake of 1925

The earthquake which took place in western Yunnan on

16 March 1925, did not present any unusual features. The greatest loss of life occurred in the urban districts. Fortunately the population was not dense, for one out of every eighteen was killed over an area of six counties. The destitute, who numbered nearly 100 000 were left without food, clothing, or shelter. Such a condition in China invariably means the starvation of a considerable number of people, and the Chinese are accustomed to regard such local distress as a famine. According to the accepted usage of the term in other countries, it is hardly correct to list a catastrophe such as occurred at Talifu as a famine emergency. It must be remembered, however, that there are few other countries where an adjustment of the destitute population could not have been so effected as to prevent any appreciable number from dying from lack of food.

Typhoons

The China coast is not subject to the tidal waves, so-called, of seismic or volcanic origin; but the southeastern coast is frequently visited by severe wind storms or typhoons, and a phenomenon not greatly different from a tidal wave occurs where the sea walls are destroyed and the lands along the shores are flooded by sea water. The average number of typhoons is sixteen a year. These cyclonic storms gather in the Pacific Ocean near the island of Guam and take a northwesterly direction, rarely reaching as far north as Shanghai. The storm centre moves forward at from 13—80 km (8—50 miles) an hour, and the wind, which blows in a circle counterclockwise around the centre, varies from 80—175 km (50—110 miles) an hour in velocity.

The damage from typhoons is restricted to a narrow area along the coast, suffering is caused mainly by the destruction of property, and loss of life by falling buildings. Many animals are killed, but the crops are not affected excepting where the sea walls are destroyed and salt water invades the fields. The loss of foodstuffs from disasters of this sort is not sufficient to cause famine, although there is some loss of life from starvation after a severe visitation such as occurred at Swatow in the summer of 1922.

6 The old industrial order

Endowed with large areas of fertile soil, valuable raw materials, and a high tradition of tests and skill, China has long possessed important manufacturing industries. Till the rise of machine production a century and a half ago, her technique was identical in character with that of the West, and, in quality, not infrequently superior to it. 'Our Celestial Empire possesses all things in prolific abundance, and lacks no product within its own borders; there is therefore no need to import the manufactures of outside barbarians' [1] – the oft-quoted reply in which her government rebuffed in 1793 the British proposal for closer trade relations, if politically naïve, had more economic justification than the West supposed. It was given at a moment when the greater number of British industries were still only emerging from much the same phase of development as those of China, and when certain among them had been striving for a century to master the lessons taught by Chinese craftsmanship.

The legacy of the past

During the three generations in which the Industrial Revolution was travelling round the world, that phase survived in China with but little modification. As far as the greater part of the country is concerned, it survives today, though with increasing erosion. No occupational census has been taken in China. Figures [2], of doubtful reliability, are available for certain provinces and cities in particular years, but both the numbers engaged in different industries, and the size of the urban [3] population, are a matter of conjecture. Factory industry, based on power and machinery, has been advancing

137

for more than thirty years in certain limited areas. Its record, with some honourable exceptions, has not been good, and the question of the conditions under which it is to develop is one of the vital problems confronting China. The standards obtaining in factory employment are necessarily influenced, however, by those prevailing outside it, and the greater part of the country stands at present on a different plane of economic civilization.

Here and there, even in the interior, where roads, rivers or railways make a highway for change, a cluster of chimneys towers over fields worn by the patient routine of 2 000 years. But the system that they represent, which in western Europe is the rule, is in China the exception. In technique and organization the major part of her industry belongs either to the pre-capitalist era or to the first infancy of capitalism. Its characteristics are not power driven machinery, joint stock finance and a hierarchy of economic authority, but primitive tools, handicraft methods, and minute investments of capital by merchants or small masters controlling a multiplicity of tiny undertakings. European analogies with which to compare it must be sought, not in the twentieth century, but from the fourteenth to the early nineteenth.

These features are found in those branches of enterprise which, in the West, are the peculiar stronghold of large-scale industry. Between one-third and one-half of the output of coal, and one-fifth of that of iron ore, have been estimated to be produced by small native mines employing a few score of workers apiece and almost destitute of machinery [4]. The Chinese iron industry has the longest continuous history in the world, and had mastered the art of making cast iron some 1 500 years before that of Europe; but nearly one-half of the pig iron produced is made in charcoal furnaces, with bellows worked by hand or water power. Cotton-spinning is the industry which first entered the factory, and in which factory production has proceeded furthest; but some of the spinning and, as in the England of the early nineteenth century, the greater part of the weaving, still continues to be done either at home or in small workshops. Side by side with machine production and large-scale organization in these, and perhaps a dozen other, branches of production, are some hundreds of industries to which western methods have hardly begun to be applied. The crafts of the worker in metal, whether iron, copper, tin or silver; of the potter and tile-maker, of the builder, carpenter, furniture-maker, painter, shoe-maker, hat-maker, tailor, tanner, wood-carver, lacquer-maker, of silk reeling and weaving, woollen-weaving, tapestry-making, rope-making, as well as the innumerable trades concerned with the production of household requirements, ornaments, jewellery, and artistic products, though often indirectly affected by changing commercial and financial methods, are still much what they were five centuries ago.

The attempts of historians to classify stages of industrial development have rarely been felicitous. The reality is too fluid to be compressed within neat boundaries of genus and species. Types overlap and melt into each other; identity of form conceals difference of fact. Hans Sachs turns out, on closer examination, to be, not the independent master crafts-man of the medieval legend, but a subcontractor, at once sweated and sweating, to a capitalist merchant. The merchant in one capacity is a factory-owner in another. The factory, so far from resembling a modern spinning mill or engineering works, may be in fact, as in China till recently it was in law, a primitive workshop, unequipped with machinery or power, housing less than forty workers. All alike may stand in a dozen different relations to the financier, the purveyor of raw materials and the market. If some 2 000 to 3 000 great concerns be for the moment ignored, what exists in China is what existed in Europe before the rise of the great industry, and still survives, if precariously, in its crannies and back-waters. It is less an organized industrial system than a lab-yrinth or spider's web of small undertakings, each working under conditions peculiar to itself, and isolated by difficulties of communication from all but those in its immediate neigh-bourhood.

Two threads in the fabric, which in Europe have slipped, are still important in China. The family, consisting, as it does, not merely of parents and children, but of a group embracing three or four generations and their collaterals living together, retains an economic significance which it has long lost in the West. It acts on occasion as an industrial unit, which supplies its own needs and produces for the market. When, twenty years ago, a Chinese economist [5] investigated conditions in his native district of Ningpo, he estimated that 40 per cent of the families cultivated cotton, which they cleaned, prepared, spun and wove in their own homes. Though family work has declined, it still survives, especially in rural districts. It is not uncommon for peasants not only to grow their own food, but to build their own cottages, to produce the material required for their clothes, to card and spin the cotton or wool, and to weave the cloth. There are, again, a multitude of isolated craftsmen who work for customers, sometimes on the premises of the latter and with materials supplied by them. They make their rounds, like tinkers or knife-grinders in the West, from dawn to dusk, and the streets of cities resound with their cries.

The characteristic organization of industry is, however, different, though the family often remains the nucleus round which it is built. It takes the form partly of handicrafts carried on in the shops of small masters, partly of work done on commission for merchants, who distribute raw materials, supply credit and market the produce. In theory distinguished by the fact that, in the first case, the master is an independent producer dealing direct with the market, and, in the second, a contractor employed by a wholesaler, in practice the two types overlap. The merchant may find it convenient at one time to buy the wares produced in a small master's shop, and at another to employ him on a commission basis. The small master may work to the order of the merchant when business is brisk, and struggle on by himself in times of depression.

Some form of what the English Commissions of the early nineteenth century, who saw it in its ruin, called the small-master system is universal in China, both in the cities and, still more, in the villages and country towns. In Tayinchen, in the south of Hopei, to give one example, the tanning of the skins collected from the neighbouring farmers is carried on in workshops, the smallest of which are staffed by the members of a single family and some two-fifths by less than ten workmen, while a few considerable firms employ a personnel of as many as 100, and the majority about twenty to twenty-five, the finished article being sold to dealers from the commercial centres. In the potting industry of P'eng Cheng, in the same province, some eighty-one potteries own 211 kilns for the manufacture of bowls, with twenty to thirty workmen apiece. In the fur and leather industry of Swanhwa, the Bureau of Economic Information reported in 1925 the existence of about sixty shops, the six largest of which employed over 100 men each, and the majority between forty and eighty. In the famous porcelain industry of Kingtchen, which has profoundly influenced the art of the Western potter, the system of small independent masters obtains [6].

But examples are endless. The traveller who explores the streets of any Chinese town passes between rows of houses open to the streets, at once workshops and homes, in which small groups of artisans are hammering metal, fashioning wood, or making clothing and shoes, side by side with their employers, whose meals they share, and with whom, when apprentices, they normally lodge. In the more pretentious establishments, and more delicate crafts, like fan-making and lantern-making, the front serves as a shop where wares are displayed; the rooms and courts behind it are the workshops where materials are stored, work is carried on from dawn to dusk, and food is prepared. There is little subdivision of labour or specialization of functions, and, in the majority of cases, no machinery or power. Work is heavy; craftsmanship fastidious; methods patient, laborious and slow; discipline slack or absent. Relations are human, not mechanical. There is much physical exertion, and little nervous strain. The product is often of singular simplicity and beauty. There is a curious contrast between the slovenliness of Chinese workmanship on western patterns — windows that will not open and doors that will not shut — and the admirable fitness and precision of the wares which it makes by methods native to its genius to meet the needs of common life. It is as though, when he abandoned tradition, the craftsman lost all standards, and when he followed it, was infallible.

An illustration of the characteristics of this type of organization is given by the handicraft industries of Peiping, described in the valuable books of S. B. Gamble and J. S. Burgess [7]. The thirty-four guilds of that city included, in 1920, some 107 000 members, consisting of masters, journeymen and apprentices, out of a total population of something over 800 000. The membership of the twenty-five among them for which complete figures are available was just

141

over 90 000, of whom about 10 000 or 11.4 per cent, were masters, 58 000, or 64 per cent, journeymen, and 22 000, or 24.6 per cent, apprentices. The number of journeymen and apprentices per master ranged from 0.9 in the case of the shoe-makers, and 1.8 in that of the jade-makers, to 73.5 among the carpet-makers, and 106.6 among the silk-dyers. But the undertakings were usually small, and sometimes minute: in ten out of these twenty-five crafts the number of journeymen and apprentices per master was less than ten, and in only five over twenty. Equally significant was the general reliance on apprentice labour: in eighteen out of the twenty-five trades there were less than four journeymen to one apprentice, and in eleven less than three, while, as already stated, apprentices formed almost a quarter of the total membership. The limitation of apprentices, which plays so large a part in the guild and early trade union history of Europe, has not apparently been among the rules generally enforced by the guilds of China.

Apart from provincial associations called by the same name, and formed of members belonging to one province to protect their interests when domiciled in another, the guilds of China have hitherto consisted partly of traders, partly of craftsmen, and most commonly, perhaps, of both [8]. In practice, as is natural when the producer of wares is also their salesman, the two types are often indistinguishable. Their number in China as a whole is uncertain, but must run into several thousand. In Canton alone there are stated to be up-wards of a hundred, covering every occupation from tailoring and shoe-making to pig-killing, pawnbroking and coffin-making; controlling prices, wages and hours; arbitrating between members and customers; and, in case of necessity, bringing pressure to bear on officials and public authorities.

7 Shanghai: modern hem on an ancient garment

Shanghai holds the commercial, financial, and industrial leadership of China. There is no rival, and none is likely to arise in the near future. In few countries of the world is there a city occupying a position of such relative national supremacy in the economic activities that are capable of record and measurement. China, it is true, is predominantly agricultural, with most of the people dependent for all their needs directly on the land and on the local village market and only remotely on any urban area; disintegration and disorganization seem to more characteristic than centralization, but foreign and interport trade, banking and modern manufacturing for the entire country are focused on Shanghai to a remarkable degree, owing to an unusual combination of political and geographical factors. The control of Shanghai carries with it the control of the valley of the Yangtse Kiang, including one-half of the area of China proper and more than one-half of the population, the most productive agricultural areas, and most of China's large-scale manufacturing.

The economic importance of Shanghai

Among the cities of China, Shanghai ranks first in population with 3.4 million people, or more than double the number in Peiping, the city of second importance. Primarily, Shanghai functions as a commercial city. It is China's principal point of contact with the world and the port through which much of China's recorded domestic trade flows. In the five-year period 1927–31, 43 per cent of China's foreign trade passed through Shanghai. Dairen, the port of second importance and the outlet of Manchuria, handled 14.5 per cent, Tientsin less

143

than 9 per cent, and Canton a little more than 5 per cent. With the loss of Manchuria and the elimination of Manchurian ports from the Chinese trade returns. Shanghai has become even more important relatively: for the two years 1933 and 1934 it handled on an average 54 per cent of the total foreign trade of China, and Tientsin, now the port of second importance, handled less than 11 per cent [1].

The bulk of Chinese domestic trade is unrecorded. Many of the commodities are transported over short distances by boats, carts, or porters to be exchanged at some roadside or village market. Only the trade that passes through the recognized customs ports is measured. Of such trade in the five years 1927–31 Shanghai handled 34 per cent; in 1933 and 1934, with the Manchurian ports excluded, the share increased to 36 per cent [2].

Finance and banking

In finance and banking Shanghai occupies a similarly commanding position. There were in the city in 1931, mainly in the International or Foreign Settlement and in the French Concession, twenty-seven branches of foreign banks, thirty-nine Chinese banks of modern type, either head offices or branches, and seventy-seven native Chinese banks of the old type. These banks hold in their vaults huge stocks of silver attracted to Shanghai by the security offered by the areas under foreign control. In the last decade the reserves of silver have increased steadily, owing to the civil wars and the bandits of the interior. In 1927 the average stocks held were a little more than $150 million, Chinese currency, and in 1934 the average had increased to more than $539 million [3]. In recent months (1936) the reserves have been seriously depleted by the shipments abroad that have followed the efforts of the American Treasury to raise the price of silver [4].

The accumulation of the stocks of silver has caused a local building boom and the expansion of industry, but a more far-reaching effect has been the development of a system of credit that has extended over much of China and has financed a large part of the foreign and domestic trade of the country. Many of the banks in other treaty ports are dependent mainly on Shanghai for their operating funds, and Shanghai is the centre through which accounts between north and south China are settled [5].

The silver stored in Shanghai has served as a reserve against which bank notes have been issued. Owing to the security of Shanghai, such notes circulate much more widely than the notes of any other Chinese centre, where there is always the danger of the seizure of the metallic reserves − when they exist − by bandits or war lords or by the government itself. Shanghai bank notes are China's nearest approach to a national currency. In 1931 the total issue amounted to some $290 million (Shanghai). The notes circulated throughout the provinces of Kiangsu, Chekiang, Anhwei, Fukien, and Kiangsi. They were accepted as far north as Tsinan in Shantung Province, as far west as Ichang on the Yangtse, and down the coast to the extreme south [6].

Manufacturing

Although statistics are not available for accurate measurement, it is certain that there has been much more advance in the development of modern manufacturing industry in Shanghai than in any other city of China, or in any other two cities. It is probable that Shanghai is almost as important in modern manufacturing as all the rest of China proper. The fairly adequate data on individual factory industries may be taken as evidence of the relative standing of the city. Of the 133 cotton spinning and weaving mills in China proper, Shanghai has sixty-one with 55 per cent of the total spindles and 57 per cent of the looms [7]. In the flour-milling industry, Shanghai has fifteen of the ninety-one modern flour mills of the country with 47 per cent of the producing capacity [8]. Shanghai's position in the industries carried on in smaller establishments, such as silk reeling, matchmaking, knitting, and rubber manufacture, is equally important, and there are a great variety of industries still in the handicraft stage. Shanghai as a manufacturing centre will be discussed more fully in later paragraphs.

The origins and growth of Shanghai

Unlike Yokohama and Kobe, the two great ports of Japan, which attained importance only with the opening of Japan to

145

world trade, Shanghai was the leading commercial centre of China long before the coming of the foreigner. The settlement apparently began as a fishing village, and its ancient name of Hu Tu indicates an estuary where rows of bamboo stakes, fastened together with cords, are placed to catch the fish borne in by the tides. In the books of the Chin dynasty (AD 300) there is a reference to the repair of the mud forts thrown up at some earlier date about 5 km (3 miles) to the north of the present city to protect the fishing estuary from pirate raids [9]. The first written reference to the name Shanghai seems to have been made in the eleventh century, when Shanghai was already important commercially [10]. The name may have a variety of translations — 'up from the sea', 'upper sea', 'above the sea', or when written 'Haishang', as it has been sometimes, 'on the sea'. Whatever the exact translation, there is no doubt that Shanghai, ancient or modern, is the product of the sea. In the sixteenth century, because of the attacks of Japanese pirates, fortifications were built and Shanghai became a walled town.

Arrival of the foreigner

In view of the antiquity of Shanghai and its early importance in the domestic trade of China, it is amazing that contact with western Europeans was delayed to so late a date. The first western European ship to reach Shanghai was the *Lord Amherst,* sent northward from Canton in 1832 by the East India Company. It entered the Yangtse almost two centuries after the arrival of the first British ships in Canton and three centuries after the Portuguese had reached Macao.

The Chinese officials received the mission from the *Lord Amherst* but informed its members that all trade must be through Canton. Another British ship, the *Huron*, visited Shanghai in 1835. The effort to open Shanghai, however, was dropped for several years. In 1842, during the Opium War, the city was captured by British troops, and in 1843 it was formally opened as a treaty port under the Treaty of Nanking, concluded in the previous year, which also provided for the opening of Amoy, Foochow, and Ningpo.

The long delay in the opening of Shanghai to foreign trade was undoubtedly due in part to the attitude of the Chinese officials. From the earliest times, even in the eighth and ninth centuries, when trade with the Arabs and the people of the South Seas had been encouraged, it had been the policy of the government to limit the contact to certain designated ports and thus minimize the dangers of penetration by foreigners. With the arrival of the western Europeans the policy had been continued, and the traders had been instructed to confine their activities to Canton. But it is likely that such restrictions would have been broken down by force much earlier, as they were eventually, if Canton had not been a convenient port. The European traders arrived from the south by way of the Cape of Good Hope and the Indian Ocean. Canton was the southernmost trading port of China. To reach Shanghai it would have been necessary to sail northward another 1 370 km (850 miles) along a coast uncharted at that time and dangerous even in the present day. The Europeans were content for a long period to have the Chinese traders assemble Chinese products in Canton. Through the sixteenth century at least, the Dutch carried on their trade with China by means of Chinese junks linking their colony in Java with the Chinese ports. They held that such a method was cheaper than direct trade and that it did not expose their merchants to the exactions suffered by other foreigners [11]. Only on the several occasions when the monopolistic tendencies of the Co-hong, the guild of Chinese merchants that controlled trade with the foreigners at Canton, became too restricting was there the threat to leave Canton for Amoy, Swatow, or Ningpo.

There was also little incentive to open up new trading areas, since there was only a small demand for Western manufactures. The Europeans paid for their outgoing cargoes in the earlier years mainly in silver and from the middle of the eighteenth century to an increasing extent in opium. Prohibited by the Emperor Chia Ch'ing in 1800, the opium trade could probably be carried on illicitly with less interference at Canton than at some port nearer the imperial capital. So great did the inflow of the drug finally become that the staple exports of China, tea and raw silk, were not enough to balance it. About 1830 the movement of silver was reversed, and the metal began to flow out of the country to pay for the opium — an added reason for the opposition of the

Chinese government to the import of opium. The efforts to suppress the opium trade at Canton led to war with the British in 1840 and to the opening of Shanghai and three other ports.

Early commercial development

The early visitors were greatly impressed by the importance of Shanghai. Gutzlaff, who visited the city in 1831 and again on the *Lord Amherst* in 1832, spoke of Shanghai as perhaps the principal commercial city of the empire [12]. The settlement was no longer a fishing village but one of the largest urban centres not only of the Far East but of the entire world. There are various estimates of the population, ranging from a total of 527 000 based on Chinese records of 1811 to the estimate of 270 000 made by Robert Fortune in 1843 [13]. Gutzlaff mentioned the numerous temples, the neat and comfortable houses, and the fact that the city was laid out in great taste.

At the time of the visit of the *Lord Amherst* in 1832, H. H. Lindsay, the supercargo of the ship, was most enthusiastic regarding the possibilities of Shanghai for trade [14]. In his report he described the commodious wharves and large warehouses that occupied the banks of the river, the fine harbour and anchorage, the accessibility of the port to the interior of China, and the magnitude of the junk trade. It was his opinion that the native trade of Shanghai greatly exceeded the trade of Canton, and he was so impressed by the number of junks in the harbour that he had the entries counted and found that in seven days some 400 junks ranging in size from 100 to 400 tons passed Woosung bound for Shanghai. If this record was characteristic of the entire year and not of the month of July alone, when Lindsay visited Shanghai, the city was one of the large ports of the world and compared favourably with London [15]. Unlike the trade of the great European ports of that day, that of Shanghai was almost entirely domestic, the junks coming from Tientsin, Manchuria, Fukien, Kwangtung, and Formosa, and, in relatively small numbers, from the South Seas, Cochinchina, and Siam.

Robert Fortune, a botanist from the Royal Horticultural Society's Garden at Chiswick, England, who visited Shanghai in 1843, described the 'forest of masts' that met the eye on the trip up the river to the town. The early observers were apparently more interested in the junks than in what they carried, for there is little mention of the commodities entering into the trade. Grain, peas (probably soybeans), and medical drugs were brought from Manchuria, and tea, silk, and cotton cloth (nankeens) seem to have been the principal exports. Foreign manufactures had evidently been brought in from Canton long before the first Europeans reached Shanghai, for the supercargo of the *Lord Amherst* saw many articles, particularly foreign textiles, on sale in the shops [16].

The eclipse of Canton

Once the port of Shanghai had been opened, development was rapid. After the Treaty of Nanking there was a period of overexpansion, when foreign officials, merchants, and manufacturers, unfamiliar with the consuming habits of the market, were much too optimistic concerning the future of the China trade. Sir Henry Pottinger, the British plenipotentiary, is reported to have said publicly that the treaty had opened to trade a country so vast that all the mills of Lancashire could not making stocking stuff sufficient for one of its provinces [17], a statement of a kind with the later famous remark of Wu Ting-fang regarding the additional inch on the shirt of the Chinese and the producing capacity of the cotton mills of the world. It soon became evident, however, that there was a real demand in the Shanghai area and in the Yangtse Valley for cotton cloth, particularly the plain goods, and that the port was admirably situated as an outlet for the products of China. It was much nearer the areas producing tea and silk, and these commodities, constituting as they did in 1842 more than 90 per cent of China's commodity exports [18], could be assembled much more readily than they could in Canton. In 1843 Fortune had prophesied that Shanghai would soon surpass Canton in foreign trade. He returned to Shanghai for a second visit in 1848 and was again impressed by the forest of masts, but this time the native junks were overshadowed by the larger vessels, chiefly from England and

America, twenty-six of which were at anchor in the harbour [19].

Within a year after the formal opening of Shanghai no fewer than eleven foreign firms were established in the port, including the American firm Russell and Company and the British firm Jardine, Matheson and Company. The increase in the export trade was immediate. In 1845 Shanghai exported 6 433 bales of raw silk. Eleven years later the quantity had reached more than 92 000 bales, a very large share of the Western demand. The export of tea from Shanghai increased from about 1 million lb in 1844 to more than 80 million lb in 1855 [20].

The rapidity with which Shanghai fulfilled Fortune's prophecy in the race with Canton was amazing. In 1842 Canton was still China's one point of contact with the West and enjoyed a virtual monopoly of the foreign trade. Exactly comparable data for these early years are not available, but it would seem that Canton still held the lead in 1851, though there was no question that a rival was arising. By 1863 the new port had established its supremacy, and eight years later, in 1871, Shanghai's share of the purely external trade of China, excluding the coastal trade, was 63 per cent of the total, and Canton's share only 13 per cent [21].

Shanghai surpassed Canton, the old established port, mainly because of a better geographical location with access to a much more extensive hinterland, but partly because of the survival in Canton of the old conservative and restricting methods of conducting trade. Canton trade with the foreigner had been through the Co-hong, and foreign merchants were not permitted to carry their business into the interior. Although the Chinese attempted to limit trade at Shanghai as it had been limited at Canton, their efforts were resisted vigorously and effectively by the foreigners. Shanghai opened with new methods and with much greater freedom to foreigners. They could send their Chinese agents into the interior to buy silk and tea, and they were not compelled to deal with any particular Chinese merchant. Although the Co-hong had been abolished by the Treaty of Nanking, and although it had been provided that British subjects should be permitted to deal with whomsoever they pleased, the treaty was in reality a dead letter for the first few years at Shanghai.

The people of Canton refused to allow foreigners within the walls of the city, and the merchants attempted to revive the Co-hong under the guise of licensed warehouses for tea. The officials made every effort to hold the trade in its old channels. The imperial government, in the hope of confining foreign trade as completely as possible to Canton and thus nullifying the opening of the new ports by the treaty, ruled in an imperial edict that on all raw silk, no matter to what port it was shipped, transit dues should be paid to the amount that would have been paid if the silk had gone to Canton. The edict had little effect, since the savings in transport charges and in loss of interest were so great on shipments to Shanghai that they much more than offset the added transit dues. By 1851 the Taiping Rebellion had so badly disrupted overland trade routes that Canton was cut off from all but its immediate hinterland. The wars with the British and French in 1856 and 1857 further interfered with Canton's trade and led to the removal of the headquarters of the remaining foreign merchants to Hong Kong.

With the opening of new ports under the terms of the Tientsin Treaties of 1858 and subsequent treaties a number of potential rivals to Shanghai were established. There are now sixty-nine treaty ports, and eleven additional ports have been opened voluntarily by China. Shanghai, however, has remained the dominant port of the import trade. By 1881 it controlled about two-thirds of the total direct foreign imports into China. The imports were mainly manufactured goods and could be handled and marketed much more advantageously through the facilities of a large city. In the export trade the smaller ports could function. Raw silk and tea were not so completely the export commodities as they had been in 1842, but in 1881 they still constituted 84 per cent of the total. A considerable share of the raw silk went out from Canton, and tea was exported from Foochow, Hankow, and Canton, the ports near the areas of production. In the early years of the twentieth century (average for 1904–08) Shanghai handled 51 per cent of the foreign trade of China and was slightly more important relatively in imports than in exports. In more recent years, with the growth of a number of small ports, particularly along the Yangtse River, in north China, and in Manchuria, the relative importance of Shanghai has declined, though the trade of the city has shown an absolute increase. In the five-year period ending with 1931, as stated in an earlier paragraph, 43 per cent of China's foreign trade passed through Shanghai. The same tendency that developed after the Tientsin Treaties is still apparent: just half of the import trade, mainly manufactured goods, was taken by Shanghai, but Shanghai's share of the export trade amounted to only 35 per cent, the smaller ports continuing to handle the raw materials. . . .

Location of Shanghai

Situated near the mouth of the Yangtse Kiang, China's principal river, Shanghai has access by water to a great delta and valley occupying the central part of the country. The area of the delta is 129 500 sq km (50 000 sq miles) and the total population some 40 million, or a density of about 800 to a sq mile. In the entire Yangtse Valley there are 1 944 300 sq km (750 000 sq miles), about one-half of the area of China proper, and nearly 180 million people, about one-tenth of the population of the world. No other port of the world has tributary to it so populous an area. Calcutta, at the mouth of the Ganges Valley, with a tributary area of some 116 550 sq km (450 000 sq miles) and a population of 145 million, is probably the nearest rival.

Within the delta of the Yangtse there are numerous urban areas important in manufacturing of both the old handicraft and the modern factory types and dependent on Shanghai as a port. In the Tai Hu area are the two great cities, Soochow, the ancient handicraft centre of the empire, with its silk weaving and luxury industries, and Wusih, a modern centre surpassed only by Shanghai. To the south on the edge of the delta is Hangchow, another old city, which still retains some of the industries dating back to its period of glory as the capital of the Southern Sung. Along the Yangtse are Nantungchow, Chinkiang, Nanking, Kiukiang, Wuhu, and Hankow, and, above Hankow, Shasi, Ichang, and Chungking. The Yangtse is navigable to all these cities. Hankow, 965 km (600 miles) above Shanghai, is accessible during the summer months by a channel of 8.5—9 metres (28—30 ft) for vessels of 8 000, or even 10 000, tons, and during low water by a channel of 2.4–3 metres (8–10 ft) for vessels of 2 000 tons. For 560 km (350 miles) more to Ichang the Yangtse is navigable by river steamers, and for 580 km (360 miles) further to Chungking, during the summer months, by specially constructed high-powered and shallow-draft vessels. Tributaries such as the Han River, which enters the Yangtse at Hankow, the Hsiang River and Tungting Lake, which join the main stream at Yochow, and the Kan River and Poyang Lake, which join at Kiukiang, add many more miles of major waterways navigable by small steamers and junks. Innumerable minor waterways — streams and canals — cover the entire alluvial plain with a network and serve as feeders to the larger streams.

The traffic from the entire valley is drawn down the tributaries and down the Yangtse as in a funnel, and back along the same channels flow the foreign imports or the manufactures of the coastal cities. A comparatively small part of the trade of the valley crosses its land boundaries, since the valley, except in its lower reaches, is isolated from the rest of China by natural barriers strengthened by the absence of adequate communication on land. To the west are the highlands of Tibet, to the southwest the high plateau of Yunnan, to the south and southeast the southern tablelands, and to the north and northwest the Tsinling Shan and connecting ranges. With the exception of small trickles of trade that may pass overland through these barriers, the valley is and will remain essentially the hinterland of the estuary of the Yangtse and of its port, Shanghai.

The many advantages of New York City with reference to its hinterland are often cited as an illustration of the importance of geographical factors in the growth of a port. It would seem that Shanghai illustrates that importance even more strikingly. Its hinterland is much more extensive than that of New York, and its tributary population is much greater. New York gained easy access to its hinterland only with the building of the Erie Canal and later of the railroads. At the present time the waterway is wholly inadequate and ineffective. Shanghai, on the other hand, possesses a natural entrance to the valley by water that will undoubtedly continue to be the main highway of trade.

Shanghai is not on the Yangtse but on a tributary, the

Whangpoo, at a point some 23 km (14 miles) above its junction with the main stream. The great port of central China has developed there partly because the tributary affords more protection from typhoons than would any location in the wider mouth of the Yangtse. Of more importance, however, has been the greater freedom from silting. On the smaller Whangpoo dredging has been necessary, but there has been a much less serious problem in combating the lighter load of silt carried by the tributary stream. The Yangtse carries a tremendous load of silt and has been building the coast of China eastward at a rapid rate for centuries. The town of Quinsan, for example, was the seaport of the district some 2 000 years ago. It is now 48 km (30 miles) from the south bank of the Yangtse and 129 km (80 miles) from the sea. Tsinglung, 32 km (20 miles) above Shanghai on Soochow Creek, was made the seat of the customs office in 1101, but in 1347 the water had become so shallow that the office was removed to Shanghai [22]. In 780 the Whangpoo was only a bowshot wide and was truly a creek, as the suffix *poo* (or *p'u*) indicates. Soochow Creek, then known as the Woosung River, was probably 8 km (5 miles) wide. Gradual silting and the shifting of deposits, to be expected in the delta of so large a stream as the Yangtse, narrowed Soochow Creek and widened the Whangpoo until by 1875 the creek had become only a few hundred metres wide and the Whangpoo more than 1 km.

In the early years after the opening of Shanghai to trade many foreigners expected that the focus of trade for central China would shift eventually to some port on the Yangtse such as Nanking, a former capital, or Chinkiang, which is at the point where the Grand Canal provides a waterway cutting the Yangtse at right angles and stretching northward to Peiping and southward to Hangchow. Chinkiang was opened to trade in 1860 and attained some importance as a collector of Chinese products and a distributor of foreign goods, but the task of keeping open a deep enough channel near the shore has been too formidable. The river is shifting northward at that point. Golden Island, where British men-of-war anchored in 1842, is several kilometres inland, and Chengjenchow Spit has grown into a mud bank completely blocking access to the landing stages along the British Concession and threatening those at the mouth of the Grand Canal [23].

Nanking, opened to foreign trade in 1899, has not had the same difficulties with silting, but the port did not have adequate means of communication with a hinterland until the completion of the Nanking-Shanghai Railway in 1908 and the Tientsin—Pukow line in 1912. Both Chinkiang and Nanking are on a river where it is wide and where there are no important tributaries. Water frontage is provided by only a single riverbank, and with any growth the ports would soon extend in a narrow shoestring along the stream and thus lose all the advantage of compactness. The Whangpoo is the only broad tributary entering the Yangtse between its mouth and the outlet of Poyang Lake, as far above Nanking as Nanking is above Shanghai. Both banks of the Whangpoo may be used for docks and warehouses and the protected waters provide anchorage space for steamers, junks, and lighters. Finally, Shanghai, situated much nearer the sea than either Chinkiang or Nanking and requiring the navigation of a shorter river channel by ocean vessels, is more favourably located for entrepôt trade and for the reshipment of goods to smaller coastal ports of north and south China. . . .

Shanghai as an industrial centre

At the coming of the foreigner Shanghai was an industrial town as well as a commercial centre. In the account of the march of the British troops to take the city in 1842 there is a reference to buildings that they believed to be distilleries [24]. Lindsay, in his account of the visit of the *Lord Amherst* in 1832, refers to the spinning and weaving of cotton carried on by every family in the many small villages dotting the area about Shanghai [25]. Cotton seems to have been the principal crop of the farmers. An account written in 1850 says that 'the husbandmen are very diligent and plant more cotton than rice' [26]. It seems to be definitely established that the cotton plant was cultivated in the vicinity of Shanghai at least as early as the Yuan dynasty (1280—1367) [27], and it is probable that the cultivation dates back even earlier, since the plant must have been brought to Shanghai from either south China or India during the centuries of intercourse by sea. At the time of the opening of Shanghai the output of cotton cloth was enough to supply several of the neighbouring provinces [28], and Shanghai nankeens were considered to be the best in China. It is reasonable to believe that they formed a part of the important export of cotton cloth to Europe that continued through the eighteenth century and well into the nineteenth owing to the superiority of the product of Chinese craftmanship over the machine-made cloth of the earlier years of the Industrial Revolution. One observer stated that in Shanghai and its neighbourhood 200 000 weavers were engaged in making plain cottons and muslins [29]. Some of the weavers were the farmers who grew the cotton, but the villagers and towns-people also manufactured cloth and yarn from raw cotton obtained in the market usually in exchange for the finished product. The principal European manufacture to enter Shanghai with the opening of the port to foreign trade was cotton cloth. In time the quality of the machine-made cloth improved, and it offered such serious competition in price to the handicraft industry that the local product gradually became of less importance. It has not disappeared, however, even with the development in Shanghai of the large modern cotton mills. Cotton is still grown around the villages and is spun and woven into a cloth that finds a ready sale in Shanghai chiefly to wharf workers and other labourers who prize the sturdier handmade material.

Development of modern manufacturing

When finally the Chinese began to accept and adopt the industrial system of the West, Shanghai was the most advantageous location for the new manufacturing industries. The Kiangnan arsenal and dockyard, were established by the Chinese government in 1865. Two small silk filatures, opened in 1862 and 1866, closed within a short time, and a more permanent filature using Italian machinery and Italian experts began operations in 1880. Agitation for the construction of a modern cotton spinning and weaving mill was begun in 1881, and after some delay the mill was finally opened in 1890. Other industries followed, and in 1895 the Treaty of Shimonoseki, concluding the war between China and Japan, gave to Japan and, through the operation of the most-favoured-nation clause, to all foreigners the right to establish manufacturing industries in China. Numerous factories were established by Japanese, Germans, British, and Americans, and Shanghai experienced its first industrial boom. A second boom came during and after the First World War when the great demand for all kinds of manufactured goods and the difficulties of importation from Europe led to a great expansion of industrial facilities.

The present importance of Shanghai in manufacturing industries has been discussed in an earlier paragraph. The rapid development of industry is shown to some extent by the increase in the electricity sold by the Shanghai Power Company from a total of 569 000 kilowatt-hours in 1901 to 743 510 000 kilowatt-hours in 1934 [30]. This index can be taken as a fairly accurate measure of growth, since in the five years ending with 1934 the Shanghai Power Company supplied, on the average, 83 per cent of the electricity sold by power companies in the International Settlement, the Western District, the French Concession, Chapei, Nantao, and Pootung, or practically the total area of Greater Shanghai, and in earlier years its share was even larger. Of all the electricity sold by the company in the ten-year period ending with 1934, 78 per cent was consumed for industrial purposes.

Among the modern industries that have been established in Shanghai, cotton spinning and weaving mills have taken the place of the old handicraft textile industry as the dominant manufacturing activity. Accurate evidence of the relative importance of the industries is difficult to obtain. One index is the consumption of power. It cannot be a final measure because of the varying power needs of different manufacturing processes, but it is a particularly significant index for Shanghai, since Chinese industrial statistics are so fragmentary.

The position of the cotton textile mills, consumers of 78 per cent of the power, is striking, particularly if the small consumption of power in a cotton mill relative to total output is considered. The other important industry is the milling of flour, and there are a great many factories, large and small, manufacturing rubber shoes, flashlights, paper, egg products, cigarettes, machinery, soaps and cosmetics, enamelware, toothbrushes, matches, phonographs, and a host of miscellaneous goods, mainly for consumption in the Shanghai area but in part for shipment to all parts of China where the difficulties of transportation do not make the freight charges prohibitive.

Industrial areas of Shanghai

In the local distribution of manufacturing plants in Shanghai and its vicinity the controlling factor seems to have been transportation facilities — a river, creek, canal, or railroad. In the original areas of the International Settlement and the French Concession there are few manufacturing enterprises other than small plants supplying the consumer directly. Those parts of Shanghai were settled by the foreigners primarily for trade, and they are still the commercial and banking centres. Long before the Treaty of Shimonoseki of 1895 gave the foreigner the right to build factories in China much more extensive areas had been added to both the Settlement and the Concession. It is in those relatively less crowded areas that much of the development of manufacturing has taken place. The most important industrial area of Shanghai is the Yangtsepoo district, which lies in the International Settlement along the Whangpoo below the mouth of Soochow Creek. The first modern cotton mill of China was located there, and below the stretch of wharves near the mouth of Soochow Creek the riverbank is now lined with cotton spinning and weaving mills and some engineering and chemical works.

A second important industrial area lies along both banks of Soochow Creek, the Settlement side and the Chapei side, above the commercial area at the mouth and near the terminus of the Nanking–Shanghai Railway. The eastern part of this area is occupied by smaller establishments — silk filatures, weaving sheds, knitting mills, machine shops, and chemical works, mainly under Chinese management. Many of the factories were destroyed during the Japanese invasion of Shanghai in 1932, and the sales of industrial power by the Shanghai Power Company dropped in that year from 506 million kilowatt-hours to 452 million kilowatt-hours. Rebuilding has been rapid, and in both 1933 and 1934 there was a substantial increase in power sales over even 1931 [31].

Along the upper reaches of Soochow Creek in the Western District beyond the limits of the Settlement and even beyond the area of external roads there is another area of large factories rivalling Yangtsepoo. Tributary to the spur of the Shanghai—Hangchow—Ningpo Railway linking with the Nanking—Shanghai line, it includes many cotton, flour, oil, and jute mills, chemical works, and the Kiangsu mint. Northeast of Chapei, along creeks and canals in the Hongkew district, there is an industrial area somewhat similar to Chapei, with small industries owned mainly by Chinese.

There is little manufacturing within the limits of the old walled Chinese city, southeast of the French Concession, but along the Whangpoo and around the terminal of the Shanghai—Hangchow—Ningpo Railway, both within the Concession and in Nantao, there is a concentration of small machine shops, stimulated no doubt by the large government dockyard and arsenal at Kiangnan nearby. Across the river on the Pootung side, stretching downstream toward the Yangtse, are many large-scale enterprises, including cotton mills, paper factories, tobacco factories, engineering works, and the storage facilities of the foreign oil companies. . . .

8 Cities as centres of change in China

Every sedentary society has built cities, for even in a subsistence economy essential functions of exchange and of organization (both functions dealing with minds and ideas as much as with goods or with institutions) are most conveniently performed in a central location on behalf of a wider countryside. The industrial revolution has emphasized the economic advantages of concentration and centrality. But is it true to say that change, revolutionary change, has found an advantage in urbanization; in concentration and in numbers? The city has instigated or led most of the great changes in Western society, and has been the centre of its violent and non-violent revolutions. In western Europe the city has been the base of an independent entrepreneur group which has successfully challenged and broken the authority of the tradional order. In China, while cities with the same universal economic functions arose, they tended until recently to have the opposite effect on the pattern of change. China has consistently reasserted itself as a single political unit, but it is otherwise the appropriate qualitative and quantitative counterpart of Europe, and provides a reasonable basis for comparison. China and Europe have been the two great poles of world civilization, and an examination of the different roles which their cities played may help to elucidate other differences between them.

The following generalized and capsulized discussion aims only to suggest this difference, as an example of what might be made of an approach to the study of society through an analysis of the city's role in the process of change [1]. By cutting a familiar pie in another way we may arrive at useful insights. In doing so in the short space of an article the writer realizes that he must raise or beg more questions than he answers, and may in particular be guilty of oversimplification or distortion. But the virtue of such an attempt may lie in its disturbing or even irritating nature; it aims less to prove than to provoke. To quote from Karl Marx with this in mind, 'the whole economical history of society is summed up in the movement of this . . . separation between town and country' [2]. In distinguishing between European and Chinese civilization, we must of course assume a complex multiplicity of causes, many of which may elude us, and many of which may have little or nothing to do with geography. The distinctions and the arguments which follow do not imply that this basic fact is disregarded, but they pursue the matter from a point of view which has frequently been neglected and which may be suggestive of important factors.

The cities of western Europe have been, at least since the high Middle Ages, centres of intellectual ferment; of economic change; and thus, in time, of opposition to the central authority. They became rebels in nearly every aspect of their institutional life. It was trade (and to a somewhat lesser extent specialized manufacturing) which made them strong enough to maintain their challenge to the established order. Their spirit of ferment was the spirit of a new group, urban merchant—manufacturers, which could operate from a base large and rich enough to establish increasingly its own rules. This setting tended to ensure that the universities, which grew up in cities originally for convenience and centrality, would frequently nourish scepticism, heresy, and freedom of inquiry [3]. Even where they did not overtly do so, the concentration of literacy and learning in the cities was a stimulus to dissent.

Most of the cities which rose out of the cultural and social chaos following the destruction of Roman unity and preceding the development of a new national unity grew in answer to new conditions, for northwest Europe was ideally situated for trade. Most of them were in their origins much older than this, and had begun as administrative, military, or ecclesiastical centres. But a score of major rivers, navigable and free from floods, silting, or ice throughout the year in this mild maritime climate, led across the great European plain to the open sea; the peninsular, indented nature of the coast critically heightened mobility. The invitation which this presented to inter-European trade furthered the ascendancy of the commercial function. The shift of commerce and associated urbanism from the Mediterranean to northwest Europe seems to have begun before the Age of the Discoveries, notably in the Hansa towns and in Flanders. This may be in part a reflection of the mobility inherent in the lands around the Baltic and North Seas, once they had learned from the Mediterranean the lessons of commerce and absorbed the civilizing influences of this earlier developed area. In any case, these northern cities came to be dominated by trader—manufacturers. Trade was a heady diet, and enabled urban merchants to command cities which had originally been administrative creations. While the cities did not alone destroy feudalism, they owed much of their prosperity and independence to its decline: freer trade, wider exchange, and failing power of the landed mobility. And their very growth as rival power bases accelerated the collapse of the old feudal order.

As the growth of national unity progressed, under the institutional and emotional leadership of monarchy, an alliance of convenience between king and city arose which met the crown's demands for funds and the city's demand for representation. Urban merchants had the money to support the king in his foreign wars and in his struggle with the divisive domestic ambitions of the nobility and the church. In return the city received an increasing voice in the affairs of state, through representation in parliaments, and indirectly through the making of policy in which the throne was obliged to follow. But while this alliance of revenue in exchange for concessions was one of mutual interest, its ultimate result was the strengthening of the urban commercial sector until it overthrew or emasculated the monarchy, and with it the traditional order as a whole. Having helped the king to power over the nobility, the city achieved a *modus vivendi* with him which left it in control of the affairs vital to it. As a current reminder of the development of urban independence, 'the city' of London retains its originally hard-won privilege of excluding the reigning monarch, who is also excluded from the House of Commons, in part the city's creation and in part its weapon. To a certain extent the king, and even the nobility, were willing to go along with the process of economic change instigated by the city since they profited from it as the principal source of wealth in which they were often investors as well as tax collectors. But the new values which the city emphasized, and their institutional expression, were in direct conflict with the traditional society based on land; the city repeatedly bred overt revolutionary movements designed to establish its new order as the national way of life.

As centres of trade, the cities were free of the land and of its social and political limitations embodied in the institutions of post-Roman society. They developed their own law which was in differing degrees independent of the traditional, rural law. Their institutions were self-made, and they were not beholden to the traditional system which they challenged. The companies and corporations which the merchants organized went far beyond the scope of guilds in their successful attempt to order most of the social and economic fabric (instead of being limited to a trade-union function, as the guilds of China predominantly were). Traditional guilds were overlaid with new merchant organizations, or were clothed with new functions and powers, although some of the older guilds remained as conservative or retarding influences. The economic institutions which arose concurrently were also new-made sources of strength: banking, letters of credit, private property, interest, speculation and investment, representing needs and ideas which were almost wholly foreign to the traditional society of the countryside, and which were the accompaniment of an ever-widening trade. For the invitation to commercial expansion overseas was as strong in Europe's geography as the earlier invitation to trade among the lands surrounding the Baltic, Mediterranean, and North Seas. A leading agent of this process was necessarily the city, where trade flowed through break-in-bulk points such as the mouths of the Rhine or the English ports facing the Channel. Merchant corporations for overseas trade became the strongest and most progressive, or revolutionary of the city's agents. Interestingly, the original charter of the British East India Company stated that 'gentlemen' (by which was meant the landed gentry) 'shall be excluded' from membership.

The city was the natural centre of political change as it had been of economic change. The growth of modern Europe may be regarded as the steady progress of a new class of urban traders and manufacturers toward a position of control in a society and economy which their own enterprise had largely created. It was they who had realized the potential of Europe's location for world trade, and they who had developed and applied the technological and economic tools which made Europe the centre of the world. The destruction of the old pattern was implicit in this process, and also implicit was the revolutionary expression, by the cities, of their claim to political power. City—country alliances were formed, and the dissident groups from the country often bore the brunt of the effort, since they were the more numerous, as well as sharing in the spoils. But the city was in the van, and even diverted or perverted rural dissent and rural force to its own ends; leadership and money were frequently more decisive than numbers. It is of course true that at least in England this city—country alliance left and perhaps still leaves the landed gentry with prestige and thus with considerable power, while it left wealth with the urbanites. Characteristically this wealth was used to acquire land and gentry status. This balance of advantage was particularly pertinent in the matter of parliamentary representation.

Revolutionary changes are nearly always the work of an alliance of groups, but the history of modern Europe is suggestive of the city's key role, despite the recurrent blurring of city—country distinctions. The first great modern revolution, in seventeenth-century England, was the work of a city—country alliance, but London was mainly Puritan, and the outcome might be regarded as the victory of urban merchants and their country confreres over the traditional authoritarian alliance of cavalier and peasant based on the land [4]. Two centuries later Manchester and Birmingham had joined London in the final stages of the contest between urban 'radicalism' and country 'conservatism', epitomized in the struggle over the Corn Laws, the Reform Bills, free trade, and the Manchester School. By this time cotton textiles had well supplanted woollen textiles as the chief manufacturing industry; since it came relatively late it was not greatly hampered by guild restrictions, as wool had been; it established itself in Manchester, which as a then unincorporated town lacked formalized controls. It may irritate many readers as a loose generalization, but still seems worth stating for argument, that representative government and the industrial revolution, perhaps modern Europe's two most significant products, were created by the city. The Low Countries provide as good an illustration of this as does England.

In France the picture was less clear since urban merchant—manufacturers were less prominent in the national economy. Even so, it was Paris which created and carried the revolution. Paris used peasant distress and rebellion, but was never dethroned by it. One may say that Paris later destroyed Charles X and Louis Philippe. By this time, however, the Napoleonic land reform had given the peasant a stake in the *status quo* and helped to keep him a conservative counter-influence to the city, after his revolutionary ardour of the 1790s had served its purpose and cooled. Thus, in part, is derived the country's role in the destruction of the Second Republic and the Paris Commune, 'radical city movements'. Across the Rhine these distinctions become increasingly blurred, as for example in the Peasant War in early Reformation Swabia and Franconia. In eastern Europe it is difficult to draw distinctions between city and country, or to find an independent urban-based group living on trade and challenging the existing order. Nevertheless even in twentieth-century Russia, while the Soviet revolution was in part carried by peasant groups, leadership remained in the urban intellectual group which had instigated the change.

In northwest Europe, which is our concern here, the city has been a consistent seat of radicalism. This is not to overlook the recurrent Jacqueries which in every society have been the desperate recourse of an oppressed peasantry. But in the West these have often been closer to reaction than to revolution — the peasants were demanding the restoration of the *status quo ante,* not the establishment of a new order. Where they did attack the old order it was characteristically on specific points, such as Wat Tyler's demand in fourteenth-century England for the disendowment of the Church. The same pattern is apparent in rural opposition in America, in uprisings like the Whiskey Rebellion or in political parties like the Populists. The removal of abuses does not necessarily mean revolutionary change, despite the violence or the 'levelling' sentiments which usually characterized rural dissidence.

In China, while the peasant and the countryside were in some respects like the West, the city's role was fundamentally different. Chinese cities were administrative centres. With few exceptions this function dominated their lives whatever their other bases in trade or manufacturing. Their remarkably consistent, uniform plan, square or rectangular walls surrounding a great cross with gates at each of the four arms, suggests their common administrative creation and their continued expression of this function. Local defensive terrain, such as at Chungking, occasionally made this common plan unsuitable, but the stamp of governmental uniformity is nonetheless apparent. This was true for cities which had originally risen as trade centres, or which became more important commercially than they were administratively. It is possible to find a clear separation in many provinces between administrative and commercial cities, where the capital is not the most important commercial base: Chungking and Chengtu in Szechuan, Chengchow and Kaifeng in Honan, Hankow and Wuchang in Hupeh, Hsiangtan and Changsha in Hunan, Soochow and Nanking in Kiangsu, Wuhu and Anking in Anhwei, Tientsin and Peking in Hopeh, and other less clear cases [5]. But despite this degree of functional specificity, little urban independence or urban-based revolutionary change appeared until the traditional fabric was rent by the growth of Western-inspired treaty ports. Even in the exceptional cases where trade or manufacturing was the sole or predominant basis of the city: Chingtechen, the site of the Imperial Potteries, or Canton, the consistent focus of foreign trade, there never developed a merchant-controlled urban base free in any significant sense of the traditional state order.

A case in point is Shanghai. Long before the city became a treaty port under foreign domination, it was the leading commercial hub of the Yangtse Valley and may even have exceeded Canton in the volume of its trade. A British visitor in 1832 maintained that it did, and his count of junk traffic suggests that Shanghai was then among the leading ports of the world [6]. It nevertheless remained well down on the list of delta cities by size despite its lion's share of the trade. Another British visitor in 1843, the year in which Shanghai was opened to foreign trade as a treaty port, estimated its population at 270 000, Hangchow at 1 million, Soochow, Ningpo, and Nanking at half a million each, and six other delta cities at figures equal to or greater than Shanghai's [7]. Shanghai has never performed any administrative functions outside its own metropolitan limits, and it may be for this reason that it did not dominate the delta until Western entrepreneurs largely took over its development. In bureaucratic China, trade alone could not rival administration as an urban foundation. Outstanding locations for trade, such as Hankow (or Shanghai), as advantageous as Amsterdam or London, were frequently not put to full use until European traders built major cities there. Wuchang, opposite the mouth of the Han, was an almost exclusively administrative city before 1850, while Hankow itself was only a moderate sized town.

Large cities seem to have been proportionately more numerous in China than in Europe until the nineteenth century, and until the eighteenth century urbanism may have been higher. Perhaps a quarter or more of the population lived in towns and cities of more than 2 500 population, and perhaps 10 or 15 per cent in cities over 10 000. The big cities of the East as a whole were huge by European standards; this was a consistent feature of what has been called 'Oriental society' [8]. In China most cities or towns of 5 000 or more had well-defined commercial or manufacturing districts, and special areas for each important enterprise: banking, metal goods, food markets. textiles, woodwork, and so on. This pattern remains in most contemporary Chinese cities. But the cities were not decisive centres of change in a commercialized economy. They served as imperial or provincial capitals, seats for garrison troops, and residences for governors, viceroys, and the ubiquitous cloud of officials and quasi-officials with their 'service-providers'. Their business was adminstration, and exploitation, of the countryside. Marco Polo, in describing the magnificence of Peking, accounts for it as follows:

This happens because everyone from everywhere brings there for the lord who lives there and for his court and for the city which is so great and for the ladies and barons and knights of whom there are so many and for the great abundance of the multitude of the people of the armies of the lord, which stay round about as well for the court as for the city, and of other people who come there by reason of the court which the great lord holds there, and for one and for another . . . and because the city is in too good a position and in the middle of many provinces [9].

Here is a clear picture of a city based on administration from a central location, where trade flows in largely in response to the existing structure of officials, troops, court, hangers-on, and the host of people necessary to support them, from secretaries and servants to bakers and dancers. Six hundred years later at the end of the nineteenth century European travellers in China reported the same phenomenon, on a smaller regional scale: large cities whose sole function appeared to be administration, or important trading cities at key locations which were nevertheless dominated by officials and the magistrate's *yamen* (office). Thus Archibald Little, describing the city of Kweichowfu in Szechuan where the manufacture of salt brine and coal dust balls, and trade on the Yangtse River, were the apparent sources of its prosperity, writes that the city was a main station for the collection of *likin* (internal customs tax) and 'the town is studded with the numerous mansions of the wealthy officials and their dependents' [10]. With the opening of Chungking as a treaty port, *likin* was collected at Kweichowu only on local hauls and the city rapidly decayed despite its apparently strong economic base in manufacturing and trade.

The trade process appears to have lacked the dynamic quality by means of which Europe's cities rose to power. Pre-eighteenth-century China had a trade as great as or greater than pre-eighteenth-century Europe, but Europe's subsequent commercial expansion left China far behind. Why this happened, and why China never produced the revolutionary economic and political changes which re-made Europe into an arbiter for the rest of the world is a vital question. An analysis of the city's role may help to suggest some relevant factors. Why was the Chinese city not a European-style centre of change?

China is geographically isolated by a formidable assemblage of barriers. To landward lies the greatest mountain mass in the world, with its extensions from the Pamir Knot, reinforced on the south by rainforests and spectacular river gorges, on the north by the barren wastes of Siberia, and on the west and northwest by a vast sweep of desert. Seaward a coast deficient in harbours faces a huge and until recently commercially underdeveloped ocean, by European standards. Chinese trade with Japan was at several periods considerable, and with southeast Asia even larger, but it did not approach eighteenth- or nineteenth-century European levels. It tended to be characterized by luxury goods, strategic goods (such as copper for coinage), or specialities such as Chinese porcelain. With these exceptions, especially the highly developed and diversified trade between southeast coastal China [11], and southeast Asia, China did not greatly extend herself commercially, and was for the most part content to send specialized goods, like silk, to the rest of the world through middlemen intermediaries: the Arabs by sea and the Turkish peoples of central Asia by land. Significantly, the largest concerted Chinese attempt in foreign trade was an imperial government project (the famous Ming expeditions of the fifteenth century), which lasted only some thirty years and apparently found no solid base in the Chinese economy or in its merchant group.

Internally, trade moved largely on the great river systems, running fortunately east and west, but there was no such close interconnection between these river basins as in Europe, by sea or across plains. Physically China is built on a grander scale, but the landscape presents no such invitation to exchange as has sparked the development of Europe. Europe is multipeninsular, each peninsula tending toward economic distinctiveness and political independence, but joined by cheap sea and river routes. This plethora of complementary areas and their transport links magnified the basis and the means of exchange. Although its early trade development was not larger than China's, by the middle of the eighteenth century commercial expansion overseas had joined and accelerated commercialization at home, and Europe stood in a class by itself. The cities of western Europe were both the creators and inheritors of this development. But in China the cities remained centres of the unitary national state and of the traditional order rather than its attackers, epitomes of the

169

status quo. As direct links in the official hierarchy, they were the props of the empire. The universities were urban, for convenience as in Europe, but they stimulated no dissent. Their accepted function was to train scholars who could staff the imperial civil service, and they fed their graduates into the imperial examination system. This, and the better economic and social position of scholars generally in China than in Europe, encouraged the universities and the literati to support the *status quo*; European intellectuals may have taken a vow of poverty, but they remained a dissident or discontented group.

Physically, China lacked Europe's outstanding advantages for trade, and on the other hand presented a base for highly productive agriculture, through irrigation. Wittvogel's revealing work on the organic connection between the need for mass organized water control and the growth of a monolithic bureaucratic state in China lends insight into the origins and pattern of the institutional structure [12]. With China's environmental advantages, water control made agriculture the massive core of the economy, and at the same time left the bureaucracy in a position of ramified command. It was not possible for urban merchants to win independence from this system. They had less economic leverage than the rising European merchants because, with the preponderant position of agriculture, they never occupied proportionately as large a place in the economy.

The state of course did its part to prevent the development of a rival group, and by taxation, requisition, and monopoly ensured that the merchants would be kept relatively impotent. This was a job which European states and monarchs, though equally determined, failed to accomplish, their merchants were in a stronger position, and the state was weaker: it was merely *primus inter pares.* Land hunger in China, as a reflection of a population too large for the available arable land (increasingly serious during the past 200 years, but even in Han times worse than in most other parts of the world, including Europe), also acted to restrict commercial development, since it meant high land rents. Capital could almost always be invested with greater profit and safety in land, or in rural loans, than in productive or capital-generating enterprises outside the agrarian sphere.

Where extra-agricultural opportunities for investment did exist, the individual entrepreneur was at the mercy of the bureaucratic state. Many of the major trade goods were government monopolies. Elsewhere the essentially Western concepts of private property and due process of law, in a word, of the entrepreneur, were lacking in a society dominated by agriculture and officials. Extortion, forced levies, confiscation, and simple financial failure as the result of arbitrary government policies were the daily risk of the merchant. Some individuals did indeed become very rich, for example the famous *hong* merchants of Canton, but their wealth came necessarily through official connection: by possession of gentry status, by office holding or official favour, or by trading as part of a government monopoly (such as foreign trade under the Canton system and at most other periods was). Even so their gains were never secure. The greatest and richest of the *hong* merchants died in poverty, having lost official favour. While this also happened to many of the pre-eighteenth-century European capitalists, it did not prevent the survival and growth of individual capitalist families or firms or of a moneyed group. The famous Ch'ing dynasty billionaire Ho Shen, said to have been worth the equivalent of nearly a billion and a half US dollars, was not a merchant at all, but a favourite minister of the Emperor Ch'ien Lung, which demonstrates the real source of wealth in traditional China. Yet he too died in poverty and disgrace (by suicide in place of a suspended death sentence in 1799) at the hands of Ch'ien Lung's successor.

In China merchant-capitalists did not use their money to establish their independence, as did the merchants of London or Antwerp, or to stimulate the growth of a new economic pattern. Unfortunately for the Chinese merchants, the imperial revenue was at most periods derived largely from the land tax and from the government trade monopolies. Agriculture was proportionately more productive than in Europe, and revenue from trade less necessary. Peking thus did not need the merchants as the king had needed them in Europe to finance the ascendancy of the national state, to pay for its wars with rival states, or to meet its normal bills. No concessions were necessary; the merchants could be squeezed dry, and were, with no harm to the state. The commanding position of the bureaucracy, and the fact of the bureaucratic state, are perhaps explainable by a similar process of default. Merchants were necessary or useful to perform essential (and, to the state, profitable) commercial functions; they were tolerated, but kept under strict control, and this was simpler and cheaper than for the state to manage all commercial dealings itself [13].

But the merchants were also identified with the state as well as being stifled by it. Their numbers were recruited largely from the gentry class, who had the capital and the official connections essential to commercial success. Gentry merchants worked willingly with gentry officials in the management of the state monopolies, including foreign trade. Outside the monopolies, the same partnership operated, as a matter of mutual interest. In addition, most gentry members, whether or not they were engaged in trade, also performed other semi-official functions, comparable in some degree to the British landed gentry. These 'services' represented a considerable part of their income; they were not likely to attack the system which nourished them. In a more general sense, the tradition of revolt in this hierarchical society did not include the reordering of social or economic groups, but concentrated on the removal of bad government. Individual or group improvement was not to be won by destroying the fabric, but by making optimum use of one's position within it.

Finally, China had maintained since Han times and with few breaks a remarkable degree of unity [14] and a central power which no single European state achieved until quite late in its modern development. In China even towns of the *chen* (market town) rank (population *c.* 3 000–5 000) were seats of garrison troops, whatever their prominence in trade. In Europe in the course of the crown's contest with the nobles, and of the international rivalries which also developed among the plethora of separate national states, urban merchants found an opportunity which contrasted sharply with the rooted monolithic nature of the Chinese state.

The cities of China were consequently microcosms of the empire, not deviants. They were not backwaters, for necessarily learning, art, and the trappings of cosmopolis were concentrated in them. Yet, each was a symbol of the imperial system, operating not only under the direct thumb of Peking, but according to its precepts. Obvious considerations of convenience made them central places, market towns, transport termini or break-in-bulk points, and exchange centres of varying degrees of sophistication. But these universal urban functions do not automatically bring with them the character of rebellion or innovation which we have rightly come to associate with cities in the West. The main distinction of the Chinese city was concentration, as the node of the traditional society and as its power base. Imperial authority filtered down more slowly into the countryside, becoming more dilute with every level. Every government with ambitions of central power attempted to control the peasant. In a largely precommercial and preindustrial society of a basically molecular character, this could never be perfect control. China lacked not only the tools of control for its huge area, such as communications and literacy, but the bond of common interest and attitude which as completely commercialized economy tends to create, often by sublimating or suppressing conflicting interests. In the absence of such tools of conditions to implement rural control in China, the importance of the city as a centre of political and military power on the side of authority was magnified.

Change in China, as elsewhere, has been the work of a city—country alliance, with the leadership coming usually from the gentry based in cities or towns. But the origins of dissent and the main force of attacks on the *status quo* have been far less urban in China than in the West. While the rebellions were in many cases closer to the usually unsuccessful Jacqueries of the West than to the really revolutionary changes generated in Western cities, they were the predominant agents of what change did take place. They were successful where their Western analogues failed because there was no more potent agent of change, no other group (if we except the several nomadic invasions and conquests) and no other economic base by which change might even superficially be forced. The similarity with the Jacqueries lies in the fact that Chinese rebellions rarely challenged the basic nature of the existing order, but only its administration. The new dynasty which resulted might mean new blood, but seldom new institutions.

173

Given a largely closed agrarian system, it is understandable that each dynasty, as it lost its momentum, lacked the means of maintaining a high productivity and effective distribution as population increased, and that it eventually declined into corruption. This was especially so in the rural sphere, easy prey to tax and rent manipulation (and the source of most of the national revenue and income), but marginal enough to be sensitive to oppression. At the same time, the lack of large extra-agricultural economic bases for an independent group prevented the growth of new ideas or new institutions to challenge the old, even while the old lay in ruins. The city—country alliance which in Europe made revolution made only a change of administration in China. The city was too dependent on the traditional order to attempt its destruction.

The accelerated impact of the West on China during the nineteenth century has by the twentieth century set in train profound changes, and it is natural to find that these are reflected also in the city's role. The Kuomintang was a largely urban based movement, and though its revolutionary aspects became less and less prominent under the more compelling problems of security against Communists and Japanese, it was far more than a change of administration. It was in fact the political vehicle of a new group, nurtured not only in Western thought, but in the essentially Western milieu of the treaty ports. Negatively also the cities have made a new impression. The present Communist regime had prominent rural roots, and came to power with an announced resentment and distrust of cities, calling them the centres of reaction (and also of degeneracy, softness, and vice), though its venom was directed particularly against the foreign-created treaty ports.

It was basically the impact of the West, including the Soviet Union, which ensured that this latest of rebellions would for the first time successfully destroy the existing fabric. In the treaty ports themselves development had been too brief, and too much limited by the inertia of the agrarian economy, to produce an effective base for change to rival Communism in its originally rural base. Nevertheless these urban centres, many of them new as large cities dependent on trade, played much the same role as the cities of late medieval Europe. They were rebels against the traditional order because for the first time in the history of China they provided opportunity for the merchant. Money could not only be made, but invested, in trade or manufacturing, with safety, profit, and prestige. Private property, and all of the values of R. H. Tawney's 'Acquisitive Society' had been enthroned in the treaty ports by the West, and to the Chinese businessman Shanghai or Tientsin were all that traditional China was not. He was prepared to work for the establishment of a government and society which would make a respectable place for a commercial industrial bourgeoisie, based, as the term implies, in cities.

This new group, shaped by the West, largely created the Kuomintang. They formed an alliance with some of the landed gentry, for example Chiang Kai-shek, who was both landed and bourgeois, but they were never in any sense a peasant party, and their ties with the land were feeble. While they answered, or promised to answer, many of the needs of the new class of treaty port Chinese, and kept peace with the gentry, they did not seriously attempt to answer the questions and strivings of the Peking intellectuals, nor the more compelling needs of the peasants. Communism ultimately rode to power in part as a crusade against the 'merchant capitalists' of Shanghai on the one hand and the Western-inspired intellectuals of Peking on the other [15].

To be sure, the Chinese Communist Party and its leaders are urban-trained Marxists operating intellectually and practically in an urban framework, and dedicated to an industrialization programme which necessarily centres in the cities. Their political control also depends substantially on their control of city populations and city enterprises. In so far as they thus push the city toward the middle of the stage as a recognized base at least for economic and technological change, they continue the about-face in the city's role which the Western impact began in the treaty ports. In any case, active urban agency for change is a recent phenomenon in China, perhaps one may say a direct transmittal from the West.

This analysis, in attempting to particularize the city's role in the two great centres of world civilization, has necessarily dealt with institutions as much as with place. The urban differences were expressions of distinct societies. It was

175

broadly speaking the bureaucratic state in China which stifled the growth of European-type cities despite the volume of trade or the regional specialization of commerce and manufacturing which existed. In Europe, too, wherever bureaucratic and/or persistently authoritarian governments ruled, commercialization and industrialization were late and/or little, and the urban-based entrepreneur usually exerted small influence. Some other common ground may exist between these bureaucracies, and the suggestion that physical conditions required or invited central control, and that geographic factors helped to minimize the opportunity of the merchant, are perhaps as applicable to eastern Europe, or to Spain, as to China. The imprint of Roman Law and of Mediterranean urban traditions may also help to account for the east—west distinction in Europe. In any case, maritime western Europe followed a course whose urban direction lay at the root of its wealth, its power, and its distinctiveness.

Sir George Sansom, in a characteristic series of lectures given at Tokyo University in 1950 and published in 1951 under the title *Japan in World History*, typifies the modern European attitude and contrasts it with the Tokugawa Japanese by quoting as follows from Alexander Pope's *Windsor Forest*, written about 1712:

> The time shall come when free as seas or wind
> Unbounded Thames shall flow for all mankind,
> Whole nations enter with each flowing tide
> And seas but join the regions they divide.

This is so revealingly and typically English, and so untypically Chinese, because it shows the world through the eyes of the London merchant. Ironically, merchant towns of a European type had begun to develop in Japan by the sixteenth century around the Inland Sea (perhaps an oriental Mediterranean?), including self-governing Sakai, living on the trade with China and southeast Asia. Sakai, with its own army and its council of merchants, was so close to the European pattern that contemporary Jesuit observers compared it with Venice. This promising development was crushed, despite its apparently strong economic base, by the feudal revival of the Togukawa and its superior armies reacting to the political threat which they felt was posed by the existence of even quasi-independent merchant cities. Here we may perhaps see an expression of Japan's insularity and strategic commercial location, and perhaps *inter alia* of the weight of influence from China. The latter was earlier expressed in the great period of Japanese borrowing from T'ang China when Nara, Japan's first real city, was built on the Yamato plain as a smaller scale copy of Ch'ang An, the T'ang capital. Nara omitted Ch'ang An's massive walls, and walled towns as such have never existed in Japan at any period, one reflection of a basically different set of geographic and social conditions.

But our purpose here has been only to suggest. The city has been a centre of change in western Europe, while it has been the reverse in traditional China, despite the broad similarity in urban economic functions in both areas. Urban character and urban roles may be useful indicators of the nature and dynamics of the diverse entities of society.

China Now

9 Population policy

After twenty-two years of Communist rule, demographic prospects in the People's Republic of China (PRC) are still in doubt. The future course of fertility and mortality depends on the direction of official policies and on the evolution of those facets of society that affect the vital rates. There can be no certainty in regard to any of these matters. Recent history is the best basis for surmise about the future, but the record is equivocal. The official attitude toward family limitation has been among the least stable aspects of Peking's domestic policy.

The specific questions most critical for China's future demographic development are whether or not a sustained programme for contraception, sterilization, abortion, and late marriage will be mounted in the cities and throughout the vast countryside, whether economic and social changes supportive of family limitation will take place, and whether administrative intervention can impose family planning on those who will not adopt it voluntarily. Related to these questions are other, more basic questions as to the degree of ideological dogmatism or pragmatism with which future leaders of the PRC will approach population policy and other issues of domestic administration, the effectiveness of the administrative system, the continuity of central leadership, and the course of economic development. None of these questions may be answered with certainty.

Domestic policies and programmes in the PRC have shown considerable variation in the past twenty-two years. In fact, there is some support for the thesis that political and economic management has followed a cyclical pattern of oscillation between extremes. At times the official position

181

has been doctrinaire; political principles have taken precedence over economic practicalities, and decision-making has been highly centralized. At other times political ideals have been sacrificed to economic necessity and considerable discretionary latitude has been allowed to local authorities to solve practical problems and achieve concrete objectives. To the extent that policy has been cyclical, it has lacked continuity. The discontinuities have undoubtedly rendered central policies less effective than they might otherwise have been and contributed to the tendency of the cadres at all levels to distrust central initiatives and to protect themselves against the hazard of policy instability by the universal bureaucratic tactics of delay, avoidance of personal commitment, superficial compliance without significant action, and deceptive reporting to higher levels. Whether the failure of the local authorities to implement the more extreme central policies has held back the drive for national economic development or has instead saved the central authorities from the consequences of their own bad judgement may be debatable, but the long term, non-cyclical decline in altruistic idealism among the cadres, who joined the regime with great enthusiasm in the years immediately after the Communist victory in 1949, must represent a dissipation of a vital administrative resource that cannot easily be restored.

Other evidence suggests that changes in domestic policy in the PRC cannot be fully explained as reactions to swings of the political pendulum. The record does not seem to justify the conclusion often reached prematurely by foreign observers during the waning phases of a period of political extremism that the leaders of the Chinese Communist Party (CCP) learn from experience and tend toward moderation. Too often an interval of apparent pragmatism has been followed by a new plunge into adventurism. Yet the new extremes have not been mere reversions to former positions. The Party leaders neither abandon their fundamental principles nor implement them in the same form in which they failed in prior trials. Hence, it is necessary to examine the total experience of the wavering family limitation efforts in the PRC before extracting from it whatever meaning it may have for the future.

This paper traces the development of family limitation

policies in the PRC in relation to population problems, population theories, economic trends, and other aspects of civil administration that seem to have influenced official decision-making. The record of population policies in the PRC can be subdivided into six fairly discrete periods: (1) from 1949 to September 1954, during which policy on family limitation was strongly negative; (2) from September 1954 to June 1958, during which the regime moved from the first indecisive steps toward support of family limitation into an all-out campaign to lower the birth rate; (3) from June 1958 to January 1962, during which first political euphoria and then economic anxiety held family limitation in abeyance; (4) from January 1962 to June 1966, the span of the second family limitation campaign; (5) from June 1966 to the summer of 1969, when birth control work was interrupted by the 'cultural revolution'; and (6) from the summer of 1969 to the present, when family limitation has for the third time become official policy. . . .

The third birth control campaign: 1969 to the present

The rationale for the third birth control campaign, as it developed during the waning phases of the 'cultural revolution', incorporated few of the arguments used in the earlier campaigns. In July 1970, an article in a pamphlet printed in Shanghai revived the contention that in a socialist country where everything is planned, population growth must also be planned [1], but most of the current arguments have been based on quotations from Mao's works used without regard to their original context and intent. The injunction 'Be prepared against war, be prepared against natural disasters, and do everything for the people' has been interpreted as authorization for promoting birth control, though the connection would seem somewhat remote. The phrase 'Show concern for the growth of the younger generation' is said to be Mao's authorization for discouraging early marriage. The exegetic freedom exercised in making such gratuitous interpretations, is necessitated by the fact that the works of Mao, like those of Marx, Engels, and Lenin, contain little that can be construed as an endorsement of family limitation.

The use of Maoist phrases to sanctify birth control clearly

indicates that the campaign now has unequivocal support at the highest level. Birth control and late marriage are repeatedly said to be 'of exceedingly great significance in changing habits and customs and transforming the world' [2]. Birth control work is 'a major event bearing on the national economy' and 'one of the important tasks of socialist revolution and socialist construction'. To promote birth control is to 'carry out . . . Chairman Mao's instructions' and to 'hold high' the 'great red banner of Mao Tse-tung thought'. Late marriage is identified with 'war preparations', 'Party consolidation', the class struggle, Mao's hopes for the young, and his opposition to revisionism. All opposition to birth control and late marriage is attributed to the pernicious influence of that 'traitorous scab' Liu Shao-ch'i and his ubiquitous 'agents'. Liu has been denounced 'with great indignation' for his 'towering crime of sabotaging planned births' and for such 'counter-revolutionary revisionist fallacies' as 'no interference with problems of marriage and love', 'no interference with early marriage either', 'match-making offices should be set up', and 'rearing sons for old age' [3].

Another feature of the rationale for the third birth control campaign is the reassertion of the connection between lower fertility and population pressures on the food supply. None of the references available thus far are as explicit as the most candid discussions of this relationship during the first birth control campaign, but the intent is obvious. One article in July 1970 related planned childbirth and late marriage to the effort of a particular production team to become self-sufficient in food grain and observed that the population of the team has not increased in the past three years [4]. A radio broadcast from Peking in November 1970 also linked grain production to the solution of over-population problems in a brigade in Chekiang Province [5]. In November 1971, Vice Premier Li Hsien-nien, in an interview with a Cairo newsman with whom he was discussing China's economic development, remarked that, 'We have been racing against time to cope with the enormous increase in population', and a little later added:

What can be said in this connection is that, despite the

enormous population, we have been able to find a basic solution for the problem of clothing needed by all Chinese, although, in our judgement, it may not be a good solution. We have also done the same thing regarding food. Thus, we have guaranteed that no citizen will die for lack of food or clothing [6].

Except for the absence of pessimism, the essential spirit of these expressions is reminiscent of the Malthusianism that marked official attitudes and Mao's own position during the Hundred Flowers period. If this is a true reflection of the mood of the current leadership, its significance goes far beyond the prospects for family limitation efforts, for it implies a return to pragmatism in domestic administration and candor in public statements.

Organization, propaganda, and popular resistance

Little has been said in the Press about the organization of birth control efforts during the third campaign. This is hardly surprising in view of the fact that local political and administrative organization has been in flux throughout this period. The Cultural Revolution incapacitated government organs and shattered local Party committees without being able to provide an effective alternative. It was only with the help of the military that order was restored in urban centres. Interim arrangements such as the political 'work teams' sent out to join in the local struggles by the Party regulars, the 'Mao Tse-tung thought propaganda teams' organized to consolidate Maoist control, the threeway alliances, and the revolutionary committees that succeeded one another through the general turmoil often involved complete changes of personnel, and the Party rebuilding and rectification efforts of the post-Cultural Revolution period seem to have been protracted and uncertain of outcome. Although most economic organs resumed normal operations in 1970—71, the power struggles initiated by the Cultural Revolution continued at the highest leadership levels. In the spring of 1971, Mao's wife, Chang Ch'ing, and his personal secretary, Ch'en Po-ta, seem to have lost power, and in September Mao's second heir apparent,

Lin Piao, was purged and may have lost his life. Since then, the central political leadership has apparently been stable, and the bold new detente between the PRC and the United States suggests that the present leaders have enough security and confidence to change some formerly inflexible positions relating to international affairs. However, it cannot be assumed that the consolidation of the new authority at local levels has been completed throughout the country. Under these circumstances, there may be no alternative but to assign the promotion of birth control and late marriage to existing agencies to be integrated with existing programmes.

As before, the health agencies seem to be the principal carriers of the message on birth control, which has been combined in some areas with schistosomiasis control and in others with the 'patriotic health movement' [7]. Shanghai designated the last week of January 1970 as a 'shock week' for mass propaganda on hygiene, health conditions, elimination of flies and mosquitoes, and propaganda for birth control and late marriage. Retired workers, 'Red Guards', 'little red soldiers', medical workers, and the 'revolutionary masses' in residential areas were organized to conduct the propaganda work [8]. In Canton and Shanghai, the municipal revolutionary committees seemed to have general charge of the work in 1969 and 1970, and in Shanghai they combined it with 'consolidation' drives in the Party, the militia, and the Communist Youth League. Cadres, Party members, and medical personnel were to set an example for the rest of the population [9].

In a rural area near Peking in 1971, the *hsien* revolutionary committee mobilized sanitation workers and 'barefoot doctors' — youthful paramedics with a few months' basic training — to conduct birth control propaganda on a house-to-house and team-to-team basis in conjunction with prevention and treatment of women's illnesses [10]. In a rural area in Hunan Province, a revolutionary committee set up a Mao Tse-tung thought study class to heighten vigilance against expensive weddings. In another rural area in Hopeh Province, the assistance of the Communist Youth League and 'Red Guards' was to be sought in promoting late marriages [11]. The Press attention given to these efforts was evidently intended to encourage other local jurisdictions to follow suit, but there seemed to be little uniformity of method in the country as a whole.

The fragmentary evidence available contains much less information than in either of the previous campaigns on the kinds of resistance encountered. This may be an indication that the current efforts, being largely directed toward thought remoulding and indoctrination, have not aroused open opposition as did the more direct efforts in former campaigns. On the other hand, the evidence suggests that the cultural barriers to family limitation conspicuous in the first two campaigns are still major obstacles. The implementation of birth control and late marriage is said to accentuate 'the struggle between the two lines and the struggle between public and private interests'. For example, when oral contraceptives were publicized in a Shanghai cotton mill, the effort 'suffered a definite setback' because some people 'with ulterior motives' spread the rumour that the pills would 'cause sterility, weaken the power of memory, and produce an appearance of "jaundiced" obesity'. The persistence of fear and distrust of government-sponsored contraceptives after years of birth control propaganda shows how little faith the people have in official reassurances. The same source also indicated that people still regard contraception as troublesome and that they continue to want children of both sexes and harbour other 'incorrect thoughts' [12].

Another source indicates that health cadres are still reluctant to undertake birth control work [13]. A foreign visitor in Canton in the fall of 1971 was told that the old problem of peasants desiring children of both sexes explained the persistently high birth rates [14]. More significant, perhaps, are the recurrent complaints about the connivance of 'evil minds' and the subversive activities of 'Liu's agents' in connection with birth control and late marriage. In the rural area in Hunan, when the 'class struggle' slackened, the 'handful of class enemies' immediately fanned the evil wind of expensive weddings again [15]. In Canton, Confucian ideas about filial piety were reportedly promoted by another 'small batch of class enemies', and as a result, 'many youths' had been 'poisoned' by their 'residual toxins' and could not handle their marriage problems correctly [16]. When Edgar Snow talked with Mao on 18 December 1970, Snow remarked that there had been a 'great change here in China' in respect to popular attitudes toward birth control compared with five or ten years earlier, but Mao replied that Snow had been 'taken in' by Chinese propaganda. Mao said that because of their preference for male children, many peasant couples go on having children until the woman is forty-five. This attitude must be changed, Mao added, but it is taking time [17]. Obviously, the force of tradition in China is still strong.

Contraception, abortion, sterilization, and late marriage

The methods of contraception used in China since the start of the third campaign include a variety of oral contraceptives. In 1970, two birth control pills based on synthetic progesterone and oestrogen became available for general use in at least some areas. They were said to have an effectiveness approaching 99.956 per cent, though there are no details on the investigations that produced this extremely high and remarkably precise figure. The pills were to be taken for twenty-two days beginning with the fifth day of the menstrual cycle. Menstruation would normally follow within one to three days after the end of the twenty-two day period. A few women reportedly experienced side effects from the pills, which were said to disappear gradually as the body adjusted to the hormonal changes [18]. On his visit to China in the winter of 1970–71, Edgar Snow was told by a Peking doctor, Lin Ch'iao-chih, that the twenty-two day pills were free of side-effects and 100 per cent effective when taken according to instructions, but that irregularity in pill-taking was 'far too prevalent' [19].

Snow was also told that a once-a-month pill was under test in Peking on a sample of 5 000 persons, which was said to be 'completely effective' except for about 2 per cent of the population, whose 'systems reject it'. Other experiments were being conducted on a once-in-three months pill, according to Lin, and she added, 'We now believe we can develop a pill or vaccine effective for about a year' [20]. The Shanghai Health Clinic reported that a once-a-month contraceptive injection using long-lasting progesterone and oestrogen was recommended for use in 1970. It was said to be 98.59 per cent effective, but in a few cases it produced side effects similar to those of the progesterone pills, and some women experienced shortening of the menstrual cycle, for which special medical treatment was required [21]. At the time of Snow's visit, Chinese medical research personnel were showing considerable interest in Japanese development of a vaginal pill utilizing prostaglandin [22]. The evidence of a serious pursuit of the latest in fertility control technology is unmistakable.

Intra-uterine devices of metal and plastic are still available in China, though they are said to be only about 80 per cent effective and are apparently no longer regarded as the most desirable type of contraceptive. The metal devices can remain in place for four to six years and the plastic ones for two years, according to Chinese medical judgement, but they are not suitable for women with ulcerated cervix, inflammation of the uterine cavity, or vaginitis. Their major advantage is convenience; users are not required to plan carefully or observe prescribed procedures. Conventional contraceptives, such as condoms, diaphragms, and spermicides are also still available, but it is apparently expected that these devices will be displaced gradually by newer devices that are less inconvenient [23].

The official position on abortion is still that this method should not be relied on instead of contraception. It may be performed 'when contraceptive measures have failed' or when a woman is 'unfit to give birth' because of too frequent births, too many children, economic problems, or problems of work or career. However, the woman is warned that the operation, though simple, can adversely affect health [24]. Actually, there appears to be a considerable effort to increase the availability of the suction abortifacient machines throughout the country. According to Snow, who witnessed several such abortions during his last visit to China, abortion is now performed without charge on demand of the mother alone [25]. There is no indication as to how widely available abortion is or the extent to which it is actually utilized.

Sterilization is available for both men and women, apparently without restriction. 'Barefoot doctor' teams in some areas were reportedly bringing the operation to the people by means of 'mobile operation rooms', which consisted essentially of carrying basic surgical equipment into the rural areas and setting up wherever patients willing to undergo the operation could be found [26]. The Shanghai Health Clinic instructions required that applicants for sterilization be subjected to the 'three-straightening-out' treatment — straightening out the thinking of the applicant, of his family, and of the 'old folk' — so as to 'remove all apprehensions' [27]. Evidently these precautions were necessitated by adverse public reactions to sterilization.

None of the available sources provides further information on the specific objectives of the late marriage drive during the current campaign. There has been no discussion of ages for marriage or possible changes in the marriage law. The essential approach seems again to have been to persuade young people to put education, career, and service to the revolution ahead of their own personal affairs. Mao's example in marrying late (he was almost twenty-seven at the time of his first marriage) has been held up for emulation [28].

Results of the campaign

The effects thus far of the third birth control campaign are even harder to judge than those of the two preceding campaigns. The few available sources contain no quantitative measures of success or failure. A number of recent visitors to China have come back with reports that the current campaign has been a startling success and that birth rates are dropping sharply. Whatever the impressions given the visitors by their guides and by the local officials with whom they talk, the central authorities make no great claims for the success of the birth control programme. Statements by returned visitors that local birth rates have dropped below 10 per 1 000 population, that the national urban rate is as low as 6 per 1 000 and the national rural rate is in the range of 18 to 20 per 1 000, make little sense except as the products of grossly defective birth registration systems. If fertility levels had actually fallen as low as these figures imply, the fact would be so obvious that, even without statistical confirmation, it would be celebrated openly as a victory for the thought of Mao. Instead, the prevailing official attitude is summed up in a sentence in the July 1970 article by the revolutionary committee of the commune near Shanghai: 'We have done something, but what we have achieved is still far from what

Chairman Mao expects from us' [29]. The same attitude was expressed in regard to the state of the economy in general by Li Hsien-nien in his interview with the Cairo newsman in November 1971, when he said: 'Actually, we have achieved some progress but we do not regard it as very great progress. When we hear from our friends that it is great progress, we look at such talk as something bigger than reality, or as courteous talk' [30].

In assessing the net effects thus far of the third birth control campaign, the significance of traditional values emphasizing early marriage and childbearing that have withstood so many years of supposedly intense indoctrination is not to be underestimated. The young people who have been the prime target of propaganda for Maoist asceticism and for late marriage and birth control give every evidence of holding persistently to their own priorities on love and marriage which they will not abandon except under strong pressure. While the Party and local government organs are being reconstructed, cadres at all levels have other duties more urgent and less unpopular than birth control and late marriage to which to give their attention. Meanwhile, all indications suggest that only a minority of urban dwellers and a still smaller percentage of rural residents are ready to use contraception effectively at present. Abortions and sterilizations may number in tens of thousands annually, but such numbers scarcely constitute a perceptible reduction in the annual cohort of over 30 million births. In judging the potential impact of birth control campaigns in China, the implications of past experience suggest that it is better to be cautious than credulous.

Implications of past policies for future trends in fertility and population growth

In the twenty-two-year history of the PRC, official population policy has changed sharply several times. The attitudes of individual Party leaders, including Mao himself, have not been constant. Yet the changes in population policy have been neither cyclical nor random. They have been associated with political, economic, and social developments that are not reversible because they represent options tried and exhausted, thus narrowing the range of alternatives open to future leaders. Hence it would not be reasonable to assume that population policy will continue to vary merely because it always has. Rather, the factors that have determined population policy or contributed to its success or failure should be identified and the prospects for each assessed as a basis for establishing the limits of possibility for the future.

Political factors

Among political factors, the most conspicuous is ideology. It has certainly had an influence on population policy, but by no means as great as might have been expected if the Chinese leaders were absolutists in matters of dogma. Mao's initial position on population given in the NCNA release of 16 September 1949, undoubtedly derived much of its optimism from the Marxist conviction that labour is the source of all wealth and the inference that a country with abundant manpower was assured of early prosperity upon conversion to socialism. Even if they were not wholly convinced of this thesis, it was important that Party leaders appear confident during the period of consolidation because of the scepticism in China and abroad about the country's prospects for economic development. However, they would not have assumed such a firmly negative position on population policy if they had thought it possible that they might have to abandon it within a few years. It was probably ideology that committed them prematurely to doctrinaire anti-Malthusianism.

Despite ideology, Mao and his associates were not deterred from changing to a thoroughly Malthusian position by the end of the First Five-Year Plan period, but they were obviously not comfortable with it. When the 'Leap' figures on food grain production promised deliverance from the spectre of famine, they quickly returned to the Maoist optimism of the early years. When the promise of the 'Leap' was broken by the food crisis of 1960–61, the optimistic attitude toward population problems was abandoned for the second time. A guarded Malthusianism intervened until the resurgence of Maoist revolutionary fervour in the early days of the Cultural Revolution. Since the end of the Cultural

Revolution, a collection of abstract and highly adaptable Maoist exhortations serves as official ideology in place of the more disciplined traditional Marxist theory. Birth control and late marriage are found retrospectively to have received Mao's endorsement in phrases written long before Mao was concerned with population problems. Thus, ideology is itself being manipulated to rationalize demographic necessity.

It was probably inevitable that the Party leaders would come to rely less and less on ideology for guidance as its precepts were tried and found wanting. The manifold problems of political and economic administration confronted them with many specific situations requiring a choice between orthodoxy and expediency in which the price or orthodoxy was found to be prohibitive. Opting for expediency made it necessary to adopt more flexible interpretations of ideological mandates. With increasing flexibility, there were increasing divergences among the leaders as to the interpretations appropriate in particular circumstances, which further weakened the authority of ideology. By now this process is so far advanced that ideology is not likely to have much influence on population policy in the immediate future.

A more significant political factor is the degree of control the central authorities have over the entire political and administrative structure down to the local level. The responsiveness of local functionaries to central command determines how far the leaders can go in imposing by force policies that meet with popular resistance and how successful such efforts will be in securing conformity. The strength of the system of authority depends in part on the unity and stability of the leadership and in part on the effectiveness of rewards and punishments and on general morale throughout the system. In earlier years, before the local functionaries had become disillusioned by being caught too many times on the horns of the dilemma of 'commandism' versus 'disobedience to Party orders', their enthusiasm may have been higher, but they lacked organization, discipline, and experience. In the latter part of the First Five-Year Plan period, sagging morale and the elaboration of obfuscatory bureaucratism had begun to be major problems, and the disillusionments of the 'Leap' and food crisis periods caused further deterioration of the system. In the period between the food crisis and the

Cultural Revolution, an unsteady trend toward decentralization preserved local administration at the expense of central authority. Hence the administrative system presumably passed its peak of effectiveness some time in the first three years of the First Five-Year Plan period, before the first birth control campaign was officially launched.

During the Cultural Revolution, the cruel humiliation of top Party leaders and the purges of their associates in lower echelons, without regard to decades of loyal service, must have impressed all but the most obtuse cadres with the uncertainty of careers in Party and government. The slowness of the current Party rebuilding probably owes something to the lesson of these events. Until the Party has been reconstituted and the morale of administrators at all levels has been restored, it may not be possible to mount a high-pressure campaign for birth control and late marriage.

The first prerequisite for an effective administrative system is a firm and stable leadership. It would be hazardous to predict at this moment what the future holds. Maoism seems to be on the wane, and Chou En-lai seems to be the effective leader of the country. While Chou remains, the country has a highly skilled administrator of national and international eminence in charge of its affairs. However, in view of the recent turmoil, no one outside China can be certain how long the present leadership will last or what sort of leadership will succeed it.

Economic factors

The main impetus toward family limitation in the PRC has been the fear of food shortages and famine. In the earliest years of the new regime, the Chinese leaders discussed their economic problems openly in the Press because they were confident that the 'socialist transformation' of the economy would bring relief in due course. However, from the start, peasant resistance to socialization posed a major obstacle to 'transformation'. In 1954, official anxieties were further heightened by the results of the census and vital rates investigations, which showed that the population was larger and growing more rapidly than had been realized, and by the widespread crop damage and consequent local famines caused by abnormal rainfall in the spring of the year. Thereafter, the priority of birth control seemed to rise or fall in proportion to the degree of pessimism with which the Party leaders viewed the prospects for agriculture, which was in turn largely determined by their assessment of the seriousness of the difficulties facing cooperativization. Later, when the Leap statistics convinced the Party leaders that the prospects for agriculture were unlimited, birth control again went into almost total eclipse. When the Leap illusions succumbed to the food crisis, birth control reappeared after a prudent interval.

Since the early 1960s, there have been no serious food shortages in China, and birth control has never quite regained the urgency it had in 1957–58. The recent increase in its priority coincides with an apparent revival by the current leadership of the comparatively pragmatic approach to economic management that prevailed during the First Five-Year Plan period. The statement by Li Hsien-nien to the Cairo newsman cited in the last section is certainly in that vein, particularly in its acknowledgement that the effort to offset population growth by economic growth is a 'race against time'. Given this attitude, any return of serious economic difficulties in China would undoubtedly result in a much greater effort to promote family planning. Without the threat of economic difficulties, it is likely that efforts to reduce fertility will continue but with a secondary priority.

Economic factors also bear on the willingness of the population to make use of the birth control services supplied by the government and to adopt the practice of late marriage. In general, the traditional peasant economy has depended upon a division of labour within the family in which larger families were able to manage their manpower more effectively and be more prosperous than small families. Large families also had an advantage in economic security. Thus, high fertility was economically rewarding for the family and the individual. As the level of mortality declined, the pressure of growing families on the available land could create economic problems at the village level and above and even for individual families, but the larger and more prosperous families were better able than the smaller families to survive these difficulties.

The socialization of agriculture was expected to establish

the supremacy of collective over family and individual interests by demonstrating the economic advantages of co-operativization. Once the peasants had 'seen their bright future' in the cooperatives, it was assumed that they would be willing to sacrifice their traditional independence for the greater personal gains assured through cooperation. But the superiority of the cooperatives failed to materialize. In order to secure maximum productivity, it was necessary to devise systems of cooperative management which relied on the family as the basic production unit, and under these arrangements the large family was able to retain its economic superiority in spite of socialization. Some recent evidence suggests that this is still the case, and as long as it is, rural population will not be motivated to adopt family limitation voluntarily.

Early marriage meant an early start on a large family and was therefore a key element in the large family tradition. Economic conditions had a direct bearing on early marriage also, inasmuch as weddings traditionally involved major expenses for gifts and feasts. In hard times, marriages were often delayed, but when prosperity returned, the marriage brokers became busy again. One of the first consequences of 'land reform' was that many poor peasants, receiving their own land, implements, and livestock for the first time in their lives, immediately spent part of their new wealth on getting married or marrying off their children as soon as possible. The relative improvement in economic conditions after the food crisis was also accompanied by an increase in the marriage rate. There is therefore reason to expect that, in the immediate future at least, any increase in affluence in rural China may be followed by a decline in the average age at marriage.

In urban areas, the division of labour within the family had less economic value, except for families engaged in home handicraft industries. However, the advantage of having a maximum number of wage earners in the family unit was probably as great for urban as for rural households if not greater, since the nonagricultural economy offered fewer opportunities for the economically productive employment of women and young children than did agriculture. The income of urban families depended mainly on the number of male members gainfully employed, and family living levels were determined by the ratio of dependent members to wage earning members. In the early stages of the family cycle, a large number of children meant a high proportion of dependents, but such families fared well in grain distribution because children were allotted the same rations as adults, a fact which was recognized as an incentive to high fertility during the First Five-Year Plan period. As soon as the older male children were able to go to work, family economic circumstances would take a more favourable turn. If the family had practised early marriage for generations past, a given generation would pass through the childbearing years while the previous generation was still actively in the labour force, hence there might be no point in the cycle of generations in which the household was dependent upon the earnings of a single member. Having more than one wage earner in the family provided greater economic security to the urban as well as the rural family. Thus early marriage and high fertility had advantages in both urban and rural areas.

The effort to induce more urban women to join the labour force as wage earners, though it has met with only limited response thus far, may have eased somewhat the pressure on urban families to produce sons for economic reasons and may in some cases have introduced an element of competition between the economic incentives for employment of wives and the economic incentives for childbearing. On the other hand, the provision of crèches and nurseries in factories where women work, and the provisions for maternity leave with pay and for mothers to nurse their infants while at work may have given working women the option of working and having children at the same time, thus making the best of both the traditional and the emancipated women's worlds.

Economic factors may also influence fertility when the earnings of workers and peasants permit them to choose between spending to improve their levels of living or assuming the expenses of additional children. Before this option can be realized, economic growth must exceed the rate of population growth by a margin sufficient to allow a significant increase in the rate of economic accumulation, and the authorities must be willing to allocate a substantial part of the surplus to the workers and peasants in the form of wages and consumer goods rather than invest the greater part of it in capital expansion or military hardware. There have been numerous reports from China indicating that in urban areas, at least, some types of consumer goods, such as radios, ball-point pens, and bicycles, have become more abundant in the last few years. Whether these are sufficient and distributed widely enough to have an appreciable effect on the urban worker's attitudes toward family planning is not clear.

In the 1960s, there were some efforts to eliminate differences between workers' and peasants' income by levelling urban wages downward, and during the Cultural Revolution Maoism strongly opposed the use of economic incentives in any form to stimulate productivity of workers and peasants. Whether the Maoist attitudes toward 'economism' still persist is somewhat doubtful, but if they do, they will tend to inhibit any rise in wages. Unless China's workers and peasants have the option of purchasing much-wanted consumer goods as an alternative to childbearing, economic growth will not have much effect on motivation toward family limitation.

In the first two birth control campaigns, a part of the propaganda effort was directed at implanting the idea that excessive birth rates contributed to the burden that the state had to bear in providing for education, public health, transportation, welfare benefits, and employment, and that this burden ultimately affected the conditions of life for individuals and families. There were apparently some attempts to reinforce this idea during the second campaign by denial of maternity leave, food and cloth rations, and other welfare benefits to couples who continued to have children after the third or fourth child. How successful 'negative' economic incentives may have been is not indicated in any of the available sources. Even if 'negative' incentives are potentially effective, their impact would depend to a considerable extent upon whether or not the welfare benefits withdrawn represented a significant proportion of the family income, whether the rationing system was tightly managed, and whether the sanctions were uniformly applied throughout all enterprises over a large area. There are reasons to be doubtful on all these counts.

In the years since the failure of the Leap, the Party leaders, while maintaining a posture of confidence, have generally not been overly sanguine about China's economic progress or prospects. For the most part, they have talked of gradual improvement to be sustained with much toil and sacrifice over a long period. If the development of China's economy lives up to their most hopeful expectations, and if domestic economic policies emphasize increased production of consumer goods and higher wage levels, the basis for a voluntary transition toward lower fertility levels will be laid and there can be little doubt that family limitation will make more progress, particularly in urban areas. However, if economic progress is slight, or if there are further setbacks like those that have occurred several times in the past twenty-two years, positive economic incentives toward family limitation may be slight, and the degree of civil control necessary to realize the questionable potential of 'negative' incentives may be lacking. The range of possibilities so far as economic factors are concerned seems to be from a moderate influence in the direction of lower birth rates to no influence at all.

Attitudes and values

The greatest single deterrent to family limitation in China has been the powerful and persistent values supporting early marriage and abundant progeny. Aside from whatever economic justification these values may have, they are so deeply engrained in Chinese culture and so closely linked to traditional concepts of family roles and to ideas about self-fulfilment, filial piety, fortune, and fate that they would tend to survive for a time after the loss of economic and functional correlates. Evidence of the persistence of traditional values relating to marriage and family formation appeared in Press discussions in all three birth control campaigns. In the first and second campaigns, when the discussion was more detailed, the power of 'feudal' thinking on these subjects was frequently recognized as a major obstacle to the work of the propagandists. Though there are also many claims of success in overcoming tradition, and some indications that at least a part of the population even in rural areas may have been predisposed in spite of tradition to adopt birth control once the means were made available, allowance must be made for the fact that Press propaganda would, as a matter of strategy, attempt to create the impression that public receptivity was greater than it actually was. Some local reports of spectacular mass conversions to the official view are too stereotyped to be credible. Others, referring to worker heroes or model female cadres, obviously recognize that these are unusual cases and do not expect them to be widely emulated.

Outside of China, there has been much speculation during the past two decades as to the ultimate effect on Chinese national character of mass indoctrination from the earliest years of childhood. Foreign visitors, shown groups of young children in schools and nurseries chanting adulation of Mao and hatred for the United States, have forecast the emergence of a nation of zealous automatons instantly and totally compliant to the will of the central authorities. Other observers have surmised that the new generations of Chinese were being socialized in roles and values that represented a distinct break from the past and that in due course China would take on an altogether new image. The first test of the success of indoctrination in China came during the Hundred Flowers period, when the attacks on the Party became so sharp that the leaders found it necessary to adopt a policy of extreme repression. The disenchanted critics included worker groups and university students long cultivated by the Party. Free criticism of authority was not permitted again until the Cultural Revolution, when university and secondary school students and graduates, many of worker or peasant background, all of whom had literally grown up under Party teaching and had been especially indoctrinated in Maoism during the 'socialist education' movement of the middle 1960s, were called upon to demonstrate their loyalty to Mao by attacking anti-Maoist authorities. The youths were only too eager to undertake this assignment, especially those for whom it meant an escape from the hardship of rural life, but when they found themselves free of authoritarian constraints, they cast aside rules and regulations and displayed an ungovernable lust for power, self-indulgence, indiscipline, and violence. Although they rarely rebelled directly against Maoist authority, they used Maoist slogans to resist Mao's efforts to bring them under control, and continued their anarchism after he had denounced and repudiated them. This is not the behaviour of a generation imbued with the principle of total obedience to authority as a way of life.

The ineffectiveness of indoctrination on young people's attitudes toward marriage and having children was apparent in the widespread disregard of the strictures against early marriage, including violations of the minimum ages under the marriage law, which continued during the second birth control campaign, and in the 'wave of getting married now' that swept through Maoist youth circles in the waning phases of the Cultural Revolution. It has also been apparent in the admissions during the third birth control campaign that the 'poison' of traditional ideas still influences the attitudes of many young people toward marriage and family. The experience of the three birth control campaigns suggests that, even among young people, traditional values will not easily be changed by propaganda except in directions which they perceive as offering personal advantage.

Development of methods and organization

The most important single factor favouring the adoption of family planning in China is the fairly steady improvement of birth control technology. During the first and second birth control campaigns the lack of effective, safe, simple, and convenient contraceptives was a major obstacle to success among people who were willing to practice contraception voluntarily. There is no doubt that the present leadership is determined to develop new methods and make them available throughout the country as quickly as possible.

Apart from the bizarre adventures with traditional medicine prescriptions and homemade concoctions during the first campaign, it has been the policy in all three campaigns to copy conventional contraceptives from the West and from Japan and to make technically advanced methods and devices available on a mass basis as soon as the necessary supplies could be produced in sufficient quantity in Chinese factories. Initial Chinese efforts at contraceptive research left much to be desired from a scientific standpoint, but the level of sophistication seems to have improved considerably during the second and third birth control campaigns. Research on intra-uterine devices began during the first birth control campaign and continued for a time even during the quiescent interval between the start of the Leap and the start of the second campaign. By the time the second campaign began, the intra-uterine ring was ready for general distribution. Research on steroids was initiated in China several years ago, and their fairly widespread availability is obviously the result of considerable planning and development. More recently, Chinese medical research has been aggressively seeking new contraceptives that may provide longer periods of protection against conception with less frequent medicine dosages or treatment.

The development and large-scale production of simple abortifacient machines that can easily be carried about and operated in remote rural areas is another indication of the priority on technologies for reducing fertility. Although official policy still opposes a casual attitude toward abortion, some people seem to prefer this method, and their wishes are being accommodated. Clearly, it is the intent of the authorities that lack of means shall not be a deterrent to the practice of family planning.

The effective promotion of birth control has been an unsolved problem throughout all three campaigns. Various forms of propaganda and organization have been tried without conspicuous success. Aggressive publicity drives and pressure tactics during the first campaign evoked much public resentment and in some cases resulted in serious reverses. The ineffectiveness of propaganda efforts was in part a result of poor organization, a problem that has not yet been solved. During the first campaign, central directives were usually issued by the Ministry of Public Health, the local organs of which also played a prominent role in the birth control guidance committees. There was no standard format for the establishment of the committees and no system for making sure that instructions from Peking were implemented promptly or conscientiously. The efforts of health organs, propaganda agencies, mass organizations, pharmaceutical plants, and pharmacies were never adequately coordinated. Aside from the repeated injunctions to local leadership cadres to involve themselves directly in the campaign, there was little indication that the central authorities recognized the seriousness of local organizational problems.

During the second campaign, much less was heard of organizational problems, but the methods seem to have been essentially the same as in the first campaign. The unstable tempo of the campaign suggest uncertainty as to its priority at the top level. In the several years since the Cultural Revolution, during which the restoration of the administrative system has proceeded slowly, it is unlikely that the organization of birth control work could have been much improved. The use of 'barefoot doctors', itinerant army medical teams, reconstituted youth organs, and local 'revolutionary committees' in crash programmes that are frequently combined with other objectives, suggests a continuation of the loose organizational patterns that have been ineffective in the past. This is probably the best arrangement that can be devised under present circumstances, and it may be followed by more effective organization in the future. In the meantime, however, birth control efforts are not likely to be well managed.

Implications for population growth

When the factors just discussed are considered in relation to each other, there is no possibility that they could be combined in the form in which each contributes its maximum potential support for family limitation. Economic adversity might assure a higher priority for family planning, but it would also tend to weaken the administrative system and inhibit the development of new consumer alternatives to childbearing. Economic prosperity would accelerate the changes in economic and other values that would make for more voluntary acceptance of family limitation, but it would also remove some of the urgency from population policies. Therefore, the weakening of cultural imperatives sustaining traditional patterns of marriage and family formation is likely to be a gradual process. Nevertheless, it seems inevitable that China will follow the course of other developing countries toward lower fertility levels.

The analysis of past policies on birth control and their relationship to political, economic, and social factors in the PRC does not lead to firm quantitative assumptions about future trends in fertility, but it does suggest the degree to which the PRC may be able to duplicate the experience of other developing countries that have successfully reduced birth rates through government-sponsored family limitation programmes. By drawing on analogous experience with appropriate modification, it is possible to reach tentative conclusions not only about the prospects for fertility but also for mortality and population growth.

Of all the world's developing countries, the one with the closest cultural resemblance to the PRC is the Republic of China on Taiwan. Despite political differences, the basic institutions, including traditional marriage and family patterns, are common to both Taiwan and the mainland. Both the government of the Republic of China and that of the PRC are committed at present to national programmes of family limitation. However, economic and social conditions in Taiwan are much more favourable to the voluntary adoption of birth control. The economy of Taiwan is more highly developed, and its rate of economic growth has been more rapid and more sustained in recent years than that in the PRC. In 1952, the gross national product of Taiwan was equivalent to about $1.2 billion in 1970 US dollars; by 1971 it had reached $6.1 billion, an annual growth rate of about 8.9 per cent for the period, with a marked acceleration in more recent years. The corresponding figures for the PRC, according to estimates by Dr Arthur G. Ashbrook, Jr., are $59 billion in 1952 and $128 billion in 1971, an annual growth rate of 4.2 per cent [31]. Between 1952 and 1971, the *per capita* gross national product in Taiwan rose from $150 in 1970 US dollars to $410, whereas that for the mainland rose from $104 to $150. During this period, both countries received foreign aid, which served to broaden the productive bases of the economies, but the amount of foreign aid received per inhabitant of Taiwan was many times larger than that received per inhabitant of the PRC.

Urbanization and literacy are the two other aspects of national development that correlate with readiness to accept family limitation. In Taiwan in 1969, 62 per cent of the population lived in urban areas, and more than 35 per cent in cities of over 100 000 inhabitants. The corresponding figures for the PRC are not available, but at the end of the First Five-Year Plan period in 1957, official data showed only 14 per cent of the population as urban, and those in cities of over 100 000 inhabitants probably amounted to only 8 or 9 per cent. Since that time, official policy has discouraged urban population growth, and there have been intensive efforts to relocate urban youth permanently in rural areas. These efforts probably have not checked urban growth altogether, but the urban population is probably still not much above 15 per cent of the total and certainly no higher than 20 per cent. In Taiwan, more than 40 per cent of the labour force is engaged in non-agricultural employment. On the mainland, according to estimates made by John Philip Emerson of the Bureau of Economic Analysis, US Department of Commerce, the proportion of the labour force in non-agricultural employment was 14 per cent in 1957, rose to 19 per cent in 1958 during the Leap, dropped back to 14 per cent by 1964, and was around 15 per cent in 1971. About 75 per cent of the adult population of Taiwan is literate as compared with an estimated 25 per cent for the PRC.

Demographic measures and estimates also indicate that Taiwan is much further advanced along the course toward lower fertility and mortality levels than is the PRC. In 1952, the birth rate of Taiwan was 46.6 per 1 000 population; by 1970, it had fallen to a provisional figure of 28.1 per 1 000. The death rate for Taiwan was already down to 9.9 per 1 000 population in 1952 and had declined to 5.1 by 1970. Natural increase for Taiwan dropped from 36.7 per 1 000 population in 1952 to 23.0 in 1970. Official vital rates for the PRC for 1952 were based on inadequate local surveys and suffered from serious under-registration of births and deaths; there are no official figures available for 1970. According to estimates made by the writer, the birth rate on the mainland in 1952 was in the vicinity of 45.0 per 1 000 population and had declined to 37.3 by 1970, while the death rate declined irregularly in the same period from about 25.0 per 1 000 population to 15.0. According to these estimates, natural increase was around 20.0 per 1 000 in 1952, has risen and fallen several times since, and is now around 22.0.

Given the differences between Taiwan and the PRC in respect to some of the factors most directly related to fertility and mortality, the PRC cannot be expected to achieve in the next twenty years the rates of decline in fertility and mortality that have taken place in Taiwan since 1952. On the other hand, it is extremely unlikely that economic stagnation could cause a virtual stalemate in demographic trends for so long a period. The most likely possibilities range from a steady decline in fertility and mortality at rates more moderate than those for Taiwan, to either steady or intermittent decline at much slower rates. These possibilities would lie well inside the boundaries described by assuming a repetition of Taiwan's demographic experience and alternatively hypothecating no change in fertility and mortality levels at all.

Four model populations: 1970–90

To test the implications of these ranges for future trends in fertility, mortality, and population growth in the PRC, four model populations have been constructed for the period 1970–90. All four models use a 1970 base total and age–sex structure derived from a single series of estimates representing probable demographic changes in China from the census of 1953 through 1970. The 1953–70 series takes as its base population the 1953 census total, distributed by age and sex according to population models reflecting assumptions about the demographic history of China back to 1750 [32]. The series assumes a slight decline in fertility by 1958, a somewhat larger decline during the crisis years 1959–62, and a rise again during the recovery period and the Cultural Revolution. Mortality is assumed to decline significantly during the First Five-Year Plan period, to rise sharply during the crisis years, to fall rapidly in the early recovery years and more slowly during the Cultural Revolution years and subsequently.

The four models begin to diverge in 1971. Model 1 assumes a decline in intrinsic fertility rates patterned on the trend of intrinsic fertility in Taiwan since 1952 and a decline in mortality patterned on the trend in expectation of life at birth in Taiwan since 1946, the year in which the officially reported levels for Taiwan approximate the level estimated for 1970 in the series for the PRC. Model 2 is also based on fertility and mortality trends for Taiwan, but the rate of decline in both parameters is only two-thirds as rapid as for Taiwan. Model 3 assumes that fertility and mortality decline at one-third the rates for Taiwan. Model 4 assumes constant intrinsic fertility and mortality levels from 1970 through 1990. The table gives midyear populations and birth, death, and natural increase rates for the base series for selected years from 1953 to 1970 and for the four models for each year from 1970 to 1990.

Table 9.1 *Estimates and projections of the population and vital rates of the People's Republic of China 1953—90 (Population figures in thousands as of 1 July; vital rates per 1 000 population)*

Year	Population	Birth rate	Death rate	Natural increase rate
1953	582 603	45.0	22.5	22.5
1955	610 881	44.0	19.5	24.5
1960	688 811	39.9	20.1	19.8
1965	750 532	37.2	16.5	20.7
1970	836 036	37.3	15.0	22.3
Projection model 1				
1970	836 036	37.3	15.0	22.3
1971	855 170	37.4	14.4	23.0
1972	875 283	37.4	13.9	23.5
1973	896 321	37.3	13.3	24.0
1974	918 236	37.2	12.8	24.3
1975	940 983	36.9	12.3	24.6
1976	964 462	36.4	11.7	24.7
1977	988 566	35.9	11.2	24.7
1978	1 013 151	35.1	10.6	24.5
1979	1 038 063	34.2	10.1	24.1
1980	1 063 159	33.2	9.6	23.7
1981	1 088 317	32.2	9.1	23.1
1982	1 113 435	31.1	8.6	22.5
1983	1 138 406	30.0	8.2	21.8
1984	1 163 122	28.9	7.7	21.1
1985	1 187 490	27.7	7.4	20.4
1986	1 211 429	26.6	7.1	19.6
1987	1 234 842	25.5	6.8	18.7
1988	1 257 649	24.5	6.6	17.9
1989	1 279 806	23.5	6.4	17.1
1990	1 301 260	22.4	6.2	16.2

Table 9.1 — *continued*

Year	Population	Birth rate	Death rate	Natural increase rate
Projection model 2				
1970	836 036	37.3	15.0	22.3
1971	855 107	37.4	14.6	22.8
1972	875 034	37.5	14.3	23.3
1973	895 788	37.5	13.9	23.6
1974	917 348	37.5	13.6	23.9
1975	939 705	37.4	13.2	24.2
1976	962 815	37.2	12.8	24.4
1977	986 587	36.9	12.5	24.4
1978	1 010 921	36.4	12.1	24.3
1979	1 035 728	35.8	11.7	24.2
1980	1 060 905	35.2	11.3	23.9
1981	1 086 386	34.5	10.9	23.6
1982	1 112 097	33.7	10.5	23.2
1983	1 137 958	33.0	10.2	22.8
1984	1 163 940	32.2	9.9	22.4
1985	1 189 971	31.4	9.6	21.9
1986	1 215 983	30.7	9.3	21.4
1987	1 241 968	30.0	9.1	20.9
1988	1 267 881	29.3	8.9	20.4
1989	1 293 678	28.6	8.7	19.9
1990	1 319 342	28.0	8.6	19.4
Projection model 3				
1970	836 036	37.3	15.0	22.3
1971	855 031	37.5	14.8	22.6
1972	874 741	37.6	14.7	22.9
1973	895 178	37.8	14.5	23.2
1974	916 374	37.9	14.4	23.6
1975	938 323	38.0	14.2	23.8
1976	960 988	38.0	14.0	24.0
1977	984 353	37.9	13.8	24.1
1978	1 008 360	37.8	13.6	24.1
1979	1 032 942	37.5	13.4	24.1
1980	1 058 042	37.2	13.2	23.9
1981	1 083 593	36.8	13.0	23.8
1982	1 109 579	36.4	12.8	23.6
1983	1 135 985	36.0	12.6	23.4
1984	1 162 754	35.5	12.4	23.2
1985	1 189 880	35.1	12.2	23.0
1986	1 217 372	34.7	12.0	22.7

Table 9.1 — *continued*

Year	Population	Birth rate	Death rate	Natural increase rate
1987	1 245 188	34.3	11.8	22.5
1988	1 273 330	33.9	11.7	22.2
1989	1 301 818	33.6	11.6	22.0
1990	1 330 648	33.3	11.5	21.8
Projection model 4				
1970	836 036	37.3	15.0	22.3
1971	854 943	37.5	15.1	22.4
1972	874 415	37.7	15.1	22.6
1973	894 504	38.0	15.2	22.8
1974	915 254	38.3	15.2	23.0
1975	936 695	38.6	15.3	23.3
1976	958 834	38.8	15.3	23.5
1977	981 663	39.0	15.4	23.6
1978	1 005 156	39.1	15.4	23.7
1979	1 029 281	39.1	15.4	23.7
1980	1 054 008	39.1	15.4	23.7
1981	1 079 310	39.1	15.4	23.7
1982	1 105 178	39.1	15.4	23.7
1983	1 131 609	39.0	15.4	23.6
1984	1 158 600	38.9	15.4	23.5
1985	1 186 159	38.8	15.3	23.5
1986	1 214 300	38.7	15.3	23.4
1987	1 243 046	38.7	15.3	23.4
1988	1 272 422	38.6	15.3	23.3
1989	1 302 441	38.5	15.2	23.3
1990	1 333 128	38.5	15.2	23.3

From the total population figures given in the table, it can be seen that all four models show a net population increase between 1970 and 1990 of almost 500 million. More startling is the fact that by 1990, the total population in model 4, in which intrinsic fertility and mortality are constant, is only 32 million larger than that in model 1, in which fertility and mortality decline at the same rate as for Taiwan. This difference is less than 2.5 per cent of the smaller total figure. The population under 20 years of age in 1990 in the two models differs by some 75 million or 12 per cent on a base total of 605 million for model 1.

However, if instead of comparing models 1 and 4, both of which seem outside the realm of possibility, the same comparisons are made between models 2 and 3, the differences are smaller still. The 1990 totals differ by only 11 million, or less than 1 per cent, and the figures for the populations at ages under twenty differ by about 24 million, or less than 4 per cent on a base total of 637 million for model 2. These models imply that even a major and successful effort at fertility reduction in the PRC is not likely to make much difference either in the size of the total population or in the size of the younger age groups, hence it cannot afford much relief from population pressure in general or from such specific problems as the need for education, employment, housing, and other services for young people. To escape from such limited prospects, the PRC would have to find a way to alter some of the factors that have thus far determined demographic experience in other developing countries.

The principal reason why these models show so little difference even for successful efforts at family limitation is that they assume a correlation between fertility and mortality trends. It is, in fact, hard to conceive of circumstances favourable to a general acceptance of family limitation which do not also result in improvement in general health and a lowering of mortality. The dissemination of family planning in the PRC has often been associated and is currently being combined with a general drive for better medical care and sanitation throughout the countryside. For countries at an intermediate stage in the mortality reduction process, as the PRC now is, mortality sometimes falls more rapidly than does fertility in the early stages of a successful birth control campaign. As a result, natural increase may rise rather than fall at the beginning of the effort, as in the case for models 1, 2, and 3 during the 1970s. When mortality has reached the levels that are characteristic of the developed world and the more advanced of the developing countries, further decline in the death rate tends to be at a much slower rate, and the rapidly falling birth rates begin to close the gap. Thus it will be seen that in models 1, 2, and 3, most of the decline in natural increase takes place after 1980, when it occurs at an accelerating rate. Taiwan is already at the point where there can be little further decline in the crude death rate; instead, changing age composition may soon cause the death rate to rise somewhat. Thus, any further reduction in the birth rate in Taiwan will result in a corresponding or larger reduction in natural increase. In the PRC, the effect on population growth of even a highly successful birth control campaign may be largely or entirely neutralized, during the next ten years by falling mortality.

Of course it is not impossible that the relationship between fertility and mortality trends in the PRC may differ somewhat from the experience of Taiwan since 1952. Though the decline in fertility may still be closely correlated with the decline in mortality, the rate of mortality decline may be faster or slower in relation to fertility decline. The differences would probably not be great but they may be significant. If mortality in the PRC declines more slowly in relation to the decline in fertility, the reduction of natural increase could occur somewhat sooner and be carried somewhat further by 1990 than is shown in models 1, 2, and 3. If instead the decline in mortality in the PRC is more rapid than in Taiwan at a corresponding stage of demographic development, natural increase would rise more rapidly in the 1970s than is shown in models 1, 2, and 3, the peak would be higher, and the subsequent decline would be less rapid.

The extreme implications of departure from the Taiwan pattern may be explored by constructing two hypothetical variants of model 1 to show the results of combining constant intrinsic rates for one parameter with declining rates for the other. The first variant assumes that fertility declines at the same rate as in the original model 1 but that intrinsic mortality remains constant as in model 4. The second variant assumes that mortality declines as in the original model 1 but that intrinsic fertility remains constant as in model 4. The first variant produces a population in 1990 that is smaller by 107 million, or a little over 8 per cent, than that of the original model 1. The population at ages under twenty is smaller by 63 million, or 10 per cent. However, the second variant results in a 1990 population larger than that of the original model 1 by 158 million, or 12 per cent and the population at ages under twenty is larger by 159 million, or 26 per cent. Thus, even if the PRC could reduce fertility at a phenomenally successful rate without lowering mortality at all, the difference in population growth after two decades would not be spectacular, whereas, if the PRC succeeds in reducing mortality but fails to reduce fertility, the increased population growth, particularly in the younger age groups, would certainly be significant.

What these models suggest is that, barring catastrophe or spectacular changes in contraceptive technology and in the means of political coercion, even the most successful family limitation effort is not likely to provide much relief from population pressure in the PRC until mortality has completed its transition to the lower levels characteristic of developed countries. On the other hand, the failure to make significant progress in family limitation while continuing to reduce mortality levels can only increase the rate of population growth in the short run and the severity of the attendant population problems. Taking into account the experiences of the three birth control campaigns and the implications of the population models, there is no reason to expect any great change in China's demographic prospects in the immediate future.

EDITOR'S NOTE

The debate concerning the size and rate of growth of China's population has engaged a number of scholars recently, prominent among them being Leo A. Orleans.* In general, the estimates published by Orleans are more conservative than those arrived at by Aird. Orleans believes that during the 1960s, despite continuing vacillation in official attitudes towards birth control, a gradual downward trend in the country's fertility was started and that within the last few years developments in the manufacture and supply of oral contraceptives have been dramatic. Propaganda against 'the evil wind of early marriage' and large families may be beginning to take effect. Abortion, too, may have increased significantly. The birth rate, according to Orleans, may therefore have fallen from about 43 per 1 000 just prior to 1949 to

* Leo A. Orleans, 'China: the population record', *Current Scene*, **10**, No. 5, 1972, 10–19.

about 32 per 1 000 at the end of the 1960s, though future decreases are likely to be slower because from the late 1960s onwards larger numbers of women would be entering the reproductive ages. The death rate may have fallen from about 35 per 1 000 in the late 1940s to about 17 per 1 000 in 1970, largely as a result of the widespread extension of simple medical services designed to reduce infant and child mortality and the incidence of infections and epidemic diseases. However, further significant reductions in the death rate are not likely within the near future unless Peking decides to invest more heavily in advanced medical training. Reasoning from these and other factors, Orleans arrives at the following population estimates:

Year	Population (millions)	Average annual growth rate
1960	655	
1965	701	1.4
1970	753	1.5
1975	813	1.7
1980	887	1.7

The most recent United Nations estimates, in contrast, are somewhat higher than Orleans, the United Nations 'medium variant' projection being:

Year	millions
1965	695
1970	760
1975	826
1980	894

DJD

10 Development of communications: the railways

Mainland China has now experienced more than a decade of Communist rule. The multiplicity of changes in this period has often bedevilled those who have attempted to assess the success or failure of the Communist programmes. While reliable information has always been meagre and difficult to sift from the mass of official releases and other fragmentary materials, new figures seem to have been given out at an ever-increasing rate. Thus China, in the course of ten years, has become more of an enigma to the world than the Soviet Union.

Among the economic achievements of the Communist regime that have been given the widest publicity, the construction of new railroads occupies an important place. In a country as large as China where waterways are unevenly distributed and motor and air transportation can still serve but a trifling minority of the population, railroad facilities, under normal circumstances, should be most indicative of the growth of the national economy and of progress in industrialization. Under a planned economy their significance is perhaps even greater. For the state may take whatever measures it deems necessary to make the maximum use of this means of transportation and to expand it in accordance with the overall economic policy and political objectives.

The pre-Communist railroad pattern

A map of railroad distribution in China before the Communist regime (Fig. 10.1) shows that the major networks were largely concentrated in two distinct areas, the northeastern provinces, or Manchuria, and north China, which together

214

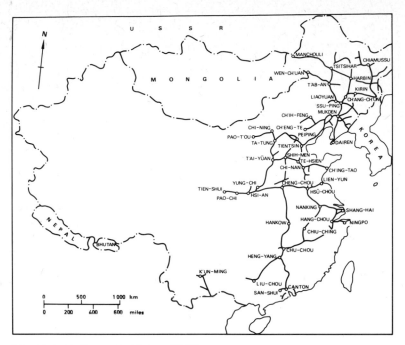

Fig. 10.1 Railways in China, 1949

accounted for more than three-quarters of the total length. South of the Yangtse River there were only a few tentacles, and west of a line from the panhandle of Outer Mongolia to K'un-ming there were practically no railroads.

The uneven distribution resulted from the interplay of a number of factors. By far the most important was the scramble for concessions by the great powers at the end of the nineteenth century (Fig. 10.2). The construction of railroads in China provided the most effective access to the interior of the country and soon led to the establishment of spheres of influence, often known as 'the slicing of the melon'. Manchuria fell within Russia's sphere as soon as the Chinese Eastern Railway and its southern branch were completed. Germany obtained the concession to build the Ch'ing-tao—Chi-nan Railway and a section of the Tientsin—P'u-k'ou line, by means of which it could exploit the minerals in Shan-tung Province. Britain attempted to open up a corridor across China from Burma to Shanghai and to bring the Yangtse Valley within the British sphere. France made it

215

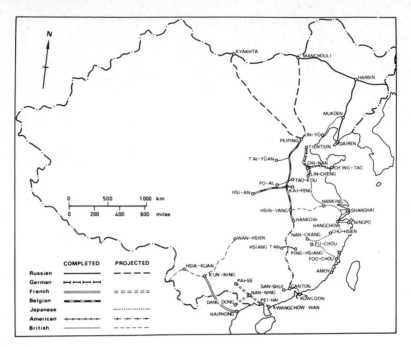

Fig. 10.2 The scramble for concessions

equally obvious that, through the building of the K'un-ming—Haiphong Railway and the seeking of further concessions in Kuang-hsi and the Lui-chou Peninsula, southwest China was to serve French interests. Japan looked on Fu-chien and the adjacent areas as its share. No less active was a Belgian syndicate that took over the project of the Peiping—Hankow Railway, and it was thought that French and Russian interests were behind it. Such a three-power collaboration could, if unchecked, easily have led to the control of the great north—south trunk line between China's northern frontier and the south coast. American capital was thus called on to build the southern section of this railroad, the Canton—Hankow line. The scheme was never realized, however, except for the building of two small branches.

This was the base on which new lines were added. In the decade that followed, railroad development took a different approach. Although many lines were built with foreign loans, their management was largely vested in the hands of Chinese directors. Popular support and private capital became in-

creasingly noticeable and gradually rivalled foreign investments.

However, the capital required for the construction of a
comprehensive railroad system was far beyond China's
financial resources. When the republic was established in
1912, the matter was taken up by Dr Sun Yat-sen, and the
pattern of development under the Nationalist government
was based largely on his concept of economic geography. Dr
Sun's programmes called for the construction of 161 000 km
(100 000 miles) of railroads through an international organization. Realizing that future economic development in China
would be inseparable from the use of foreign capital and
trade with the West, he proposed that railroad networks of
the first order should radiate from three projected seaports,
on the Gulf of Chihli, Hangchow Bay (Hang-chou Wan), and
the Hsi Chiang estuary [1].

In view of the rapid silting of the Yangtse estuary and the
Huang-p'u Chiang, Dr Sun proposed the construction of the
'Great Eastern Port' on the north shore of Hangchow Bay.
This port, when completed, would be the terminal of the railroad network in central China [2]. The construction of the
Shanghai—Hangchow—Ningpo Railway and the Che-chiang—
Chiang-hsi Railway was in accordance with his programmes,
as was that of the Canton—Hankow line in relation to the
proposed construction of the 'Great Southern Port' in the Hsi
Chiang estuary near Canton. Even the wartime efforts did not
alter the pattern. The Hu-nan—Kuang-hsi line can be looked
on either as a major branch of the Canton—Hankow Railway
or as an extension of the Che-chiang—Chiang-hsi Railway.
And the Kuei-chou—Kuang-hsi line is in fact tributary to the
Hu-nan—Kuang-hsi Railway. Through the construction of
these two lines, southwest China was linked for the first time
with the Yangtse and Hsi Chiang valleys by railroad. Dr Sun's
programmes also stressed that future railroad development in
north and northwest China should be associated with the
construction of the 'Great Northern Port' on the west shore
of the Gulf of Chihli, which would provide the chief outlet
for the products of Hsin-chiang, Mongolia, and the Hwang
Ho valley [3]. The lack of substantial progress in this direction is mainly attributable to the prolonged disunion and
political uncertainty in these areas. The only significant

accomplishment was the extending of the Lung-Hai Railway into Kan-su to reach T'ien-shui.

The Communist railroad pattern

Soon after the Sino–Japanese War, which not only hampered railroad development but also caused immense damage to the lines already in existence, a second serious blow was struck during the destructive war through which the present regime rose to power. In 1948 the total length of railroads in China was given by responsible sources as 26 448 km (16 434 miles), including all lines in operation or damaged [4]. When the Communists took over the mainland in 1949, the railroads bore the scars of the military campaigns. The total length of lines in operation in that year has been given by Communist sources as 21 715 km (13 492 miles) [5], which may be accepted as reliable in view of figures subsequently released. This 1949 figure, then, may serve as a starting point for a study of the Communist railroad programmes and policies in the past ten years.

By the end of 1952 the lines in operation had increased to 24 232 km (15 056 miles). One could easily be misled by these figures to think that until then the Communists were doing nothing but rehabilitating or repairing the existing lines. Actually their efforts were concentrated on a few key lines that were to them most strategic. It is interesting to note that up to the end of 1958, the 'Year of the Great Leap Forward', the Hangchow–Ningpo section and the K'un-ming–Haiphong Railway, to mention only two, had not yet been opened to traffic. On the other hand, several new lines had been completed even before the end of 1952, notably the Lai-pin–Mu-nan-kuan section of the Hu-nan–Kuang-hsi Railway, linking the Yangtse and Hsi Chiang valleys with the Tonkin Basin, most of which was already under the control of Ho Chi-minh's forces; the Ch'eng-tu–Chungking Railway, completed on 1 July 1952; and the T'ien-shui–Lan-chou Railway, opened to traffic before the end of that year. No information has yet been given as to when the construction of the Chi-ning–Erh-lien line began; in fact, the construction of this railroad to Outer Mongolia was not announced until it had been completed, toward the end of 1954 [6]. Consider-

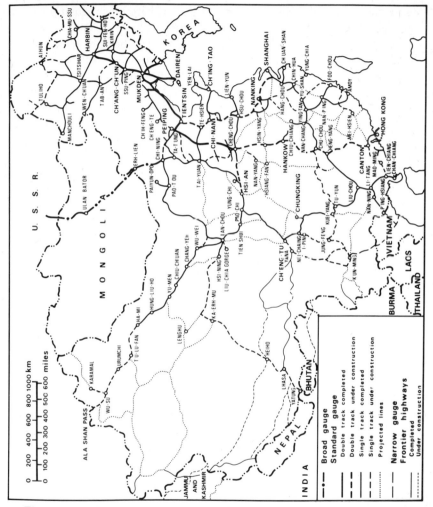

Fig. 10.3 Railways in China, March 1960

ing the length of this line and the aridity in the Gobi, work must have begun before 1952. According to Communist sources released at a later date 1 316 km (817 miles) of new railroads had been finished by the end of 1952 [7], which constituted about two-thirds of the total increase during the so-called 'Rehabilitation Period' (1949–52).

Although the few lines completed in this period are sufficient to reveal the priorities in the Communist railroad programmes, the nature of the overall policy and planning may be gleaned from additional construction in the following years. As the First Five-Year Plan drew to a close at the end of 1957, more than 5 000 km (3 110 miles) of track had been laid [8]. With a few exceptions all the major new lines were either in the northwest or in the southwest (Fig. 10.3).

One of the significant things to bear in mind is the manner in which these railroads were constructed. Many of them were completed far ahead of schedule. As a rule, the more important a railroad, the faster it was built and finished. The Li-t'ang–Chan-chiang line, the Kuei-yang–Tu-yün section, and the Pao-t'ou–Lan-chou Railway were all completed five to six months ahead of time [9]. The bridge over the Yangtse at Chungking, which links the Ssu-ch'uan–Kuei-chou and Ch'eng-tu–Chungking Railways, was built ten months faster than had originally been planned [10]. The Pao-chi–Ch'eng-tu Railway, the only vital link between the northwest and the southwest, was completed seventeen months ahead of schedule [11], in spite of the barriers imposed by the Ch'in Ling and the Ta-pa Shan.

Haste often makes waste. The waste that resulted from this rapid construction was astounding. The Pao-chi–Ch'eng-tu Railway was finished on 12 July 1956, but the opening of the line to traffic was delayed for a year and a half [12]. The official Press, to quiet the furore, went so far as to admit that in 178 places 'there is faulty engineering work which needs to be improved, as these places where the line passes through were ill chosen' [13]. The T'ien-shui–Lan-chou Railway was so hastily constructed that it took one year's work of reconstruction, and a 120 km (75 miles) length of track had to be rebuilt [14]. These facts, selected from many, may give some idea of the urgency of railroad construction for northwest China.

Soviet aid

Special mention must be made of Soviet aid in this enterprise. On 12 October 1954 a communiqué was issued to the effect that the government of Communist China and the Soviet Union had decided to build a railroad from Lan-chou through Urumchi to Alma-ata and that the section inside China would be built 'by China with all-round Soviet assistance' [15]. A similar arrangement was made known with regard to the construction of the already completed international line from Chi-ning to Ulan Bator [16]. One cannot help being bewildered by such an official announcement, for it seems to have no bearing on the actual construction programmes. As one can see now in retrospect, it came at a time when the Chi-ning—Erh-lien line had been nearly completed. And the Lan-chou—Hsin-chiang Railway will join the Turko—Siberian system at Aktogay instead of at Alma-ata. In fact, Soviet assistance had entered this programme long before 1954. The 190 km (120 miles) Lan-chou—Wu-chiao-ling section, which was completed by the end of 1953, had been laid with Soviet machinery [17], and so had the rest of the tracks in the Kan-su corridor [18].

No less prominent was the role played by the Soviet advisers during the construction of the Pao-chi—Ch'eng-tu Railway. Their decisions have been hailed as the determining factor in the hastening of its completion, but were never held responsible for the high cost and low quality of the finished work [19]. The Feng-t'ai—Sha-ch'eng line, an alternate loop on the Peiping—Pao-t'ou Railway designed to lighten its burden, was also completed with substantial Soviet help. As an official organ stated: 'Soviet specialists contributed to the successful completion of this different line. They gave guidance, in both designing and construction and helped solve problems' [20].

Information has been rather scanty concerning Soviet assistance in the construction in the southwest. The Li-t'ang—Chan-chiang line, which provides the most important outlet for this area, and which was completed far ahead of schedule, was probably built with considerable Soviet help. The official sources revealed only that, under the guidance of Soviet experts, Chan-chiang has been made one

221

of the largest seaports in Asia, capable of accommodating vessels of more than 10 000 tons [21].

A few more words should be said about the Lan-chou–Hsin-chiang Railway. It was in this undertaking that Soviet assistance was most conspicuous. In addition to the use of Soviet track-laying machinery, which speeded up the project, Soviet experts gave substantial help in facilitating the surveying, designing, and construction of the line. In 1955 they even made an aerial survey of the route between the Jade Gate (Yü-men) and the Hsin-chiang border. Says the *Peking Review*: 'What would have taken a whole year by ground survey was actually done in two months' [22]. A study of the speed of construction in different sections of this trunk line reveals that work was done progressively faster beyond the Jade Gate, where aerial survey and track-laying machinery were used. Now a survey of the section from Urumchi to the Ala Shan Pass, on the Soviet border, has been finished, and the roadbed has reached the northern side of the T'ien Shan [23]. If the construction continues at its present speed, the Lan-chou–Hsin-chiang line will probably join the Soviet section at the Ala Shan Pass before the end of 1961. When completed, it not only will serve as the third link between mainland China and the Soviet Union but will also provide the Communist bloc with one more outlet to warm water, running diagonally across China to the great new seaport of Chan-chiang.

Economic objectives

Associated with the construction of the two international lines through Hsin-chiang and Mongolia are a few railroad programmes centred on steel production and the exploitation of mineral resources. Among the listed exports from mainland China to the Soviet Union and its European satellite countries, minerals such as tin, zinc, lead, mercury, antimony, and tungsten constitute an important part. Except for tungsten, which comes largely from southern Chiang-hsi and northern Kuang-tung, the others are mined mainly in Yünnan, Kuang-hsi, Kuei-chou, and Hu-nan. Ssu-ch'uan is a great source of those agricultural products, such as meat, tobacco, oilseed, raw silk, and citrus fruits, which the Chinese

Communists also send to the Soviet Union in exchange for machinery and heavy equipment. Thus the Nei-chiang—K'un-ming, Ch'eng-tu—K'un-ming, and Ssu-ch'uan—Kuei-chou lines, supposedly part of the Second Five-Year Plan (1958—62), have actually been under construction since 1956 [24]. Added to these are the Chu-chou—Tu-yün and San-shui—Mao-ming lines, which are also presently under construction, and which, when completed, will link the south-western and northwestern networks with the great vertical trunk line, the Canton—Hankow Railway.

The vehement drive to increase steel production and to build up other types of heavy industry has been reflected in the construction of several new railroads. The Lan-ts'un—Yen-t'ai line, which provides an alternate route to southern Manchuria for the already overburdened Peiping—Mukden line, was, in all likelihood, intended for shipping the rich iron ore of central Shan-tung to the blast furnaces in Dairen. Since An-shan alone accounted for more than 50 per cent of China's steelmaking capacity, and since many heavy industries are concentrated within sixty miles of Mukden, the Peiping—Mukden Railway had to be double-tracked in order that the key industrial area might efficiently serve the other regions. The double-tracking was accomplished as early as 1954 [25].

A new steel-producing centre has arisen recently on the Great Bend of the Hwang Ho. Based on local iron ore from Paiyun-opo and coal from Shih-kuai-kou, and again with 'all-round Soviet assistance', Pao-t'ou has been made the largest steel town on the Mongolian Plateau [26]. The role it was about to play became clear when the construction of the Pao-t'ou—Lan-chou Railway was begun in 1954 and, like that of several other vital lines, was completed well ahead of schedule [27]. The city will serve as the supply base of steel to Kan-su, Ch'ing-hai, and even Hsin-chiang for the various heavy construction projects.

One of the significant recent developments in the economic geography of northwest China has been the discovery of some rich oilfields in the Tsaidam Basin, at Yiu-sha-shan and Leng-hu in particular. The oil reserve seems so promising that the Communists have called the area the 'Second Baku' of China. For the purpose of exploiting the oil, as well as of extending railroads into Tibet, a new line called the Lan-chou–Ch'ing-hai Railway, which was originally part of the Second Five-Year Plan, has been under rapid construction since 1956. Groundwork has now been pushed beyond the Ch'ing Hai (Koko Nor), whence it will run across the basin to the oilfields. From Ka-erh-mu (Golmo), a point on the projected Lan-chou–Ch'ing-hai line in the western Tsaidam, the future Ch'ing-hai–Tibet Railway will be built over the Tibetan Highlands to Lhasa and ultimately to the border city of Yatung (Fig. 10.3). Aerial survey of this route, according to various sources, has been underway since as early as November 1956, with Soviet help and with advanced instruments such as the radio elevation indicator [28].

Strategic significance

No mention has ever been made by the Communist planners of the strategic significance of their railroad programmes, yet one cannot fail to recognize certain conscious designs behind the emerging pattern. There is no secret about the purpose for which the Ying-t'an–Amoy line was hurriedly built facing Formosa Strait. When this line was about to be completed, toward the end of 1956, official newspapers reported that henceforth 'rich iron ore, timber and figs' produced in Fu-chien could be shipped out for the benefit of other parts of the country [29]. But no sooner had the line reached Amoy than the announcement was made that it would not immediately be open to civilian traffic. The official reason given was that the railroad was being set aside for a year of 'experimental operation' [30], and it could not have been a coincidence that, not too long afterward, the newly deployed coastal batteries began their furious bombardment of Quemoy and other offshore islands in the summer of 1958. And, incidentally, the railroad does not even go near the mining areas [31].

Actually, the Ying-t'an–Amoy Railway is only one finished section of a projected system aimed at the effective control of the entire coastal region from Hang-chow Wan to Kuang-chow Wan (Kwangchow Bay). Another section, the Nan-p'ing–Foo-chou Railway, has also been opened and is a branch of the Ying-t'an–Amoy line. New sections now under survey or construction will ultimately form a giant arc extending along the coast, linking the provinces of Che-chiang, Fu-chien, Kuang-tung, Kuang-hsi, and Yün-nan.

The speedy construction of the southwestern railroad network also seems to have its strategic undertones. The long coastal arc will eventually reach Yün-nan and join the projected Burma—Yün-nan Railway, and three lines will also intersect it from the north, the Nei-chiang—K'un-ming, Ch'eng-tu—K'un-ming, and Ssu-ch'uan—Kuei-chou Railways. This projected network will give Yün-nan a commanding position in the Communist strategy with regard to the countries in the Indo—Chinese peninsula, committed or otherwise. It is not difficult to visualize what an important role the southwestern railroad complex would play in the decisive struggle if an all-out economic offensive in southeast Asia should be launched against the free world. Its military significance is obvious even to the layman.

There is little doubt that the Communists will before long extend the northwestern network into Tibet. The Ch'ing-hai—Tibet Railway, when completed, will probably change the geographic orientation of the area greatly. The world's highest plateau is no longer a 'forbidden land', not even in the strategic sense. Two major highways criss-crossing it have been completed. Another mountain road is being built north of the one in the Tsangpo valley, and the two will converge in western Tibet before reaching into Hsin-chiang and the Soviet Union.

The military expert would certainly not look at the railroad complex in mainland China from Peiping only. The completion of the Chi-ning—Erh-lien, Pao-t'ou—Lan-chou, and Ying-t'an—Amoy lines, the southwestern network, and a large part of the Lan-chou—Hsin-chiang Railway seems to have unfolded a new pattern, a pattern that is well beyond national dimensions. Since the Chi-ning—Erh-lien Railway and the Russian-built Trans-Outer Mongolian line were connected, the journey between Peiping and Moscow has been shortened by 1 145 km (710 miles) or two and a half days of travel time [32]. From the Kuznetsk Basin and other newly developed industrial regions in the 'Heartland' of the Soviet Union to northwest and southwest China the shortest route will be via the Lan-chou—Hsin-chiang Railway. Both lines are shorter and less exposed than the old route from Peiping through Manchuria to Novosibirsk. It was at least partly due to this consideration that the Trans-Mongolian Railway, the Pao-t'ou—Lan-chou Railway, and many sections of the Lan-chou—Hsin-chiang Railway were either completed far ahead of schedule or built under a veil of secrecy.

Effect on population distribution

The impact of the new railroad programmes has already been felt in several respects, among which is the rapid redistribution of population. A large number of people have been moved, by force or otherwise, to Inner Mongolia, Kan-su, Hsin-chiang, and Ch'ing-hai. Lan-chou was a city of about 190 000 inhabitants in 1949; now it is a great industrial and urban area of 1 180 000 people [33]. Ten years ago there were about 279 000 people in Chang-chia-k'ou (Kalgan); now the number is set at 630 000 [34]. Pao-t'ou during the last decade has increased its population nearly seven times, to more than 700 000 [35], and is expected to reach the million mark shortly. Urumchi has increased two and a half times, from 80 000 in 1949 to 200 000 at the present time (1961) [36]. Besides these and many other planned urban centres, the trend in the Tsaidam Basin, the Dzungarian Basin, southern Kan-su, the Inner Mongolian steppes, and northern Manchuria is nearly the same. The scale of forced migration may be discerned from a few scattered official dispatches.

'On 5 March 1959', says a Ho-nan newspaper, '52 000 youths of both sexes in Junan Hsien submitted applications and decided to settle down in frontier areas' [37]. On the same day, interestingly enough, the same newspaper quoted an editorial from the *Tsaidam News* saying that 'the party and government organs and the people in the Tsaidam Basin are actively making preparations to welcome the youths from Ho-nan Province who will be going to Ch'inghai to take part in construction' [38]. Similar duets have been heard between 'volunteers' in Chiang-su, An-hui, and Hu-pei and official newspapers in Kan-su and Hsin-chiang [39].

The future pattern

If railroad construction is more indicative of long-term Communist objectives than the ideological divergencies among the leaders at different times, then the railroad programmes and the resultant new patterns fail to reveal any signs of breakdown in the partnership between Peiping and Moscow. In addition to the new lines just completed, the double-tracking of the two major north—south trunk lines, from Peiping to Canton and from Peiping to Shanghai, and of the horizontal Lung—Hai Railway, and the ready Soviet assistance in the Ch'ing-hai—Tibet project, will further facilitate trade and close cooperation between the two strongest members of the Communist bloc.

And all this seems to be only the beginning for more ambitious undertakings in the future. It has been announced that 8 370 additional km (5 200 miles) of new railroads were to be constructed under the 1960 Economic Plan [40]. As one looks a few years ahead, the most important thing is not to discover whether the plans will be fulfilled according to schedule but rather to discern the patterns that will emerge both from the planning table and from the labours of the millions impressed into the massive undertakings.

EDITOR'S NOTE

Due to the Sino—Soviet dispute, work was stopped on the railway running from Lanchow northwest towards Russia through Sinkiang province at Fukang, shortly after the line had reached Urumchi. Though the collapse of the Great Leap Forward curtailed expansion for several years, railway construction revived in the mid-1960s but was interrupted again by the Cultural Revolution. Only a limited number of major new projects have been started since Dr Chang wrote the above paper. However, a line linking Chengtu directly with Kunming was completed recently after more than a decade of construction work. The most important new line at present under construction is that between Wuhan and Chungking, which when completed will provide the first direct rail route between the Szechuan Basin and the middle Yangtse area.

DJD

11 Industrial expansion: coal, a case study

In 1958 the government of the Chinese People's Republic claimed a production of coal of 270 million tons (Table 11.1), greater than that of the United Kingdom.* A subsequent Press report has stated that output in 1960 reached 400 million tons, a figure that would mean that China had now superseded the United States as the world's second largest coal producer. It is the purpose of this paper to outline some of the major geographical features of the rapidly expanding Chinese coal industry. It will not be possible to give a complete picture because of the scarcity of the official information of geographical significance. Indeed, most of the details presented here are derived from what would normally be considered secondary sources of doubtful value, namely reports in the Chinese Press. As Shabad has pointed out, however, under Communist governments publishing is a state monopoly and the main newspapers are, in effect, official publications (Shabad, 1956, p. 271).† In this sense the Chinese Press can be regarded as primary source material for research workers. This is not to deny that it is usually extremely vague in its geographical, economic and statistical information, heavily loaded with propaganda and sometimes self-contradictory. The reader will doubtless sense the difficulties of relying on such a medium in the incompleteness of the present paper. The only argument for its presentation is that already used by Chandrasekhar in connection with Chinese population studies (Chandrasekhar, 1960, p. 5): that it is better to have a glimmer of light on this and similar important subjects than no light at all.

* All tonnage figures refer to metric tonnes.
† Details of references are given on p. 459.

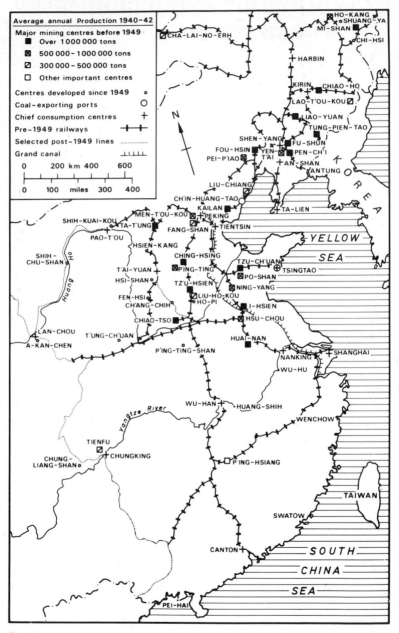

Fig. 11.1 The coal industry in mainland China

The growth of output

By 1936, the year prior to the outbreak of the Sino–Japanese War, the production of coal in China and Manchuria had reached an estimated level of 35 million tons [1]. Although the situation during the war years remains obscure in its details, it appears that coal production generally expanded further, at least in the early part of the period. Manchurian production would seem to have risen from about 13 million tons in 1937 to about 25 million tons in the early 1940s as the mines were rapidly developed at Fou-hsin (Fousin), Liao-yüan (Liaoyuan, Sian), Ho-kang (Hokang), Mi-shan (Mishan) and Yen-t'ai (Yentai); to supplement production from the older centres of Fu-shun (Fushun) and Pen-ch'i (Penki) [2]. In that part of China occupied by the Japanese during the war several mining companies were reorganized for greater output. For example, the Kailan [3] miners were obliged to produce 1.5 million tons of coal above their usual 4–5 million tons yearly, with special emphasis on coking coal. Ta-t'ung (Tatung) coal production was also pushed up, though not, it seems, as much as the Japanese had hoped, perhaps because of the resistance of the miners (Chin Yu-kin, 1954, p. 9). In Free China, in the south-west, the coal industry had to be expanded through desperate necessity, and new manufacturing industries built around it. To this end, mining equipment was transferred from Honan into Szechwan by the retreating Chinese forces; the mines of the Tienfu Company, for example, were re-equipped in this way. It is probable that, as a result of the various wartime drives for more coal in China and Manchuria, the total output of the industry was near to, or slightly exceeding, 60 million tons by 1943 [4].

The coal-mines, in common with most other Chinese industries, suffered heavily during the latter part of the war and the chaotic period of civil strife that followed its conclusion. Production had fallen as low as 15 million tons by 1946, and the coal industry in Manchuria had almost entirely stopped working (UNECAFE, 1952, p. 49). The Russians added to the industry's difficulties through their policy of massive reparations from Manchuria at this time. By 1949, at the time of the change of government in China, the output of the industry had recovered only to 32 million tons.

Table 11.1   *Production of coal in mainland China 1949—60*

Year	Million metric tonnes
1949	32.4
1950	42.9
1951	53.1
1952	66.5
1953	69.7
1954	83.7
1955	98.3
1956	110.4
1957	130.0
1958	270.0
1959	347.8
1960	400.0

Source: 1949—58: State Bureau of Statistics: *Ten Great Years; statistics of the economic and cultural achievements of the People's Republic of China.* (Chinese edition), Peking, 1959, p. 84.

1959—60: *Peking Daily*, 23 January 1960 and *Chinese Youth Daily*, Peking, 10 February 1961 (quoted in *China News Analysis*, Hong Kong, No. 374, 2 June 1961, p. 2).

The major problem posed by the industry during the first years of the Communist regime was thus one of rehabilitation, and this task largely occupied the period up to the opening of the First Five-Year Plan in 1953. By June 1952, it was reported, 83 per cent of all the damage suffered by the industry had been repaired (Jen Pi-shao, 1952, p. 32). As was to be expected, the Manchurian mines received the first and greatest attention. They were probably restored almost to their pre-1943 condition by 1952 (Chao Kuo-chun, 1953, Table 1, p. 173) and with their rehabilitation total output (see Table 11.1) reached a new high level that year. Half the mines in Manchuria, it was claimed, had received mechanized equipment by 1950 (*People's Daily*, 23 May 1951). This was followed in 1950—51 by the modernization of the Ta-t'ung, Huai-nan (Hwainan) and some Shantung mines; the P'ing-hsiang (Pingsiang) mines, the only ones south of the Yangtse, were also restored (ibid.). Much of the rehabilitation of the industry was said to have been carried out under the guidance of Russian experts and the Ho-kang mines in Heilungkiang in particular to have been especially heavily equipped by them

(*China News Analysis,* 8 February 1957, p. 4). Russian combined cutting, crushing and loading machines were introduced into the Chi-hsi (Kisi), Fou-hsin, Chiao-ho (Chiaoho), Ta-t'ung, and Huai-nan mines; and at the Second Coal Mining Conference in April 1951 all other mining administrations were officially urged to follow the directions of their Russian experts (*P.D.* 23 May 1951). As part of the First Five-Year Plan, Russia subsequently agreed to equip twenty-seven coal-mines and coal-washing plants in China (*First Five-Year Plan,* 1956, p. 68), and her experts, as will be outlined below, have been active in introducing new techniques into the industry.

Starting from a base of 66.5 million tons in 1952, the First Five-Year Plan provided for an increase in coal production to 112.9 million tons by 1957. The Plan called for an additional 53.85 million tons of coal-mining capacity to be completed by 1957 (*First Five-Year Plan,* p. 68), but this rate of expansion was said to have been exceeded and, in the process of pushing output by the latter year up to 130 million tons, 124 new shafts with an average yearly capacity of 420 000 tons each to have been completed by the central government, and ninety-four smaller shafts (of 93 000 tons average annual productive capacity) by local authorities (*P.D.* 3 March 1958). Unfortunately, location information on these and later developments is extremely hard to find. Some will, however, be given in later sections of this paper.

Besides the rapid increases in output, two other marked features of the First Five-Year Plan and the years following it have been the search for more coal, often, it seems, by comparatively untrained prospectors, and the introduction under Russian guidance of more mechanization and new techniques into the larger mines. China's reserves of coal in seams 1 metre (3 ft) thick and over, down to 914 metres (3 000 ft), had been estimated by the National Geological Survey in 1945 to be 265 311 million tons (UNECAFE, 1952, p. 48). By 1959 the Chinese Press could claim that 'current estimates' of 1 500 000 million tons would themselves have to be increased 'several times' in view of the great expansion in prospecting (Chang Yang, 1959, p. 8). But, as is common with such reports, no further details were given. Figures for the progress of mechanization in the mines are quite startling. Only 4 per cent of the coal mined in China in 1950 was obtained by mechanized methods; by 1954 the figure had been increased to 33 per cent (Shabad, 1956, p. 56), and it has since been claimed that, by the end of 1958, 97 per cent of the extracting work and 90 per cent of the lifting of coal to the surface had been mechanized in the larger mines (*Daily Worker*, Peking, 2 September 1959). A major technological development in recent years has been the introduction of hydraulic mining, though as yet it accounts for only a small proportion of the total output (7.85 million tons in 1959: Liu Hsi-ching, 1960, p. 29). One report has stated that at a working face at Kailan a monthly output six times that of normal was achieved for part of 1960 as a result of the introduction of hydraulic mining (*New China News Agency*, 25 September 1960), while another has it that twelve large mines (not, however, named) have recently been converted to this method of working (Liu Hsi-ching, 1960, p. 29). Improved methods of working inclined medium and thick seams have been announced, also from Kailan (*NCNA*, 6 April 1960). The system, it is claimed, eliminates manual labour at the coal face by employing a new type of machine to make holes in the seam and insert the explosives. The broken coal slides down a specially prepared, sharply inclined face directly on to the haulage system without being touched by the miners.

A call to 'overtake Britain in fifteen years' in the production of coal, steel, machinery, cement, and electric power went out to the nation in 1957. The next year coal output was pushed beyond that of Britain. The tremendous spurt in coal production recorded in 1958 was, of course, directly related to the official 'Great Leap Forward' of that year, and in coal it partook of one of the principal characteristics of the Leap, namely the prominence given to local production by indigenous methods. As both the large-scale and 'backyard' steel furnaces and other industries sought more and more coal, the number of local mines increased from 20 000 to 110 000 in 1958 alone (Chang Yang, 1959, p. 6). Local mines have since held a prominent place in the production pattern, though there has been some modification of the wild enthusiasm for them of 1958, when 20 million people were said to have been mobilized to dig coal (Union Research Institute, 1959, p. 59).

The Great Leap Forward of 1958 resulted in the coal target for the Second Five-Year Plan, 190–210 million tons, being exceeded in the Plan's first year (Table 11.1, p. 232). But it has been reported that in 1959 as much as 40 per cent of total production came from the small, locally run mines (*NCNA,* 26 January 1960). This raises an immediate doubt as to the quality of much of present Chinese coal production. In the third section of this paper a detailed description of one set of local mines will be quoted which will do nothing to dispel this doubt, and examples will later be presented of complaints of poor quality that have found their way into the Chinese Press. As Hughes and Luard (1959) have pointed out, local enterprises 'for a country such as China, short of capital but rich in labour . . . may well, at least temporarily, serve an important function'. But clearly it is unreal to compare, as the Chinese Press has repeatedly done in triumphant tones, the total coal production of China since 1958 with that of Britain and the USA. Apart from the fact that planned contractions in some branches of the industry have been taking place in both Britain and the USA, the long-term basis of the coal industry in China, as in other countries, must remain the large mines rather than the small, local workings. And it is to the former that attention will now be directed.

The large mines

The present distribution of the larger mines shows some important changes from that before 1949 (see Fig. 11.1, p. 232). Before the Second World War the coal industry in Manchuria had been highly developed by the Japanese, while in China itself Hopeh and Shantung provinces had become the main centres of the industry. The largest coal deposits, however, lie in Shansi and Shensi (United Nations Dept. of Econ. Affairs, 1953, pp. 145–8), and it is the policy of the present government to introduce new, large mines into these provinces, partly for defence reasons, but mainly to broaden the geographical distribution of the industry and so ease its transport problems. The Shansi deposits, in particular, seem to be undergoing very rapid development. A modern mine was reported finished in 1956 at Hsien-kang (Hsienkang) in the northwest of the province [5]. The first large shaft at Fen-hsi (Fensi) was completed in 1958, and further construction is expected there to help supply the Wu-han (Wuhan) steelworks. Fen-hsi is said to be promising in coking coal and is, moreover, on a railway line. The sinking of a shaft at Hsi-shan (Hsishan), to the southwest of T'ai-yüan, began in 1959, presumably to supply the latter's expanding steel industry. Reserves at Hsi-shan are claimed to be as much as 20 000 million tons, of which 600 million tons are coking coal. Four shafts have also been started at Ch'ang-chih (Changchih, Luan), in southeast Shansi, and are linked by rail to the Wu-han steelworks.

Further to the west are several new mines associated with recent railway building and the drive to develop industrial centres in the interior. At Shih-kuai-kou (Shihkwaikow), convenient to supply the new steelworks at Pao-t'ou (Paotow), the first three shafts were sunk in 1958. Reserves there are put at 700 million tons. No less than eight shafts have been started since 1953 at Shih-chü-shan (Shihtsuishan), and by 1962 they were expected to produce 5 million tons a year. They will largely feed railways, especially the Lan-chou (Lanchow)—Pao-t'ou line, and, eventually, the projected steelworks at Chiu-ch'üan (Kiuchuan) in Kansu. Other large new mines have been reported from A-kan-chen (Akanchin), south of Lan-chou city, and Shan-tan (Shantan), even further west, along the Sinkiang Railway; while at T'ung-ch'uan (Tungchuan) in Shensi, where there are 9 100 million tons of reserves, much of it railway coal, one new shaft has been constructed and two old primitive mines renovated since 1959. The 1962 target for T'ung-ch'uan was 6 million tons.

To complete this summary of new mines, the following may be mentioned. At Ho-pi (Hopi) in northern Honan two modern shafts were under construction in 1957—58: but the coal from Ho-pi is expected to be of rather poor quality and so will be mixed with rich coal from P'ing-ting-shan (Pingtingshan) in central Honan for coke making. Coal production from P'ing-ting-shan was expected to rival that of Kailan by 1962 and was mostly destined to Wu-han. In the southwest, an area poor in good coal, a large mine is being developed at Chung-liang-shan (Chungliangshan) to the west of Chungking.

In Manchuria, Chi-hsi has been described as developing into one of China's largest coal centres and the population there is now said to be 'several hundred thousands' (*NCNA,* 25 November 1960).

Although the Peking Press has often claimed speed records for coal-mine construction, even in China a mine of about 900 000 tons yearly capacity still requires at least forty-four months for building and planned production cannot be reached until the eighth year (*PD,* 3 March 1958). The older mines, therefore, have played, and continue to play, the leading part in the drive for more coal. Fifteen coal-mining complexes were said to have produced over 5 million tons each in 1959 and seven of them reached 10 million tons (*NCNA,* 26 January 1960). It is likely that these were all old-established centres. Five of the seven leading ones were Fu-shun, Kailan, Fou-hsin, Ta-t'ung and Huai-nan (*NCNA,* 17 December 1959), while the other two were probably Ho-kang and the Ching-hsi (Chingsi) collieries to the west of Peking, which include the Men-t'ou-kou (Mentoukou) and Fang-shan (Fangshan) mines.

In Manchuria the exploitation of the thick, horizontal seams of the great open-cut at Fu-shun, the largest coal-mine in the Far East, has been vigorously pushed forward. Its 1958 goal was 11 million tons (Table 11.2) but production that year is said to have reached 15 million tons [6]. Fu-shun coal is used on the railways; it supplies the towns and cities of the northeast; and it is mixed with that of Pen-ch'i for coke for

Table 11.2 *Production and targets of the major coalfields (In million metric tonnes)*

	Production 1934	*Production 1957*	*Target 1958*
Fu-shun	7.5	9.2	11
Kailan	4.7	9.7*	11
Fou-hsin	0.1	8.6	10
Huai-nan	0.2	4.9	6.9
Ta-t'ung	0.2	6.5*	*not available*
Ho-kang	0.3	*not available*	6

Sources: Wang (1947); Shabad (1956); *Financial and Economic Research* (1958).
* = Target figure.

the An-shan (Anshan) steelworks. More spectacular, because
it started from lower levels, has been the recent development
of the Fou-hsin field to the west [7]. Reserves at Fou-hsin
are estimated at 4 000 million tons, as opposed to Fu-shun's
1 400 million tons. They were first exploited by the Japanese
as late as 1931, production by 1938 reaching 1.5 million tons
(Schumpeter, 1940, p. 410), In 1953 a new open-cut, in
preparation since 1951 in seams 64 metres (210 ft) thick,
came into production there. The plans for it were drawn up
by Russian specialists and Russian machines employed were
said to have speeded development by two years. Two other
open-cuts are currently being built at Fou-hsin, as well as two
vertical and thirteen inclined pits, and a new city of 300 000
people is in the process of rising there. Fou-hsin's 1958 production target was 10 million tons, but actual production
during the Great Leap Forward was probably greater. The
other major development in Manchuria concerns the important Ho-kang field near the northeastern border of Heilungkiang. Reserves there are now said to total 5 000 million
tons, mostly of coking quality. During the First Five-Year
Plan the original three working areas at Ho-kang were increased to six. Six million tons of coal were expected in
1958, taking this field to sixth place among China's producing areas.

In north China, the Kailan mines have been enlarged to a
point at which they now rival Fu-shun in production. In
1958 they produced 13 million tons. The reserves there total
3 000 million tons. Much of the coal is going to Peking and
Tientsin for power production and railway use and also to
the Shih-ching-shan (Sihkingshan) steelworks near Peking.
Kailan appears to be a major centre for training workers for
other parts of the country, for of the 20 000 new workers
said to have been taken on there since 1958, 2 400 were
trained for eventual transfer to other mines (*Peking Review,*
8 December 1961, p. 3). The First Five-Year Plan provided
for the sinking of fourteen new shafts in the Ta-t'ung coalfield, each yielding 900 000—1 500 000 tons annually and
also for a fourfold increase from the existing mines there
(Chin Yu-kin, 1954, p. 11). The new shafts were to 'conform
in construction and equipment to the standards of the Don
Basin' (Chin Yu-kin, 1954, p. 11) which suggests Russian

assistance with the project. Reserves at Ta-t'ung have been recently given as 40 000 million tons (*Financial and Economic Research*, 1958, pp. 58—60), much of it coking coal, and mineable seams are now thought to extend in places as far north as the Great Wall. It appears that further expansion at Ta-t'ung is to be partly on the basis of demand from the Pao-t'ou steelworks. Details of the larger projects south of the Huang Ho (Hwang Ho), of which the Tzu-ch'uan (Tzech-wan), I-hsien (Yihsien, Chungsing), Huai-nan and P'ing-hsiang mines are the chief, are few. Five new pits have, however, been added at Huai-nan since 1949, and production there was expected to reach 10 million tons a year by 1961, double that of 1957. Output in 1958 was 8 million tons. Huai-nan serves Shanghai, Wu-han and Huang-shih (Hwangshih) with coking and railway coal. The P'ing-hsiang mines, the only large ones in the south, were reported in 1961 to have been completely re-equipped with modern coal-cutting machinery (*NCNA*, 27 April 1961).

The small mines

According to Ho Ping-chang, Vice-Minister of the Coal Industry, it is on the basis of small, local mines that the industry is to build south of the Yangtse; in other areas small mines are to play an important supporting role supplying the needs of local industries and fuel for peasants' domestic use (*NCNA*, 27 December 1959). Two hundred and fifty such mines were recently said to have been established in one month in Fukien province (*NCNA*, 21 June 1960); in May—June 1960, 'about 1 000' were opened up in Kwantung province alone (*NCNA*, 27 July 1960). What is not at all clear from published information, however, is the precise distribution of such workings, the regional variations in their output and, above all, the quality of the coal they produce. Small mines are presumably now to be found in greatly increased numbers in almost every province, but clearly, from the published information about Fukien and Kwantung quoted above, many can at present amount to little more than surface scratchings. Some confirmation of their extremely small scale of working comes from Honan province (*Financial and Economic Research*, 1958, pp. 58—60). There, one of the

objectives of the Second Five-Year Plan is to bring into production 1 000 village coal workings with a total annual production of 2 million tons, that is, an average of only 2 000
tons each. As for the probable quality of the output of many
of the small mines, the following example of one such set of
mines will serve better than any general comment.

During the Great Leap Forward of 1958 the Chief
Engineer of the Honan Provincial Coal Industry Bureau
visited Pao-feng (Pofeng) county for three days. During that
short period he managed to make plans for the construction
of nine open pits and 200 small shafts. Then:

> An army of 70 000 peasants went to the mine sites and
> camped there, bringing its own tools. In scores of places
> people swarmed with pick, shovel and carrying pole, and
> carts on iron, ceramic and wooden rails shuttled off
> with earth and coal. Some shafts were sunk vertically,
> others horizontally or on an inclined plane. They were
> generally not deep, 80 metres (262 ft) at the most. All
> kinds of contraptions were designed to cut down labour.
> From the vertical shafts the coal was brought up in
> baskets on local-type pulleys 'modernized' with ball-
> bearings. The hoist rope was simply wound round mill-
> stones pulled by circling bullocks. Underground water
> was brought up in the same way in leather bags. Ventila-
> tion was supplied by a hand-operated blower through
> sleeves made of sacking. All these methods proved both
> effective and safe.

And within two months the coal output of the county had
rocketed from seventy to 'several thousand' tons a day
(Chang Yang, 1959, p. 7).

Problems of the industry

The coal industry of mainland China seems to be facing
several serious problems. First and foremost, largely because
of the present policy of developing the industry 'on two
legs' — that is, through small, local mines using indigenous
methods as well as large mechanized units — must be that of
the overall quality of the greatly increased production of
recent years. As early as June 1953 it was being urged in the

Chinese Press that the decline in the quality of coal must be halted. The coal shortage of that year was said later to have been due to qualitative rather than quantitative under-production (*PD*, 5 October 1955). The 1956 Press reports carried many more specific complaints. Coal coming from the Pei-p'iao (Peipiao) mines was reported to have an ash content as much as 30—38 per cent at times, while some shipments from Fu-shun were found to contain 30—40 per cent stone (*PD*, 8 January 1956). When 200 tons of coal from Yang-ch'üan (Yangchuan) (Shansi province) were unloaded at Hsü-chou (Suchow), half of the shipment was found to be stone; while in January—April 1956 the ash content of coal from Lung-feng mine in the Fu-shun mining administration became so great that coke made from it could not be used (*PD*, 23 June 1956, *Daily Worker*, 15 June 1956). With the rapid growth of demand for coal in China even since 1956, it is not likely that there have been favourable opportunities to take action on the complaints about quality, which have grown in volume every year. The fear now seems to be that the mines will be unable to produce enough coal of any quality. Industry in 1952 consumed 32 million tons of coal, but by 1957 its demands had risen to 69 million tons; during the same period the consumption of coal for heating and cooking rose from 24 to 52 million tons: 'Thus, owing to the growth of the national economy, a new problem arose' (*PD*, 2 November 1957). The miners have, therefore, been asked to work longer and directives have been issued calling for the drastic reduction of the amount of coal used for non-essential purposes.

Complicating the problem of raising coal output to keep pace with demand, is the strain that rapid national economic development is placing upon the transport system. Because of the large measure of geographical separation of the production from certain of the largest consumption centres, coal is the principal commodity using the railways. A major policy objective of the coal industry has therefore become the reduction of the volume of coal transported (Li Fu-chun, 1960, p. 12). In 1960, 40 per cent of the total freight on the railways was coal; if the planned rail freight figure for 1960, 720 million tons, is accepted as realistic, this would mean that 288 million tons of coal out of a total production of 400

million tons were transported by this means alone (*PD*, 3
December 1960). Coastal shipping is undoubtedly important
in the traffic also. Large quantities of coal were shipped
coastwise before 1937 from the Hopeh mines (Kailan especially) to Shanghai, the Yangtse Valley and the coastal regions
of Kwantung and Fukien. Because of the danger from the
Nationalists in Taiwan, China's coastal shipping routes have
now been divided into two zones — a northern one stretching
from Wen-chou to An-tung (Antung), and a southern one
from Hsien-t'ou (Swatow) to Pei-hai (Pakhoi) (Chang Yuan-
kuang, 1958) — so it is unlikely that much coastwise coal
today goes further south than Shanghai. The northern ports
are, however, still active in the trade. Coal from Kailan and
Fou-hsin, for example, accounts for about 80 per cent of
Ch'in-huang-tao's (Chingwangtao) outbound cargo, and at
Ch'ing-tao (Tsingtao) special jetties have recently been built
for the traffic (Chang Yuan-kuang, 1958). As for the inland
waterways (Dwyer, 1961, pp. 165–7), an extension is being
made to the Grand Canal to take it northeast of Tientsin to
the Kailan mines, while at Wu-hu (Wuhu), a river town on the
Yangtse served by a branch from the Peking–Shanghai Railway, a new port was constructed during the First Five-Year
Plan, specially for coal.

On the railways the main movement of coal is from the
large Hopeh, Honan, Shantung and Shansi mines to the lower
Yangtse Valley. The greatly expanded Wu-han steelworks
form a particular focal point in the latter area, and Shanghai,
still the nation's most important manufacturing centre
despite efforts to decrease the rate of its industrial growth by
the present regime up to 1956, is another. The two main lines
from Peking to Wu-han and Shanghai respectively are now in
the process of being double-tracked (Chang Kuei-sheng,
1961, p. 538), but an acute shortage of rolling stock may still
prevent the solution of what has, up to the present, been a
major difficulty. The problem of coal transport and the rapid
expansion of demand may perhaps best be illustrated by
reference to Shanghai (*Daily Worker,* Shanghai, 24 February
1961). The city required 300 000 tons of coke for its industries in 1958, two-thirds for its iron and steel industry alone.
It produced, however, only 40 000 tons. Coke was recorded
that year as coming into Shanghai from Wu-han, from Shan-

tung and even from Inner Mongolia (presumably from Pao-t'ou). During the Great Leap Forward the production of coke on a local basis in and around the city was boosted and by the autumn of 1959 output had reached the equivalent of 540 000 tons a year. But as the industrial expansion of Shanghai had by then progressed further as a result of the Leap, it satisfied only 87 per cent of the city's requirements. A recent report (*NCNA*, 27 April 1961) tells of the rapid development of the coal industry in the neighbouring provinces to meet the needs of Shanghai and states that, besides local mines, the large ones near Tzu-po (Tzepo) (Shantung province) at Tzu-ch'uan and Po-shan, Huai-nan and P'ing-hsiang have received special attention for this purpose. Even before the Second World War the annual consumption of coal in Shanghai was in the region of 3 million tons (UNECAFE, 1952, p. 48); it now may well be as much as three times this figure.

Within the general problem of expanding output to meet demand, that of coke production is especially important in view of the priority that has been given to the steel industry since 1949. There is some evidence that the supply of coke is by no means satisfactory, despite a reported increase in output from 8 to 23 million tons between 1957 and 1958 alone (*Liberation Daily*, 14 November 1959). Plants for the large-scale production of coke by modern methods have been built at Fen-hsi, Ch'ang-chih, Hsi-shan, Hsien-kang and Shih-kuai-kou since 1953 (*Financial and Economic Research*, 1958), to supplement those of the older mining centres. But the bulk of the great increase in output since 1957 has undoubtedly come from local production by indigenous methods. According to one source, 70 per cent of the total coke production of 1958 was obtained in this way (*Liberation Daily*, 14 November 1959), and it has been admitted that 'the quality of the native coke cannot be compared with coke produced in the modern way, and the cost of the native coke is higher' (*Daily Worker*, Shanghai, 24 February 1961).

Conclusion

The years since 1949 have seen a remarkable development of the Chinese coal industry. Unfortunately this cannot be documented fully because of the lack of detailed official information. From the partial picture that has been presented here, it is clear that few of the current Chinese claims about the industry can be accepted without reservation. In this respect, it has been suggested that it is, to say the least, unwise to compare the total output figures of China with those of the United States and the industrialized countries of Western Europe. In China's present race for accelerated development many strains are being placed on the economy. Today's coal industry shows evidence of this, especially in its transport difficulties. Between 1949 and 1960, when the unsatisfactory state of the agricultural sector of the economy caused some reconsideration (Dwyer, 1962, pp. 301–5) increased production at almost any cost seems to have been the ruling criterion in Chinese heavy industry, and several policy decisions regarding coal have been taken in recent years that, at best, will benefit the industry only in the very short run. The small mines are again the outstanding example.

But when all this is said, the most important aspect of the whole picture remains the striking effect vigorous government has had since 1949 upon the development of China's natural resources. The present policy for the coal industry has been stated to be 'readjusting, consolidating, filling out and raising standards' (*Peking Review,* 17 November 1961, p. 3). If it is carried out thoroughly, a solid core of real progress should then stand revealed. The challenge to be faced by the democracies lies in the fostering of effective alternative means to the same end in those underdeveloped nations with more liberal systems of government.

EDITOR'S NOTE

Since the above paper was written there seems to have been little change in the distribution of the major coal-mines. The south of China remains a coal deficient area. In order to minimize transport requirements, current policy continues to emphasize the working of small mines throughout the country but on a much more conservatively planned and carefully implemented basis than in the heyday of the Great Leap Forward. Coal production declined drastically during the Cultural Revolution but is thought to have since regained a level of about 300 million metric tons. It is now obvious that the 1958, 1959 and 1960 production claims quoted from the Chinese Press in the above paper were gross exaggerations.

DJD

12   Sinjao: a commune near Canton

Whilst much has been written about the Chinese communes in general [1], little geographical information is available about individual examples. Reasons for the lack of detailed information on individual communes are not hard to find, the major one being the difficulty of access to China. The account which follows is based on information gathered by the writer during a visit to the Canton area in April 1965. The time spent in the Sinjao commune, one day, was not long enough to cover all the ground in detail, thus this study is not complete, but efforts to arrange a second visit to the same commune were unsuccessful.

Sinjao lies immediately to the southeast of Canton and is made up of an island complex on the edge of the delta of the Si Kiang extending as far as the outport of Whampoa. The larger part of the commune occupies the eastern portion of the major island, the western part of which forms the south-eastern suburbs of the city of Canton. The commune is of average size with a total area of 65 000 *mow* (about 4 400 hectares, 11 000 acres) of which 45 000 *mow* are cultivated. As might be expected in a delta area the land is generally flat and lowlying, although there are a few small hills up to about 30 metres (100 ft) high, and cultivation would be impossible without an adequate system of drainage.

The commune of Sinjao was set up on 16 August 1958 by the amalgamation of sixteen pre-existing cooperatives. The population is made up of about 11 000 families, each of which lives and feeds as an individual unit, and has a total population of some 48 000 of which 20 000 form the work-force. Most of the population lives in one or other of the seven major nucleated villages which form a part of the

246

commune. The workforce is organized into seventeen production brigades which are subdivided into production teams with an average membership of between thirty and fifty individuals. The production teams normally work an eight-hour day for six days a week, but longer hours are worked during the busy periods of the year. As the visit coincided with the planting of the first rice crop, the length of the working day at that time had been temporarily lengthened to nine hours.

The activities carried on at Sinjao are unusually varied and even rice growing is a comparatively minor agricultural interest. Of the cultivated land, some 16 000 *mow* are devoted to fruit growing and fruit trees are a major feature of the otherwise flat landscape. The major fruit trees are lychees, longans and peaches, whilst pineapples are also grown in quantity and some bananas were also seen. The fruit trees are grown on banks about 5 metres (15 ft) wide between ditches some 2.5—3 metres (8—10 ft) deep which give adequate drainage to the tree roots and prevent water-logging of the soil.

In order of cultivated area vegetables form the second most important crops of the commune and some 11 000 *mow* are devoted to the growing of green vegetables of various kinds, especially those of the cabbage family, as well as beans and onions. The vegetables are largely grown in carefully tended beds some 2—3 metres (5—10 ft) wide between ditches which are used for both drainage and irrigation as necessary. Depending on the type of vegetable, up to eight crops per year can be grown and the fertility of the soil is maintained by the combined use of chemical fertilizers, which are produced in Canton, night soil from the city, humus from decayed vegetable matter and alluvium from the bottom of the drainage and irrigation canals. Additionally, widespread use is made of alluvium derived from the beds of the larger rivers which is brought to the fields along the larger canals in flat-bottomed boats.

The production of vegetables per *mow* is said to be increasing almost every year and in 1963 reached 7 100 catties [2] per *mow*. This was on the land used for growing vegetables all the year round, but additionally vegetables are grown as a catch crop in the dry winter season between the second rice

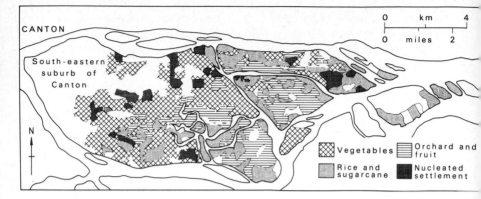

Fig. 12.1 Land use in Sinjao

crop of one year and the first rice crop of the next. The ready market for vegetables in nearby Canton certainly influences the size of the area which this commune devotes to vegetable growing. An excellent metalled road which links the commune with the city ensures rapid transportation of the green vegetables which are subject to deterioration especially in the summer heat. As the land use map shows, much of the land devoted to vegetable growing is in the western part of the commune, nearest to Canton, although other vegetable areas are scattered elsewhere in the commune.

At the time of the visit some 8 000 *mow* were under padi and 7 000 *mow* under sugar cane, but since conditions for the growth of these two crops are much the same, they alternate to some extent on part of the cultivated land. The land under these two crops tends to be closest to the rivers and on the margins of the islands. The yield of rice in 1963 was said to average 1 020 catties per *mow*, about double that of fifteen years ago. Naturally, yields vary to some extent from year to year and 1963 was generally a good year for rice. The cultivation cycle on the padi land in Sinjao is typical of south China in that two crops of rice and a catch crop of vegetables can be grown on the same land in one year. The first rice crop is sown in the nursery in March, transplanted in early April and harvested in late June and July; whilst the second is sown in July, transplanted in early August and harvested in late October and November. After the second harvest the land may be used for a catch crop of vegetables until it is ploughed in March for the first rice crop of the next year.

The increased yields of vegetables, rice and other crops was said to be made possible by a number of factors including the less frequent occurrence of flood and drought due to better water control. Twenty-eight electric pumps are in use to control the level of the water in the irrigation/drainage ditches which were in excellent condition. During late 1959 and in 1960, 300 labour days were spent on building a bund some 15 km (9 miles) long to give greater protection against flooding. Sinjao has an agricultural technical committee under whose guidance agricultural techniques have improved and the use of better quality seeds, together with improved methods of cultivation have combined with better water control and the increased use of fertilisers to make the higher yields possible.

A feature of the commune was the 'reserved land' which is kept and cultivated by the peasants for their own use. This is allotted to individuals on the basis of 0.01 *mow* for every member of the family, with adjustments made at the end of the agricultural year according to births and deaths. This land is used mainly for raising vegetables for the family and for the growing of pig feed since most families keep for their own use one or two pigs and a number of chickens and ducks. When individuals sell pigs, 40 per cent of the cash so obtained is retained by the owner.

Other commune agricultural activities also include the keeping of freshwater fish on a small scale, partly in the moat which surrounds the house of the former landlord. Some 7 000 pigs are kept by the commune at any one time, whilst ducks and chickens are also bred. An unusual feature was the 600 cows kept for their milk, which is sent to Canton. These cows, said to be a cross between Friesian and Chinese stocks, were of excellent quality and appeared to be almost pure bred Friesians. They are stall-fed, in open-sided sheds, on rice straw, cut grass and some artificial feed. Some bulls are kept but artificial insemination is also used.

Although agricultural interests form the major activity of the commune, there is also some minor industry. Food processing in the form of preserved fruit is linked with the fruit growing activities, whilst sauces are also produced. The embroidery of traditional colourful designs, principally for export, is also carried on. The rate of pay of the embroidery workers varies according to skill and experience, but the young girls learning this skilled work are paid 35 yuan [3] per month and obviously prefer this type of work to labouring in the fields. Other minor industries of the commune include the making and repairing of small boats and simple agricultural machinery.

The commune is run by a management committee which in part consists of people sent by the state but also includes elected members of the commune. It would appear that the elected members have more authority in the purely agricultural decisions. The leaders of the commune are paid by the state, the head earning about 70 yuan per month and the ordinary cadres about 50. In return, some 8—10 per cent of the income of the commune goes to the government, but since selling prices are also controlled there is complete financial control of the whole operation. One per cent of the commune's income is given to retired workers. The real income of the workers is difficult to assess since part is in kind, whilst the cultivation of individual plots also contributes to it. We were told that the actual cash income is rising steadily and that in 1963 it amounted to 450 yuan per worker per year, with an average cash income per family, since most women work, of about 800 yuan per year.

The commune is of course a social as well as an economic unit and this short account would not be complete without some mention of the social services which are provided. In Sinjao there is compulsory primary education and 90 per cent of the children attend school. There are thirty-five nursery schools provided where children may be left whilst their mothers add to the family income. There are also fifteen primary schools and two junior middle schools which provide the first three years of secondary education. No senior middle schools are provided on the commune because it is so near to Canton and the older children can go there, not only for their second three years of secondary education, but also for higher education. The teachers' salaries in all the schools are paid by the state and the school fee of 1 yuan per month is used to pay for books.

Sinjao has two small comprehensive hospitals with a total of eighty-two beds and judging from the number vacant, this appears to be more than adequate. Additionally there are fourteen clinics for outpatients. The commune had forty-four 'doctors' (not always as highly trained as Westerners might expect) who provide a choice of Western or Chinese treatment for the patients. Maternity, dentistry and X-ray facilities are provided, medicines are dispensed and there is an operating theatre for minor surgical cases, the more serious being taken to the larger hospitals in Canton. Preventive medicine, especially against cholera and malaria, is not neglected. We were told that the workers pay for medical treatment but that none go without because of inability to pay. On the whole, medical facilities appeared adequate although somewhat primitive by Western standards.

Every peasant is allowed to attend a free film show once a week and shows are held in different parts of the commune every evening for this purpose. Judging from the entertainment provided in Canton, these film shows are as much a means of political education as entertainment for virtually all the films appear to have a large propaganda content.

It has been said that Western visitors to China are only taken round 'show' communes and this may be true, for there is a worldwide tendency to show visitors the best rather than the worst. Colleagues on a separate visit at another time were, however, shown round another example. Certainly it is true that visitors are frequent at Sinjao and this in part may be due to its accessibility to Canton. The general impression was that the peasants were happy and well fed, if rather shabbily dressed. It would seem likely that the nearness of Sinjao to Canton, which has such a marked influence on its agriculture, in the concentration on the comparatively highly priced and high-yielding products of fruit and vegetables, makes the people more prosperous than those in communes which concentrate on the production of rice. However, a brief and superficial tour of parts of other communes producing rice near Canton showed little obvious difference in the living standards of the people.

13 The Great Leap Forward

In 1958 the Chinese Communist leadership launched the so-called Great Leap movement with the aim of increasing production on all economic fronts at an unprecedentedly high rate. As a result, the nation plunged rapidly into a deep economic quagmire.

Under the new programme, production targets for many commodities were repeatedly adjusted upward, and maximum pressure was applied on production units to achieve assigned output quotas by whatever means necessary. Another salient feature of the Great Leap movement was a greater emphasis on indigenous methods of production and labour-intensive investment projects. This policy, officially called 'walking with two legs', represented a sharp departure from previous development strategy which had stressed only modern production techniques and large-scale investment projects. The technical dualism introduced in 1958 was based on the assumption that native and small plants require less capital and a shorter construction period and that such plants can make use of local resources and labour that might otherwise be unemployed. These arguments were even more persuasive because of the discontinuation of Soviet loans which led to restraints on the importation of modern equipment for the ambitious economic development plans. Theoretically, the technical dualism envisaged by the Great Leap programme is not inherently unreasonable. In a country like Communist China, the rate of economic growth could be maximized, assuming a fixed amount of investment, by developing labour-intensive production. Misallocation of resources would occur only if this strategy were carried too far and conducted in a chaotic fashion.

The Great Leap movement, lasting about two years, was abandoned in 1960 after the country had been afflicted by a prolonged and serious agrarian crisis. The economic situation made continued industrial expansion impossible. The most obvious consequence of the Great Leap was the enormous waste involved. Indigenous production methods often proved either too costly in comparison, with their counterparts in the modern sector or capable of producing only low quality goods. A large number of the backyard furnaces hastily built in 1958 dissolved into piles of mud and brick after a few rains. Others were given up by the local authorities because of prohibitively high operation costs. Only a small portion of the indigenous blast furnaces survived and then only after some renovation. Similar situations prevailed in other industries, such as the small coal pits utilizing primitive methods of production that had been opened in 1958.

Another serious form of wastage was created as a result of inter-industry imbalance. Because the Great Leap movement was improvised rather than well planned in terms of inter-industry coordination, and because bottlenecks came sooner in some industries than in others as the movement proceeded, the economy was completely off-balance toward the end of 1958 and during 1959. Stocks piled up in those industries which had overproduced, while production capacities could not be fully utilized in other fields due to material shortages.

Resource misallocation due to industrial imbalance may be only temporary since the Communist leadership can avoid further waste of this type by altering or discontinuing the programme. However, from official statements and non-official disclosures, we know that in addition to the waste of resources incurred in the Great Leap movement, there were more profound shocks to the economy, some of which lasted for a considerable period after the movement was discontinued and which could be corrected only through serious readjustments.

Unfortunately, it is very difficult to make a full assessment of these more fundamental factors even today, four years after the Great Leap movement was abandoned. However, certain preliminary evaluations can be made. The Great Leap followed immediately after nation-wide decentralization in industry, commerce, finance and other areas in the economy.

It was also at this time that the commune system was introduced. All these drastic institutional changes in mainland China have had profound effects. Moreover, some of the damaging effects became noticeable only after 1959 when extremely unfavourable weather conditions and other natural calamities were also devastating the country. Since 1960, the Communist authorities in China have withheld all economic information so that an outside observer is unable to evaluate these developments in quantitative terms.

Clearly, one far reaching result of the Great Leap movement was the statistical confusion that ensued, creating new difficulties for future planning. Since the founding of the State Statistical Bureau in 1952, the Chinese Communists had striven to establish a workable statistical system over the whole nation to facilitate economic planning. The avowed objective of the State Statistical Bureau was to collect reliable and comprehensive data by standardizing statistical schedules, methods of computation, and definitions of terms and designations. Undoubtedly, the statistical system was greatly improved during the First Five-Year Plan period. However, these efforts were partially nullified in 1958 and 1959 by decentralization and the Great Leap [1]. Under the decentralization policy, more than 80 per cent of the centrally controlled enterprises were transferred to provincial jurisdiction. Local party cadres, who had been given greater responsibility and independence in handling production statistics, did not always follow the rules set by the State Statistical Bureau. Standard statistical schedules, computation methods, and commodity designations were frequently changed by the local governments to suit their own needs and purposes.

The Great Leap movement, on the other hand, created additional burdens for the State Statistical Bureau. Under the 'walking with two legs' policy, more than 700 000 tiny industrial units emerged throughout the country in 1958 [2]. These native industries utilizing indigenous methods produced non-standardized goods. The lack of well-trained accountants and statisticians to provide regular statistical reports was common. In some small-sized industries, there were not even instruments to measure output [3]. More serious was the tendency among production units to exaggerate output because of the intense pressure to fulfill targets. Local cadres, hoping that the glowing reports would stimulate other units to accomplish spectacular results, were unwilling to check on, and in some cases connived in, the statistical exaggerations made by individual enterprises.

The statistical confusion reached its climax in 1959 when the central government openly admitted surprisingly large errors in some of the 1958 figures, and consequently adjusted the planned targets for 1959. However, this confession merely exposed the chaotic situation; it did not change it. Several years were required for the Communist planners to remove fully the statistical confusion created. Meanwhile, massive statistical errors increased the difficulties of economic planning. Communist planners have been deprived of reliable current production data from which to work out consistent plans for the future. To formulate the so-called material balance tables, moreover, the planners need fairly accurate technical coefficients indicating how much of one commodity will be required as material input in producing one unit of another commodity. However, with the technical dualism that rapidly developed in 1958—59, most technical coefficients or input-output ratios had so greatly diverged between modern and native industries that national averages became less meaningful. As a result, it became more difficult for the planners to maintain inter-industry balance even when production figures were well controlled.

Quality control

One universal phenomenon in the Great Leap era was the drastic decline in the quality of commodities. A number of factors were responsible. Shortages of raw materials existed in varying degree in practically all manufacturing plants during this period. As a remedy, producers were asked to use inferior materials, poor substitutes, or scrap materials, which would inevitably lower the quality of finished products. At the same time, a larger number of new workers were recruited by industries from the countryside and were immediately put to work without having received sufficient training in production techniques. Deterioration in quality was also attributed to the fact that in many plants the normal process of production and technical requirements were not strictly observed [4]. But, more important was the tendency for some producers to deliberately lower quality as the only possible means of fulfilling the unreasonably high output quotas. The deterioration in the quality of products reached such an alarming level that six nationwide conferences were held by various industrial ministries in June 1959 to correct the situation.

Except for a few cases, this problem may have been a temporary one without any long-lasting impact on the economy. One might expect the quality of production to return to normal when the production drive was discontinued, shortages of materials were relieved, normal production processes and technical requirements were carefully observed, and regular quality control was reinstated.

One probable exception, however, is machine production in which the quality of output may have been affected for a number of years. Machines of inferior quality tend to make poor products. Some plants in Communist China have reported that they constantly have difficulty in stabilizing the quality of their products because they are using non-standard machinery built in the Great Leap period [5].

Still worse is the problem of quality in water conservation projects. The inferior quality of ordinary goods at most makes them defective or useless articles. Even the injurious effects of defective medicines can be prevented by not using them. But the poor quality of water conservation projects can be far more serious and their damaging effects can hardly be prevented, once construction has been completed. In 1958, more than 100 million people were mobilized to construct dams, reservoirs, and other irrigation projects. Most of these were small projects hurriedly approved without adequate advance surveys or proper designs. During that period, even for large-scale, well-planned projects, normal construction procedures were altered under the pressure of speeding up the work. Precautionary measures were often labelled 'superstition' and were abandoned. As hydraulic engineers know, unsatisfactorily designed and poorly constructed flood-control projects may make the control of floods more difficult and the results of floods more disastrous. Improperly built water reservoirs may raise the underground water level in the neighbouring area above its critical point resulting in the land becoming too alkaline. Similarly, irrigation systems with inadequate drainage may also cause alkalinization or salinization [6]. In fact, some hydraulic engineering experts had warned the Communist cadres before and during the Great Leap about the dangers of building water conservation projects without careful planning survey and design. Since 1959, articles have appeared in leading Communist journals and newspapers condemning the heavy damage in agricultural production caused by re-alkalinization and other manmade disasters. Today, certain observers on both sides of the bamboo curtain are inclined to believe that the abnormal weather conditions in the past few years would have been less disastrous if the Chinese Communists had not built so many indigenous and defective water conservation projects during the Great Leap period.

Lack of maintenance

Under heavy pressure to increase output during the Great Leap, all industrial enterprises overused or abused their machinery and equipment. Regular maintenance and check-ups were reduced to a minimum in order to gain more time for operation [7]. Some machines were operated at such a high speed as to exceed the technically permissible limit. It was also very common in the transportation system that vehicles were overloaded and kept running with little or no normal maintenance.

Repair and maintenance departments in large enterprises were converted into manufacturing workshops. This was partly because an illusion had been created that maintenance services could be abandoned without affecting the conditions of the machinery. Since workers in the repair and maintenance departments knew more than the newly recruited workers about the equipment and production skills, those departments were frequently converted into production units as a very convenient way to increase production. These conversions were euphemistically termed the promotion of repair and maintenance departments. In this period, a great number of independent repair shops in the cities were also encouraged to become production units by local authorities [8].

The impact of reduced maintenance and repair activities was extensively felt only after a period of time; conversely, it will also take time to reverse the trend. Unfortunately for the Communists, the corrective measures taken after 1959 were modified by another factor, that is, a shortage of spare parts. Great Leap targets assigned to machine-producing enterprises were assigned only on the basis of major machine parts; the output of accessories and attachments was usually not taken into account. Hence, individual enterprises naturally concentrated all their efforts on increasing the production of the essential machine parts at the expense of the output of appurtenances and accessories [9]. Consequently, in many large enterprises, workshops producing spare parts and accessories were converted into units manufacturing machines proper. One Communist source has reported that almost all iron and steel enterprises established in 1958 lack inspecting devices, spare parts, and other necessary accessories [10].

A very serious impact was first felt in the transportation system in the latter part of 1959 when official reports disclosed that thousands of motor vehicles could hardly be kept in normal operational condition due to the above mentioned difficulties [11]. Within approximately one year, similar problems arose, with varying intensity, in other industries [12]. As a result, beginning in 1961, the Communist leadership launched a new campaign urging all production and transportation units to place a higher priority on maintenance than on production [13]. They were ordered to restore their repair departments or to establish new ones, and were also instructed to observe strictly the normal maintenance schedules and regular check-ups of equipment. In 1961 and 1962, a coordinated plan was mapped out among three machine industry ministries to produce more parts and accessories [14]. All parts-producing units which had changed their production lines during the Great Leap period were ordered to shift back to their original line, or to be re-equipped with new lathes or machines for the production of spare parts.

Diversification of production

Another undesirable result of the Great Leap movement was

an unnecessary diversification of production in most large enterprises. One of the main features of industrial development in Communist China prior to 1958 was the emphasis on specialization. Most state enterprises were so designed as to specialize in one or several products, and each was subject to the direct control of the industrial ministry concerned. However, this principle was somewhat negated in 1958 by more diversified production or what the Chinese Communists called 'multiple-lines of business'.

Diversification of production is not necessarily bad if carried out properly. Indeed, it is quite common in large enterprises in the Western world. There is some saving in cost if a manufacturer produces several commodities which are joint products of the same materials or are related to each other in the production processes or in the requirements of machinery, laboratory equipment, and technical personnel. This type of diversification, which may be called horizontal diversification, provides some protection for the producer against the risk of a sudden decline in the market demand for the commodity in which he might otherwise have specialized. However, except for certain giant industries such as the iron and steel complexes, it is less common to find vertical diversification — i.e., the production of all kinds of raw materials required in making industrial end-products. This type of diversification may not provide any appreciable cost-saving, and even little or no protection for the firm in case of a sudden decline in demand for the end-product.

Industries in Communist China pursued vertical diversification after 1958. This was a consequence of the failure by most plants to obtain sufficient quantities of materials needed for production during the Great Leap period. As a result, factories were inclined, under the decentralized administration, to establish a number of subsidiary units, known as satellite plants, around each main plant in order to supply materials needed by the main plant. Thus, railway bureaux began to run cement plants and steel mills in order to make their own cement and rails. Cement mills began to establish paper mills to supply paper bags. Paper mills began to produce sulphuric acid and caustic soda in their satellite plants. This development was further encouraged by a speech of Mao Tse-tung in September 1958, in which he applauded

259

the operation of multiple businesses as an ingenious idea to make plants self-sufficient and to overcome the shortage of raw materials [15]. In about one year, thousands of complex industries had been formed, each trying to produce whatever materials were in short supply.

Since the satellite plants were quite different from the main plant in capital and technical requirements, there was little cost saving. In fact, a great number of satellite plants were hurriedly built to meet exigent needs without any serious consideration being given to the geographical distribution of natural resources and other relevant conditions. Consequently, production costs in such plants were abnormally high. Of course, cost considerations had been relegated to secondary importance during the Great Leap period and it seemed justified for an enterprise to fulfil its assigned target even at a high expense. It was only when the Great Leap was over that the Communist planners began to worry about the disequilibrium caused by the undesirable diversification in industries. It has subsequently been suggested that the principle of industrial specialization should be restored, that waste in satellite plants should be eliminated, and that diversification should be confined only to those industries were cost savings may be induced by diversified production [16].

Labour morale

Finally, the Great Leap caused a demoralization among workers, managerial and technical personnel that has also had a long-lasting effect. A large number of new workers were recruited into industry in 1958. They differed from the old workers in that most of them were so-called contract workers, hired on a contract basis for a specified period of time [17]. They lacked a feeling of security. Most important, they were not entitled to all of the benefits enjoyed by the old workers such as free medical care, compensation for injury and disability, retirement pensions, and special allowances for dependents. On the other hand, the number of work accidents greatly increased during the Great Leap period due to the relaxation of safety measures under the pressure of the production drive [18]. Demoralization among workers became even worse when the Communist authorities began to repatriate superfluous workers to the countryside in late 1959.

The factors that impaired the morale of managerial and technical personnel were different. Under the slogans 'politics takes command' and 'reliance on the mass line', the administrative system within an enterprise underwent considerable disruption. Technicians and engineers were humiliated by the existence of a situation under which experts had to listen to non-experts in technical matters, scientific laws were replaced by political demands, and production fell into the hands of a group of 'fanatics'.

Several years after the Great Leap era, the situation has still not returned to normal in many enterprises. The Communist leadership has recently repeated the necessity to overcome management chaos in those enterprises in which there is no one person responsible for any specific job or assignment [19]. Emphasis is again being placed upon a managerial system in which the entire factory is subordinate to the unified leadership of a general manager, and each staff member is responsible only for those tasks assigned to his post. Workers have been instructed to respect the professional opinion of the engineers and technicians and to observe strictly the normal order and technical requirements in each production process.

The above problems represent some consequences of the Great Leap movement on the subsequent economic development of mainland China. However, one should not describe the Great Leap as a total failure. It is undeniable that output increased remarkably in that period even after official claims have been subjected to an intensive and sceptical scrutiny. More important from a long-run point of view perhaps is the fact that the Great Leap movement, like most blunders made by men, has had its educational effect. Chinese Communist planners must have learned a lesson from it and, presumably, they will try to avoid the same mistakes in the future.

14　The three bitter years

In 1960, for the first time since the Communist regime came to power, China's production plans for agriculture and for light industry based upon agricultural raw materials were not fulfilled. Two reasons have been advanced for this. The official report cited 'natural calamities of an order unknown for the last century'. Non-Communist observers, in contrast, have tended to ascribe a large part of the failure in agriculture to the malfunctioning of the system of rural communes established in 1958. This note presents some evidence relating to both contentions and summarizes the major consequences of the 'natural calamities' of recent years upon China's rapidly developing economy.

From reports appearing in the Chinese Press the food crisis, which developed in 1960 and has since caused so much world comment, appears as the cumulative result of three bad agricultural years. In 1958 400 million *mow* (see p. 91) of the total cultivated area of 1 600 million *mow* were affected by extremely adverse weather, floods or insect pests, and conditions reached disastrous proportions on as much as a quarter of this area. The next year was described as the worst of the decade for the farmer and the total area affected rose to 600 million *mow*. Nevertheless, increases in agricultural production were reported in both years, and the commune system received the credit for these achievements. In 1960, however, the total area affected by 'natural calamities' rose to an unprecedented 900 million *mow*, of which 300—400 million *mow* suffered very heavily. There is some evidence — though no direct official statement has been made — that the production of food grains reached only the level of 1957 (that is, about 185 million tons as against the 1959 produc-

262

tion of 270 million tons) and that the cotton crop was particularly small also. The worst of the 'natural calamities' of 1960 was undoubtedly drought, which prevailed over widespread areas of north China. The provinces of Hopeh, Honan, Shantung and Shansi, all important wheat producers, were affected over areas totalling 60 per cent of their cultivated land. In some parts dry spells lasting more than a year were reported. In Shantung, for example, there was no water in eight of the twelve principal rivers for part of the year. The province had to receive continuous help: foodstuffs, medicines and clothing were supplied from Chekiang, Kiangsu, Fukien, Kiangsi and Anhwei provinces as well as from Shanghai, and units of the army were sent from Fukien to help with relief work. Central Honan experienced a 300-day drought which started during the winter wheat sowing in 1959. A report from Honan in late June 1960 described the drought situation as serious and stated that some areas had not been sown with summer crops. The volume of flow of the Hwang Ho through the province at this time was only two-thirds that of the previous year. In Shensi a drought of 100 days' duration in the autumn of 1959 was followed almost immediately by a similar dry spell extending well into 1960.

Typhoon damage during 1960 was unusually severe in the northeast and in the coastal provinces of Kwantung, Fukien, Kiangsu and Shantung. Between 1 and 5 August the heaviest rain in living memory fell in south Manchuria during the passage of a typhoon and flooding occurred on such a wide scale that even industrial production was interrupted. Fushun received 203 mm (8 in) of rain in six hours on 4 August. The waters of the Hun and Tungchow rivers burst the dykes flooding the great West opencast coal-mine and many smaller pits. The Penki mines and some factories there were also flooded, while at Anshan the steelworks had to suspend operations. The damage to farmland can best be judged from the interruption of railway services. The Shenyang–Dairen line was cut in no less than forty places by flooding and that from Shenyang to Changchun in twenty-two places. In the south, Kwantung, the country's second largest rice producer, which in 1959 had experienced the worst floods of a century along the East River, was struck in May and June by typhoons in the Swatow area and in October by two that passed across the south of the province within a week. As a result of the May typhoon 1.82 million *mow* of crops were inundated on the Swatow plain. The damage from that of June extended north into Fukien; in the Swatow area alone 60 000 homes were reported damaged. The destruction caused by the autumn typhoons can be gauged from the fact that they flattened 70 per cent of Hainan Island's late rice crop. Serious floods occurred along several rivers during the year. To take one example, along the Han river, the Yangtse's largest tributary, the biggest water crest for twenty-five years was experienced early in September and a million people had to be mobilized from the farms to strengthen the dykes and fight the floods. In addition, an important consequence of the drought and floods was the rapid increase in insect pests over large areas. Shantung, Honan, Kiangsu, Anhwei and Liaoning were all reported to have been badly affected.

As late as the first months of 1960 the commune system was being praised in the Chinese Press for averting the worst effects of the 'natural calamities': 'The vivid facts of 1959 show that with the benefit of the enormous collective force of the people's communes, plus the sky-rocketing enthusiasm of hundreds of millions of our heroic people, we are able to surmount all natural calamities' (*People's Daily*, Peking, 10 February 1960). But more recent indications point to the fact that some shortcomings of the communes are now being realized and that as a result the whole system of agricultural organization is undergoing fundamental changes. One of the chief criticisms is the size of the communes (on average 64 000 *mow* of agricultural land and 5 000 households) and the unified systems of cultivation that have been introduced with them. In Fukien province, for example, the *People's Daily* (4 January 1961) has admitted that the general principles of the Party regarding agriculture were badly applied. The rule adopted there was that all sowing and other farmwork should be done uniformly throughout each special district, which comprised a number of counties. In reality, however, the *People's Daily* states 'not in a special district, nor in one county, one commune, or one great labour brigade, hardly even within a small labour brigade, could the work of cultivation be thus unified'. Another issue

(12 November 1960) admits that in south China:

> There were places where the nature of the soil was dis-
> regarded and methods of cultivation which did not suit
> the nature and condition of the place were adopted. . . .
> They [the commune leaders] did not look at the natural
> conditions and rigidly insisted on [the Party policy of]
> 'change over to wet rice'.

It is thus likely that the commune system bears at least
some responsibility for the failure to achieve crop targets in
1960. This view would seem to be confirmed by a current
lack of enthusiasm for the communes in the Chinese Press. As
a result of the agricultural disasters of 1959–60, production
brigades, subordinate groups within the communes, have
become the basis of agricultural organization. Now, it seems,
the production brigades too are losing their importance, to
yet smaller production teams. This basic change follows logically from the criticisms of the communes quoted above. The
brigade can still assign quotas to the team, but it cannot
interfere with the manner in which the team works.

> The small labour brigade should have, under the general
> production plan laid down by the large brigade, the
> right of sowing what the soil demands, the right of
> determining technique and the number of the labour
> force, the right of managing animals and implements,
> the right of handling part of the funds. The masses must
> daringly be trusted. (*People's Daily,* 12 November
> 1960.)

A second major consequence of China's recent natural
calamities has been the re-focusing of the attention of the
national planners upon agriculture. In recent years agriculture
has tended to be relatively neglected and most available
capital has been put into developing heavy industry and the
transport system. As a result of the experiences of 1960,
however, it has now been decided that 'the whole nation
must concentrate on strengthening the agricultural front and
must carry out the policy of taking agriculture as the foundation of the national economy. . . . In heavy industry the
scope of capital construction in 1961 should be appropriately
reduced' (Li Fu-chun). Some planned slowing down in the

rate of growth of China's heavy industries is therefore to be expected besides that imposed in the light industries by shortages of raw materials derived from agriculture. The effects of the present shortages of agricultural raw materials are probably the reason why no statistics have yet been published for industrial production in 1960 except those for steel (18.45 million tons) and coal (400 million tons). . . .

Lastly, as a result of internal shortages China became a major importer of wheat and barley during 1961 and this resulted in a sharp increase in her trade with the non-Communist countries. She is currently Australia's best wheat customer, having purchased 40.3 million bushels against the United Kingdom's 27.4 million in the 1960—61 season (Table 14.1). Canada has now also become a major supplier of wheat to China, while smaller quantities of food grains have been obtained from France, West Germany and Argentina. It seems likely that China will remain a heavy food importer for several years to come: but at the same time food is also being exported. Small amounts of the wheat China has bought have been shipped directly to Albania and East Germany and more may be intended for delivery to other Communist countries in Europe in fulfilment of commitments to supply foodstuffs

Table 14.1 *China's food purchases for delivery in 1961 (thousand tons)*

	Wheat	Barley	Flour	Oats	Maize	Rice	Milk powder	Sugar
Argentina					45			
Australia	2 285	360	40	60			0.03	
Burma						300		
Canada	1 720	620						
France		260	25					
W. Germany			250					
New Zealand							0.60	
UK							1.00	
USSR								500
TOTAL	4 005	1 240	315	60	45	300	1.63	500

China is now unable to meet herself (in 1959 she supplied 2.2 million tons of foodstuffs to Russia in return for industrial capital goods and in repayment of loans). China is also buying Burmese rice and transhipping some of it to Ceylon to meet trade obligations there.

EDITOR'S NOTE

An estimated 7.6 million tons of grain was imported by China in 1973 compared with 4.8 million tons in 1972. The previous highest figure was 6.6 million tons in 1964. The 1973 imports included 2.8 million tons of wheat from Canada; 0.8 million tons of wheat from Australia; and 2.6 million tons of wheat and 1.4 million tons of maize from the United States. Even with good harvests, because of its growing population China will probably require relatively large agricultural imports for at least the remainder of the present decade.

DJD

15 Developing the interior: the growth of Urumchi

'The city of Urumchi,' wrote Mildred Cable in 1944, 'important though it has been for generations as a centre of the caravan trade of central Asia, has remained all but unknown to the Western World until recently' [1].

Although numbers of Western travellers have visited this centre during the last three decades and have brought out short descriptions of this pivotal oasis centre and city on the northern flanks of the Great T'ien Shan range, the last two words of the quotation probably could safely be removed even today without damaging the essential truth of the quotation. The importance of this city, currently carrying the name of Urumchi, and its oases has become greater today than at any time in past history. It constitutes the nerve head of Chinese Communist development of the vast territory with 7 million people [2] fronting Soviet central Asia and now deceptively termed the Hsin-chiang Uighur Autonomous Region. This article attempts to accord to this significant city and its oases some of the attention that they deserve by gathering the strands of their historical evolution, presenting a picture of their commanding development today, and pointing to their rising role for the future of this far west frontier region of China.

The physical situation

From the Pamirs in the west, the mighty T'ien Shan range reaches a distance of 1 697 km (1 054 miles) eastward into China's northwest desert lands. Of this length, only some 1 130 km (700 miles) border Dzungaria, the basin north of the T'ien Shan. Along this 1 130-km wall of mountains separating the Tarim basin from Dzungaria and its gateways to Soviet central Asia, there are only two relatively easy routes that cut through the barrier. One crosses the eastern T'ien Shan northwestward from Ha-mi and Ch'i-chiao-ching, east of the Turfan basin. As a connecting link between Dzungaria and the important western oases of the Tarim basin, this eastern route is 480—560 km (300—350 miles) longer than the Urumchi route which is situated near the centre of the 1 130-km T'ien Shan wall. The eastern route also must traverse the length of the Turfan basin, an unbearably hot stretch during the summer season, to reach the western Tarim regions. The Urumchi route, therefore, is the commanding gateway between the two great basin lands of Hsin-chiang or Chinese central Asia.

Urumchi is situated at the northern end of a broad corridor, the Chai-wo-pao Valley, separating the eastern and western T'ien Shan. The corridor is over 120 km (74 miles) long and averages about 20 km (12 miles) wide. It divides the north slopes of the Kara Uzun Tau lying southwest of the city from the high Bogdo Ula east of the city. The Bogdo Ula reaches a peak of 5 437 metres (17 847 ft) [3], a rise of 4 558 metres (14 946 ft) within a distance from the city of about 65 km (40 miles). To the southwest the high water divide of the Kara Uzun Tau lies about 76 km (47 miles) distant, and its highest peak 4 317 metres (14 156 ft) above sea level, towers 3 427 metres (11 255 ft) above and almost due south of Urumchi. A number of short, broken ranges running east—west extend from the eastern end of the Kara Uzun Tau to the southern and lower slopes of the Bogdo Ula. These short ranges lie generally between 1 614—2 681 metres (5 300 and 8 800 ft) in altitude. Carving a canyon between the easternmost two segments, a small river flowing southward into Chio-lo-huan (a sink) drops about 220 metres in 32 km (720 ft in 20 miles) from Ta-pan-ch'eng (Dawan Ch'eng or Pass City) to Hsiao-ts'ao-hu ('Small Grass Lake') on the northwest rim of the Turfan basin. Urumchi Hsièn (district) limits, according to a 1909 atlas of Hsin-chiang [4], lie 2—5 km (2—3 miles) northwest of Hsiao-ts'ao-hu village.

The strategic passes protecting the approaches to Urumchi lie in the narrower part of the route between Ts'ao-yang-hu and Ta-pan-ch'eng. From the latter to Urumchi City, the route rises only very gradually some 77 metres (252 ft) in a distance of 64 airline km (40 miles) to the mountain saddle occupied by the village of Ch'i-ch'i-tsao. From this saddle the road begins its descent of 261 metres (859 ft) in the remaining 13 airline km (8.6 miles).

Urumchi River in its upper reaches is known as the Arkhoto Gol. North of the city, the river becomes the Lao-lung Ho (Old Dragon River) before it unites with the T'ou-t'un to enter Pai-chia Lake (the ancient Lake Erbantolo) in the sandy desert of south-central Dzungaria. This lake probably is mostly a vast marsh much of the time. The several patches of irrigated land that together make up the oases region of Urumchi are found between the city and the junction of the two rivers to its north.

The slope of the present municipal area is steep. In the south the Ulabai district stands at an elevation of 1 033 metres (3 395 ft). This falls to 600 metres (1 968 ft) at the lower end of the city. Because the broken folds of the main T'ien Shan range included in the municipality have suffered the erosive force of mountain streams through many millennia, an uneven surface of scour depressions alternates with depositional mounds. The Yao-mo (Demon) Mountains on the west bank of the Urumchi River reach 1 388 metres (4 592 ft) above sea level, with steep local relief of up to 499 metres (1 640 ft). This section comprises the highest part of the present Urumchi Municipality. On the east bank of the river, a tongue of the Hung Shan (Red Mountains) has developed a high fault escarpment [5].

Urumchi, at 43° 45'N, 87° 40'E, is shown to have considerable differences of altitude in different parts of the city. In connection with the city's weather and climatic records, however, the elevation generally given (possibly at its former weather station) is 915 metres (3 003 ft). The following statistics of the climatic record must, therefore, be recognized as properly applying to this elevation and site rather than as true for all parts of the city. This site is likely to have been in the vicinity of the old provincial government quarters within the former main city walls. Here the annual average temperature is 5°C (41°F). The January average is −19°C (−2.2°F) [6] with the absolute minimum reaching −41.6°C (−42.7°F) in February [7]. The July average is 24°C (75.2°F) but the maximum can reach 43°C (110°F) during this month. The number of days with below-freezing average temperatures are 140, and the growing season (free of killing frost) is 165 days. Killing frost on the average begins 5 October and ends in spring on 22 April. However, frost has occurred as early as 29 September and as late as 6 May. Such severe winter temperatures reflect the exposure to the boreal winds that sweep south from Siberia through the Dzungarian basin. This oasis region has forty-five more days averaging below-freezing temperatures than K'u-ch'e (Kucha) on the southern, protected slopes of the T'ien Shan, only two degrees of latitude further south. Probably by the end of September freezing temperatures have stopped much of the snowmelt and glacial runoff from the T'ien Shan, since Menon [8] wrote that in 1957 the Urumchi River was devoid of water on 27 September.

Urumchi is subject to frequent light valley winds. At night these are south winds, whereas daytime winds come from the north. Aside from these, north and northwest winds are the dominant winds the year round except for December and January. December is the only month when winds show no marked predominance of direction, although southwest winds tend to be most frequent then. In January southwest and southeast winds are most prominent. Very strong winds may sweep over Urumchi through the pass southeastward, and at Ta-pan-ch'eng (Pass City), winds with speeds reaching 6 or 7 on the Beaufort Scale drive sand to sculpture rocks into grotesque shapes. At times these winds have caused death of many livestock as well as destruction of crops and houses [9]. Scorching hot winds from the Dzungarian desert in summer, spring, and autumn, seldom exceeding a few hours, may blow through the corridor. Even more scorching and desiccating winds, which at their maximum may reach gusts of 39 metres (130 ft) per second or almost 145 km (90 miles) per hour, blow northward through the Chai-wo-pao corridor from the Turfan basin. These southeast winds occur most often in spring, frequently in fall, rarely in winter, and never in summer. They are highly destructive and, if they persist for a day or more, will sear crops to death if irrigation is not promptly applied [10].

Based on records for ten years, the average annual precipitation at Urumchi is 240 mm (9.4 in) [11]. At Chi-t'ai and

Shih-ho-tzu, northeast and northwest of Urumchi, with alti-
tudes respectively of 612 and 445 metres (2 007 and 1 452
ft), the annual precipitations are 183 and 178 mm (7.2 and 7
in). This shows the influence of altitude here on the precipitation, since all three cities are on the north slopes of the
T'ien Shan. (Chi-t'ai is further east in Dzungaria than Shih-
ho-tzu and should be drier, but, because of almost 120
metres (394 ft) greater elevation, is benefited by increased
condensation.) Precipitation at Urumchi is relatively well
distributed the year round, with the winter period having
least. The minimum month is January with 8 mm (0.3 in) in
contrast to the October maximum of 46 mm (1.8 in). Sunny
skies prevail much of the time, with total hours of sunshine
during the year averaging 2 607, or 59 per cent of the possible total, including 118 cloudless days.

The region around Urumchi has a natural vegetation of
short steppe grasses of the feather-grass and fescue varieties.
The Chinese names for the grasses include han-kao, chi-chi-
ts'ao, pai-tz'u, and lo-t'o-feng (camel grass) [12]. Grass cover
reaches up to some 1 400 metres (4 600 ft) altitude above sea
level, when forests take over on the northern slopes of the
T'ien Shan east and southwest of Urumchi. The forest grows
up the slopes to some 2 800 metres (9 200 ft) altitude. Within about 97 km (60 miles) of Urumchi the forests, comprised
mainly of T'ien Shan fir with some Siberian firs and pines,
occupy 13 per cent of the slope areas, interspersed with grass-
lands. Pure stands of willow or mixed birch and willow
forests often take over as second growth after forest fires. In
these secondary forests may be found wild rose and plum
trees and evergreen shrubs. Above the 2 800 metres (9 200
ft) altitude rich, long meadow grasses with some scrub forests
take over the vegetation cover up to about 3 500 metres
(11 500 ft). At and above these elevations mosses and lichens
and some herbaceous plants known as 'tiger ears' and 'dragon
livers' may be found. Above 3 965 metres (13 000 ft) bare
rock or ice and snow prevails on the north slopes of the
Bogdo Ula east of Urumchi [13].

Political history

The name 'Urumchi' is derived from the Dzungar dialect of

272

Mongolian, 'uru' meaning 'beautiful' and 'mchi' meaning 'pasture'. However, this area has been known by a great number of different names and is characterized by long occupation by various ethnic groups in its 2 200 years of history. Among the earliest people using the area were pastoralists who established a nomadic 'state' here during the early Han period about 200 BC. The records of the western regions in the *History of the Han Dynasty* tell of a Pei-lu Kingdom situated at the present oases of Urumchi. There also are records telling of a Ch'e-shih Kingdom here in 60 BC [14]. Subsequently there was a Chin-man-ch'eng (Chin-man City) situated in the same area [15].

From the end of the second century AD to the beginning of the fourth century, the Oelot branch of the western Mongols grazed their flocks and herds here. A Communist Chinese report asserted that these nomads built a 'city' here in AD 176 [16]. It seems doubtful that the early nomad 'cities' here were anything more than large encampments. However, during the fifth century the T'ieh-le tribe (Turkic Töläs) migrated here [17], possibly from the Turfan and Ha-mi area to the southeast where these seminomads apparently were present with their flocks and herds [18]. They also were farmers, and their arrival at the Urumchi oases marked the beginning of agricultural crops here and settlement that more truly could be called a town or small city. These people, according to Ch'en Pu-ch'ing, were ancestors of the Uighurs now dominant in the Tarim basin. Perhaps it was at about this time that the settlement here acquired the name Beshbaliq which, according to Mildred Cable, constantly recurs in the historical annals of Dzungaria [19].

By AD 552 the Kök or Eastern Turks in the Altai Mountain region had freed themselves of their former overlords, the Jou-juan tribe, and had founded a vast empire. This empire stretched from the Orkhon (Mongolia) across western Turkestan to the shores of the Sea of Azov and was the power domain of the Türküt [20]. Presumably the Türküt dominated the oases along the northern piedmont of the T'ien Shan. However, they were ousted as masters of the oases at Urumchi by the early T'ang dynasty armies from China. The T'ang Chinese brought new and more advanced agricultural techniques to this region and set up garrisons

273

to ensure their grip on these patches of irrigated desert.

During the T'ang period the vast reaches of Hsin-chiang and presentday Soviet central Asia were known to the Chinese as Hsi-yü or western regions. The Tang–Chinese empire tried to control the many tribes of this huge area occupying lands reaching to the Persian borders. Politically, the entire region was under the cognizance of Chinese officials of Lung-yu Tao (Lung-yu Province), one of sixteen Tao into which the T'ang empire was organized. Responsibility for this control was in the hands of the Hsi-an Military Governor situated at what was called Chiu-tzu, the present-day K'u-ch'e (Kucha) in the southern piedmont of the T'ien Shan southwest of Urumchi. The latter was then called T'ing Chou (T'ing Department). Subsequently during the T'ang, the Dzungarian basin and the lands west of the Altai in present Soviet central Asia were placed under the jurisdiction of a military governor at the site of Urumchi, then called Pei-t'ing. Thus, as early as the T'ang, the strategic situation of Urumchi was recognized by Chinese officials. Still later during the T'ang, the military governor (tu-tu-shih) was replaced by a commissioner of revenue (chieh-tu-shih) at Pei-t'ing. The Hsi-an (K'u-ch'e) military governor was replaced by a similar commissioner resident at An-hsi in northern Kansu Province [21].

The Türküt empire north of the T'ien Shan was destroyed in the eighth century by the ancestors of the modern Uighurs who, between AD 745 and 854 (i.e. during the latter half of the T'ang period), ruled over Mongolia and Dzungaria and at times over the Turfan basin oases. Such periods marked a temporary Chinese retreat from the Urumchi region. When the Uighur empire was broken up by the Kirghiz tribes in the middle of the ninth century, part of the Uighurs fled to north China where, in the course of time, they presumably became absorbed by the Chinese. Another group of Uighurs moved to Kansu where they founded a small kingdom without building any distinctive culture. They were unable to raise protecting walls against the alien tribes that roamed or passed through the Kansu (Ho-hsi) corridor between east China and Hsin-chiang. The third and largest group of Uighur tribes fled from the Kirghiz to the Turfan oases. In this restricted arena they promptly won the upper hand politically [22].

The last group of Uighurs migrated into the Turfan basin as seminomadic Manichaeans. They found a Buddhist culture here which they soon took over. Beginning in the eleventh century, however, they were subjected to a cultural and religious transformation which has lasted to the present. This was brought about by the Turkic Karachan tribes who first took over Kashgar and then moved eastward through the Tarim basin, spreading the religion of Islam [23]. This movement was furthered by the overriding might of the Mongol empire in the thirteenth century, so that Islam gained a strong body of adherents throughout northwest China as well as in China proper itself. At the end of the twelfth century there was a migration of Turfan agriculturalists (presumably Uighurs) northward across the T'ien Shan to the Urumchi oases. They brought with them crops new to the area, such as cotton, flax, and melons [24].

Under the Mongol conquerers of China and central Asia the strategic situation of Urumchi was recognized anew when Beshbaliq became the site of the Mongol Pei-t'ing military governor's headquarters. Then, when the Mongol empire began to collapse at the end of the Yuan dynasty, the Mongol chieftain Mungo Timor occupied the Urumchi oases and city and established there the so-called Hu-la Kingdom [25].

The earliest city walls and more recent suburban sections of pre-Communist Urumchi were constructed during the Ming dynasty. These walls are reported to have been 3 li (about 1 mile) in circumference. The Ming were unsuccessful in retaining this western region in their empire, and these early walls have long since disappeared [26].

In the seventeenth century, at the beginning of the Manchu rule over China (Ch'ing dynasty) the region north of the T'ien Shan was again occupied by a member of the Oelot branch of the Mongol tribes who had come here before, during the Later Han dynasty. These more recent Mongols were the Dzungars. They also overran the Islamic Uighurs south of the T'ien Shan. During this period there were four Oelot tribes in Hsin-chiang. The Cho-lo-ssu pastured their flocks in the I-li Valley; the Durbot occupied the Kurgis River drainage in the southwestern Altai; the Turgut occupied the T'a-ch'eng (Tarbagatai) region, and the Hosht occupied the Urumchi region. The latter were descendants of

Habut Hasar, younger brother of Genghis Khan. During the reign of the Manchu Emperor K'ang-hsi (1662–1723), the Hosht, who at the end of the Ming period attacked and occupied the Ch'ing-hai (Kokonor) region and the region of Kam to its south, became involved in warfare with the other Mongol tribes in Hsin-chiang. Galdan, a chieftain who rose to power over the Dzungars of I-li by assassination of his nephew, now attacked the Hosht and killed their king, Ch'e-chen. Galdan thus became lord of all four Mongol tribes as well as of all of Hsin-chiang. Not satisfied, he next attacked the Khalkha Mongols of Outer Mongolia and threatened the Manchu frontiers in Inner Mongolia. In various campaigns, the Manchu forces and their allies among the northwest tribes defeated Galdan and his successors and drove the Dzungars westward [27]. In 1755 the 'West-pacifying-general' (Ting-hsi chiang-chün) of the Manchu armies based on Urumchi attacked the Awachi Mongols, and it was at Urumchi that the Kumnoyat tribes' Anchi Kolola-durchi surrendered to Manchu forces. Further campaigns by forces of Manchu Emperor Ch'ien-lung resulted in the complete rout of the Dzungars and the reoccupation of the I-li valley in 1758 [28].

Because of the strategic control that Urumchi provided in the corridor connecting north and south Hsin-chiang, the Manchu at this time stationed a military governor there with two subordinates, one at Ch-t'ai and the other at Pa-li-k'un. A policy of military colonization or militia farmers was established and there were two vice-superintendents of military farmers to supervise the total of some 238 600 mu (15 150 ha/37 433 acres) of land farmed by them in Dzungaria [29]. A civil service system also was established. Urumchi became the seat of what was called Ti-hua Chou (Ti-hua Department) and within the *chou* were included the four hsien (districts) of Ch'ang-chi, Fu-k'ang, Sui-lai, and Chi-t'ai. Ti-hua Chou was a department of the larger unit called Chen-ti Tao which in turn was a subdivision of Kansu Province. The military governor at Ti-hua Chou was concurrently commander of the army and head of the *Chou* civil administration [30].

Political and criminal exiles from mainland China were the chief elements in the militia farms, just as today political opponents of the Communist Chinese regime are exiled to these same remote regions to serve as compulsory labour battalions. Much of the credit for the rapid construction and reclamation activities in post-1949 Hsin-chiang probably belongs to former Nationalist army units under T'ao Shih-yüeh, who surrendered to the Chinese Communist army in 1949. Their 're-education is to last a lifetime and it takes the form of the military colonization of Sinkiang' [31].

Just about 200 years earlier, in 1758, a rebellion by Chinese exiles in Dzungaria took place at Ch'ang-chi, a district governed by Urumchi and only about 48 km (30 miles) northwest of it. Apparently, drunken Manchu–Chinese army officers at a merrymaking during the Autumn Festival compelled local wives of the exiles to sing and dance for them. The incensed exiles killed the officers and seized their arms, and over 1 000 of the rebels marched the same night on Urumchi, only to be slaughtered at Hung Shan Pass by troops under Military Governor Wen Fu [32]. Two years after this rebellion, in the summer of 1760, the military commander for Shensi and Kansu, Yang Ying-chü, memorialized the Throne to establish a civil subprefect at Urumchi. This was established under the jurisdiction of An-hsi Tao [33].

In 1763 the former small walled fortress was enlarged to a small city of about 10.8 sq km (4.2 sq miles) in area, and the name Urumchi was discarded in official Chinese usage and replaced by the name Ti-hua [34]. The Communist Chinese Press has termed this action 'an insult' to the Hsin-chiang minorities. Nevertheless, the meaning of the new name, i.e. 'to direct the transformation', seems very appropriate to its present role as the spearhead of the development and exploitation of Hsin-chiang.

Later, to strengthen their control, the Manchu–Chinese constructed a garrison fortress for Manchu troops in 1772 called Kung-ning. This Kung-ning was situated about 8 km (5 miles) northwest of Ti-hua (Fig. 15.1), but was destroyed by rebel tribes not many years later [35]. Ti-hua was secure under Manchu control for almost a century thereafter, during which no major uprisings threatened its position.

In 1863 a 'Chinese city' was constructed north of the earlier defence fortress and received the name Ti-hua, and the An-hsi provincial commander-in-chief's office was moved there [36]. During this period, unrest among the Islamic adherents (variously called Tung-kan, Dungan, or Hui) in China's northwestern provinces was increasing and beginning to evolve into a major rebellion. In 1864 (third year of Emperor T'ung Shih), a Tung-kan from Lin-hsia district southwest of Lan-chou by the name of Ahung Toming entered Ti-hua surreptitiously and conspired with So Huan-chang, the son of the former governor of Kansu Province. They stabbed the governor to death and seized the 'Chinese city', and Ahung proclaimed himself King of Urumchi with the title Ch'ing Chen (Clear and True). He brought under his control the adjoining oases and towns of Chi-t'ai, Sui-lai, Ch'ang-chi, and Fu-k'ang. Two years later, Uighur and Tung-kan at I-li also revolted, but leaders of the two fell out with each other, and the Uighur Abdur proclaimed himself sultan [37].

The leaders of the Tung-kan rebellion built an 'Imperial City' outside the south gate of Ti-hua in 1868, so that three cities existed concurrently adjacent to one other [38].

With the Tung-kan rebellion weakening Manchu control over their central Asian territory, the Russians seized the opportunity to extend their empire in this region. They ousted the Uighur Abdur from I-li in 1871, taking over control themselves in this strategic western T'ien Shan Valley. Although the Manchu were so discouraged that they were ready to abandon all attempts to retain Hsin-chiang within their Chinese empire, one of their Han Chinese generals, Tso Tsung-t'ang, was determined to win back the northwest. His zealous stand won him permission from the emperor to attempt to pacify the Hsin-chiang rebels in 1875. General Tso's deputy, Chin Shun, recaptured Ti-hua from Ahung Toming, who then committed suicide. General Chin Shun was appointed governor of Ti-hua [39].

In the meantime, the Uighur chief, Abdur, held the Tarim basin oases. In 1877 when he was attacked from the 'east and south routes' (presumably via Ha-mi and An-hsi), he countered by attacking Ti-hua from his base at Ta-pan-ch'eng, the southern end of the trans-T'ien Shan corridor. Fate had deserted him, however, and he fled in defeat to T'o-k'u-sun (Toksun) in the Turfan basin where he too committed suicide.

Through negotiations involving many humiliating conces-

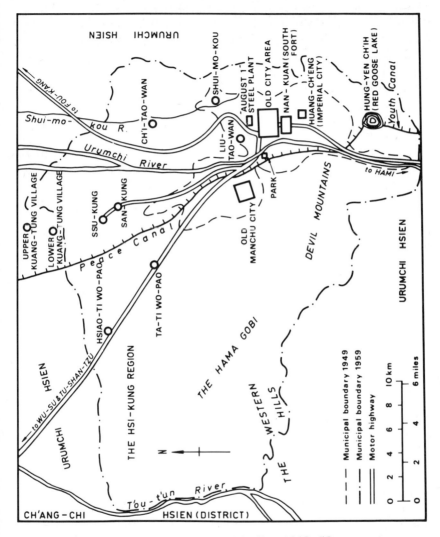

Fig. 15.1 Expansion of Urumchi municipality, 1949—59

sions by the Manchu–Chinese to Russia, war with Russia was avoided on the I-li frontier. The Russians agreed to evacuate I-li and return it to Manchu rule. In the I-li Treaty of 1881, the Manchu Court opened Hsin-chiang to Russian trade and conceded the Russian's rights to establish consulates and mercantile houses at the five cities of I-li, T'a-ch'eng, A-shan, Kashgar, and Ti-hua [40].

In re-establishing their rule over Hsin-chiang, the Manchu in 1885 constituted their central Asian colonial territory a regular province of their Chinese empire and called it Hsin-chiang or New Frontier. To form a provincial capital, the 'new Manchu city' was united with the existing Ti-hua city into one municipality of some 23 sq km (8.8 sq miles) of area [41]. Ti-hua city became the chief *fu* (prefecture) within a *hsien* (district) of the same name, and the former *chou* (department) was abolished [42].

Hsin-chiang continued to be ruled from Ti-hua following the Republican Revolution of 1911 which ousted the Manchu from their two and a half centuries of rule over China and the adjoining regions in central asia to China's west. (Although Chinese in the past and present always have been ready to denounce imperialistic colonialism practised on them by alien powers, whether Mongol, Manchu, Japanese, or European, few Chinese statesmen or politicians have ever been ready to recognize or relinquish their position of colonial master over imperial territory inherited with their succession to the Manchu rule. Nor are the present Communist Chinese less hypocritical in this respect.) Following 1911, however, the breakdown of centralized rule with the Manchu overthrow was also reflected in the situation at Ti-hua. The British consular officer Sykes wrote in 1915 that Hsin-chiang was ruled by a *chiang-chün* (general) or provincial governor who resided at Urumchi. Under him were *tao-yin* or prefects at Urumchi, Tarbagatai (T'a-ch'eng), I-li, Aksu, and Kashgar [43]. 'The situation is complicated', he stated, 'by the fact that the commander of troops in the districts south of the Tian Shan is independent of the Governor of Urumchi, taking orders direct from Peking.' All the officials mentioned above were Chinese, but their subordinates, known as Begs, Ming Bashis, and Yuz Bashis, were Muslims, mostly Uighurs, entrusted with the collection of taxes, the administration of justice in minor cases, and the arrangement of forced labour. They also controlled the irrigation system and were men of considerable influence. The nomadic people, however, were administered quite independently of the provincial governors by an official known as the I-li Tartar General. Sykes continues: 'The system sketched above, by which there are three independent authorities in the province, is bad enough; but it is made infinitely worse by the corruption which prevails, especially in the collection of revenue. On the other hand, the taxes are generally light, and the condition of the people is one of acquiescence in Chinese domination.'

It is clear from the above that the conditions for a new power struggle in China's 'New Frontier' were present following the destruction of Manchu domination, and that Ti-hua, or Urumchi, as the strategic pivot in the province, would again be the centre of the struggle. Numerous political uprisings had occurred during the latter half of the nineteenth century and the beginning of the twentieth. Much of this turmoil arose from corruption and maladministration, as revenge for savagery practised by Manchu and Chinese officials, or from hopes by Turkic and Mongol tribes to reassert their independence from Manchu and Chinese domination. Secret societies such as the Ko-lao Hui, and Nationalist, and, subsequently also, Communist agents and subversives stirred up civil commotion. Russian agents intrigued to gain territory and influence in the Hsin-chiang borderlands.

Yang Tseng-hsin, who became governor of Hsin-chiang at the beginning of the Republican period, is reported to have been a clever man in solving the complex political problems of Hsin-chiang by diplomatic manoeuvrings as well as by force and terror. He also took advantage of the Russian revolution to reduce Russian privileges and power in Hsin-chiang gained during the Manchu period. Yang, however, was assassinated in 1928 to be succeeded at Ti-hua by a less able man, Chin Shu-jen. Chin's ineptness and his arbitrary and finally outrageous conduct started a revolt at Ha-mi which spread to the entire province. He had also yielded to Soviet threats or promises to sign a much-denounced 'Temporary Commercial Treaty' with the Soviet Union, whereby China lost the diplomatic ground regained by former Governor Yang. On 12 April 1933 subordinates of Governor Chin revolted at Urumchi and caused him to flee to T'a-ch'eng and from there via Siberia to China proper. After a brief interim when the commander of the Northeastern Army Corps, Cheng Jun-ch'eng, was acting Commissioner, General Sheng Shih-ts'ai, who commanded a strong body of troops, was appointed *tu-pan* or military governor. Liu Wen-lung, chief of the Education Office, was appointed 'chairman' of the provincial government. At this time, the Tung-kan rebel, Ma Chung-ying, entered Hsin-chiang for the second time and joined with the rebel Hokaniyatz in seizing control of the districts of Ku-ch'eng and Fu-yüan, after which they marched on Urumchi. General Sheng led his forces to battle at the small settlement of Tz'u-ni-ch'üan (Purple Mud Springs) in Fu-yüan district. A political manoeuvre by the provincial government to divide the rebels in the meantime had succeeded. Hokaniyatz accepted a provincial appointment as 'Chief Defence Commander for South Hsin-chiang', and he refrained from joining in the battle at Tz'u-ni-ch'üan. When he observed that Ma Chung-ying was being defeated, he led his own troops to occupy T'o-k'u-sun. When Ma withdrew to the Turfan basin, he forced Hokaniyatz to retreat to south Hsin-chiang [44].

In the meantime, the Nationalist government at Nanking was becoming much concerned over the turmoil in Hsin-chiang and sent intermediaries to try to reconcile Sheng Shih-ts'ai and Ma Chung-ying, but they were unsuccessful. In September 1933 Sheng drove southward through the corridor from Urumchi and attacked Ma's forces entrenched at strategic Ta-pan-ch'eng. This attack was unsuccessful and Sheng had to retire again to Urumchi. That winter Ma Chung-ying and the Commissioner for Military Colonists at I-li, General Chang Pei-yüan, joined forces to overthrow Sheng. Ma's forces invested Urumchi for an entire month, while Chang led his forces to fight against Sheng's provincial troops at Wu-su about 402 km (250 miles) west of Urumchi. Sheng had been wooing Moscow and now sent his chief of the aviation school, Yao Hsiung, and his special commissioner for foreign affairs, Ch'en Te-li, to Moscow asking for Soviet assistance against his opponents.

The Soviet Red Army responded by attacking I-li, and T'a-ch'eng. Faced with certain defeat, Chang committed suicide. Ma Chung-ying, however, was not so easily quelled. Reportedly, it was not until Soviet aircraft attack and Soviet use of poison gas that Ma's troops were routed. He fled with the remnants of his army to Kashgar. In a curious turn of events that points strongly to the Soviet's intrigues to better itself in all sectors of Hsin-chiang, Ma Chung-ying now deserted Hsin-chiang for refuge in Moscow. Urumchi and Dzungaria thus returned to Sheng Shih-ts'ai's Soviet-bolstered control. Revolts and the power struggle based on Kashgar and Khotan continued in south Hsin-chiang, but, with further Soviet aid, Sheng gained control over these rebels as well. In return for Soviet aid, Sheng increasingly oriented his social and political policies toward socialism. Under two treaties, in 1933 and 1938, the Soviet Union gave aid to Sheng in return for concessions which greatly extended Soviet influence in Hsin-chiang [45].

When during the Second World War Soviet fortunes in the German invasion of Russia seemed to falter, Sheng had second thoughts about his Soviet ties. He was persuaded then by Chinese Nationalist envoys to re-establish his subordination to the Chinese government in Chungking. Then, in 1944 when the German Army was suffering reverses in their Soviet campaigns and the Chinese Nationalists were faltering before Japanese drives, Sheng appeared again on the verge of switching his allegiances. He had loosened his control too far by then. The Nationalist government was able to shift him from his post as governor of Hsin-chiang to a politically innocuous post as Minister of Agriculture and Forestry at Chungking and to appoint Chu Shao-liang acting governor of the frontier province [46].

The final historical drama in Hsin-chiang marked the triumph of the Chinese Communists over this frontier province. Chu Shao-liang took over the post at Urumchi, but in two months was succeeded by Wu Chung-hsin. During Chu's tenure, the Soviet Union stimulated and supported a new revolt at I-li on 7 November 1944, establishing the abortive East Turkistan Republic. Both north and south Hsin-chiang were involved in the uprising. Rebel forces reached as far as the Urumchi region, but the arrival of five groups of Ch'ing-hai cavalry eased the situation [47].

Under Wu Chung-hsin and his successor, Kuo Chi-ch'iao,

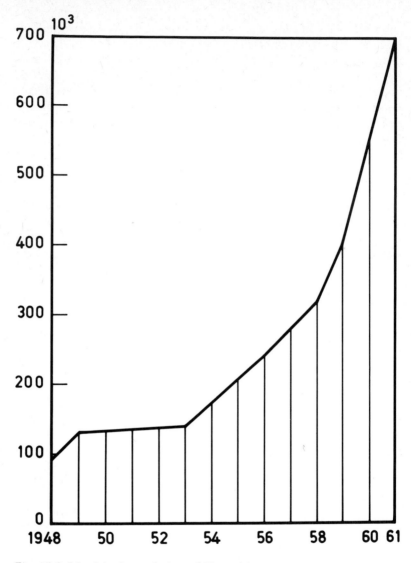

Fig. 15.2 Municipal population of Urumchi

the rebels were driven back. However, for fear of arousing greater Soviet intervention, the rebel strongholds at I-ning, T'a-ch'eng, and A-shan on the Soviet frontier were left alone. In 1945 Chang Chih-chung was sent to Urumchi to try to resolve the rebellion. An unhappy compromise from the

Chinese standpoint, was arranged on 2 January 1946, and a peace treaty was signed, supplemented by an 'Appendix II' on 6 June. Under this arrangement a so-called 'United Front Government' was formed for Hsin-chiang on 1 July at the urging of the Soviet Union. One of the I-li rebels, Ahomaiti-jang, became vice-governor under Chang Chih-chung. Saifudin, whom the Chinese Communists since have made vice-chairman of the Hsin-chiang Uighur Autonomous Region, was then made provincial vice-secretary [48].

At the beginning of 1949 Chang Chih-chung strongly urged the appointment of a pro-Tartar named Barhan to succeed the much-disliked Uighur Maiswudeh as governor of Hsin-chiang. According to Kuang Lu, this was done to placate Soviet Russia because of Soviet dislike of the pro-Uighur nationalism of Maiswudeh. That same year, when the Nationalist armies lost Lan-chou to Communist troops, Barhan and the pro-Soviet Chief of Defence T'ao Ch'i-yo (appointed in 1947) were among the first to welcome the entry of the Chinese Communist Party and Army to Hsin-chiang [49]. With their entry, a completely new phase of Urumchi's development began.

Population and character

Little is available to the present writer on the early population of Urumchi. Ch'en Pu-ch'ing [50] reported that in 1886 the city had some 23 000 inhabitants. He also gave the 1909 population as 23 097. Wang Chin-fu in 1935 listed an estimated population of 50 000 [51]. By 1948 the population is reported by Ch'en to have reached only 87 710. Thereafter, rapid expansion occurred (Fig. 15.2) as the Communist Chinese poured in political exiles and youthful 'volunteers' for the development of the northwest frontier region. The growth as described by Ch'en was as follows:

		Increase
1948	87 710	
1949	131 360	43 650
1951	135 064	3 699
1953	140 658	5 599
1955	207 519	66 861
1957	280 088	72 569
1958	320 000	39 912

In 1959 the population of the city had further expanded to 402 000 [52], an increase of 82 000 over 1958, and an amazing April 1961 report told of the municipal population enlargement to 700 000 [53]. If this, indeed, is true, there was an increase of the city population within less than a year and a half by some 298 000. However, the figures in part are deceptive, since considerable numbers of the population represent a mere paper increase from the political enlargement of the municipal bounds to enclose many pre-existing farm settlements that were outside the pre-1949 municipal boundaries (Fig. 15.1). Nevertheless, such a large municipality in a steppe and desert setting based upon a very restricted local agricultural base is possible only where food imports can be brought in to support the urban population. Its development to such major rank can only mean that the Communist Chinese government recognizes its site and situation as the most satisfactory for political and strategic control of its colonial region and for the economic and industrial exploitation of the promising resources of the great territory of Hsin-chiang.

The multinational character of Urumchi is shown in a 1956 report [54] which also indicated the predominantly Han—Chinese character of this Communist Chinese colonial centre in Hsin-chiang. At this time there were sixteen nationalities represented at Urumchi. Among these, Han—Chinese constituted 62 per cent, Uighurs 20 per cent, Hui (Tung-kan) 15 per cent, and the lesser nationalities 3 per cent.

At the end of September 1957, the Indian diplomat Menon [55] was told at Urumchi that 74 per cent of the city's 270 000 population then were Han—Chinese. If we take the 1956 population as half of the two-year increase from 1955–57, or 243 804, then 38 per cent of this, or 92 645 of the 1956 population, were of minority nationalities. If in 1957 some 74 per cent of the population were Han—Chinese, then the minorities numbered only 70 200 at this date, or a reduction from the year before of 22 445 in non-Han population. Menon wrote that when he was in Urumchi in 1944, he 'hardly saw a Chinese face in the bazaar; the few Chinese who were in Urumchi lived herded together in a separate quarter'.

It would seem from the above that after an initial increase in non-Han minority peoples at Urumchi, their percentage of the total municipal population decreased sharply, and there appears to have been an absolute reduction in minority peoples from 1956—57. If the percentage change continued subsequently, and this appears most likely, one may conclude that by 1960—61, the ethnic composition of Urumchi was over 90 per cent Han—Chinese.

To the eye of the traveller, Urumchi makes an impression that varies somewhat with the season. 'City of sinister repute', wrote Eric Teichman in 1935 [56], when Urumchi was a city of about 50 000 people, 'it looked a pleasant spot; grey city walls along a mountain stream, trees, cultivated fields and groves, surrounded by low hills and backed by the snows of the Celestial Mountains and the three majestic peaks of the sacred Bogdo Ula.' After the end of the Dzungarian summer, the pleasant aspect changes to the eye. Menon [57] wrote: 'On 27 September 1957 . . . I flew over the Heavenly Mountains [Tien Shan] from Alma Ata to Urumchi. It was like passing from paradise to purgatory. Alma Ata is a spot blessed by nature; there all was green and luxuriant. In Urumchi everything was bleak and bare; there were no trees, and even the river was devoid of water. The only sublime object was Bogdo Ula.'

Most travellers appear to agree with Mildred Cable [58] when she writes of pre-Second World War Urumchi as hot and smelly in summer, covered with alternate layers of snow and rubbish and garbage in winter, and in the transition seasons of spring and autumn having streets that became 'expanses of the vilest mud'. The rise in the level of the street in winter resulted from the practice of householders of throwing domestic rubbish out on to the street, since there was no adequate way to dispose of it otherwise during the long, cold winter. Until the snow melted, most people had to step down from the street level to reach their front door. The flat-roofed houses built of mud also had to be quickly swept of snow after each fall, since the neglect of this brought the percolation of snowmelt through every crevice and crack into the house interior in the obviously poorly constructed Urumchi houses.

The long, narrow triangle that comprised Urumchi prior to

1949 was about 21 km (13 miles) from north to south, with a maximum width in the north of 6 km (3.6 miles), but narrowing upslope to a few hundred metres in the south [59]. From north to south, Urumchi comprised three adjoining towns, beginning with the main walled Chinese city. Then came the walled Muslim city, followed by a bazaar section called Nan-kuan. In the northern walled Chinese city, one could in many sections imagine easily that one were in any north China city. The Muslim city was almost entirely inhabited by Tung-kan. Teichman [60] found Nan-kuan, commonly known as the 'Foreigners' Quarters', resembling a small Siberian town, with Russian houses and shops and the Soviet Consulate. He thought both Chinese and Muslim cities rather small, whereas the Russian settlement area was a narrow strip a mile or two long. Cable [61] described this strip as a congested section around the shops of which crowded all the central Asian ethnic types of people, 'but the middle of the road is thronged by heavy freight carts from central China, light vehicles from the town cart-ranks, long strings of camels, numberless men on horseback, and bullocks ridden by Kazakhs'. Even the Soviet government had a department store in Nan-kuan, stocked with Soviet manufactures and, according to Cable, served by wives of Soviet consular officials. However, the best houses in Nan-kuan then were occupied by Russian emigrés who hated the Soviet regime.

Across the Urumchi River which ran over a wide bed of many interlacing channels, a narrow strip on the west bank also formed part of the city. In the north part of the west bank was a public park in 1935, with an ornate pavilion, pleasure grounds, and a zoo containing specimens of T'ien Shan fauna (including bear, wild ass, wapiti, deer, wolves, and foxes) [62]. In all, the whole pre-Communist municipality covered about 75 sq km (29 sq miles) of surface [63].

Reported development of the municipality since 1950

Although the glowing self-praise of the Communist regime for its achievements in Hsin-chiang must be read with some grains of scepticism, there appears to be little doubt that important and far-reaching changes have been made in this burgeoning metropolis, both in physical and industrial aspects. Figure 15.1 shows the 1958 municipal area, which, according to Ch'en Pu-ch'ing, had been enlarged to 587 sq km (266 sq miles) to accommodate the influx of people and industrial plants, governmental, educational, and other buildings. The municipal district boundaries in 1958 reached to the foot of the Bogdo Ula in the east and to the T'ou-t'un River in the west, where it borders Ch'ang-chi district and the coal-mines of the western hills. In the south it reached Ulabai and in the north Hsiao-ti-wo and Ssu-kung villages, including large areas of pre-existing agricultural land and villages.

One of the first important developments was the water supply system, which involved work on the middle sections of the Urumchi River near the city suburbs. A large network of piped running water led through the municipality. To this was added in 1959 some 11 km (6.7 miles) of public water mains and 36 km (22.3 miles) of distributary pipelines [64].

The old and dilapidated city wall had been completely demolished and removed by 1955. At the site of the old South Gate a park now stands, with a new theatre accommodating 1 200 spectators at the 'front' of the park. More than ten of the large streets of the city have been paved with asphalt (presumably from the new Karamai oilfield). White willows have been planted on both sides of the streets, and municipal bus transportation has been provided. Along a 10-km (6-mile) stretch of road running from the residential section of Nan-liang to Ming-yüan (Ming Park) in the western sector of the city there is a succession of newly built office buildings, schools, theatres, movie houses, and hospital buildings. The hospital in 1956 was reported as being expanded to contain 6 000 beds [65].

Included among the multistoried buildings are those of the Hsin-chiang Petroleum Company, the Hsin-chiang Coloured Metals Company, the Military Hospital, the Institute of Languages, the School of Mineralogy, and the Hsin-chiang Medical College. The latter is a branch of Hsin-chiang University, enlarged from the amalgamation of Hsin-chiang College which in 1956 had an enrolment of 1 200 students, with new departments [66]. Another Communist Chinese report asserted that in addition to Hsin-chiang University, there were eleven other 'institutions of higher education'. These were not defined, but most probably are technical institutes for mining, engineering, and other applied sciences [67].

Aside from the above types of buildings, there were reportedly about 800 shops and industrial plants, including various types of small mills as well as the larger factories and repair shops. Thirty-five per cent of the entire built-up area of the city was said to have been added between 1951 and 1954, and large areas have been built up since 1954, so that the western suburbs of the city have been transformed from arid wastelands to urban residential, administrative, and industrial land use areas [68]. Of presentday Urumchi, the Communist Chinese author Shih Man writes glowingly: 'There were two different Urumchi before and after liberation: one was impoverished and the other rich; one was dirty, and the other is beautiful.' This, of course, overlooks much that still is dirty. Even pro-Communist Basil Davidson, after a rare conducted tour of this central Asian sector of China seldom seen by Western visitors, concluded that Urumchi remained

> a melancholy place. Its colours help towards that: they are gravel grey and the brown of hot dust, the buff of mud walls, the pink and primrose splash of new buildings here and there: small faded colours for the most part as though the place had not as yet quite succeeded in believing in its new respectability. Perhaps it is simply that in 1956 one could all too easily imagine from its surviving squalor what the miseries of the past must have been [69].

Agricultural base and development

In the desert heart of Chinese central Asia, the productive agricultural base of a city is very localized and restricted and dependent upon irrigation. Within approximately 65 km (40 miles) of the centre of Urumchi there are seven oasis patches, the largest of which is around Fu-k'ang district town, and the second largest stretching north from the northern suburbs of Urumchi City. The oasis patches include settlement areas as well as cultivated areas and the generalized boundaries indicate the 'limits of cultivation' [70]. The exact acreage cultivated, thus, cannot be computed from these patches of oases. They provide only an indication of the order of size of the cultivated area. The total of the seven patches amounts to about 107 000 ha (265 000 acres). The oasis patch immediately north of Urumchi City covers about 22 825 ha (56 400 acres), and the T'ou-t'un river oasis to its west has about 11 575 ha (28 600 acres). These two patches formerly outside Urumchi's municipal area were included within the municipal boundary in 1959. In 1944 the irrigation canals in Ti-hua Hsien (Urumchi district) were reported to number 193, with a total length of 4 418 km (2 744 miles) [71].

With the above figures in mind, one is puzzled by the Communist Chinese assertion that prior to 1949 (pre-Communist era), the area under irrigated agriculture at Urumchi (and any cultivation requires irrigation here) was only about 3 959 ha (9 800 acres). The report goes on to assert that, after great efforts and achievements in reconstructing the canal system and constructing new canals, the area of irrigated land at Urumchi was expanded by 1958 to some 43 107 ha (106 700 acres), or over ten times the pre-Communist area of irrigated land.

Without doubting that much renovation and new construction have been done to improve and enlarge irrigated agriculture in the Urumchi region, one still must suspect a distortion of the truth. The report does not define the boundaries of the compared pre-Communist and post-Communist municipal or district areas. If municipal boundaries are used in the comparison, then it is true that the pre-1949 municipal area included very little irrigated land as shown in Fig. 15.1. On the other hand, the 1958 municipal bounds had been much enlarged to include pre-existing oasis land in the two patches immediately north and northwest of pre-1949 Urumchi. Together these two patches comprised an area of over 34 144 ha (85 360 acres), much of which presumably was cultivated land prior to 1949. Thus, merely the enlarging of the municipal boundaries apparently would have enlarged the statistical figure of irrigated land 'at Urumchi' in 1958 by several tens of thousands of acres. The true post-Communist-control achievements at Urumchi may well be much padded.

If Urumchi Hsien (district) rather than Urumchi Municipal

areas are the ones used in the comparison, at least the two small oasis patches in the upper Urumchi River drainage must be added to the 34 144 ha (85 360 acres) to form a total of some 46 864 ha (116 000 acres), of which a large part was probably cultivated prior to 1949.

Although one must treat the Communist Chinese claims with great reservation, one can still accept the probability that significant additions and improvements in irrigated land at the Urumchi oases have been made since 1949. It has long been known that the available volume of runoff from snow and glacial melt in Hsin-chiang could support a much-enlarged agricultural base. Political instability led to neglect of irrigation systems, and the established system of water-use rights prevented much change and improvement. According to a New China News Agency report [72], some 70 per cent of the estimated 420 million cu metres (14 831 million cu ft) of annual flow of the Urumchi River was lost through seepage. Moreover, because there were no significant storage reservoirs to preserve the summer snowmelt runoff, the potential agricultural land could not be put to production.

Work in improving river control at Urumchi was started in the winter of 1950 following the Communist takeover in Hsin-chiang. Since labour was mostly available in the vicinity of the city, work was first started on the middle reaches of the river and on improving existing facilities for irrigation. The river channel was straightened, and a new bed 60 km (37 miles) long was lined with concrete and pebbles to check the seepage loss. In the lower reaches of the river plain, where artesian water could be brought to the surface, eight small- and medium-sized reservoirs were built. Each year between 1954 and 1957 a definite area of land was selected for improvement and irrigation. By the end of March 1962 there had been built thirteen small- and medium-sized reservoirs with a storage capacity totalling 200 million cu metres (7 062 million cu ft) almost half the annual runoff of the Urumchi River [73].

After 1958 a great effort put into the upper reaches of the river, plus the over 1 100 branch and subsidiary canals and ditches, reportedly resulted in the enlargement of the irrigated acreage 'at Urumchi' to some 43 000 ha (106 680 acres) [74].

Among the important reservoirs were the Ulabai Reservoir, south of the city, which existed as a small storage pond earlier and was greatly enlarged after 1955. Leading the water through the southern part of the city is the so-called Youth Canal, which was built in 131 days by some 30 000 young boys and girls including children as young as fourteen years of age, working under hazardous and cruel conditions, at times when air temperatures were reported as low as −40°C (−40°F). The original estimate of cost was 2.2 million yuan, but by squeezing free labour from the 'volunteer' students, the cost only came to a reported 0.75 million yuan. A total of 800 000 man-days of labour on this canal involved the handling of some 500 000 cu metres (17 657 000 cu ft) of earth [75].

Two other significant reservoirs were the 'August First' and the Meng-chin reservoirs whose waters were attributed with the responsibility for the increase in crop production of 21 per cent between 1960 and 1961 [76]. At the end of 1962 a 20-km (12-mile) stretch of the bed of the San-t'un River flowing past the west side of Ch'ang-chi city northwest of Urumchi was concrete lined, and a network of connecting branch canals was being added. Having an annual flow of 310 million cu metres (10 947 million cu ft), this river adds significantly to the local agricultural production for feeding the population of Urumchi. Prior to this project, an estimated two-thirds of this water had been lost in seepage [77].

According to Communist Chinese reports, the total area of agriculture in the Urumchi oases comprised some 42 900 ha (106 000 acres). This, if divided by the reported 700 000 people of Urumchi Municipality, amounts to about one-seventh of an acre per capita. Low-standard subsistence agriculture in north China in the past required about 0.2 ha (0.5 acre) per capita or in central China about 0.16 ha (0.4 acre). Chang Chih-yi indicated that at Khotan a 'middle' status peasant farm contained an average of 2.3 ha (5.7 acres). According to the deputy-director for the Hsin-chiang Department of Agriculture in 1956, the pre-Communist 'middle peasant' had a farm averaging in size from 8–19 *mow* [78]. If a median be taken, this farm size would be 13 *mow*, or a little over 0.8 ha (2 acres). Presuming that the average Hsin-chiang family size is four, the per capita cultivated land on a subsistence basis would be 0.2 ha (0.5 acre), and if the family size be taken as five, the per capita requirement would be 0.16 ha (0.4 acre) in Hsin-chiang.

Now, assuming the 0.16 ha (0.4 acre) per capita as a minimum, the agricultural land in the Urumchi oases can support at most a population of about 262 500 people. It would appear, therefore, that about two-thirds of the Urumchi municipal population must be supplied with food from outside their oases, and only one-third can be supplied from local resources. (If Chang Chih-yi's figure is accepted as indicating the farm size for median peasants, then per capita land requirements in Hsin-chiang would be about 0.4 ha (1 acre).) In any event, the importance of good supply lines to transport food to this large urban population is highly essential and can brook no interruption for any considerable length of time. Interruption would mean drastic food shortage in a very short time [79].

Industrial resource base

Urumchi has become the greatest industrial production centre of Hsin-chiang. The choice of this centre for large-scale industrial development is not only because of its other strategic aspects and because of the large proportion of immigrant Han—Chinese, but also because of favourable resource location in the immediate vicinity (Fig. 15.3). The amount of coal reserves in Hsin-chiang are reported to be second only to that of Shansi among China's provinces [80]. A 547-km (340-mile) stretch of the northern slopes of the T'ien Shan from Wu-su (Usu) in the west to Chi-t'ai in the east forms one of the largest coalfields in Hsin-chiang and is said to have economic reserves of 32.4 billion tons, mostly of high quality bituminous coal, but including forty-five deposits of anthracite as well. Much of Urumchi's present construction overlies coal strata, and Urumchi's coalfield covers an area of 118 sq km (46 sq miles) [81].

Coal is exploited at Liu-tao-wan, Ch'i-tao-wan, Pa-tao-wan, and Wei-kuo towns of the Urumchi oases. The Liu-tao-wan field extends over 96 km (60 miles) in more than thirty

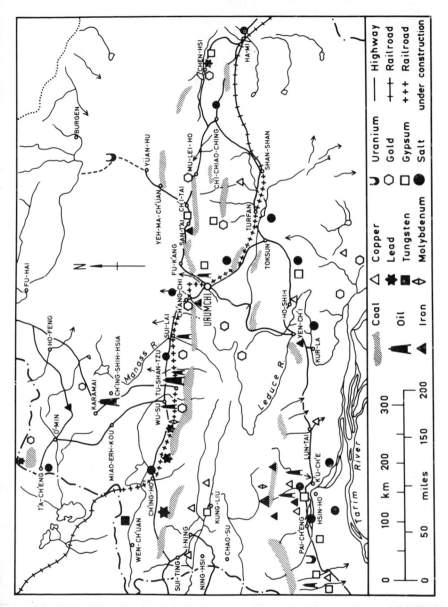

Fig. 15.3 T'ien Shan communications and minerals

layers, the thickest of which is reported to measure 40 metres (130 ft), constituting one of the largest coalfields in China. Coal is so near the surface, that it is being mined by the open-pit method [82].

In another form of fuel, it is asserted that 1.5 billion tons of Hsin-chiang's estimated 4.5 billion tons of oil shale, equivalent to 75 million tons of liquid fuel oil, are situated at Ya-ma-shan near Urumchi. These are supposed to have thicknesses of several hundred feet and are close enough to the surface to permit open-cut extraction methods [83]. The Ya-ma-shan field is described as also 96 km (60 miles) long and from 5–11 km (3–7 miles) wide. It is situated in the southern part of the coalfield and on the slopes of the Bogdo Ula, stretching from the Yao-mo (Demon) Mountains and Hung-yen Ch'ih (Red Salt Pond) (Fig. 15.1) in the municipality eastward to the gulch west of the waters of the Chimsar [84].

Among the metallic minerals are important iron ore deposits. Hsin-chiang has long been known for its large iron ore resources waiting to be exploited. Hematite deposits near Urumchi are reported to contain more than 50 per cent iron content [85]. Three iron ore mines are being exploited in the Urumchi area: the Mo-t'o-sha-la iron mines, the Hsi-kou iron mines, and the Cha-kan-sha-la (Jagan-shala) mines. They supply the ore for the moderate-size 'August First Steel Plant' in the northern part of the city [86].

Among the other minerals reported at Urumchi are the limestone within the municipality and the gypsum of the Pai-yang (white willow) River southeast of Ta-pan-ch'eng at the southern end of the Chai-wo-pao corridor and northwest of Turfan. At Ta-pan-ch'eng itself there are salt deposits [87]. Finally, local deposits of green and blue jade rocks offer materials for jade-working artisans and craftsmen [88].

Power for the developing industries of Urumchi is furnished by both thermal and hydroelectric power plants. At the end of 1953 the Wei-hu-liang thermoelectric power plant was constructed for the Chinese Communists by Soviet technicians [89]. At Ulabai south of the city is the only significant hydroelectric power plant in Hsin-chiang up to 1962 (so far as the writer is aware). This had a generating capacity of only some 20 000 kW [90]. At the end of 1959 it was reported that a new large thermal power plant was being added at Ulabai [91], but figures on the generating capacity are unknown to the present writer.

Little information on the nature of the industries at Urumchi is available. The steel plant is described as 'small' and of 'only local significance' by the Soviet writer Ovdiyenko [92], and Yen Kuan-yi writes of it as manufacturing modern farm machinery on a modest scale. These include mowing machines, a ten-row seed-drill, double-wheel ploughs, and cotton-cultivating machinery. The 'October Motor Repair Plant' probably is merely a glorified garage that uses a factory system for rebuilding old motor vehicles. Chemicals and 'construction materials' are among other heavy industries. The 'construction materials' very likely is mainly cement. Machinery plants manufacture machine frames, mining machinery, hauling equipment, and ball bearings, among other things. After the construction of the station for the approaching railroad, plans were under way for the construction of railroad cars and locomotives [93]. Probably the largest single industry in Urumchi is the cotton textile industry, using cotton from Dzungaria and the Tarim basin as well as from local production in the Urumchi oases. The so-called 'July First Cotton Mill' has modern machinery partly imported and partly manufactured in eastern China. It was to have over 30 000 reels and 1 000 looms when the first phase of construction was completed [94]. Other light industries at Urumchi include leather processing and manufacturing, foodstuffs, and soap.

Ch'en Pu-ch'ing has provided some data showing the increase in the number of industrial labourers and in the increase in value of Urumchi manufactures [95]. In the stagnant economic era of political turmoil before the end of the Second World War, six old plants of a 'semi-handicraft character' had a total of 895 labourers at Urumchi. By 1958 the number of industrial labourers had increased 46.9 times. On the basis of the 895 figure for the pre-Communist period industrial labourers, this would mean that in 1958 the 'civilian' industrial labour force at Urumchi was some 41 900.

The increase in the value of manufactures is reported on a comparative basis, using an index of 100 for the base year 1949 when the civil war had brought production to a state of collapse. Ch'en's tabulation shows the following rise in indices:

1952	2 337.5
1955	12 179.8
1957	19 918.5
1958	28 128.5

On 19 August 1961 a report from Urumchi stated that the industrial output value had increased to 460 times that before Communist control [96]. The index for 1960 thus would appear to be 46 000 on the same base as the above.

That the above list gives only a partial picture of the industrial production is indicated in a note added by Ch'en saying that the figures did not include the production or the manpower of the plants and mines operated by the Military Construction Corps. Since these involve the large number of ex-Nationalist troops who surrendered in 1949 and who are a 'captive labour force', there is a major unknown factor in the Hsin-chiang industrial picture. It seems clear, in any event, that very rapid increases in production have accompanied the rise in the population of Urumchi municipality.

Communications and trade

In scrutinizing the situation of Urumchi as a communications centre in Hsin-chiang (Fig. 15.3) one must compare it with equally large or larger oasis centres along the various routes of trade to see what it has that the others do not have to like or greater degree. Kashgar, Yarkand, and Khotan, for instance, as well as other oases in the western half of the Tarim basin, have much larger cultivated and irrigated land areas. Since there are only two possible routes between the eastern and western ends of the Tarim basin, almost any major town along one of them shares in the 'control' of the route concerned. But it is only when one gets to the western limits of the basin that a single centre, Kashgar, has the ultimate control over the pass leading into the Fergana valley of Soviet central Asia, just as Yarkand, or perhaps more properly, Yeh-ch'eng to its south, controls the access to the Karakorum pass into India. Although of considerable importance in the past caravan trade, neither of these is a major trade route in the period of modern transportation. Their passes across the borders are too high and difficult. Neither one is in a position to control or intercept the internal trade of the province east of them.

To the north of the T'ien Shan the border gateways to the Soviet Union are via Sui-ting in the I-li Valley or via T'a-ch'eng some 240 km (150 miles) further north. For trans-border trade, Sui-ting has the added advantage of being on the main highway and planned railroad route. However, again, neither has a strategic position with respect to the internal communications routes of the Hsin-chiang territory. It is in this respect that Urumchi has superiority over all other centres. Both of the alternate routes north and south of the Eastern T'ien Shan which lead from Ha-mi and China proper to the Soviet frontier in the Dzungarian basin must run through Urumchi or its immediate vicinity. Urumchi also holds the 'throat' of the corridor between the Tarim and Dzungarian basins. Thus, no other communications centre in Hsin-chiang has such strategic advantages with respect both to domestic and transfrontier trade.

Urumchi is the hub of the Hsin-chiang motor highway network. Before the Communist Chinese conquest, Hsin-chiang had some 5 955 km (3 700 miles) of motor highways [97]. Owing to deterioration, the usable highway network in 1949 is asserted to have been only half this length. During the following decade of reconstruction and new construction, however, the total network reportedly was increased to almost 20 000 km (12 400 miles) [98]. Among the new stretches is the highway leading southward from Urumchi to Kurla, bypassing the hot Turfan basin and shortening the route to Kashgar by 200 km (120 miles) [99].

By 1955 truck transport was carrying most of the territory's freight along the highways, amounting to the movement of 5 295 266 tons [100]. Although figures for ton-km would have been more meaningful, much of the above tonnage probably was long-distance haul. This seems indicated by Davidson's report [101] that, while travelling between Turfan and Urumchi in 1956, he made a two-day count of truck traffic on the highway connecting the advancing railhead with Urumchi. He estimated that not less than 2 000 trucks crossed the desert weekly here (although he did not indicate whether this was movement in one or in both directions). It would appear also that the bulk of the freight transport went through Urumchi, part of it for the Karamai oilfields in the northwest beyond, and, undoubtedly, much of it for the construction work in Urumchi itself.

The 1955 highway freight transported was reported to be twenty-seven times what it was in 1950 [102]. Five years later, in 1960, the volume of freight was said to be about forty-eight times what it was in 1950 [103]. This would indicate that the tons of freight transported would have been around 9 413 000 tons, an increase according with the large increase in population and industrial needs of expanding Urumchi. Aside from the freight transport, there also is reported to be regular bus service linking 90 per cent of the district centres of the territory [104].

When the railroad finally reaches Urumchi (this apparently has been completed, since a 1962 Nationalist Chinese atlas shows it completed [105]) the pattern of truck transport undoubtedly will change, since much of the past transport has been from the end of the advancing rail line to Urumchi. Until further railroads are constructed as planned to connect the Tarim oases as far as Kashgar and Khotan with Urumchi, truck transport will distribute the industrial manufactures of Urumchi as well as of eastern China to the farflung reaches of Hsin-chiang. Both of these developments will enhance the position of Urumchi in its dominating role in the Hsin-chiang economy.

Data on Urumchi's trade with the Soviet Union or Mongolia are not known to the writer and only vague indications of its importance have been provided. According to Ch'en Pu-ch'ing, following the eradication of the capitalistic economy, the foreign trade of Urumchi has multiplied and been transformed. As of 1959, some fifty types of local products were involved in this trade with 'fraternal countries' (Soviet bloc). In exchange came imports of 'large amounts of industrial and agricultural products. Hence, it has become the country's great northwest trade portal. This trade has had a notable increase in the last few years. Thus, if 1952 be taken as having a trade index of 100, by 1958 this had increased by 4 185 per cent or forty-one times.' [106] No information, however, is available on the trade trends since the 'fraternal clash' with the Soviet Union began.

A final aspect of Urumchi's communications meriting mention is the air transport which had already had a small start during the period of Sheng Shih-ts'ai's governorship and during the Second World War. At the end of 1954 a 'Civil Aviation Company' was formed as a joint Soviet–Chinese company and was thus operated at least until the end of 1955, when it was still entirely adjusted to the Russian system. From Urumchi, twice-a-week flights made connections via I-li with Soviet Alma Ata, and, in the eastern direction, had links via Ha-mi, Chiu-ch'uan, and Lan-chou with Peking, on the one hand, and Hsi-an (Sian), on the other. There also was a run within the province from Urumchi via K'u-ch'e and Aksu to Kashgar [107]. In April 1961 it was reported that civil airlines then linked Urumchi 'not only with Peking, Shanghai and other major cities of China, but also with every important centre in the region'. Although no definition or list is made of the 'important centres', the statement appears to indicate a considerable extension of air transport over that existing in 1955.

Conclusion

The preceding account has shown Urumchi to be the centre of political storms for over 1 000 years between Chinese and central Asians, and the bastion for extending and maintaining imperial power over central Asia by the rulers of China. Its strategic situation straddling the T'ien Shan corridor, set in well-watered oases producing food and cotton, and sprawling over key mineral fuels, metals, and raw materials, provides some of the necessary requirements for a moderately large industrial and commercial base. The impending or completed connection by rail with China proper, on the one hand, and the Soviet rail net, on the other, also links it with two of China's chief petroleum-producing and refining centres, Lan-chou (and the Yü-men, Chiu-ch'uan field) in the east, and Tu-shan-tzu (and Karamai) in the west.

Finally, its selection as the chief focus of Communist Chinese immigration and industrial development in Hsin-chiang will add to its momentum as the spearhead of siniciza-tion and now of communization in China's great colonial realm in central Asia.

16 Problems of urbanization

Although China is generally considered to be a rural country, she is also a country of great cities. In 1960 there were about 120 million urban dwellers [1], a figure larger than the total population of either Japan or Indonesia. While an official urban census is lacking in mainland China, it is very likely that China has more cities with a population of 1 million or more than any other country except for the United States. According to various estimates, there were fifteen cities in China with a population over 1 million in 1958 [2]. By 1960, two rapidly growing industrial centres, Changchun and Lanchou, were added to the list of the million city [3]. In 1960, therefore, there were seventeen municipalities in China with a population over 1 million, as compared with twenty-four Standard Metropolitan Statistical Areas in the United States with a population of 1 million or more [4]. These seventeen cities contained about one-third of the total urban population in China. The remarkable increase in the number of million cities has been perhaps the most striking pheno-menon of urbanisation in mainland China in the last two decades (Figs. 16.1 and 16.2). This paper attempts to trace the origin and growth of the Chinese million city, to evaluate its role in the process of political, economic, and cultural transformation in mainland China, and to analyse the major problems associated with the rapid growth of the million city.

Historical development of the million city in China

With a highly centralized bureaucratic government of enormous size and numerous functions housed in the

302

imperial capital, it is very likely that China contained the first million city in the world. While ancient Rome registered only approximately 350 000 residents at its peak [5], the city of Changan at the beginning of the eighth century accommodated a population well over 1 million [6]. Recent archaeological excavation has shown that the walled city of Changan extended 9.5 km (5.92 miles) east and west and 8.5 km (5.27 miles) north and south [7], which is about four times as large as the walled city of Sian, the present city in this location. The remarkable size achieved by the city of Changan represented the zenith of Chinese cultural development. Since the ebb of the Tang dynasty, no imperial capital in China has ever reached the size of Changan.

The first million city in modern China was mainly created by international commerce and, to a certain extent was associated with industrialization. The city of Shanghai, originally a county seat opened as a treaty port in the 1840s, experienced a rate of urban growth unprecedented in history

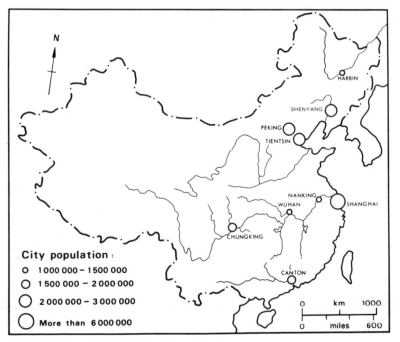

Fig. 16.1 The million city in China, 1953

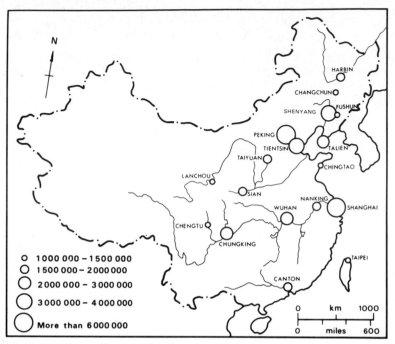

Fig. 16.2 The million city in China, 1960—66

by any other Chinese city. The city population of Shanghai reached half a million around 1895 and, with the establishment of modern factories in the following two decades, achieved the million mark [8]. Shanghai, with the whole Yangtse Valley as its hinterland, enjoyed the locational advantage of a primate city. For a period of two decades prior to 1930, Shanghai distinguished itself as the only million city in China.

The first half of the decade of 1930—40, which was a relatively peaceful period in China, saw significant growth of urban population in spite of the fact that the urban population in many Western countries had stagnated or even declined due to the effect of world economic depression. Five cities had reached the status of the million city either in the late 1920s or the early 1930s (Table 16.1). The city experiencing the most remarkable growth during this period was Nanking which became the seat of the Nationalist government in 1928. Being the new political and military headquarters of the nation, Nanking tripled its population in

Table 16.1 *Population of million cities of mainland China*

City	1922	1935	1946	1953	1958	After 1958
Shanghai	1 500 000	3 480 018	4 447 015	6 204 000	6 977 000	6 000 000 (1966)
Peking	850 000	1 564 869	1 672 438	2 768 000	4 148 000	6 800 000 (1959)
Tientsin	900 000	1 067 902	1 707 670	2 694 000	3 278 000	3 000 000 (1961)
Shenyang	250 000	526 879	1 120 918	2 300 000	2 423 000	3 200 000 (1965)
Chungking	252 000	281 272	1 002 787	1 772 000	2 165 000	1 970 000 (1959)
Wuhan	750 000	1 352 639	1 061 560	1 427 000	2 226 000	2 500 000 (1960)
Canton	829 500	1 156 786	1 413 460	1 599 000	1 867 000	1 994 000 (1966)
Talien	237 100	444 666	772 950	766 000	1 590 000	3 000 000 (1960 include Port Arthur)
Harbin	200 000	431 250	760 000	1 163 000	1 595 000	1 800 000 (1961)
Nanking	300 000	1 013 320	1 037 430	1 092 000	1 455 000	1 670 000 (1965)
Sian	250 000	154 541	520 988	787 000	1 368 000	1 500 000 (1965)
Chingtao	90 000	527 150	759 057	917 000	1 144 000	1 050 000 (1959)
Chengtu	500 000	480 821	620 302	857 000	1 135 000	1 030 000 (1959)
Taiyuan	80 000	139 458	251 566	721 000	1 053 000	1 500 000 (1961)
Fushun	(no data)	117 699	729 604	679 000	1 019 000	1 050 000 (1961)
Changchun	70 000	(no data)	605 279	855 000	988 000	1 000 000 (1959)
Lanchou	110 000	150 558	156 468	397 000	732 000	1 200 000 (1959)

a decade. Peking, almost at the same time, also became a million city. The removal of the national capital from Peking in 1928 had hardly any effect on the size of the city's population, as the rank-and-file of the old regime still remained with their properties and associates in the old capital. In the meantime, the takeover of Manchuria by the Japanese in 1931 had made Peking a shelter for thousands of Chinese refugees. Besides Peking and Nanking the other three new million cities in the 1930s were all regional centres which had been opened as treaty ports at earlier dates. Located at the nodal points of major regions, the three centres had identical functions of collection and distribution for their vast hinterlands. Tientsin was to the North China Plain what Wuhan was to central China, and Canton to south China. The population of these three cities reached the million mark almost simultaneously. (Table 16.1)

The process of urbanization in the decade following 1936 was somewhat hampered by the prolonged Sino—Japanese war. Some cities, such as Nanking, experienced a retardation of growth; others, such as Wuhan, even suffered a drastic decline of population. However, positive urban development was taking place on both sides of the war zone: the great interior of western China as a strong base against Japanese invasion, and Manchuria as a new industrial region under Japanese control. It is little wonder, therefore, that the two 'million' cities newly emerged during this period should be the wartime national capital of Chungking and the largest industrial city of Shenyang in Manchuria. The latter doubled its population in eleven years from 1935—46 and the former increased its population more than three times.

The period from 1946—53 witnessed both devastating military destruction and drastic political reorganization. The sizeable population increase in several major cities was merely a result of the influx of thousands of refugees from rural areas in the midst of civil disorder as well as the initial stages of collectivization. Only the city of Harbin, however, advanced to become a million city during this period. Its rapid growth may partly be attributed to the fact that the city did not suffer the severe military struggle between the nationalists and the Communists which spread over wide areas in southern Manchuria in 1946 and 1947. The city was controlled by the Communists as early as the spring of 1946. Thus as a trade and industrial centre of northern Manchuria Harbin appeared to have grown at a faster rate than many other Chinese cities during that particular period.

China's urbanization since 1950

There has been a rapid rate of urbanization in mainland China during the decade of 1950–60 [9]. For the period of 1949–60, the urban population grew at an annual average rate of 7.6 per cent [10], more than three times the rate of population growth for China as a whole. This enormous growth has been attributed to the higher rate of natural growth of urban population compared with that of rural population, and to migration from rural areas. The natural growth rate of urban population during 1953–57 was estimated at more than 4 per cent, or twice that of the national average [11]. The urban death rate has been lower than rural areas due to relatively adequate hospital facilities, medical personnel, supplies of medicines, and better sanitation in the cities. Furthermore, the urban birthrate may be higher than the rural rate due to the fact that the overwhelming majority of the new immigrants to the cities have been young men and women who comprised the most fertile age group of the population.

Migration from countryside to town also contributed significantly to rapid urban growth. During the First Five-Year Plan period from 1953–57 the influx of rural population to the cities numbered more than 8 million [12] and accounted for nearly one-half the total population growth in the cities. The peasants were not only pulled by the demand for labour in the cities and by the attractiveness of industrial employment, but also were pushed by the violence of collectivization and natural calamities in the countryside. Judging from the widespread phenomenon of urban unemployment the 'push' effect may have exceeded the 'pull' effect in the formation of the urban population during the decade of 1950–60. The most impressive growth of urban population has occurred in the largest cities. The number of million cities increased from nine to fifteen during the period of 1953–58 (Figs. 16.1 and 16.2), whilst the number of the cities with a population between 500 000 and 1 million gained only from fifteen to eighteen, and the number of cities with a population between 100 000 and 500 000 from seventy-seven to eighty-one [13]. The rapid increase of population in the million cities reflected both the superior locational advantages of these cities and the ideology of a centrally planned national economy [14].

Reasons for the formation of the million city

One factor partly responsible for the concentrated development of a few selected cities was the well-planned growth of provincial capitals and the capitals of autonomous regions. Traditionally, the administrative centres at the provincial level, being the cultural and economic as well as the political headquarters of each province, were usually the most populous urban centres of the province; and the tradition has been well maintained in the People's Republic of China. The majority of the provincial capitals today have been administrative centres of regional importance for some 2 000 years or so. The concept of province or region in China is traceable to the feudal period of the late Chou dynasty around 700—500 BC. The domain of a feudal kingdom often occupied a fertile river valley and, by and large, coincided partly or wholly with what is the province today. The headquarters of the feudal lord often took the site of the most productive and most strategically important point of the valley such as the confluent point of a tributary and the main river. After the feudal period terminated around 220 BC, the capitals of the feudal kingdoms became administrative centres of prefectures or provinces in the later dynasties. Through more than 2 000 years of regional development as well as boundary adjustments, provinces in China have gradually evolved into largely capital-oriented nodal regions. Comparing a map of China's administrative divisions with a map of China's landforms, one will find that most of the provincial boundaries of China are strikingly identical with the most difficult terrain. Perhaps partly due to poor communication facilities between provinces and partly due to the ancient heritage of regional tradition, each province has gradually developed within the common framework of Chinese culture a distinguished regional culture which may have been manifested in such elements as dialect, cuisine, handicraft, etc. [15]. The perfection and standards of these cultural elements were often found in the capital cities. Since the new regime stressed the important role of large cities in the social and economic transformation of the vast rural areas, the priority developing provincial capitals is not at all surprising.

The cultural importance of provincial capitals in mainland China has been greatly enhanced with the concentration of higher educational institutes in these cities. Table 16.2 shows the distribution of universities and colleges in major cities. Among the 220 universities and colleges in mainland China in 1961, 164 were located in the two independent municipalities and twenty-three provincial capitals, accounting for nearly 75 per cent of the total. Thus, the numbers of students and teaching staffs must have contributed greatly to the rapid growth of these urban centres.

As the provincial capital performed numerous functions, its population size was often several times larger than that of the second largest city in the province. Virtually all the capital cities have been the primate cities in each province. According to the population estimates in 1958, the exception to this generalization occurs only in the Inner Mongolian Autonomous Region, Shantung, and Szechwan. In Inner Mongolia the steel centre of Paotou was larger than the capital city of Huhohaote. The primacy of the capital city in each province is measured in Table 16.3.

Since 1958 a few provincial capitals in the interior have grown even faster. For instance, Lanchou's population had increased from 732 000 in 1958 to 1 200 000 in 1959; Urumchi's population from 320 000 in 1958 to 700 000 in 1961 [16]. It is very possible, therefore, that the primacy of a number of provincial capitals has further increased in recent years. It is not surprising that in 1960 out of seventeen 'million' cities in mainland China eleven were provincial capitals. In view of the fact that many medium size provincial capitals, such as Kunming, Hangchou, Changsha, and Chengchou, had already recorded their estimated population between 700 000 and 1 million in 1958 [17], it is likely that, if there is any increase in the number of million cities in the next few decades, it must include several provincial capitals.

Table 16.2 *Chinese cities with three or more universities or colleges, 1961*

City	No. of universities or colleges	Independent municipality or provincial capital	Million city
Peking	28	X	X
Wuhan	13	X	X
Shanghai	11	X	X
Sian	11	X	X
Nanking	10	X	X
Harbin	9	X	X
Canton	8	X	X
Chengtu	8	X	X
Shenyang	7	X	X
Taiyuan	7	X	X
Paoting	7		
Changchun	6	X	X
Changsha	6	X	
Chinan	6		
Chungking	5	X	X
Tientsin	5	X	X
Chingtao	5	X	X
Talien	5		X
Kunming	5	X	
Huhohaote	4	X	
Hangchou	4	X	
Lanchou	3	X	X
Urumchi	3	X	
Hofei	3	X	
Fuchou	3	X	
Kueiyang	3	X	
Kaifeng	3		

Source: Chi Wang, *Mainland China Organisations of Higher Learning in Science and Technology and their Publications*, Library of Congress, 1961, pp. 11–33.

The traditional provincial capitals were so well situated geographically and their positions in relation to transportation routes were so strategically important that they still hold high nodality in their own provinces even today. New technology and modern transportation seem to have altered very

Table 16.3 *Ratio of population of the capital city to population of the second largest city in each province, 1958*

Ratio	1—1.5	1.5—2	2—2.5	2.5—5	5—10	10+ over
Number of provinces	4	4	4	7	2	2

Statistical source: Morris B. Ullman, *Cities of Mainland China, 1953 and 1958* (see note 2, p. 470).
Data for Tibet and Ninghsia Hui autonomous regions are not available. Peking and Shanghai are not taken into account as they are independent municipalities under the direct jurisdiction of the central government.

little the pattern of regional centres. The feverish railroad construction during the last two decades certainly created new important industrial communities but, what is even more significant, it greatly enhanced the centrality of the older provincial capitals. As traditional China relied mainly on waterways for transportation, provincial capitals were often situated at the hub of several rivers. The 100 years of railroad construction, in a spatial sense, resulted largely in a network connecting treaty ports with provincial capitals, or provincial capitals with other provincial capitals (Fig. 16.3). The completion of these railroads, especially during the last twenty years, has greatly strengthened the position of these capital cities as interregional trade centres. Upon the completion of the First Five-Year Plan, railroads have largely replaced waterways as the most important means of cargo transportation. In 1966, out of 600 million tons of commodity which had been moved in China, 400 million tons were moved by railroad [18]. Those cities located at the junction of rail lines have gained population very steadily. At the present time all of the seventeen 'million' cities are connected by at least one rail line; fourteen of them by two or more lines; and five of them by four or more lines. Undoubtedly, railroad building has become the most important single factor in creating the million city.

One of the salient features in the Chinese industrialization programme which contributed to the further growth of large cities has been the high concentration of new factories and

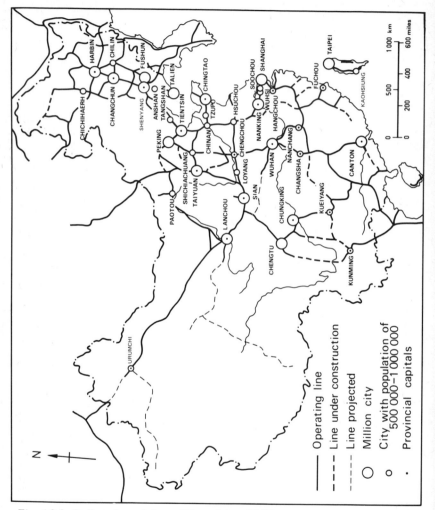

Fig. 16.3 Railroads and the million cities, 1966

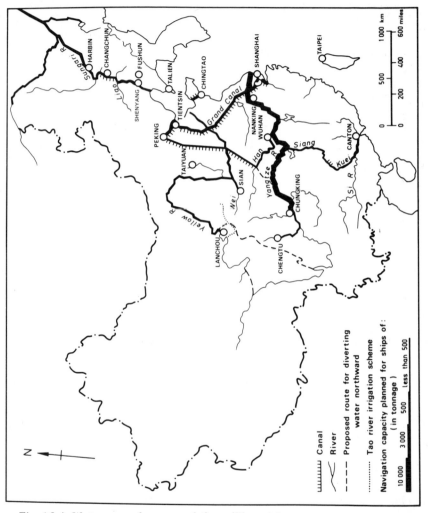

Fig. 16.4 Waterway schemes and the million cities

other establishments in a small number of cities. Virtually all the new construction projects for industry in the First Five-Year Plan were distributed in some 120 cities and a majority of the above-norm (large) projects were clustered in eighteen cities, most of which were the largest cities in the country [19].

Since 1958 the concentration of industrial construction in a small number of cities may have been intensified with the formation of the so-called 'economic cooperative regions' and the selection of the key industrial centres for each region. The idea of economic cooperative regions was initiated by the Central Committee of the Communist Party and was more or less patterned after the system of economic regions in the Soviet Union. The purpose was to develop national industry with seven regional divisions and to establish an integrated industrial system in each region [20]. These regions were delimited with a view to supplying them with an adequate raw material base for industry and allowing them at least one or more economic centres that could serve as levers for further industrial development of the region as a whole. Each region was expected, according to the committee, to develop a modern industry corresponding to the regional population and natural resources and including all basic sectors with a specialization insuring a rational division of labour among regions. Each region must have its own iron and steel industry. The location of the iron and steel centre was supposed to be carefully considered, as the distribution of nearly all other sectors of industry depends on it. The establishment of large steel centres, surrounded by a complex of enterprises of heavy and light industry, was planned to be the prerequisite for the development of the entire regional economy. A few of the key iron and steel centres were located in newly developed cities of medium size such as Anshan for northeast and Paotou for north China. However, many more iron and steel centres have been deliberately located in the largest metropolises in the nation, such as Shanghai for east China, Wuhan for central China, Canton for south China, Chungking for southwest China, and Tientsin, Taiyuan, and Peking for north China [21] — all million cities. The diversified industrial activities in these cities, with the iron and steel plant as the backbone of the economy, have been developed with a sort of linkage or snowball effect.

Another reason for the increase of urban population was the expansion of city boundaries, resulting often in the annexation of adjacent districts and counties, and including a significant population engaged in agricultural activities. The phenomenal growth of Peking's population from 4 148 000 in 1958 to more than 6 million in 1959 was accompanied by inclusion of nine counties in the surrounding areas to form the so-called 'far suburbs' of the city [22]. Shanghai, the other independent municipality in China, annexed ten counties in the Yangtse delta in 1958 [23]. The expansion of large municipal boundaries was aimed at strengthening the coordination of the industrial and agricultural enterprises in the city. It was to make the urban population self-sufficient by supplying them with the secondary foods such as vegetables and fruits. It was also to supply the urban centre with sufficient local construction materials. The reasons for areal expansion of each city may have been varied. The northward expansion of the municipality of Peking to include large hilly areas north of the Great Wall in 1958 had been intended, at least partially, to include several large reservoirs within the municipality for supplying water to the city [24]. The southward expansion of the city of Chungking to the border of Kueichou province in 1959 was purposely designed to include the largest coal-mine in the southwest, the Nantung mine, within the city [25]. In 1958, 'in order to form a comprehensive production area for the industrial city of Harbin', four counties were incorporated into the jurisdiction of the city [26]. The expansion of the city boundary in different localities has had a profound impact on the rural land use pattern of the incorporated counties. After the ten counties were annexed to the city of Shanghai, for example, these 'far-suburb' areas began to increase vegetable acreage at the expense of grain crops. The business of raising chickens, ducks, and hogs also began to flourish in order to make the city of Shanghai self-sufficient in producing secondary food supplies [27]. The annexation of nearby counties into large cities facilitates better coordination between industrial workers and farmers, a policy aimed to maximize the utilization of the labour force and to diffuse agricultural innovations to the rural areas.

315

The nature of the million city in China

The seventeen 'million' cities in China represent an historical profile of Chinese urbanization. Based on their diversified origin, development, and functions, these cities can be grouped into a few simple categories. Four of the seventeen cities, Peking, Nanking, Chungking and Sian, are either the present national capital or the former imperial capitals of China. Nine are provincial capitals of the present day: Shenyang, Wuhan, Canton, Harbin, Nanking, Sian, Taiyuan, Changchun, and Lanchou. Five have been treaty ports opened in the nineteenth century: Shanghai, Tientsin, Chungking, Wuhan and Canton. Two have been leased territories of foreign countries near the end of the nineteenth century: Talien and Chingtao. Four have been developed for a certain period under the influence of capital and technology supplied by the Russians or the Japanese: Shenyang, Harbin, Fushun, and Changchun. All of the seventeen cities are important industrial centres in the nation.

Among the four national capital cities Sian was the imperial capital for the longest period. It became the site of the Chou dynasty as early as 1100 BC and served, on and off, as the imperial capital for eleven dynasties, for a total period of more than 900 years. The last time when the city of Changan was the capital of China can be traced as far back as the Tang dynasty, more than a millennium ago. Thus, the ancient glory of Changan has little to do with the present population size of Sian. The other three capital cities, Peking, Nanking, and Chungking, have been the national capital relatively recently; as such, their administrative function has contributed importantly to the present size of these cities. Nanking became the site of a ruling house as early as the third century but its status as an imperial capital has been maintained only sporadically through history. It became the headquarters of the nationalist government from 1928—49 with a short interruption of eight years after 1937 when Chungking became the wartime capital. Both of the cities of Nanking and Chungking gained their more than a million population in the period when they were the capital cities respectively. Peking has been the seat of the ruling houses almost continuously since the twelfth century, and also the most important cultural centre in modern Chinese history.

Like the four national capitals, most of the nine provincial capitals discussed here are also cities of antiquity. Except for the three provincial capitals in Manchuria, all the capital cities trace their origins as walled towns to the third century AD or earlier, and many have continuously functioned as regional administrative centres, retaining their position of unchallenged supremacy to the present day. Shenyang started as a prefectural seat in the eighth century and became a strategic administrative centre of the Manchu people in 1621 when the first ruler of the Manchu dynasty moved his capital from Liaoyang to the city [28]. Upon his subsequent occupation of China, the Manchu ruler moved the capital to Peking, but still kept Shenyang as the 'second capital', a capital city in his own homeland. Both Changchun and Harbin are relatively new towns; Changchun became a market town for agricultural products in the early nineteenth century and Harbin as a city was entirely the product of the Chinese Eastern railroad which was built by the Russians at the turn of the century.

The great impetus to the rapid urbanization in nineteenth-century China was the opening of treaty ports, which not only shattered the self-sufficient rural economy of China, but also altered the traditional urban patterns which were mainly based on the development of administrative centres at different levels. However, the five port cities which now have a population over 1 million were all walled towns. Canton and Wuhan were the seats of provincial capitals during the Manchu dynasty. Chungking was a prefecture city in Szechuan. Shanghai and Tientsin were both county seats. Among all treaty ports created in the nineteenth century, Canton had the longest history as a port of trade with foreign merchants. The first walled town of Canton was built in Han times and as early as the third century AD, Arab merchants appeared in the city to collect Chinese goods [29]. For several centuries Canton was the only city designated by the court where foreign merchants could conduct their business. In the 1840s, the city, as did Shanghai, became one of the five ports opened for trade with the British. Two decades later Tientsin and Wuhan became treaty ports, whereas Chungking was not opened for trade until 1891. By the early 1930s, the peak trading period in the era of treaty ports, Tientsin, Wuhan, and Canton all joined Shanghai in becoming million cities. The inland port of Chungking, however, did not join the list until it became a wartime capital in the late 1930s.

The seaports of Chingtao and Talien, with their deepwater and natural harbours, were developed as urban communities entirely under the administration of a foreign country. The Germans were the first to appreciate the excellence of the harbour at Chingtao when in 1897 they occupied Chiaocheu Bay, where Chingtao was situated. As the First World War broke, the city was taken over by the Japanese, who held it until 1922. Under German and Japanese control Chingtao was linked with the interior by railroad and was developed as a textile manufacturing centre. In recent years heavy industries such as locomotive and rolling stock manufacturing have been added to the city's industry. The port of Talien experienced similar development. It was the site of a fishing village up to the last decade of the nineteenth century. In 1898 Russia leased Talien and Lushun (Port Arthur) as her entrance to the Pacific. After the Russo—Japanese War the Japanese took over the city. In the forty years following, Talien's population increased from 18 882 to 700 000 [30]. With rapid agricultural and industrial development of Manchuria in recent years the city of Talien became the only year-round open harbour for the rich land of the northeast. In terms of total tonnage of export and import commodities, Talien recently has ranked second only to Shanghai [31].

The four industrial cities in Manchuria, Shenyang, Changchun, Harbin, and Fushun, were all developed rapidly under the Japanese administration during the period from 1931 to 1945. In these years Shenyang, surrounded by important mining towns and steel centres, became a manufacturing centre of heavy machinery. Changchun, with its central location in Manchuria, was selected as the administrative headquarters of Manchukuo, a political unit for Manchuria created by the Japanese. Harbin, at the junction of important railroads, became a trade centre for northern Manchuria. Fushun, traditionally a small county seat east of Shenyang, has been developed as the largest coal-mining town in China.

The role of industry in the million city

While the Chinese cities with a population over 1 million in the first half of the century were mainly a result of commercialization, it was mainly due to the extensive programme of industrial development in the First Five-Year Plan that new million cities have come into being in the 1950s. As the number of persons employed by industrial enterprises in each city is not known, the only information available concerns the industrial plants in each city. Generally speaking, there is a proportional relationship between the size of city population and the number of plants in the city as shown in Table 16.4. The fact that the cities of Harbin, Taiyuan, and Changchun have a greater number of plants in relation to their population may probably indicate a larger proportion of industrial workers in their population than many other cities. The largest number of new plants added since 1949 has been in the city of Peking, reflecting the regime's determination to make the capital city a strong industrial base. The high percentage increase of the number of plants since 1949 occurred in the cities of Sian, Chengtu, and Lanchou. The rapid growth of these inland cities indicates a new trend of industrial location in mainland China.

Except for the old treaty ports of Shanghai and Tientsin and the Japanese-developed cities of Talien and Fushun, in all the other million cities the number of new plants built since 1949 exceeds the number of old plants. Most of the cities which gained twenty new plants or more since 1949 are the cities which already had a population over 1 million by 1953. In other words, the most vigorous industrial construction in China during the 1950s still occurred in the old metropolises where existing facilities and skills were readily available. The cities of Taiyuan and Sian were the only two new million cities which gained more than twenty new plants each. These two inland cities are both located near the largest coalfield in China.

All of the seventeen 'million' cities are among the most important manufacturing centres in China. Out of a total of 542 units of machinery manufacturing plants in 1959, 403 units were located in the seventeen 'million' cities [32], accounting for 74 per cent of the total. As most of the million cities

319

Table 16.4 *Distribution of industrial plants in seventeen cities, 1960*

City	Old plants expanded since 1949	New plants since 1949	Total
Shanghai	168	43	212
Peking	40	66	106
Tientsin	40	37	77
Shenyang	37	34	71
Chungking	15	25	41
Wuhan	17	29	47
Canton	35	38	73
Talien	23	10	33
Harbin	28	21	49
Nanking	8	24	32
Sian	7	24	32
Chingtao	7	11	18
Chengtu	2	12	14
Taiyuan	11	22	33
Fushun	13	6	19
Changchun	13	16	29
Lanchou	3	15	18

Source: Yuan-li Wu, 'Principal industrial cities in Communist China, their regional distribution and ranking', *Contemporary China*, 5, No. 1, 1961, 1–32.

were originally commercial ports and regional centres, the industries in these cities are characteristically diversified. The distribution of various industrial units in these cities is listed in Table 16.5.

Chinese industries which were developed before 1949 were mainly composed of light industries such as textile manufacturing and food processing. The First Five-Year Plan largely changed the industrial patterns in major cities. A shift of emphasis from light industry to heavy industry can generally be observed. The growth of heavy industry is partly indicated by the presence of steel mills. Except, probably, for the cities of Chengtu, Changchun, and Lanchou, there is at least one steel plant in each million city. In spite of the phenomenal growth of the steel centres of Anshan and Paotou, the cities of Shanghai, Peking, Chungking, Wuhan,

Table 16.5 Plants of selected industries in million cities of mainland China, 1965

City	Iron and steel	Ferrous metal products	Heavy machinery	Precision instruments	Electric machinery	Transport equipment	Chemicals	Petroleum products	Textile
Shanghai	19	35	90	42	56	28	105	2	65
Peking	9	12	28	17	22	7	26	–	19
Tientsin	7	11	30	10	29	11	45	–	30
Shenyang	3	37	65	4	20	–	23	2	4
Chungking	1	3	12	–	7	4	10	1	9
Wuhan	6	8	22	3	12	5	15	–	6
Canton	2	1	16	5	12	10	42	–	8
Talien	2	2	6	–	2	13	9	3	–
Harbin	1	9	19	1	9	–	–	–	5
Nanking	2	–	11	10	5	4	18	2	4
Sian	1	7	5	2	8	3	7	–	14
Chingtao	1	2	3	1	3	7	5	–	8
Chengtu	–	1	8	1	6	1	5	–	10
Taiyuan	2	4	13	1	5	3	11	–	3
Fushun	–	1	–	1	2	–	6	3	–
Changchun	–	5	–	3	–	7	2	–	1
Lanchou	–	1	2	–	2	–	2	1	5

Source: Chūgoku kōgyō Kōjō sōran (A total list of industrial plants in China), Tokyo, Ajia Kenkyūjo (Asia Research Institute), October 1965.

and Taiyuan all have steel mills capable of producing at least 1 million tons of ingot steel annually [33].

Generally speaking, the million cities which newly emerged in the period of 1953—60 show more specialization in industrial products than those old million cities. The city of Fushun, with fuel industrial output accounting for 53.6 per cent of the total value of industrial output and with 60 per cent of its population in fuel mining and production, is essentially a city of coal and oil shale mining [34]. The city of Changchun, where 45.5 per cent of the total industrial product was in machinery and 30 per cent of this machinery production was contributed by the First Automobile Manufacturing Plant alone, is the automobile centre of China [35]. The city of Shenyang, easily accessible to the steel centre of Anshan and the coal-mines of Fushun, has become the most important manufacturing centre of heavy machinery and ferrous metal products in the northeast (Table 16.5). The port cities of Talien and Chingtao, where the transport equipment manufacturing plants outnumbered any other industrial establishments, were centres of shipbuilding, rolling stock manufacturing and automobile parts manufacturing and assembly. As indicated by the number of various industrial plants, the industrial development in the city of Nanking has been concentrated in the petrochemical industry, while the city of Taiyuan, located in the middle of a rich coalfield, has emphasized manufacture of heavy machinery. The former treaty port cities, such as Shanghai, Tientsin, Wuhan, and Canton, have still kept a balanced industrial development of diversified nature. A similar pattern of development has been followed by the newly emerged manufacturing centre of Peking. The city of Shanghai since 1949 has drastically reduced its share of the total industrial output of the nation. Nevertheless, the city is still the most important single city in industrial output in mainland China. Shanghai possesses more plants almost in every branch of manufacturing industry than any other city in the nation (Table 16.5).

The million city and the planning of national construction

While the First Five-Year Plan has promoted the emergence

of a number of new million cities, the future plans for major capital construction as well as the projects which have been already undertaken seem to be directed more toward promoting growth of the above-mentioned seventeen 'million' cities than toward creating new million cities.

The plans for railroad construction are mainly concerned with lines connecting inland provinces. Among several projects underway at the present time, two of the most important ones are the Lanchou–Chinghai line and the Chengtu–Kunming line. The city of Lanchou, being near the geometric centre of the nation, is considered to be an important railroad centre linking the densely populated eastern half with the sparsely-settled western half. It is already connected with the eastern provinces by the Lunghai railroad, and with the steel centre of Paotou and the city of Urumchi. The recent completion of the Lanchou–Tibet highway has made the city of Lanchou an important gateway to the vast Tibetan plateau. The construction of a railroad through the oil rich Tsaidam basin and eventually to the city of Lhasa will certainly strengthen the central position of Lanchou in the transport network of China. The railroad from Chengtu to Kunming has been under construction for several years. Once the whole line is finished, Chengtu will become the transport centre linking the northwest and the southwest (Fig. 16.3).

Perhaps the projects for river control and the utilization of water resources will have great effects on the economic landscape of China as well as on the nation's urbanization. The major schemes of water conservancy include control of the upper and middle portions of the Yellow River, development and utilization of the Yangtse Gorges, and the more ambitious plans for an inland waterway connecting the major river systems. The construction of the Sanmen Gorge Dam in the middle section of the Yellow River was scheduled to be completed in 1962. If the original plan to have 1.1 million kW electricity generated at the dam site can become a reality, the nearby million cities such as Sian and Taiyuan and other industrial centres such as Loyang and Chengchou will obtain ample supplies of electricity [36]. The control of the upper streams of the Yellow River involves the construction of the Liu-chia Dam about 65 km (40 miles) west of the city of Lanchou. The planned generation of 1.05 million kW will be mainly transmitted to the city of Lanchou. Upon the completion of the projected forty-six dams along the tributaries of the upper Yellow River, the city of Lanchou is expected to become an inland river port for ships up to 500 tons [37].

The plan for the development of the Yangtse Gorges was initiated as early as 1944. The revised plans under the present regime call for the construction of three major dams along the 200 km (124 miles) course of the gorges and the generation of as much as 15 million kW electric capacity [38]. The preliminary survey works of the area have already been done, but no major construction work has ever started. The project would enable ships of 10 000 tons to reach the city of Chungking and the hydro-electricity generated would be transmitted to the cities within a distance of 1 046 km (650 miles) from the gorges. The cities of Chungking and Wuhan, both being within 320 km (200 miles) from the gorges, would probably benefit most after the completion of this multipurpose river control project.

The most ambitious plans ever laid out by the present regime to effect changes in the landscape of China are probably those to divert water from the Yangtse to the Yellow River and to construct an inland waterway network linking the four most important drainage systems of the country. One of the crucial problems in developing north China is to achieve a balanced supply of water. While the Yangtse basin drains ample water into the ocean, the annual discharge rate of the Yellow River system is equivalent to only one-twentieth of that of the Yangtse [39]. The quantity of water which is planned to be diverted northward is given as 140 million cu metres (5 000 million cu ft) per annum [40]. Many routes for diverting water from the Yangtse have been suggested. The four most likely are (Fig. 16.4) [41]: (1) From Yushu on the upper Yangtse to the Yellow River near Chishihshan by way of Kantze; (2) from a northward bend of the Yangtse in Yunnan to the Yellow River at Tingsi in Kansu by way of the Yalung River and the northern part of Szechuan; (3) water from the Yangtse Gorges is to be led to connect with the Han above the Tanchiangkou Dam and northeastward to Chengchou; (4) water is to be taken up the Grand Canal near Yangchou. If any of the first two routes were selected, water will enter the Yellow River in the vicinity of Lanchou, a newly emerged million city whose expansion of industries demands water supply of both better quality and greater quantity.

The city of Lanchou will also benefit by the completion of the Tao River project which has been under construction since 1958. The project was aimed at irrigating the arid areas of the western part of the loess plateau by constructing a 1 125 km (700 miles) long canal with water supply from the Tao River and, eventually, from the upper Yangtse [42] (Fig. 16.4). This extensive area under irrigation was planned to become an important agricultural base to supply food for the ever growing urban population in the northwest, including those in the city of Lanchou.

Traditionally the long distance transport of China has mainly relied on water. The Grand Canal formed the main north—south route and thus allowed the imperial court in Peking to be fed by tribute rice from the south. Although the canal had been replaced by the railroads from Peking to Wuhan and from Tientsin to Shanghai in modern times, the increasing traffic on these two routes in recent years has made China's transport network far from adequate. The failure of present transport arteries to meet the load of raw materials may have obliged the regime to draw a plan to develop inland water navigation all the way from the Amur River in the northeast to the Si River in the south (Fig. 16.4). The northern portion of this waterway is made up of the Sungari—Liao canal which will link Harbin with Changchun and Shenyang and gives access to the sea at Yinkou. From Yinkou a short sea passage leads to Tientsin. The line is continued to Peking by the Grand Canal. From Tientsin—Peking area to the Yangtse there will be two routes. The east route follows the Grand Canal which is to be enlarged to accommodate ships up to 3 000 tons [43]. The west route runs from Peking to Chengchou and then to the Han River at the Tanchiangkou Dam and to Wuhan. South of the Yangtse the route will pass through the Tungting Lake and the Siang River to Hsingan, where a short canal will run across to the Kuei Riving at Lingchuan. From that point the route follows the Kuei River to the Si River and the city of Canton. Upon the completion of this scheme, the million cities of Harbin, Changchun, Shenyang, Tientsin, Peking, Wuhan, and Canton will all be linked together by the inland waterway. As this water route will cross the major river systems of China, practically all the seventeen 'million' cities will be connected by water transport. This giant scheme, if it can ever be carried out, will likely strengthen the key positions of the seventeen cities in transport networks of China, thereby generating further growth of these cities.

Problems of the million city

1. Inadequate transportation

While the majority of the large metropolises in the United States are concentrated in the manufacturing belt in the northeast, the million cities in China are much more dispersed; they are scattered in twelve different provinces. Though the distance between Peking and Tientsin is less than 160 km (100 miles), the average distance between two 'million' cities via railroad is well over 480 km (300 miles) [44]. The wider spacing between the million cities in China reflects their chief function as regional distribution and collection centres. As mentioned before, however, all of the million cities in China are also important industrial centres and most of them are equipped with iron and steel plants and machinery manufacturing plants. Only low quality coal is relatively widely distributed in China, and therefore many million cities with active industrial activities are not easily accessible to the fuel supply or raw materials for manufacturing. The situation is particulary true for the industrial cities in the south such as Shanghai, Wuhan, and Canton, where large quantities of coal, especially coking coal, had to be shipped from north China. Thus the creation of industrial centres out of regional metropolises has accentuated the major commodity movement in north—south direction, putting an enormous burden on the sea route and particularly on the nation's two major railroads which run from north to south. Even with the recent completion of the double tracking of both lines, the supply of raw materials to many industrial centres still causes congestion.

2. Housing shortages in urban centres

The rapid growth of urban population in the last two decades has never been matched proportionately by the rate of new house building. During the period from 1949 to 1962 only 13 million sq metres (3 212 acres) of residential housing have been built in the urban areas [45]. During the same period the urban population has increased from 60 million to more than 120 million. The new housing projects were distributed in different cities not quite proportional to the rate of population increase. Generally speaking, those cities which have grown more rapidly have suffered more from a housing shortage. The population of Sian increased more than three-fold from 490 000 to 1.5 million during the period 1950 to 1965, while the floor space of dwelling units only doubled during the same period [46]. In the seven-year period after 1949, the total floor space of dwelling units in the city of Taiyuan had a 140 per cent increase compared to the 400 per cent increase of the city's population in the same period [47]. A serious housing shortage also occurred in the city of Lanchou where the floor space shared by each resident in 1958 was only 1.6 sq metres (16 sq ft) in contrast to the better situation in 1949 when each resident had 3.1 sq metres (33 sq ft) of accommodation [48].

Most new residential units in large municipalities since 1949 have been constructed in the suburbs near the sites of newly developed industrial plants, so that the workers can easily reach their working places. With newly constructed schools, stores, and recreational facilities of its own, the new industrial unit became virtually an independent community, without much intra-urban relationship with the old city district. The old walled sections of large muncipalities have witnessed relatively little change except perhaps for the public buildings in the centre of the town. The dwelling units in the old residential areas, though centuries old in many cases, have experienced repeated repair rather than complete renewal. The lack of new houses in large cities may have been reflected in the municipal programme for exchanging houses which has been set up in recent years. The employees and workers at all levels were encouraged to live near the places where they were employed. The policy was aimed to cut down transportation cost, to save time in commuting, and to reduce traffic on the streets. As there were few vacant dwelling units available in the cities, it was not easy for every

327

family to be housed at the place of its own choice. In order to remedy this situation a house exchange working group has been set up in the Municipal Housing Administration Bureau in large cities such as Peking. The housing administrative offices in the suburbs of various cities also handle house exchange business. Quite often three or four parties were involved in swapping their residences in order to insure mutual satisfactory locations. However, since many people often use this opportunity expecting to get better living conditions through the exchange, satisfactory exchanges have been seldom accomplished [49].

3. Shortage of land for urban use

The Chinese walled cities often occupied a lowland site which was immediately surrounded by the most productive and most expensive agricultural land in the area. The recent urban expansion which involves the construction of building almost entirely outside the city walls has been done at the enormous cost of fertile land. As most cities in China are located near the bank of a river, the newly developed areas are often extended from the walled districts along the waterway. The urbanized areas in many large cities have been developed astride both banks of a river. Shanghai, Tientsin, Canton, Wuhan, and Chungking are classic examples of such development. More recently, Lanchou, Taiyuan, and Changchun have added their industrial establishments across the river from the old city [50]. The intrusion of urban land use into productive agricultural land has alarmed the planning authorities of the regime. A principle of 'using first the hills then the lowland and little farmland' was promoted for the construction of all transportation lines, industrial sites, and residential districts [51]. The idea of using hills and slopes for urban construction has begun to change the traditional urban landscape of China as these rugged terrains near the city were relatively little used for any major construction. Architects were urged to study the possibilities and methods of constructing industrial plants and public buildings, as well as residential units, on various slopes and hills near the large cities. The city of Chungking, where little level land is available, has extended its new construction up the hills at an unprecedented scale.

4. Deficient urban utilities

The installation, maintenance, and management of various municipal utilities for industrial and residential uses have been a new experience to the municipal authorities of large cities in China. Prior to 1949 most urban utilities in a few large cities such as Shanghai, Tientsin, Chingtao, Talien, and Shenyang were mainly constructed and managed by the British or Japanese who were in charge of the administration of a concession or in actual control of a whole city. The rapid growth of many large cities in the 1950s demanded utility facilities on a much greater scale. Generally, all the seventeen 'million' cities and many medium size cities have, at least partially, the convenience of electricity, sewer, and the modern water supply system. However, the water supply is often inadequate, and the purification of water for industrial and domestic consumption in large cities still poses a problem. Many cities have to rely partly on water from wells for direct domestic consumption. Perhaps the most serious problems concerning utility facilities in large cities lie in the low standard of construction and the short operational duration. A great percentage of the newly installed facilities required constant repair and inspection. During the year of 1960—61, for example, 67 per cent of the equipment of the water supply enterprises in Wuhan, Sian, and Taiyuan has been repaired [52]. In the first half of 1962, the city of Shenyang cleaned 143 000 metres (469 000 ft) of open and underground sewers and repaired 452 000 sq metres (4 864 000 sq ft) of street [53]. In the meantime, the demand for more public utilities still far exceeds the supply, and an overall plan is often needed in the management of urban construction in various large cities.

Conclusions

The growth of the seventeen 'million' cities in the 1950s has been an important phenomenon in the history of Chinese urbanization. Each of these cities, with its numerous economic, cultural, and political activities, has virtually become the primate city of the province or even the region in which the city is located. As the present regime has constantly stressed the role of cities in making social and material transformations of vast rural areas, these cities have become strong bases and backbones for nationwide construction, and their growth and associated problems may become a useful thermometer for measurement of China's economic conditions. The transport facilities serving these cities very likely will be further improved and strengthened with the new plans for inland waterways and with the construction of more railroads in the inland provinces. Thus each city will not only function as a regional centre, but, with the centralized economic planning and at a great cost of national capital investment, will more and more become an integrated part in the national economic structure of mainland China as well.

Since 1960 there has been a continuous paucity of the quantitative information of city development on the China mainland. However, in view of the regime's constant campaigning for returning urban residents to the countryside and the emphasis on the self-reliance policy at the commune and brigade levels, it is likely that the process of urbanization has been slowed down in the 1960s. Therefore, the present urban patterns which were mainly developed during the 1950s, as described above, will probably exist as they are for some time to come.

17 Eyewitness of the Cultural Revolution

Drawing a picture of China on the basis of personal experience alone presents several problems. First, 'foreign experts' generally did not have access to much more material or information than did foreign journalists; when the movement began to make itself felt in foreign language institutes, in March or April, we were told categorically that it had nothing whatever to do with foreigners. Second, our outstanding advantage as observers — contact, and on the whole good relations, with students — was in general little exploited, in the beginning because we did not appreciate the importance of what was happening, and later, for fear of provoking our employers. Third, much of the most interesting 'news' came as rumour from somewhere within the large body of foreigners living in the Friendship Hostel, and these sources were inevitably imprecise in their dating.

The advantages we did have over non-resident observers lay partly in what we saw and heard at first hand, which often did not reach the newspapers, and partly in the opportunity to compare notes with a large number and variety of foreigners. I estimate that at some time I discussed the Cultural Revolution, at length, with some thirty or more people of various nationalities and from four cities apart from Peking. Of these, about a third had a fair knowledge of spoken and written Chinese; all were interested in what was happening. We differed widely in our interpretations, but regularly exchanged personal experiences, which were all the more valuable since we worked in different institutions, including both translation bureaux and Peking University*.

Phase one: November 1965 to August 1966

The first three or four months of newspaper criticisms which grew into the Cultural Revolution made little impact on the self-contained and highly artificial world of the 'foreign experts'. Nor was there much indication elsewhere that great matters were afoot. I doubt if anyone considered the movement very important before April when students began to devote more of their time to criticizing Wu Han and less to language study. By the end of April, however, posters and essays had appeared on selected walls within educational establishments, though still only as echoes of criticisms in the daily Press. Certainly nothing dramatic seemed to be happening in any of the language institutes at which we taught.

The attack on Teng T'o in early May threw the movement into higher gear. This was reflected in the ratio of time spent by our students on political meetings as opposed to academic study. The number of posters, slogans and essays grew. Lessons were interrupted or cancelled to make way for 'reports'. There was an increasing loss of concentration, and evening meetings lengthened. My own students were not loath to talk to me about the movement, but did so entirely in terms of slogans and political theory. When at one point I asked whether P'eng Chen had been critized, the suggestion was vehemently denied as quite impossible. In the streets there was still little sign of activity. Indeed, as the campaign grew steadily more serious, its literary manifestations were more zealously guarded. Few foreigners — and only selected Chinese — could view many of the innumerable posters written within educational, and later cultural, establishments.

It was not until late in May that we encountered any signs of violence, and even then it was confined to Peking University. The publication on 1 June of the poster attacking the Chancellor, Lu P'ing, and other officials was a signal for greater activity everywhere. But we were not allowed to see it. Those institutes which had not already suspended lessons now did so very quickly. A few foreigners continued to work in middle schools, and one or two still had access to their places of work. But on the whole, except for translators and 'polishers' who continued to work as usual, we were strictly barred. Many of us began to wonder whether, or when, we would be dismissed from our jobs and sent home. (In fact this never happened, though many left, some with the prospect of returning later.)

It was soon clear that Peking University was to be the centre of the Cultural Revolution, at least as far as Peking students were concerned. The anti-Lu P'ing poster, written by cadres and students from the philosophy department, was put up on 25 May — a week or so before it was actually published in the Press — and it was torn down the same night. On the whole there does not seem to have been a great deal of resistance to the Party line, though there was some. The working party sent in by the new Peking Party Committee was not questioned or refused entry, as at Ch'ing-hua University. The evening mass meetings, now little more than hysterical denunciations of an increasing number of people and equally hysterical protestations of loyalty to Mao, lengthened into all-night sessions. Those at Ch'ing-hua were often reinforced by large contingents from Peking University.

Virtually all academic staff and many administrators were criticized in varying degrees. Those guilty of the most serious 'crimes' were placed in special compounds or fields and made to do the lowest menial work. They were also subjected to constant ridicule and humiliation. It was estimated that within a week or two of the denunciation of the Chancellor 20 000 'sightseers' were visiting Peking University each day, partly to read the wall-posters, partly to watch and abuse the 'criminals'. (A seasonal variant of pulling up grass, cleaning lavatories and carrying night-soil, was picking up melon seeds spat out at random by the visitors.)

Although Peking University seemed to have been deliberately chosen as the focal point of the movement, a measure of what seemed to be spontaneous chaos soon erupted there. A mass meeting planned for a redenunciation and trial of Lu P'ing in the Workers Stadium was somehow turned into criticism of the head of the outside working party, Comrade Chang. In early June Chang and his companions were apparently responsible for saving a number of people from severe physical punishment, denouncing students who went too far as counter-revolutionary. In other institutes too there was soon friction between the indigenous population and members of the groups sent in by the reorganized Peking

Party Committee. In late July Chou En-lai is reported to have all but apologized to a meeting of Peking student representatives for having sent in the working parties.

Some very curious stories emerged from both Peking and Ch'ing-hua Universities and personalities played a large part. Liu Shao-ch'i's wife, Wang Kuang-mei, and Ch'en Po-ta are said to have taken up residence at Ch'ing-hua early in June. Mrs Liu was bitterly criticized for her bourgeois ways. The student leader at Ch'ing-hua, K'uai, was rumoured to have criticized Mao himself in a poster commenting on the scandal, involving both Peking and Ch'ing-hua Universities, of exposing 'volunteers' to uranium 273 isotopes for testing purposes in 1961. (I imagine that what he actually said was that Mao could not have sanctioned such experiments, as was claimed at the time, because they were inhuman — not that Mao was inhuman for having done so.) Mao's wife certainly visited both universities fairly often, usually in the company of Ch'en Po-ta. At first she consistently referred all questions from the students to Ch'en, claiming that she was a mere housewife and had no authority to speak. Later, however, she took the belated initiative of denouncing Lu P'ing, and possibly others.

This period, from May till August, was an extremely noisy one in Peking generally, but the gongs, cymbals, drums and flags were not accompanied by physical violence. Credible reports appeared of suicides within the universities, as well as severe physical maltreatment, though the few deaths at this stage seem to have been caused largely through neglect of old or sick 'criminals'. In the rest of the country there was a timelag, and generally the lead was taken from Peking. The few foreigners outside Peking stopped working several weeks after we did.

Although youth was at the centre of the movement, it was now no longer confined either to the young or to places of education. Everywhere there were signs of activity behind the scenes as well as the constant parades in public. A glimpse into a courtyard would reveal the writings of a diligent street committee. A restaurant window might overlook a passage or yard plastered with the literary efforts of the cooks and waiters. The middle-aged and the old also marched and paraded, though with noticeably less panache than the young. They also attended all-night meetings, contributing to the regular nocturnal hubbub throughout the city.

Phase two: August to October 1966

By mid-August many of us were convinced — and some had been mistakenly convinced several times already — that the Cultural Revolution had now reached a period of consolidation and that nothing new would happen. The launching on 18 August of the Red Guards, composed of students and schoolchildren who already looked exhausted from interminable meetings and much parading, took us by surprise. By then the movement had become more boring than stimulating, and we hoped for a return to some sort of normality before very long. Even when we learned that there would be no teaching in September we did not envisage a greater role for the students than that of ambassadors to the country at large. On the whole we regarded the antibourgeois movement as a necessary evil, at least when viewed from the Party's point of view. A struggle for power among the leaders was not then an obviously important ingredient of the Cultural Revolution. Some harm had already been done, and perhaps some good; but the sooner it ended the better it would be for China.

Reactions to the Red Guards differed though most, I think, felt some fear during the first two weeks. Many of us were involved in minor skirmishes with them, generally for taking photographs or pausing to read particular posters. Three days after the Red Guards began their activities in Peking we heard that three had been killed, and the mood of the youngsters hardened. As far as I know only very few foreign Pressmen and diplomats were actually manhandled, and these incidents all centred on the demonstrations outside the Soviet Embassy. But the hostility to foreigners was evident everywhere and a fair quantity of film was surrendered to avoid physical violence. There were exceptions however. Our treatment seemed to depend largely on the particular group of youths rather than on a general policy. In some cases foreigners were actually escorted about the city while they filmed.

Violence, torture and humiliation seem to have been less

335

marked — or better concealed — in Peking than elsewhere, though we saw enough. In Tientsin, for instance, people were seen being made to kneel, either in the street or on narrow raised planks for several hours at a stretch, heads bent and arms raised. They were constantly reviled, prodded and beaten, made to confess their crimes, then paraded round the town in groups. When asked how they chose their victims, one Red Guard said that a group would think hard about the people they knew until someone remembered, for instance, that in the past a certain woman had worn cosmetics or frequently had her hair permed. The group would then proceed to the woman's home and point out the error of her ways.

Among the many posters we read, a large number were either impractical or completely irrelevant, and often amusing. The condemning of all leather shoes, irrespective of style, did not last. But all save the plainest spectacle frames remained taboo. A large number of girls and women lost their plaits, if necessary at the hands of an enthusiastic amateur barber in the street. Not a few young men appeared with heads shaved bald — but caps are frequently worn in China, irrespective of time or place.

Stamps bearing the Queen's head, imported from Hong Kong and offered for sale to collectors, were displayed as a sign of ultimate decadence. Outside restaurants not only the customary steaming towels but even toothpicks were condemned as bourgeois. The number of roads newly named 'The East Is Red Street' or 'Red Flag Road' would have created an administrative nightmare if officially adopted. All foreign cars, buses and lorries — that is the majority of vehicles — were labelled either 'Anti-Imperialism Brand' or 'Anti-Revisionism Brand', according to their origin.

The revolutionizing of the Friendship Hostel was among the most comical sights. Solemn processions of youths, each bearing a part of the new name, marched to the front of each building and duly pasted up appropriate titles. But the food in the Revolutionary Dining Hall was not noticeably different the next day; and the cheaper Yenan Dining Hall was now forbidden to Chinese.

Despite the occasional comedy, the first two weeks of the Red Guards was not a pleasant period. The treatment of ageing nuns — accused of spying, though they had not left their convent since Liberation — was uncivilized and unnecessary. So too was the razing of the foreign cemetery out in the suburbs. We saw people of all ages, bound and wearing placards or the tall conical hats of shame, being marched or driven in lorries about the city. Children too young to take an active part in the movement and thus on prolonged holiday from school, were eager observers of acts of cruelty and humiliation. From Peking University we heard a Chinese estimate of 200 suicides in that establishment alone. Posters which appeared later — that is, after 1 September — confirmed reports of terrorism on an appreciable scale.

The attitude of the Red Guards towards foreigners and to a large extent towards Chinese too changed dramatically after the second mass rally on 1 September. It was difficult to believe we were among the same people. The emphasis placed by the leadership and the newspapers on 'literary struggle' as opposed to 'physical struggle' produced smiles, cheers and handclaps for us, and a marked diminishing of personal violence for the Chinese. We now know that this was a lull, not the end, and with hindsight we can see that it could not have been the end. A great deal of heat had been generated, and relatively little of positive value accomplished.

From midsummer on, the adoration of Mao and the sanctity of his writings were taken to incredible lengths. By 1 October most young people were Red Guards and everyone seemed to possess a badge and a copy of Mao's *Quotations*. The parade on National Day was a fascinating psychological experience. The young Chinese in the stands close to us who shouted slogans in cracked, hysterical voices continually from 9 a.m. till 4 p.m. were clearly experiencing an emotional event of great power. Contrast this with the dutiful, luke-warm applause or — as in my case — the unutterable boredom displayed by most foreigners. For us it had neither impact nor relevance. But for the couple of million unsophisticated young people who took part — most of them from the provinces — I am certain it was the moment of a lifetime.

The overall impression I retain of Peking during an unusually warm September and October is one of shambling chaos, punctuated by outbursts of feverish, if purposeless, activity. Most shops had returned to normal; virtually the only items no longer available were books — particularly secondhand ones, which had all disappeared — works of art, and the more extreme luxury goods such as jewellery. But the city itself had changed, if temporarily, for it accommodated a shifting population of some 2 million provincial Red Guards, perhaps more. They came to 'exchange revolutionary experience' with their Peking counterparts. They travelled about the city in lorries or buses, many of which they had brought with them. The vast majority must have visited Peking University, for they formed a constant procession along the road leading there. Within the establishments where they were billeted they often clashed, verbally at least, with the original inhabitants. They also toured the city, had their photographs taken in front of T'ien An Men, read the posters with which most available wall space was plastered, and bought PLA hats and badges depicting Mao in profile. They cluttered the streets and clogged the public transport system. Some wrote posters and handbills, for which people would fight when they appeared on the streets. They were also roused to an air of purposeful dedication for each of the several mass rallies. But in general the atmosphere seemed sluggish. Behind the scenes there was doubtless more action, as was shown by the growing dissatisfaction with the Peking Party Committee's handling of the Cultural Revolution. But this seemed only to be coming to a head as I left; in fact the last new poster I saw, stuck to a lamp-post, said 'Dismiss Li Hsueh-feng', the new first Party secretary of Peking.

I left China depressed rather than frightened or stimulated by the prevailing atmosphere. So much anger and activity seemed to have produced, and to be likely to produce, so little. With this feeling was mixed one of slight disbelief that so many people could regard so much ballyhoo with such seriousness. Perhaps by the end I was no longer in a condition to judge rationally, but two final incidents in the process of departure half persuaded me that I was dreaming. One was the singing of revolutionary songs and recitation of Mao's works by a plane-load of Chinese officials and a delegation to Cairo. The other was the request at the customs house, not only to tear out of several volumes a few pages of worthless articles by Chou Yang and others, but to obliterate every last trace of these poisonous weeds in the index too. I suppose it did happen; the faces around me as I scribbled at the offending names were certainly tense with righteous concern. On the whole though I doubt whether many Chinese find much that is comical about their Great Proletarian Cultural Revolution.

18   China's economy in 1970

The writer on Chinese economic affairs may be forgiven for
recalling an incident from early schooldays when the head-
master, introducing his pupils to *The Odyssey*, mused about
its author: 'Nobody, he said, knows for certain whether
Homer ever lived; what is known, though, is that he was
blind.' Turning to China, the student of contemporary affairs
is similarly uncertain of his facts. He is facing the most populous, yet one of the industrially least advanced and statistically least well documented countries in the world. At the same
time, China not only succeeded within two decades in developing its own nuclear striking force, but at the end of this
short period of development it launched its first earth satellite. We are thus confronted with an entirely new situation,
the study of which requires certain adjustments of the techniques of analysis usually applied. Today's 'China-watchers'
find themselves where twenty years ago the analysts of the
Soviet scene were when they had to guess Stalin's intentions
and successes on the strength of misleading indices related to
unknown starting dates.

Economic intentions undisclosed

This is not to say that we know nothing firm about China. It
is true that in statistical terms a near-blackout has persisted
for a decade. Worse still, one searches in vain for any meaningful statement from official sources as to economic intentions, successes or failures. Chou En-lai's last revelation of
this kind dates back to the end of 1964 when he gave his
economic progress report to the National People's Congress.
More recently, the editorial published on New Year's Day —

traditionally a significant statement of intent — merely revealed that 'in the economic sphere, we will consolidate and develop the socialist economic base and, in a planned way, deal blows at the corrosive and sabotaging activities of the bourgeoisie' [1].

Equally unrevealing have been the public pronouncements emanating from the all-important Ninth Party Congress which sat through the better part of April 1969 and brought the Great Proletarian Cultural Revolution to a close. Lin Piao, Vice-Chairman of the Party's Central Committee, devoted much space to denouncing as a 'renegade, hidden traitor and scab' [2] Liu Shao-ch'i, China's Head of State and the Party's ideologue for many years past, but dismissed from his post and from the Party at the twelfth session of the Eighth Central Committee in October 1968. By comparison the Ninth Party Congress had little, if anything, to say for public consumption on the economic condition, past, present or future, of the nation that is due to complete by the end of this year its Third Five-Year Plan.

Lin Piao quoted at length from the writings of Lenin, particularly when attacking small-scale production which, after years of suppression, still causes concern and apparently still 'engenders capitalism and the bourgeoisie continuously, daily, hourly, spontaneously and on a mass scale' [3] — as in the bygone days before Lenin discovered its usefulness in his country's recovery from war communism. In this situation it is perhaps not to be wondered at that Mao's heir apparent was pessimistic regarding the final victory of 'socialism', i.e. communism, over capitalism which seems not within reach for some decades to come. In the meantime Lin Piao gave high priority to the task of 'struggle—criticism—transformation' which is apparently being carried out by the chief organ of the new order, i.e. the 'three-in-one combination' of the Revolutionary Committees, embracing representatives of the revolutionary cadres, of the People's Liberation Army and of the revolutionary masses.

Politically less weighty subjects, such as the country's economy, were apparently passed over in silence. If they were discussed, they were not considered subjects suitable for a mention in the communiqué on three weeks' work of the country's most important gathering of the recent past. In consequence, during the year in which the Third Five-Year Plan draws to a close, there is no certainty that there is in fact a plan; and if so, that it is in operation. Its priorities can only be guessed at even though, during the last few months, China's mass media have been a little more forthcoming about the country's economic performance than in the recent past.

Selected economic information

Whereas no overall data can be had, information in quantitative terms is available for a few selected industries, for some urban and industrial areas and for certain, though not necessarily representative factories, communes or work brigades. This is not to say that everything that goes into print or on the air can be relied upon. Most of it is interesting, nevertheless, since it reflects, if nothing else, the intentions of those who are charged with serving the mass media; and of late these intentions have become a little more discernible than during the tumultuous years of the Cultural Revolution.

To quote at random: At Anhwei some 150 000 people, working during the winter along the Yangtse River, apparently completed no more than a foot each of a new dike. In Honan a pumping station driven by water-wheels seems to provide irrigation for 30 ha (74 acres) per wheel; against this, in Hopei, 400 wells equipped with power-operated pumps irrigate 5 ha (12 acres) each. In Hunan a commune applies 200 tons of compost per hectare of farmland — an enormous undertaking; another commune claims a yield of 10 tons of paddy per hectare — approximately four times the national average. In Kansu almost 2 million people have been engaged in the construction of terraced fields, each 500 persons on average creating 1 ha (2.4 acres) of land. In Kiangsu duck-weed is used in lieu of nitrogen fertilizer, each 100 tons of the aquatic product serving in place of 1 ton of ammonium sulphate — another huge transport operation. In Kiangsi small hydroelectric power stations provide on average 250 households each with electric light — a small-scale industry *par excellence*. In Honan fertilizer is produced by several small chemical plants, each being approximately one twenty-fifth the size of the Indian plant at Sindri. In Hopei the output of a small ironworks amounts to approximately 8 tons of pig iron per working day, and farm equipment works employ an average of 150 factory hands, one-fifth of whom work on a full-time basis. In Fukien the average generating capacity of a large number of small hydroelectric stations ranges from 10–20 kW per power plant. In Hupeh a printing press produced 20 000 copies of *Quotations from Chairman Mao* a month ahead of schedule, and in Inner Mongolia an inland revenue office collected the year's taxes forty days ahead of time [4].

These items show that:

(a) reports published and broadcast are not necessarily chosen because of their representative character, but they may be selected for their publicity value;

(b) manpower is readily and amply available and it is used lavishly;

(c) agricultural activities are featured prominently in all provinces;

(d) production by small-scale industries is fostered on a broad front;

(e) economies of scale and labour productivity are given low priority;

(f) large-scale industrial operations, for both civilian and military purposes as well as global national data, are not reported.

To aggregate and analyse material of this kind requires large research establishments endowed with substantial financial resources. It is thus not surprising to find that most publications on the Chinese economy bear the imprint of American institutions. Students of Chinese affairs everywhere find their work eased both by the translation services of US government agencies and the analytical work undertaken at universities in the United States (to deny one's debt to these sources is merely to reflect a political bias).

It is hardly the fault of scholars concerned with Chinese affairs if there is less consensus among them than there is by now among those working in the Soviet field. Even so, the conclusions derived from the same sources sometimes differ to an uncomfortably great extent. To quote only one example: in the studies prepared in 1967 for the Joint Economic Committee of the US Congress, estimates of growth of income per head of population range from a modest 1.4 per cent a year during the period from 1952 to 1965, as given by Professor Ta-Chung Liu of Cornell University, to a rate of at least 4 per cent put forward for a similar period of time by Professor J. G. Gurley of Stanford University. Whereas there is a somewhat greater measure of agreement on industrial aggregates, the gap is widest in the demographic and agricultural areas. Here the degree to which students of contemporary affairs differ in their views is all the more disturbing as China, in spite of some marked progress in the industrial sphere, is still one of the most agrarian communities on earth.

Any error committed in the areas of population and farming is bound to be reflected in any overall estimates of national aggregates. Not only are population and food supplies closely interrelated, but where foreign aid is not forthcoming — and this applies to China nowadays — the villages are bound to serve as the prime source of what Marx called the process of 'primitive accumulation'. Without this process central government can hardly function and industrialization cannot progress. As budgets — like plan targets, achievements in industry, agriculture and trade, or wages and prices — have not been published for a decade, the student of Chinese affairs treads uncertain ground; yet, unless he elects to ignore the development of 'a most mystifying but enormously important country' [5] and thus abdicates his chosen task, he has to make do with what evidence comes to his attention.

China's population

At the time of Stalin's death most Western observers of the Soviet scene, on the advice of experienced demographers, estimated Russia's population to be 220 million; yet when later Khrushchev had the first postwar statistical yearbook published, the population was given as 200 million. Considering that for many years a complete blackout had hidden all Soviet statistics from view, an error of 10 per cent might seem small, but it meant that Western sources tended to exaggerate the shortage of foodstuffs and other consumer goods in Russia and to underestimate the per capita supply of industrial goods and equipment and the national income per head of population. To recall this incident might serve as a reminder to those speculating about China's population.

Nobody within or without China is likely to know the true size of the country's population. In 1953 the first proper census ever taken yielded a figure of 583 million. This was followed, up to 1957, by data covering annual net increases in population. For over five years thereafter, official Chinese statements used a constant figure of 650 million. This was raised to 700 and eventually to 750 million, but the editorial published in the *People's Daily* on New Year's Day 1970 reverted to quoting a figure of 700 million. None of these round numbers can be regarded as belonging to a series of population statistics. In 1967 and 1968 Chinese Press and radio reports revealed population data of a more serious type. These emanated from the Revolutionary Committees in China's chief administrative regions. China's population derived from these figures totalled approximately 710 million but there was no indication as to the dates to which the regional population figures referred. The suggestion has been made that they represented a belated publication of a population registration which is supposed to have taken place in 1964 [6]. In fact, no evidence of an administrative registration on a nationwide scale has ever been traced; it seems to have been limited to a few localities. No global results were published during the four years following the alleged mass registration. It seems therefore more probable that the regional Revolutionary Committees gave the best figures available at the time of publication, i.e. in 1967—68. None of the Committees indicated that out-of-date figures were being published, and none made any adjustments for a lapse of time between the date of any registration and the date of publication. It would thus appear that the Chinese authorities estimated the population at the end of 1967 (rather than in 1964) to be a little over 700 million. This seems a plausible figure, though it is by no means accepted by all demographers concerned with China.

A check on official Chinese claims entails both the starting figure of 1953 and the net increase in population during the ensuing years. Whereas Irene Taeuber concluded from her examination of the census of 1953 that China remained a country without statistics [7] and Leo A. Orleans summarized his findings by saying that China's population will continue to be an enigma and a subject for academic guessing games for many decades to come [8], John S. Aird, after detailed analysis of all available census data, reckoned with an undercount of up to 15 per cent [9]. Against this, L. A. Orleans in a recent article accepts as reasonable the result of the census of 1953 and presumes any errors to have cancelled each other out [10].

Undercount in rural areas

Whereas J. S. Aird has shown that evasion undoubtedly took place in urban areas, he and other demographers seem to discount contrary trends in the villages where the census authorities were given permission to consult earlier registers in case their own records were unsatisfactory. In the villages they were bound to fall back on the land reform investigations which had been carried out prior to the census by the Rural Work Department of the Chinese Communist Party. In some provinces cultivators were known to have divided their families and to have exaggerated their numbers in the hope of raising their claims during the period when landed properties were redistributed. At least 100 million villagers were involved in this operation. As cultivators — like ration-card holders — are known to register their 'dead souls', if this is to their advantage, the exaggeration of the rural population during the census of 1953 might well have exceeded the undercount due to evasions of census registration in urban areas [11].

Apart from the starting figures at the base year, in any population projection the annual net increase has to be considered. This was probably exaggerated by the Chinese authorities in the few years for which data were released, although any error made in the annual projections at the time was probably small by comparison with possible faults in the census results of 1953. However, if wrong projections are carried on for a long period of time, the orders of magnitude of the two errors might well be reversed. Assuming an undercount, owing to cultivators' manipulations during the census of 1953, amounting to, say, 5 per cent, and allowing, in the years after the end of the Great Leap Forward, a slightly higher net increase in population than L. A. Orleans has put forward [12], one arrives at a population of approximately 700 million at the end of the calendar year 1966 [13], of approximately 750 million at the end of 1970 and slightly more than 800 million in 1975 (as against 715, 757 and 800 million respectively as estimated by L. A. Orleans). Any estimates higher than these, e.g. those by J. S. Aird, do not seem to tally with estimated available food supplies. To accept uncritically official Chinese claims in the agricultural field but to dismiss out of hand Mao Tse-tung's claim, when talking to Edgar Snow in 1964, that China's population was less than 680 million [14] seems rather inconsistent. One cannot rule out the possibility that on this occasion Mao was briefed better by his officials than when talking to, say, Viscount Montgomery — not too well briefed himself — on foodgrains in 1960.

Food supplies

To say that food supplies and the number of people to be fed are two aspects of one and the same problem is stating the obvious. But the reasoning becomes 'circular' [15] only if one set of figures is manipulated for the sake of proving the other set to be correct. The proper procedure is to use the estimates on both sides as a means for mutual check and crosscheck. This requires more expertise than is generally at the disposal of the individual writer. Interdisciplinary consultation ought to take place and there is thus a strong case for demographers, agronomists and nutritionists getting together on this checking operation [16].

If some demographers have erred in their assessment of China's population, so too have those who have written about China's food supplies without sufficient knowledge of either farming or nutritional techniques. To relate food output, without adjustment, to population can lead to gross errors, particularly in periods of steeply rising or falling production, since seed, waste, feed, industrial use and foreign trade in foodstuffs follow patterns different from those that apply to the consumption of foods of various kinds. The amount of seed is related to the acreage sown or planted and resown and replanted, and the seeding or planting rates which are applied. Waste depends on the size of the crop, on the weather during harvest time and on storage conditions. Industrial use changes in line with the size of the crop, the industrial needs of the community, the manufacturing facilities and export possibilities of the country. Food — like foreign trade in foodstuffs — is usually a residual, but large herds and favourable conditions for sideline production can make inroads into stocks of grains, pulses, tubers, oilseeds and sugar crops, irrespective of the claims of other users. Finally, as all those who have lived through two world wars know only too well, the milling rate can be raised greatly in times of scarcity, as it is lowered in years of plenty. These alternatives affect not only the vegetable part of the human diet. Pig numbers and thus pork output change in relation to the amount of offal available. In 1958 grain extraction rates were probably the lowest in Chinese history. Conversely, after the Great Leap Forward extraction rates increased to close on 90 per cent, thus keeping the calorie intake well above the starvation levels then claimed by some writers. As a corollary the animal protein contents of the diet declined substantially.

In view of these complexities, to apply a flat rate of reduction for non-human consumption or 'processing' [17] does injustice to the considerable amount of knowledge which agricultural economists and nutritionists have transmitted to those concerned with the movement and use of foodstuffs from the point of production to its final destination. The food balance technique — designed to eliminate the impossible and to reveal the probable [18] — is being applied with benefit throughout the world by national and international agencies alike. There is thus no justification for using cruder techniques in the case of China for which food balances were already calculated by the Food and Agriculture Organization for the period prior to the Communist seizure of power [19].

Input—output relations

On the side of food production, certain calculations published in recent years also leave much to be desired. Some of them have been unnecessarily crude, and others have been downright misleading. It seems, for instance, impermissible to relate, directly and without qualification, grain output to fertilizer input, ignoring what little is known of the needs of China's soils and of the supplies of farm inputs available. Whereas at least four-fifths of all soils in China can be regarded as deficient in nitrogen, two-fifths also lack phosphorus and one-fifth potassium. Yet, the bulk of the fertilizer produced in China today is of the nitrogenous kind; phosphates are often of poor quality; and potassium is hardly used at all. In these circumstances no agronomist can support with a clear conscience the view that a 'conservative' yield response of 15 kilos (33 lb) of grain for every kilo (2.2 lb) of fertilizer nutrient applies in China on a nationwide scale [20]. Responses of this magnitude can be found in highly developed agricultural communities which dispose of accurate soil, water, farm management and marketing surveys and apply fertilizers at high rates and balanced ratios. Many years will have to pass before these conditions will apply to China. In this situation to embroider statistical material of dubious origin and suspect quality with the mathematical formulae of marginal product and least square does not strengthen the argument.

The application of chemical compounds is a highly skilled operation, and so also are other modern farm techniques. Many farm managers and cultivators have learned this to their cost in recent years in countries as far apart as Russia and India. Volumes could be written about the setbacks suffered by the scientifically untrained due to products which can poison plants having been applied at the wrong time in the wrong quantities to the wrong crops. Party cadres, demoralized after having been exposed to vicious attacks by Red Guards during the Cultural Revolution, are not necessarily the most suitable agents to teach the cultivators in China's 600 000 villages the highly sophisticated techniques of the chemical age. This is not to say that fertilizers applied well above average rates have not had their favourable effects on scientifically grown 'commercial' crops, such as tea, tobacco, cotton, sugar or soya. The first satisfactory results are also beginning to accrue in some of the well-irrigated paddy areas of south China, which also use fertilizers in quantities well above the national average.

Where yields have increased, this is not due to one single input, such as fertilizer, but it is invariably the result of a

well-balanced programme of closely interrelated inputs, i.e.
the regulated supply, throughout the season, of irrigation
water, the allocation of improved seed ahead of the sowing
season, the use of the right type of insecticides and pesticides, the adjustment of farm management and the tactful
effort, over a number of years, of advisory or extension
officers trained and retrained in the rapidly changing art of
modern farming.

The 'package' concept

Those interested in the rate at which a farming nation in Asia
can change its ways and improve its performance can usefully
be guided by the history of Japan's agriculture since its first
modern agricultural research station was set up in 1895, and
by the — more recent and much shorter — history of the
International Rice Research Institute at Los Banos (Manila)
which, though working under exceptionally favourable
circumstances for ten years, has yet to produce the answers
to some of the questions which have arisen in connection with
what is commonly, and rather misleadingly, known as the discovery of a miracle seed variety. The list of setbacks suffered
in the course of attacks from insects, pests, rodents, mill
owners and rice consumers is too long to be enumerated here.
To overcome them is a wearisome and formidable task.

When all the apparent obstacles connected with matching a
'package' of inputs with the desired output have been
removed, a series of what is now commonly known as
'second generation' problems tends to show up. Among them
the lack of feeder roads, linking railheads and trunk roads
with the centres of village communities, and the absence of
market facilities, such as warehouses, silos, harbour facilities,
short-term credits, price reporting and all the other parapher-
nalia of modern marketing, are the most outstanding [21]. If
the Chinese leaders have thought of all these first and second
generation problems and have tackled them in the midst of
their preoccupation with the ideological and political issues
of such long-drawn-out interruptions of normal economic
development processes as the Great Leap Forward and the
Cultural Revolution, they have been astonishingly discreet
about their foresight and their good fortune. Until these are

better documented than they are at present, it would seem prudent to approach the phenomenon of China's agricultural development along conventional lines.

When this is done, China's successes and failures tend to fall into place. But before dealing with them, it might be worth remembering that agriculture is still China's largest single industry, providing work for at least three out of every four, or altogether well over 100 million, families and creating almost one-third of the country's total national product. Instead of shrinking in the course of intensive industrialization, the agrarian population is likely to have increased in the last two decades, since cities and industries have been unable to absorb the full annual net increase in population. The numbers given as having returned to the land are probably exaggerated, but the general trend can hardly be in doubt. Agriculture therefore continues to determine to a large extent the character of the country and the speed at which it changes to a non-agrarian society.

Inept agricultural planning

In spite of their original reputation of being agrarian reformers rather than professional revolutionaries, Mao and his associates have shown an unhappy hand when turning to the problems of the countryside. To be sure, the confiscation of the landed property of 'landlords' and 'enemies of the revolution' and its distribution among many millions of smallholders, tenants and landless labourers gained the political leaders sympathy and support in the villages. But much of this was lost in the course of mass collectivization which in China took as few months as it had taken years in Soviet Russia. The communes finally destroyed any illusion that the cultivator was entitled to determine his farm pattern or the disposal of his crops. In agricultural planning the Chinese leaders showed themselves unbelievably inept. The twelve-year agricultural plan, introduced in 1956 and adopted in 1960 by the National People's Congress after the Great Leap Forward had failed, was supposed to produce, *inter alia*, some 450 million tons of grain by 1967, the year in which in fact little more than 40 per cent of this amount was harvested [22]. The ambitious targets of the plan were expected to be achieved as the result of simultaneous improvements, ranging from the increased use of fertilizers and pesticides, the improved supply of irrigation water and the provision of high quality seeds to land reclamation, mechanization and multiple cropping. Due to the cumulative effects of the inputs envisaged, the crop yields were expected to more than double within twelve years. The Chinese leaders, like some of their Western interpreters, did not understand that the effects of one input depended upon the presence of all the others and that double counting could only make fools of them and their supporters outside China. This happened sooner than expected.

If agricultural planning was faulty in the extreme, actual steps taken in the countryside were no less disastrous. The worst case of all was in the withdrawal, at the time of the largest harvest ever experienced in China, of large numbers of farmhands for the sake of the ill-considered backyard production of iron scrap. Those Western commentators who in the face of seasonally fluctuating needs suggested an overall agricultural 'labour productivity of zero' misjudged China's requirements in the year of its first bumper crop. If the experience of tens of thousands of country folk 'burning their fingers' in a primitive industrial process produced the avant-garde of an industrial proletariat, this exercise in mass education was bought at the price of a manmade harvest failure of unexpected dimensions. This blunder was part and parcel of the Great Leap Forward, that gigantic experiment in social engineering, which delayed China's economic development by several years and led to the premature termination of the second plan and the delay of the start of the third plan from 1963 to 1966.

Agriculture as the 'foundation'

Since the failure of these early policies, China's farming industry has been treated with somewhat greater discretion by its leaders. In 1960 it was elevated by the then head of the Planning Commission to the publicly proclaimed position of 'foundation' of the nation's economy. In the meantime it has apparently been allocated investment goods and working capital at a somewhat more generous rate than during the first decade of Communist rule. If it has not done as well as some of its Western wellwishers would have liked to see, nor has it done as badly as some critics seem to have deduced from estimated gross production figures. There have been certain savings in the use of grain crops. These are unlikely to have exceeded, to any great extent, the exceptionally good harvest of 1957, a record by all accounts and thus no suitable yardstick for subsequent years, but except for the three 'bitter years', following the Great Leap Forward, the average Chinese consumer is unlikely to have had less than 210 kilos (460 lb) of grain most of the time. This equals 170 kilos (375 lb) of product at the normal extraction rate or 1 650 calories a day. If other items are added, the average annual individual food intake is unlikely to have fallen below 2 100 calories except in the years 1960–61 to 1962–63. It may be slightly higher at present. Whilst this is less than the consumption level attained prior to the Japanese invasion of China, considering the climate of the country, the average body weight and the age composition of the population, it still provides the Chinese people with what they need to keep fit at work.

If no disruptions occur in the transport and distribution system, there is little cause for concern and no need for Western experts to upgrade production estimates for the sake of arriving at increased per capita supplies. These are not in jeopardy. On the other hand, as long as China imports every year 4–5 million tons of wheat and expends up to US $400 million in the course of this operation, it is unlikely that the production of grains and pulses (including potatoes in terms of grain equivalent) exceeds 200 million tons. If this amount is surpassed substantially, China will probably appear on the world grain market as a net exporter, and China's livestock production will increase well beyond present levels.

Non-agricultural activities

As long as the bulk of China's industry rested on raw materials produced on farms, the performance of the industrial sector was directly tied to the previous year's agricultural record. To the extent to which China's industry develops its own raw material base, this interdependence between agriculture and industry loses much of its significance. As a corollary, the extent to which students of contemporary affairs agree on China's industrial performance is growing as China's industry gains weight. To be sure, certain differences remain. In the reports prepared for the Congressional Committee on the Economy of China, Ta-Chung Liu and Robert Michael Field set the increase of China's industrial production between 1957 and 1965 at 35 per cent, or 3.8 per cent a year [23]. Against this, Dwight H. Perkins estimated the industrial growth for this period at 45–50 per cent, or 4.8–5.2 per cent a year [24]. In the meantime R. M. Field has raised his earlier estimates to approximately 50 per cent [25]. This faster rate of growth seems reasonable in view of the fact that China's industry was able to utilize unused capacities when the Great Leap Forward was called off and thus to recover rapidly the ground lost in 1960–62 [26].

Although information on industry, mining, handicraft and public utilities is not easy to come by, a fair degree of consensus exists as to the level of production in the major sectors of industry and with regard to the weight to be given to them. Certain industries have grown faster than others. This applies in particular to mineral oil, fertilizers and cement, as well as to the machine-tool industry. Other industrial sectors have lagged behind. Whereas, during the first plan, the industrial raw material basis was laid, and the interval between the Great Leap Forward and the Cultural Revolution was devoted to the creation of a modern machine-building industry, more recently the emphasis has been shifted to the expansion of the chemical industry. In the course of this development the traditional handicraft and cottage industries have lost ground, but new small-scale industries are being set up side by side with the modern sector which produces the bulk of China's industrial output nowadays. The shift of China's industry into the interior has materialized less than was originally planned. The eastern and northeastern regions are still the most industrialized parts of the country. The transfer from traditional to modern industry, the creation of new products at initially high prices and the practice of sub-contracting tend to inflate the volume and value of production. Thus any official claims have to be considered with this

aspect in view. This applies as much to the last overall statement on industry made by Chou En-lai at the end of 1964, as
to the more recent claim that in 1968 China's industrial
production was more than a dozen times larger than in 1949
(when it was, of course, exceptionally low) [27].

Progress in selected areas

Considerable achievements can be recorded in highly selected
areas, such as the nuclear field. In October 1964, i.e. in the
interim between the defunct second plan and the anticipated
third plan, China became the first backward agrarian country
to place itself side by side, in the nuclear field, with some of
the most highly developed industrial nations in the world.
This achievement was greatly helped by the development of
the machine-building industry, one of the most dynamic
sectors of the Chinese economy, which is supervised by no
less than eight ministries. In addition, certain ancillary
sectors, such as the fuel and power, cement and chemical
industries, played a significant role in this development. As
the Soviet Union had shown under Stalin thirty years earlier,
centralized economies can advance greatly on a narrow front
once the political choice has been made and the necessary
administrative decisions have been taken.

By implication, other targets have had to be given lower
priority. This applies of necessity to the industrial sector concerned with the supply of consumer goods. If producer goods
are supposed to rank behind consumer goods and both in
turn behind agriculture, this order of priorities should be
taken with a pinch of salt. The consumer goods industries
were probably never meant primarily to meet the task of
'serving the people', but rather the call of the Exchequer to
earn foreign exchange. In any event, the demarcation
between producer and consumer goods industries is imprecise, open to interpretation and bound to alter in changing
circumstances. Nowadays economic self-sufficiency and military preparedness unquestionably rank higher in the order of
priorities than any other economic targets.

The Cultural Revolution was meant to remain strictly
within political bounds, but unavoidably by the end of 1966,
as large numbers of Red Guards moved up and down the

country, China's rather weak transportation system began to be disrupted, affecting the movement of such bulky goods as coal and iron ore. In the first half of 1967 industry, unlike agriculture, was in the throes of the political dispute between opposing factions. A large number of leading figures in the industrial sphere became political casualties of this dispute [28], among them the head of the State Economic Commission, the Chairman of the Capital Construction Commission, the Director of the State Statistical Office and several of the Ministers in charge of important sections of the machine-building industry. Even the nuclear establishment was not spared the effects of the political upheaval. At the same time, China's programme of general education, vocational training, and last, but not least, academic work was set back severely. Thus the full impact of the Cultural Revolution will only be felt in the 1970s and 1980s. In the second half of 1967 the People's Liberation Army was given certain strictly limited powers over the civilian authorities, but order was not restored fully until the second half of 1968 when the decline in industrial production was halted and eventually reversed.

This is not the place to recapture the historical sequence of China's industrial development [29]. Suffice it to say that at the end of 1969 overall industrial production had recovered from the setbacks suffered during the Cultural Revolution. It was probably some 15 per cent above the level attained at the beginning of the Third Five-Year Plan in 1965 and thus some 70 per cent higher than in 1957, the year before the Great Leap Forward was supposed to double and treble production, thus making China an industrial equal of Great Britain within a little over ten years. In the meantime the Chinese leaders have revised their views more than once, and the period during which parity is to be achieved with Western industrial nations is set in terms of decades rather than years.

Industry's share of national product

At present, close on 70 per cent of China's overall economic activities are probably non-agricultural. Half of this amount is likely to be accounted for by industry, the other half being within the sector of transport, trade and communal services. Employment figures are unknown, but one-sixth of the total working population is likely to produce the one-third of the national product defined as industrial goods. A yardstick of the low labour productivity of agriculture can be found in the fact that two-thirds of the working population, engaged in farming, produce less than one-third of the national product. In industry the productivity of labour, though still low by Western standards, is probably five to six times as high as on China's farms. This is a measure of the support by mechanical power from which the worker in industry, but not yet the cultivator on the land, benefits in China.

A comparison with Western nations shows the length of the way which China has yet to travel before it can count itself among the industrialized countries of the world. Energy available per head of population equals less than 300 kilos (661 lb) of coal or little more than one-twentieth of the energy available per capita in Britain, where one person has at his disposal as much electricity as fifty people have in China. The disparity is even greater when the output of steel is compared. At approximately 20 kilos (44 lb) per head of population in China, the supply equals one-thirtieth of that in Britain. The gap is still wider in the case of some of the less measurable ingredients of industrialization. Thus China's industrial base is narrow, its technical knowledge patchy and its industrial production small by comparison with second-class industrial nations, let alone with the major powers China, though an industrial nation, is not yet industrialized in the sense that it is not yet endowed with the supply of mechanical equipment per head of the working population which is the mark of full industrialization. Even so, China in the short span of twenty years has created enough civilian and military industrial capacity to be a factor with which to reckon in the context of the industrial rivalry and political balance of power on the continent of Asia.

Foreign trade

As economic and political self-reliance is one of the corner-stones of China's concept of its national self-interest, it is not surprising that China's foreign trade figures rather low in the list of economic priorities. It accounts for hardly one-twentieth of the total national product. Within these limits there have been great changes in recent years. From small beginnings the Soviet share rose rapidly to almost half the total trade turnover in 1959, the other communist countries' share accounting for yet another one-fifth. Soviet aid was never large or generous, but the blunder of Soviet Russia's dismantling policy in Manchuria immediately after the Second World War was corrected when Soviet capital equipment was supplied in the years that followed. Between 1950 and 1955 China accumulated a debt on account of her trade with the Soviet Union equal to US $1 000 million. This debt was repaid by 1962. The withdrawal of Soviet technical personnel in 1960 brought China's capital investment programme almost to a halt. Since then the level of trade, its origin and composition, have undergone dramatic changes. Today China's trade turnover stands at close on US $4 000 million, with almost four-fifths of the total tied to non-Communist countries. Sino–Soviet trade turnover has declined from its peak of US $2 000 million in 1959 to less than US $100 million at present. As a corollary, the import of complete Soviet plant has dropped from US $400 million in 1959 to zero. Approximately one-fifth of China's current volume of imports consists of grains, and a similar portion of China's exports is needed to pay for these purchases. Textiles account for two-fifths of China's exports, whilst machinery and equipment account for two-fifths of China's imports. Developing countries make up one-quarter of China's trade with non-communist countries. Hong Kong is the main source of foreign exchange earnings. China's foreign debt probably stands at present at a mere US $500 million, and her gold and hard currency reserves are probably of a similar order of magnitude.

Economic balance sheet

In the absence, for a decade, of any firm data it is exceedingly difficult to be definite about China's overall rate of economic growth and its annual fluctuations. The political uncertainty which has hung over the country for almost three years makes it well nigh impossible to arrive at national aggregates, that have any meaning, for the Five-Year Plan period which ended in December 1970. At mid-point, transport, communal services, domestic and foreign trade were seriously disrupted. Unavoidably industry suffered most in the turmoil of 1967 and 1968. Agricultural distribution rather than production was affected, though less than during the Great Leap Forward. Thus the various sectors which contribute to the gross domestic product fared unevenly at different times. Its use must also have undergone different changes in its component sectors. Personal consumption is bound to have been affected by the Cultural Revolution, though less than during the Great Leap Forward.

Assuming that the normalization of economic life which began during the second half of 1968 continues until the end of 1970, an increase of gross industrial production by 30 per cent during the period of the current plan could still be achieved. This would imply an average annual industrial growth rate of 5.5 per cent. Transport, commerce and public services are unlikely to match this average rate of progress. The record of the economy as a whole continues to depend to a considerable extent on the performance of the farming industry, where nature rather than man still determines the outcome. Assuming average growing and harvesting conditions, the best that can be expected is an increase by 15 per cent over the Five-Year Period or an average of less than 3 per cent a year; it might be less. In the aggregate this would mean an increase of gross domestic product and expenditure by a quarter, or by an average of 4.5 per cent a year — a good deal less than the growth rate attained during the first Plan, though more than during the interim period between the first and the third Plan [30].

Nothing at all definite can yet be said about the 1970s, which are shrouded in political uncertainty. The readily available economic resources seem to be fairly fully utilized at present, and new investment projects will therefore have to be set in train even if the relatively modest current rates of growth are to be maintained. However, if China can be spared any more experiments such as the Great Leap Forward and the Cultural Revolution, significant advances ought to be possible in the years following Mao's departure from the centre of power. China's resources are larger, the means of mobilizing them are more readily available and the structure of the economy is more balanced than in the past. Thus,

Table 18.1 *China: agricultural and industrial production (in million physical units)*

Commodities	1952 (Official claims)	1957 (Official claims)	1965 (Estimates)	1970 (Estimates)
Grains (tons)	154.5*	185.0	185.0	200.0
Sugar (tons)	0.5	0.9	1.3	1.7
Veg. oils (tons)	1.0	1.5	1.8	2.4
Cotton (tons)	1.3	1.6	1.6	2.0
Cotton yard (tons)	0.7	0.8	0.9	1.2
Cotton cloth (000 m)	4.2	5.0	5.2	6.6
Coal (tons)	66.5	130.7	230.0	255.0
Electricity (000 kWh)	7.3	19.3	45.0	60.0
Crude oil (tons)	0.4	1.5	9.0	12.5
Iron ore (tons)	4.3	19.4	33.0	45.0
Pig iron (tons)	1.9	5.7	15.0	20.0
Crude steel (tons)	1.3	5.3	15.0	15.0
Cement (tons)	2.9	6.9	11.0	13.5
Fertilizers (tons)	0.2	0.8	4.5	6.5
Paper (tons)	0.6	1.2	1.8	2.5

* Probably understated. (Notes on p. 362.)

Table 18.2 *China: Population and food supplies*

Population and foods	1952–53 (Estimates)	1957–58 (Estimates)	1965–66 (Estimates)	1970–71 (Estimates)
Population (mill.)	550	600	685	750
Grain prod. (mill. tons)	160	185	185	200
Grain prod. (kilos p.h.)	291	308	270	267
Grain cons. (mill. tons)	115	130	145	160
Grains cons. (kilos p.h.)	210	217	212	213
Grain cons. milled (kilos p.h.)	168	169	170	170
Grain cons. milled (cal. p. day)	1 630	1 640	1 650	1 650
Non-grain foods (cal. p. day)	420	460	450	500
Total food consumption (cal. p. day)	2 050	2 100	2 100	2 150

(Notes on p. 362.)

Table 18.1

Note: Production data for 1952 and 1957 are official Chinese claims. My estimates for 1965 differ slightly from those given by Robert Michael Field; they are based on published information as quoted in his article (*The China Quarterly*, No. 42). The figures for 1970 are forecasts based on estimates up to 1968, allowing for recovery from the effects of the Cultural Revolution since then. Production estimates for the years between 1957 and 1967, not reproduced in the table above, but published previously (in articles quoted in references 29 and 30) were shown to the US Consulate General in Hong Kong and were partly amended in the light of their comments. Industrial production for 1966–70 (1965 = 100) has been estimated as follows: 1966: 110; 1967: 95; 1968: 105; 1969: 115; 1970: 130. Agricultural production is assumed to have been affected less by the Cultural Revolution, but this does not apply to the supply and distribution of farm products; nor to public utilities. According to Soviet estimates (*Pravda*, 18 May 1970), production in 1969 was: grains, 185–190 million tons; coal, 210–225 million tons; electricity, 60 000–65 000 million kWh; crude oil, 12–13 million tons; crude steel, 12–13 million tons.

Table 18.2

Note: Population estimates not previously published except for the end of 1966 (for which see my 'Comment' in *The China Quarterly*, No. 31) were revised after 1965 in the light of reports from Chinese refugees according to which census counts were exaggerated in some villages in south China in 1953. The grain production estimate for 1952 has been raised above the official Chinese claim (which was probably too low), but not as much as by Owen L. Dawson in *Communist China's Agriculture* (New York, Praeger, 1970); for 1957 and 1965 the figures are as I have estimated previously (see *The China Quarterly*, No. 35); the forecast for 1970 is based on the assumption of favourable weather throughout the season and during harvest time. The grain and non-grain consumption are estimated on the same pattern as in the food balance for 1966–67 (as previously published in 'Comment' in *The China Quarterly*, No. 31).

Table 18.3 *China: Domestic product and expenditure 1952–70*

Sectors	1952 (Estimates)	1957 (Estimates)	1965 (Estimates)	1970 (Estimates)
	(000 million yuan of 1952)			
Gross domestic product:				
Agriculture	33.5	40.0	40.0	46.0
Industry, mining, construction*	19.0	30.0	45.0	59.0
Trade, public utilities	22.5	30.0	45.0	55.0
Total	75.0	100.0	130.0	160.0
Gross domestic expenditure:				
Personal consumption	52.5	65.0	78.0	95.0
Government consumption*	7.5	10.0	19.5	25.0
Domestic gross investment	15.0	25.0	32.5	40.0
Total	75.0	100.0	130.0	160.0
	(per cent of total product and expenditure)			
Gross domestic product:				
Agriculture	45.0	40.0	30.0	29.0
Industry, mining, construction*	25.0	30.0	35.0	37.0
Trade, public utilities	30.0	30.0	35.0	34.0
Total	100.0	100.0	100.0	100.0

Table 18.3 – *continued*

Sectors	1952 (Estimates)	1957 (Estimates)	1965 (Estimates)	1970 (Estimates)
Gross domestic expenditure:				
Personal consumption	70.0	65.0	60.0	59.0
Government consumption†	10.0	10.0	15.0	16.0
Domestic gross investment	20.0	25.0	25.0	25.0
Total	100.0	100.0	100.0	100.0
		(1952 = 100)	(1957 = 100)	(1965 = 100)
Gross domestic product:				
Agriculture		120	100	115
Industry, mining, construction*		160	150	130
Trade, public utilities		135	150	125
Total		135	130	125
Gross domestic expenditure:				
Personal consumption		125	120	120
Government consumption†		135	195	130
Domestic gross investment		165	130	125
Total		135	130	125

Table 18.3 – *continued*

Sectors	1952 (Estimates)	1957 (Estimates)	1965 (Estimates)	1970 (Estimates)
	(growth rate: per cent per annum)			
Gross domestic product:				
Agriculture		3.7	0.0	2.8
Industry, mining construction*		9.9	5.2	5.4
Trade, public utilities		6.2	5.2	4.6
Total		6.2	3.3	4.6
Gross domestic expenditure:				
Personal consumption		4.6	2.3	3.7
Government consumption†		6.2	8.7	5.4
Domestic gross investment		10.5	3.3	4.6
Total		6.2	3.3	4.6

* Includes handicraft.
† Includes communal services (communes). (Notes on p. 366.)

Table 18.3

Note: Domestic product and expenditure data are given in round figures so as to indicate the highly tentative nature of these estimates. For 1952 and 1957 these are close to those given by Yuan-li Wu in *The Economy of Communist China* (London, Pall Mall Press, 1965). See also: Ta-chung Liu: 'Quantitative trends in the economy', in Alexander Eckstein *et al.*, *Economic Trends in Communist China.* The estimates for 1965 and the forecasts for 1970 (published earlier in articles quoted in references 29 and 30) have been revised in the light of what little has become known of the effects of the Cultural Revolution on the main sectors of the Chinese economy and of their rates of recovery since the termination of this disruptive political campaign. The estimates are meant to indicate no more than the orders of magnitude believed to apply to the period from the end of the first to the end of the Third Five-Year Plan (annual fluctuations not shown). Indices, rates of growth and shares of economic sectors have been derived from estimated volume data, but the various sets of figures have been checked against each other in an attempt to achieve internal consistency. The estimates are subject to further revision in the light of more detailed information than is available at present.

barring external warfare and internal upheavals, such as those of recent years, China ought to be able to become, before the end of the century, a major industrial nation. How much power China will wield in Asia will not entirely depend, however, on its own economic performance and political attitudes. Others in Asia and elsewhere are unlikely to stand still whilst China marches forward.

19 China as a trading nation

Communist China, despite its size, cuts a minor figure in the commerce of the world. In 1970 it accounted for only some 0.7 per cent of total international trade. Chinese exports and imports together in that year are estimated to have reached US $4 225 million, the highest level recorded for Chinese trade except for 1959. Yet this was equivalent to only 78 per cent of the total trade of the small colony of Hong Kong, or to 43 per cent of Australia's international trade, or to 11 per cent of that of Japan. On a per capita basis the smallness of China's trade is even more striking. Its value in 1970 amounted to US $5 per head of the population, compared with US $7 per head for India, US $369 for Japan, US $789 for Australia, and US $1 355 for Hong Kong.

The smallness of this foreign trade stems from the fact that China is a large, underdeveloped and inward-looking country with an economic system that has strong autarkic leanings. The vast size of China and the variety of natural resources it encompasses facilitate a higher degree of self-sufficiency than would be possible for smaller lands. Its poverty — China has a per capita income of around US $100 per annum — means that both productivity and purchasing power are low. Although the planners of China's foreign trade are not un-mindful of comparative advantage, this concept is allowed only a limited sphere of operation. Both national and local self-sufficiency is strongly encouraged.

Japan is China's largest trade partner, taking 12 per cent of China's exports and supplying 26 per cent of the country's imports. Chinese exports to Japan comprise foodstuffs, raw silk and other fibres, and miscellaneous raw materials. Over 80 per cent of Japanese exports to China in 1970 consisted of steel, machinery and equipment (including some 4 500 trucks), and chemicals (fertilizers, synthetic fibres, plastics, and organic chemicals). Trade and politics have been closely enmeshed in Japanese commercial dealings with China. Some 90 per cent of Sino—Japanese trade is conducted on the Japanese side by 'friendly firms' which, at least overtly, support Chinese politics. The rest of the trade is governed by the semi-official Memorandum Trade Agreement.

Hong Kong is China's largest single export market, taking US $467 million worth of Chinese goods in 1970. Nearly a quarter of this total was subsequently re-exported, leaving China's net exports to the colony at US $354 million, or 17 per cent of the country's total exports. Food and live animals constitute the major items in these exports, but manufactured consumer goods are also important. The Chinese government controls a number of retail stores in Hong Kong as well as a network of wholesalers, banks, insurance companies, and other interests. The profits from these, as well as remittances from local Chinese to their families on the mainland, and overseas remittances channelled through Hong Kong, all add to China's foreign exchange earnings from the colony, which were estimated at around US $675 million in 1970. China's export surplus to Hong Kong enables it to finance deficits with the industrial countries of Europe, notably West Germany, the United Kingdom, and France, as well as with the suppliers of its wheat imports. Steel, non-ferrous metals, chemicals, machinery, vehicles, and other transport equipment comprise China's major imports from western Europe, while foodstuffs and raw materials are prominent among exports to these markets.

In 1970 China had a large import surplus with both Australia and Canada owing to heavy wheat imports. Rubber is China's main import from southeast Asia, while exports comprise a wide range of consumer goods directed largely to the Chinese communities.

Sino—Soviet trade fell in 1970 to US $45 million, the lowest level for twenty years. Textiles, clothing, and footwear, with some foodstuffs, comprise most of China's exports to the Soviet Union, while, in return, machinery and equipment and iron and steel are the chief items of import.

There are few countries for whom China is a major trade

partner. Trade with China constitutes around 70 per cent of Albania's foreign trade and between 25—40 per cent of that of north Vietnam and north Korea. Apart from these, Ceylon, with 12 per cent of its trade with China, is thought to be the only country for which in 1968/69 Chinese trade accounted for as much as 10 per cent of the total. Only three others — Hong Kong, the Sudan, and Singapore — conducted over 5 per cent of their trade with China [1].

Foodstuffs constitute nearly a third of China's exports, with textiles and clothing accounting for just under a quarter, and various raw materials together for a little over 20 per cent. Other export items include a wide variety of manufactured consumer goods together with some machinery. Among foodstuffs, rice exports reached 885 000 tons in 1970. Exports of rice have counterbalanced some, but not all, of China's wheat imports — an arrangement that has made commercial sense because of price differentials. Most of these rice exports have gone to other Asian countries (notably to Hong Kong, Ceylon, Malaysia, and Singapore) although some have been shipped further afield (e.g. to Cuba and the UAR).

Wheat imports have figured prominently in China's imports since 1961, comprising some 13 per cent of total imports in 1970. Their volume fell in 1971, but it is too early to be certain that this trend will continue, although recent reports of increased grain yields in China suggest that it may do so.

Machinery and equipment accounted for 17 per cent of China's imports in 1970, and is the fastest growing group. Japan supplied a third of the goods in this category. Peking appears to be giving high priority to transport equipment and the 1970 import list included some 10 000 trucks (around US $90 million in total value) and also forty French locomotives. Japan supplied three-quarters of China's purchases of iron and steel — another growing category of imports — and somewhat more than half of the US $170 million imports of chemical fertilizers.

From 1951—55 Soviet credits enabled China to run a trade deficit. While these credits were being rapaid in the years 1956—65, substantial export surpluses were the rule, except during the agricultural disaster period of 1960—61. Since then China's trade has usually been in surplus, although

Table 19.1 *China's international trade*

Direction of exports

	Total	To Communist countries	To non-Communist countries
	US $m	%	%
1952	875	69	31
1959	2 205	72	28
1966	2 170	27	73
1967	1 915	24	76
1968	1 890	24	76
1969	2 020	24	76
1970	2 060	25	75

Composition of exports

	US $m	
	1969	1970
Foodstuffs	615	645
Crude materials, fuels and edible oils	450	n.a.
Textiles	305	300
Clothing	195	200
Other	455	915
Total	2 020	2 060

Direction of imports

	Total	From Communist countries	From non-Communist countries
	US $m	%	%
1952	1 015	70	30
1959	2 060	66	34
1966	2 035	25	75
1967	1 945	17	83
1968	1 820	19	81
1969	1 835	15	85
1970	2 165	15	85

Composition of imports

	US $m	
	1969	1970
Wheat	260	290
Iron and steel	265	315
Machinery and equipment	240	360
Non-ferrous metals	170	110
Rubber	145	n.a.
Chemical fertilizers	205	170
Other	550	920
Total	1 835	2 165

deficits occurred in 1967 (during the Cultural Revolution) and in 1970. According to Japanese estimates, China's external reserves amounted at the end of 1970 to some US $600 million.

The Chinese government does not have an expansionary attitude towards foreign (or internal) trade. Some of the primitive Marxist disapproval of commerce as being necessarily capitalist in tendency still persists. Yet alongside this attitude Peking is capable of very shrewd assessments of where its advantage lies in trade, and is aware of the latest shifts and prospects in world markets. However, it would not want to push purely commercial considerations to a point which would make China excessively dependent on supplies from a single country.

The role of politics in China's trade is not easy to define. Basically the Chinese conduct their dealings on commercial principles. When they can afford the luxury of political discrimination, or when they judge the issue is sufficiently important, politics may exert influence. Thus it was not until their need for wheat imports became less urgent that they began to discriminate against Australia. The stage at which this point is reached differs according to the trading partner. From Japan, which stands in a special relationship to China owing to ancient cultural links, the Chinese demand a greater degree of at least verbal sympathy from their commercial contacts than is expected from nationals of other lands.

The future prospects of trade with China must not be exaggerated. No sudden great expansion need be expected. Those in past generations who have been deluded by the mirage of the China market — and such there have been at many periods since at least 1842 — have had their hopes sadly disappointed. However, a gradual, if unspectacular, growth can be expected in line with the general growth of the Chinese economy.

20 Mao's goals

More than a decade has passed since the end of the Great
Leap Forward, and it has been more than a dozen years since
China completed its first and, for all practical purposes, last
Five-Year Plan. During this time must of the rest of east and
southeast Asia has worshipped at the altar of a high rate of
growth of gross national product (GNP) and the importance
of concerted government action toward that end — and with
considerable success. Japan's performance is well known, but
such countries and areas as Korea, Taiwan, and Hong Kong,
have for some years now kept pace with the Japanese, and
others (e.g. Malaysia, Singapore, and Thailand) have not been
far behind.

But China has not kept up, and in the year 1971, with the
apparent end of the Cultural Revolution, it is worth pausing
to ask why. Before attempting an answer, however, it is
necessary to point out what China's rate of growth has been
in the years since 1957. The well-known dearth of statistics
emanating from the Chinese mainland is a problem, often an
insurmountable one, for economists interested in careful
analyses of such subjects as changes in China's industrial
structure in the 1960s, the rate and pattern of investment,
and the like. But there is enough information to establish
reasonably clear limits on a range of estimates of the growth
rate of national product.

Agriculture is perhaps the easiest sector to deal with. Anna
Louise Strong told us in 1967 China expected to produce
230 million tons of grain. Miss Strong is not the State
Statistical Bureau but there is no reason to believe that
she would make up such a figure and even less reason to
think that she would underestimate China's agricultural

performance. Thus, this figure can be treated as something like a maximum estimate. When compared with the commonly used figure of 185 million tons for 1957, Miss Strong's 230 million-ton estimate gives one a growth rate of 2.2 per cent a year for the decade 1957—67 — a rate that probably matched but did not greatly exceed the increase in mouths to be fed [1]. Certainly there is no reason for believing that grain output grew significantly faster than population either up to 1967 or in 1968 and 1969. If such was the case, how then would one explain the continued importation of wheat at an annual cost of several hundred million dollars in foreign exchange? [2] Many analysts, of course, do not accept the 230 million figure, but few argue that per capita grain consumption in China dropped dramatically in the 1960s and even a 1 per cent decline a year in per capita intake over a twelve-year period would have ı noticeable impact [3].

Cash crops, vegetables and other forms of agricultural production are more difficult to deal with, but here again there is little evidence in recent years of major increases (or declines) in per capita consumption. Thus, if population growth was in the neighbourhood of 2—2.5 per cent per year, overall farm output probably grew at somewhere between 1.5—2.5 per cent a year between 1957 and 1969. Light industry is closely tied to agriculture and hence could not have grown much more rapidly than the farm sector [4]. Heavy industry is more difficult to estimate, but we do have tentative figures for 1965 [5], and it is unlikely that there was a large increase in output or capacity after that date. The early demise of the Third Five-Year Plan would suggest that relatively few new plants were built or that major additions were made to old plants in the 1967—69 period, since one of the main purposes of a Five-Year Plan is precisely to direct such expansion. By 1969 disruption of the economy had begun to subside [6], and production probably had recovered at least to pre-Cultural Revolution levels, perhaps a bit more. This is rather vague, but whatever numbers one uses, provided they are consistent with the above statements, the reflect an average rate of growth for all industry (including handicrafts) of between 4 and 5 per cent a year for the years 1958 through 1969 [7]. Other sectors of the economy include trade, transport, and government services, including education. If anything, education and other services provided by the government have declined since 1965, and there is no evidence of major improvements in either the trade or transport networks. Thus, an estimate of the rate of growth in national produced based on industrial and agricultural output alone would tend to be biased on the high side.

The only really hard data we have are the foreign trade figures collected by China's trading partners. These indicate that China recovered to the 1959 peak level in 1966, again fell below it in 1967 and 1968, and bounced back part of the way in 1969 (see Table 20.1). Trade is such a small proportion of China's GNP that one must be careful about generalizing from trade statistics. In principle, for example, China's campaign for autarky may have proved such a success that the country can now maintain a high growth rate without any need for an increase in imports of machinery and steel above the levels of the early 1960s. But such a turn of events is not likely, particularly when one takes into account the fact that in the 1950s China could devote over 90 per cent of its imports to its industrial investment programme, whereas in

Table 20.1   *China's foreign trade (in millions of dollars)*

Year	Exports from China	Imports to China
1957	1 595	1 430
1958	1 910	1 825
1959	2 205	2 060
1960	1 945	2 030
1961	1 525	1 495
1962	1 525	1 150
1963	1 560	1 200
1964	1 770	1 475
1965	1 955	1 740
1966	2 245	2 045
1967	1 890	1 920
1968	1 860	1 760
1969	2 060	1 825

Sources: The 1957—65 figures are from R. L. Price, 'International trade of Communist China, 1950—1965', in *An Economic Profile of Mainland China*, p. 584. The 1966—68 figures are from 'China's foreign trade in 1968', *Current Scene*, 1 July 1969. The 1969 figures are from 'China's foreign trade in 1969', *Current Scene*, 7 October 1970.

the late 1960s large amounts of foreign exchange were expended for the purchase of wheat and chemical fertilizers. Therefore, the trade figures provide further support for a picture of modest economic growth.

Even if the most favourable of the above estimates are used, the pace of industrial and agricultural development between 1957 and 1969 averages out at about 3—3.5 per cent per annum. Whether such a rate is fast or slow depends on one's perspective. The pace is higher than that achieved by China in the 1900—49 period [8], and it is similar to that achieved in the nineteenth and early twentieth centuries by many industrialized countries [9]. On the other hand, China's rate of growth during the First Five-Year Plan (1953—57) was roughly twice as high. Further, as already indicated, in much of Asia economic growth has reached 7—9 per cent a year or double and more that of China.

Explanations of China's performance

There are three kinds of arguments that are commonly heard when analysts outside China try to explain what has happened to the Chinese economy since the optimistic years of the mid-1950s. One line of argument is that the economic successes of the 1950s could not have been sustained in the 1960s, largely for economic reasons. A second is that the slowdown after 1959 was a result of the mistakes and excesses of the Great Leap Forward. A variation on this argument is that the Chinese leadership and Mao Tse-tung in particular did not understand the requirements of a developing economy. Finally, there is the proposition that Mao Tse-tung and at least some of his associates have been pursuing other goals, not because they have failed to grasp the requirements for rapid industrialization, but because they have felt that other objectives were more important. Much of this article will be devoted to expounding this third theme, but the argument is more convincing if one first gives the other two theories their due.

Could the rapid pace of economic development of the 1950s have been maintained, or was it a one-shot spurt not capable of being repeated? Certainly there is no easy answer to this question. The issue turns in part on how one estimates the prospects for raising farm output in China. The slowing pace of agricultural development in 1956 and 1957, for example, was a major element bringing the 1956 investment boom to a halt and leading the government to institute a variety of cautious policies. Again it was the drop in farm output in 1959 and 1960 that more than any other single factor necessitated abandonment of the Great Leap. The issue, however, is not whether China's farm sector retarded growth in the rest of the economy, but whether this had to be the case and will continue to be so in the future. Throughout the 1950s, China's leaders attempted to solve the farm problem without resorting to the use of large investments in modern inputs (e.g. chemical fertilizer and modern dams), which instead were mainly used in support of heavy industry. In the 1960s, investment policies were changed, and the rural sector began receiving a larger share of available funds, with the result that farm output has increased, but at a pace that has done little better than to keep up with population growth. If China is ever to sustain rapid industrialization, however, the farm sector will have to do better than it has to date [10].

Certainly an increased rate of growth will only be possible if the government devotes even more modern resources to agriculture. But even if resources are so used, will it prove possible to raise farm output, and, if so, will the effort starve other sectors of funds? There is no reason to believe that this was or will be the case. Rates of return on many kinds of investment in agriculture tend to be high, although there may be a point beyond which returns decline as the capacities of extension services to introduce change and of farmers to adapt to it are taxed to the limit. It is not likely, however, that such limits have been or will be reached in China at rates of growth in yields of say 3 or 4 per cent a year [11]. Thus it is unlikely that the Chinese government has had or will have to allocate vast sums of capital to achieve modest rural gains. There should be plenty left over for industry; in fact much of the investment in agriculture will itself be in industries that support agriculture. It may be that rural society is organized in such a way as to hamper efforts to raise output, but such retarding elements are not the result of 'underlying economic conditions' and hence belong under one of the other two

377

categories of explanations of China's performance in the 1960s.

Another possible interpretation of the slowdown of the 1960s is that China's rate of investment was too high, hence was bound to fall and the growth rate with it. There are several facets to this argument. One is that the poor perform-ance of agriculture may have been a direct result of excessive pressure on that sector to produce a surplus for investment — a pressure that materially reduced the incentive to raise out-put. A second facet is that the Sino—Soviet dispute has both cut China off from significant quantities of foreign aid and has necessitated large expenditures on armaments to defend the homeland against surrounding hostile forces. However, it is difficult to see why China cannot maintain a combined rate of investment and military spending that exceeds that of, say, India by a significant margin even without any foreign aid. India is poorer than China, and its government is less central-ized and hence less capable of extracting a surplus for invest-ment. For all of its problems, India in the 1960s has been able to sustain an average growth rate of 3.3 per cent a year on an investment of 16.7 per cent of gross domestic product [12]. If underlying economic conditions had been the only retarding factors, China, by comparison, should have been able to do better than that.

If agriculture and the investment rate were not insur-mountable problems, is it possible that there is something about China's people, her labour force, her scientists and managers, that created barriers to economic development? Sociological explanations of China's 'failure' to respond to the Western challenge more or less along Japanese lines have always been popular with China specialists. The Chinese family system, the low status of merchants, and any number of other values regularly get trotted out when analysts try to solve the 'why Japan and not China' puzzle. The modern variation on this theme is that all or most of the changes in China's social structure instituted since 1949 have been necessary in order to overcome such barriers to economic growth [13].

This article is not the place to attempt to refute these argu-ments point by point, but a few brief remarks are in order. First, the Chinese labour force from the point of view of its potential for industrialization is among the best in the developing world. It is hard working, disciplined, and easily trainable, all qualities which made it a popular export item to southeast Asia and beyond in the late nineteenth and early twentieth centuries. Nor will China have to wait for a generation or more before being able to produce her own scientists, technicians, and managers. No one yet really knows what it is in a culture that makes it possible to develop large numbers of scientists and engineers, but whatever it is, China has it. American science faculties have large numbers of Chinese who were born and raised in China, the scientific and engineering departments of universities in such countries as Malaysia are completely dominated by Chinese, and in China itself Chinese scientists and technicians are building missiles and nuclear weapons and operating advanced industrial enterprises usually without the help of any outside technical support.

It is, of course, possible that China's underlying economic conditions were and are much worse than the essentially optimistic picture painted above. What is even more likely is that China's leaders have only gradually become aware of the nature of the economic problems which they face. China, after all, encompasses a large and complex society, and few Chinese Communist leaders had had any experience with economic planning and management when they came to power. Further, even in the West in the 1950s the study of economic growth was only beginning to emerge from its century-long slumber.

As indicated above, the second of the three standard explanations of China's slow growth in the 1960s is that the Chinese leadership's understanding of economics was imperfect and mistakes were made. All national leaders make mistakes, particularly in the area of economic policy, but the implication of this line of argument is that China's economic mistakes were on a grander scale than most. What were these mistakes, and do they really account for China's economic performance in the 1960s? Probably at the head of the list belongs the leadership's fascination with China's mammoth labour force and its large pool of underemployed labour. In the 1950s many Western economists, Nurkse and Myrdal to name only two [14], placed great emphasis on the advantages to be gained from mobilizing this labour for rural capital formation. Mao Tse-tung, presumably independently, reached much the same conclusion at about the same time. The main *economic* objective of the cooperatives of 1956—57, and even more of the communes of 1958—59, was to mobilize China's underemployed labour for water control construction. In 1958 the possibilities seemed boundless, so much so that there was even talk of a labour shortage. But the gains in terms of an improved water control system were modest, and a high price was paid in the form of disrupted farmwork, increased managerial and incentive problems, and the like. Another feature of the 1958—59 period was a belief in the powers of decentralization — in the spontaneity of local cadres as a source of great gains in productivity. But the tasks of coordinating inputs and outputs and of insuring product quality were neglected, and the statistical reporting system was virtually abolished.

There seems little reason not to describe the above measures as mistakes. When combined with the Soviet pull-out in 1960 and bad weather in 1959 through 1961, they plunged China into a severe economic crisis. Recent attempts to rehabilitate the Great Leap may succeed in showing that the movement did have some positive features [15], but by no stretch of the imagination can the programmes of 1958—59, as they were actually carried out, be considered an economic success either in the short or long run. We shall return to Mao Tse-tung's own view of the Great Leap later. The fact is that in 1960 and 1961 the Chinese government made major policy changes which effectively eliminated many of the key features of the Great Leap. Acknowledging the major mistakes were made during the Great Leap Forward, however, does not by itself explain China's economic performance throughout the 1960s. To do that, one must further argue that the mistakes were so serious that their effects were felt for many years after they had been corrected. Yet agriculture had recovered by 1962 or 1963, and industry by 1964 or 1965. Slowed development in the early 1960s would, of course, affect average rates for the decade as a whole, but it appears that, if anything, the rate of growth since 1965 has been even slower than before that date.

Little effort is required to find an explanation for the retarded growth of the years 1966 through 1969. The Cultural Revolution aborted the Third Five-Year Plan scheduled to begin in 1966 and turned the attention of China's leaders, at all levels of authority, from economic to political matters. In addition, periodically in 1967 and 1968 and to some extent even in 1969, factories and transport were disrupted by factional disputes. But can the Cultural Revolution be considered a mistake? In particular was it a result of mistaken economic policies as contrasted to, say, errors in political strategy? To ask the question is virtually to answer it. If Mao Tse-tung initiated the Cultural Revolution in order to accelerate the rate of increase in China's national product, then his efforts have certainly been a failure in the short run and give no indication of great success in the longer run either. The Chinese economy would have to grow at nearly 9 per cent a year in the 1970s in order to achieve a modest average rate of increase of 5 per cent over the whole twenty-three-year period (1957–80). But it is unlikely that Mao started the Cultural Revolution with mainly economic gains in mind.

The goals of Mao Tse-tung

Neither underlying economic conditions nor mistaken economic policies adequately account for China's performance in the 1960s. Both factors may have depressed growth below the high rate of the 1950s, but not to a level that barely exceeded the increase in population. That leaves us with the theme of this article, namely that the slow pace of development in the 1960s has been in part at least a result of Mao Tse-tung's determination to pursue a set of goals among which economic growth does not get top priority. To establish this point from analysis of Mao's statements and of events and policies with which Mao's name has been associated is not easy because economic topics are not among Mao's favourites [16]. *Quotations from Chairman Mao Tse-tung*, for example, contains almost nothing on economics beyond a half-dozen remarks such as, 'we must learn to do economic work from all who know how, no matter who they are' [17]. Nor does Mao make speeches on the 'I have a dream' theme in which he spells out how he would like his good society of the future to look. Still there is enough upon which to base a rough outline of what it is that Mao wants the Chinese economy and society to become.

The subject of Mao's economic priorities is best treated historically because, like most of his thoughts, those on the economy and society appear to have evolved over time. No attempt, however, will be made to trace this evolution before 1949. The first point that needs to be made is that prior to 1958, that is for the first eight years of Communist rule, Mao Tse-tung was not intimately involved in economic policy making. In his own words: 'Prior to August last year [1958], my energy was primarily devoted to the field of revolution. I was a layman on construction and knew nothing about industrial planning' [18]. Apparently in 1949 the Party leadership was divided informally into two groups, the responsibilities of one encompassing the economy while the other devoted itself to completing the revolution of China's society [19]. Mao chose the latter.

Concern with revolution meant concentration on such problems as thought reform for intellectuals. Mao was directly involved in the 1955 attacks on the writer Hu Feng, for example [20]. It also meant involvement in the campaign to collectivize agriculture. It was Mao himself who pushed a reluctant Party into the rapid collectivization programme of the winter of 1955–56. The nationwide establishment of cooperatives, of course, involved important economic considerations, but to Mao they must first of all have been the key to the consolidation of the revolution. How could one have a truly socialist country in which 80 per cent of the population were small capitalist farmers?

Mao in 1955, however, saw no conflict between completing the revolution and achieving economic growth. In fact, to him, one was necessary to the other. 'Members of agricultural producers' cooperatives must obtain higher yields than individual peasants and those working in mutual-aid teams. Output certainly cannot be allowed to remain at the level reached by individual peasants or mutual-aid teams: *that would mean failure. What would be the use of having co-operatives at all?*' [21] (emphasis added).

With the success of the cooperativization movement, Mao

in 1956 and 1957 returned to activities that only indirectly involved the economy. In 1956 he launched the Hundred Flowers campaign apparently in the belief that thought reform had done its job and hence criticism from intellectuals and others could be counted on to be constructive. Disillusion with the results of 'blooming and contending' in turn led in 1957 to a major political rectification campaign. If Mao was not yet involved in economic policy, however, he seems to have been giving the matter some thought. In the statement 'On the Ten Great Relationships', made in April 1956, half of what he has to say concerns economic matters. One can even find traces of the Great Leap Forward in this statement. There is a concern, for example, with excessive centralization in the control of industry and with the belief that, 'if we can fully mobilize [the] enthusiasm [of factory cadres], it will be of great advantage to our industrialization' [22]. But the main themes of the statement are also consistent with the decisions of Eighth Party Congress (September 1956) which ushered in a brief period of caution in economic policy. The statement, for instance, urges greater attention to the development of light industries and to industries along the coast (as contrasted to the interior) [23]. Mao was later to describe the caution of late 1956 and 1957 as representing 'the dreary, tragic disappointment and pessimism of the bourgeoisie' [24].

The most important document of this period as far as Mao's economic theories are concerned is the 'National programme for agricultural development, 1956–67', which was proposed in January 1956, although not actually adopted until April 1960 [25]. It directed that the cooperatives were to rely largely on their own initiative and resources to expand the irrigated area from 390 million *mow* in 1955 to 900 million *mow* in 1967 and 'rely as far as possible on their own efforts for the supply of fertilizers' [26]. The objective of rapidly expanding the irrigated acreage by means of locally mobilized labour power was to play an important role in the decision to promote the communes in 1958.

If Mao was beginning to think about economic policy in this period, he was not yet prepared to become involved except in such cases as the collectivization of agriculture where basic revolutionary goals could only be accomplished through changes in economic institutions. From 1950 through 1957, China's leaders introduced the Soviet system of planning and Soviet-type investment priorities. They debated the relative merits of physical and financial controls and the pace of industrial investment. In but few of these decisions does Mao appear to have been involved except perhaps in a very general way.

Mao and the Great Leap

In 1958 this state of affairs changed dramatically. To quote Mao: 'In the past the responsibility rested with others, such as [Chou] En-lai . . . but comrades, the principal responsibility rested with me in 1958 and 1959' [27]. There is little doubt that most of the key features of the Great Leap Forward and the commune movement reflected his thinking.

What were these features? First, there was the commune itself, a rural organization which represented an important step closer to the ideal of a Communist society and one that, it was hoped, would more effectively carry out the transformation of agriculture along lines suggested in the 'National Programme' [28]. Mao said at the 1959 Lushan Plenum: 'The people's commune was not invented by me, but I suggested it. When I was in Shantung, a correspondent asked me: Is the people's commune good? I said, "Good", and he published a report on the strength of this in a newspaper. From now on I must shun reporters' [29]. Mao's lament at the end of this statement does not alter the fact that it was he who gave the initial impetus to the spread of the communes and continued to give them active support from then on. Second, Mao promoted the construction of small-scale industries throughout the countryside including the backyard iron and steel furnaces. As Mao himself says, he 'advocated the promotion of small undertakings with indigenous methods by the masses', and earlier in the same speech he asks, 'Is the inventor of taking up iron and steel smelting on a large scale K'o Ch'ing-shih or I? I say it is I' [30]. Finally, the very spirit of the Great Leap Forward was in keeping with Mao's ideas of how a campaign should be carried out: with speed and with emphasis on the enthusiasm and creativity of the masses [31]. In January 1958 he is quoted as saying: 'On the question of cooperation, some advocate that it should be carried out at a faster rate and some at a slower pace. I think the former one is better. It is better to strike while the iron is hot. It is better to accomplish something at one stroke than resort to procrastination' [32].

The policies of 1958 and 1959 represented China's first full-scale attempt to break away from dependence on the Soviet model and to develop policies and organizations based on Chinese experience. The move was deliberate and was led by Mao Tse-tung, not without resistance. In a speech in June 1958, he criticized an earlier resolution on technical reform, arguing that:

> there is something improper with this passage because it overemphasizes Soviet assistance. While it is necessary to solicit Soviet assistance, we must mainly rely on our own efforts. If too much emphasis is laid on Soviet assistance, will somebody tell me on whom did the Soviet Union depend for assistance at that time? [33]

There seems to be little doubt that at least through 1958 Mao Tse-tung saw few serious contradictions between his programmes and rapid economic growth. In mid-1957 he had justified the rectification campaign in part because it would 'make it easier (for) . . . modern industry and modern agriculture [to] be built in China at a faster rate' [34], and economic slogans, such as catching up with Britain in fifteen years, dominated the Great Leap. It is probably fair to say that accelerated economic development was *the* overriding goal of the Great Leap Forward and the communes, but it was not the only goal. Mao had not lost his interest in the continuing Chinese revolution and the creation in the not too distant future of a truly Communist society, however vague his picture of what that society would be like. In 1958, however, he believed that the two goals of revolution and accelerated growth would reinforce each other. This optimistic outlook did not last for long. By August 1959 Mao's policies were under severe attack at the Lushan Plenum. From that time until the fall of 1962 economic conditions deteriorated. By the end of 1960 Mao had removed himself or had been removed from his command position over the economy and his colleagues struggled with the problems of recovery.

We do not know precisely what lessons Mao Tse-tung drew from the 1959–61 difficulties. At the Lushan Plenum he explicitly recognized that many mistakes had been made in the previous year both because of his own ignorance of planning and because of the excessive enthusiasm of low-level cadres. Outright egalitarianism, for example, had been instituted by many commune cadres in late 1958, but this move was stopped and at least partially reversed in 1959 [35]. Production targets, particularly those for small blast furnaces, were recognized to be unrealistic and lowered (although not necessarily to realistic levels), and Mao acknowledged the necessity of such moves. But in July 1959, Mao still looked on the events of the previous year and a half as more of a success than a failure. At a minimum it had been a valuable educational experience. Quoting again from his Lushan Plenum speech:

Have we failed now? All comrades present at the meeting have learned that ours is not a complete failure. Is it a failure for the most part? No it is only a partial failure. We have paid too high a price, but a gust of Communist wind has been whipped up, and the people of the whole country have learned a lesson [36].

The movement's most severe critic, Defence Minister P'eng Teh-huai, was purged and an only slightly modified Great Leap plunged on for another full year.

The Tenth Plenum

The next indication of Mao's views on the economic situation comes in September 1962, when he talks of 'the situation at home [being] not very good in the last few years', because 'things were blindly directed both in agriculture and industry [and] a number of mistakes were made through taking up work on a large scale' [37]. He also points out that the situation in 1960 was made much more difficult by the battle with Khrushchev. This speech to the Tenth Plenum of the Party is also interesting because Mao makes a clear distinction between the pursuit of economic development ('work') and of revolution ('class struggle') and recognizes that the two goals are not always fully compatible. 'We must this time pay attention to telling all places and departments that they must give first place to work, that work must rank equal with the class struggle, and that the class struggle must not be given too salient a place' [38].

Although at that difficult time he seems to be suggesting that economic development be given top priority, it was also at the same Party gathering that Mao apparently called a halt to some of the more extreme forms of retrenchment that had occurred after the end of the Great Leap [39]. The revolution was to be slowed, not abandoned, in a rush to promote something approaching individual peasant agriculture in the country (i.e. the 'responsibility farm system' of 1961). The country as a whole was asked to concentrate on work, but Mao himself went back to building a base from which to renew the revolution. Throughout the first half of the 1960s Mao Tse-tung was preoccupied by one main theme, the power of bourgeois modes of thought to make a comeback and to destroy the revolution, thereby reversing progress toward the ideal of a Communist society. To Mao the Soviet Union was the prime example of such apostasy, but the events since mid-1959 had made it clear that his own Party and people were riddled with similar tendencies. He is said to have told André Malraux: 'Humanity left to its own devices does not necessarily re-establish capitalism . . . but it does re-establish inequality. The forces tending toward the creation of new classes are powerful' [40]. In Mao's view, the only possible solution to this problem was to cleanse the minds of the Chinese people, washing away bourgeois ways of thinking and replacing them with true socialist values. First, the PLA was 'reformed' and then the rest of the country was told to 'learn from the army'. The Socialist Education Campaign was launched, and then in late 1965 and 1966 the Cultural Revolution began.

To say that Mao had lost interest in economics would be to overstate the case. In a statement in 1964 he referred to the continued need for something like a Great Leap Forward.

We cannot take the old path of technical development followed by various countries in the world and go at a crawl after other people. We must break with conventions and make maximum use of advanced techniques, so that our country can be built into a socialist modern power within not too long a historical period. We mean precisely this when we talk about the Great Leap Forward [41].

But if Mao was still confident that a new and faster path to economic growth existed, he apparently lost some of the assurance he had in 1958 that he knew where that path lay. That at least is one plausible interpretation of the events of 1966, when an effort was made to insure that the Cultural Revolution did not interfere with the economy [42].

When it became clear, however, that opponents of the Cultural Revolution were using fear of economic disruption to undermine the movement, it was economic growth that was jettisoned, at least for the time being, not the revolution. Few events in the history of the Chinese Communist movement give a clearer indication of Mao's sense of priorities. When, in addition, one considers the sheer volume of Mao's speeches and remarks in the 1960s stressing themes such as the dangers of bourgeois thought and the need to re-educate youth, and the paucity of his remarks on subjects related to economic development, there seems little reason to doubt where Mao's basic interests lay. Thus, by the late 1960s Mao had apparently set himself against the dominant national development ideology of the post-Second World War era. Mao, of course, was not uninterested in economic development. He was deeply concerned with making China a great power and that could not be done without a modern industrial economy. He was also interested in a higher standard of living for the Chinese people. But this latter goal could be postponed, and the former would be dealt with, for the time being, by investing in nuclear weapons and emphasizing defensive guerilla warfare.

What Mao felt he could not postpone was the pursuit of his revolutionary social goals, or they would be buried in a rush toward 'revisionism' by his successors. 'In this battle,' he said to Malraux, 'we are alone. I am alone with the masses. Waiting' [43]. But what were Mao's social goals by the late 1960s? The central goal seems to be the complete destruction of classes in China and of modes of thought that tend to recreate a class structure. There is much more to this than a

'bourgeois liberal's' desire to ameliorate the excesses of industrialization or to eliminate rural—urban income differentials.
Yet it is not necessarily out-and-out egalitarianism, either.
Most of all it is a society where all people work for what has
been defined from above as the common good regardless of
whether they receive 'adequate' material rewards for their
efforts. Such a goal, in Mao's mind, cannot be achieved overnight. It must be pursued relentlessly with the reform of
education, with prolonged stays in the countryside for urban
intellectuals, and with experiments with new systems of
income distribution such as those of the Tachai brigade [44].
Will such efforts accelerate the rate of economic growth?
Mao probably does not even think of the problem in those
terms. A great China to him is much more than just a rich
China. But what this great China will look like is not
altogether clear even to him. When Malraux asked Mao
whether it will be the China of the great empires, he replied:
'I don't know; but I do know that if our methods are the
right ones — if we tolerate no deviation — China will be
restored to greatness' [45].

Prospects for the future

Will Mao achieve his objectives, and what will be the effect
on China's rate of growth if he does? There is no certain
answer to these questions, but the range of possibilities is not
a complete mystery either. Even modest social experiments
fail more often than they succeed, and Mao Tse-tung's social
experiment has been anything but modest. It is possible, of
course, that Mao may discover a way to pursue his social
goals without exacting such a high economic price. A discovery of that kind would greatly enhance the prospects for
success of Mao's non-economic goals, but the likelihood of
such a discovery is not great. Too much of what Mao would
like to see for Chinese society would seem to be in direct
conflict with the requirements of modern economic growth,
at least as that process is understood today. Whatever
happens in the future, to date Mao seems to be little further
down the road toward his most important goals than he was
fourteen years ago, just after the successful completion of
collectivization. In fact, he has probably lost ground. For the

past four years he has had to decimate his own Party just to insure that there would not be further backsliding, and he may not have entirely succeeded even in that endeavour. As he himself is acutely aware, his time is running out. No successor will possess his power even in the unlikely event that they possess the same vision of a future China.

Given uncertainty about how long Mao Tse-tung will remain in control of China and how vigorously he will (or can) pursue his social programmes while he is in control, there is little point in trying to predict a growth rate for China in the 1970s. It does not seem likely that China's leaders can afford a much slower pace of development than that of recent years. If true, this will put some limits on the pursuit of political and social goals, albeit rather broad ones. But there is no clear upper limit to how fast China could grow if a new leadership wanted to pay the price. Economic bottlenecks and military needs would probably keep the pace below that of Japan, but how far below is anyone's guess. The question is whether China's leaders will want to pay the political and social price for rapid growth.

21 International reactions to the new China

Although the United States had decided early in 1950 to aid France in resisting the Vietminh insurgency in Indo—China, it seems almost certain that, but for the outbreak of the Korean War, the Americans would soon have followed the British action of 5 January 1950 in recognizing the new government in Peking. But after 24 June 1950 the American attitude changed. Besides taking the lead in supporting United Nations intervention in defence of South Korea and itself providing the bulk of the armed forces needed for this purpose, the United States ordered its Seventh Fleet to prevent any attacks either by Communist forces against Taiwan or by Taiwan-based forces against the mainland. Subsequently the United States began discreetly to build up in Taiwan ('the unsinkable aircraft-carrier off the China coast') a model of what a non-Communist regime might be. However, MacArthur's action in ordering his commandos in Korea to advance to the Manchurian frontier resulted in October 1950 in a massive intervention of Chinese Communist 'volunteers' against them. It was not until two years after MacArthur's dismissal that an armistice was signed which for all practical purposes merely restored the *status quo ante*.

Meanwhile the United States pressed forward with its plans for a Japanese Peace Treaty which was signed, though with some abstentions — notably the Soviet Union and both Chinas — on 8 September 1951. Thereafter Japan, while continuing until very recently to eschew any significant re-armament, advanced almost miraculously to the commanding position it now holds as the third ranking industrial and economic power in the world.

By 1954, a year after the Korean armistice, the outlines of

the new China were beginning to emerge with more clarity. The success of the 200 000 Chinese 'volunteers', whose action in Korea apparently prevented yet another invasion of the Manchurian industrial nucleus, had contributed powerfully to the strengthening of national solidarity. Moreover, besides emphasizing China's continuing interest in a former tributary state, the campaign had enabled Peking to make sure that the Soviet Union fulfilled the undertaking given in the 1950 treaty to relinquish within two years the main Manchurian positions regained at Yalta. This restoration of Chinese authority in Manchuria was paralleled by the reimposition of effective control over Tibet and Sinkiang, though the 1952 Treaty of Economic and Cultural Cooperation with the Mongolian People's Republic implicitly accepted that the latter had become an independent republic, politically aligned with the Soviet Union.

In these circumstances, the decision already implemented in 1949, to make Peking the capital of the Chinese People's Republic, may perhaps have been even more significant than was generally assumed. For while it undoubtedly involved an important element of historical imitation, a deliberate attempt to break away from the Western influence associated with the port cities of the coastal fringe, and a desire to be close to the industrial heart of the country, it may also even then have reflected a concern to watch over the security of China's frontiers with the Soviet Union.

Meanwhile the pattern of economic development as initiated in the First Five-Year Plan of 1953—57, which gave overwhelming priority to heavy industry, was strongly influenced by Soviet precedents and relied heavily on the USSR for both financial and technical assistance. But the new regime did not neglect rural development. Having already reclaimed extensive areas of flooded land along the Huai River, it drew up plans for a much more ambitious conservancy scheme to control and exploit the resources of the vast Hwang Ho basin.

Against the background of decades of chaos interrupted only by what had proved to be a false dawn under the Nanking government, these achievements and prospects won over many who were disturbed by the extent to which the Communists were going beyond the principles of Sun Yat-sen, whose heirs they claimed to be. Much the most significant aspect of this tendency concerned the land reform programme under which, by the end of 1952, some 47 million ha (117 million acres) had changed hands. For while this had ostensibly made each cultivator the owner of his fields – a goal which Sun Yat-sen had regarded as the final stage – the authorities had begun to proclaim the advantages of larger scale organization and to move towards this by promoting 'voluntary' mutual aid teams and agricultural producer cooperatives.

Taken as a whole, these manifold activities suggested to neighbouring countries that China was modernizing much more effectively than India, though whether they themselves wished to adopt such drastic measures was a different matter. Furthermore, other aspects of the new China gave rise to some concern. In 1954 the results of the 1953 census, certainly the most thorough count yet made, showed a population of 583 million within mainland China. This was a far higher figure than had hitherto been suspected. Yet although a majority of Western observers had long held that, even with much smaller numbers than this, China had been seriously overpopulated, the new People's Republic laid the blame for famine and poverty exclusively on the crimes of 'the imperialists, feudalists and bureaucrats in the old China' and regarded birth control as being both unnecessary and immoral, and contrary to the interests of the State. This view was in line with Marxist orthodoxy, which claimed that 'under socialism overpopulation simply cannot exist' [1]. Perhaps even more significantly it was an echo of Sun Yat-sen's hatred of 'the poisonous Malthusian theory' which he regarded as an invitation to 'race suicide' since in his view 'within the last 100 years China has begun to suffer from the population problem; the Chinese people are not increasing while other populations are growing' [2].

To the governments, if not to the ordinary people, of neighbouring countries, mostly much smaller than itself, a China with so vast a population now apparently bent on increasing it still further was a disquieting prospect. And this situation was certainly not improved either by the fact that the new government had already declared in 1949 that it would re-examine foreign treaties concluded by its predecessors and 'recognise, abrogate, revise or renegotiate them' [3] as seemed appropriate. Nor was it helped by the publication in 1952 of a map of 'the Chinese territories taken by the Imperialists in the Old Democratic Revolutionary Era (1840–1919)' which appeared in Liu Pei-hau's *Brief History of Modern China* [4]. And finally, the provision under China's new 1954 Constitution that the National People's Congress should include representatives of Chinese resident abroad seemed to suggest ominous implications for the southeast Asian countries, all of which contained important Chinese minorities.

For all these reasons, therefore, China's southern neighbours were less concerned with the ideological change that had taken place in that country than with the fact that it was now becoming simultaneously more powerful and more efficiently organized. But while this seemed likely to make China a more difficult neighbour to live with in the future, they took refuge in the hope that the change need not necessarily imply any positively aggressive designs on its part.

The rise and fall of Indian influence in postwar Asia

In adopting this stance, the southeast Asian countries took their cue primarily from India, on whose cooperation in postwar Asia the Americans had originally entertained high hopes. Some basis for these had existed since the publication in 1943 of K. M. Panikkar's book *The Future of South-East Asia* [5]. This had argued that India's security depended primarily upon sea power, and hence that in the new era of independence after the Second World War it would be necessary to preserve the continuity of the Indian Ocean defence system previously built up by the British. Moreover such a new regional organization centred in India would not only be concerned with defence but would also serve the economic needs of both an industrializing India and a still mainly primary producing southeast Asia. Geopolitically and economically, therefore, India should in large measure replace Japan in southeast Asia, and though Panikkar recognized that postwar China would also have aspirations in the same area he implied that they would not clash with those of India.

Clearly Panikkar's views showed considerable parallelism with the ideas expressed in Spykman's posthumous book [6] of the same year and were also echoed by Nehru in *The Discovery of India* written in 1944 [7]. But by the later 1940s Nehru no longer looked at these matters in the same way. Thus, while still sharing Panikkar's view over extending India's economic links with southeast Asia and other parts of the Indian Ocean region, he was above all concerned to keep India — and if possible the wider region as well — outside the ambit of the Cold War. Partly with this in mind, therefore, and partly also in order to build up India's national self-esteem (which had suffered greatly from the trauma created by partition) he developed the theme that, in contrast to Japan which had betrayed Asian ideals by itself adopting Western militaristic values, India should follow the truly Asian way of advancing Asian interests by applying the Gandhian doctrine of non-violence to international relations. It was in this context that Panikkar, who had meanwhile become Indian ambassador to China, and in the spring of 1949 was caught in Nanking between its two regimes, used the opportunity to draw up a memorandum, 'the main argument of which was that without immediate and adequate help in the economic field, the political structure of southeast Asia would provide no more than a frail barrier to the expansion of communism'. Since he knew that his own government 'could not move in the matter effectively' he enlisted the help of the British and Australian ambassadors, the latter of whom apparently attributed the origin of the Colombo Plan to this initiative [8].

In effect the Colombo Plan was both an economic variant of Panikkar's original mainly strategic concept, and a collective Commonwealth rejoinder to the Communist takeover of China, although within a few years all the south and southeast Asian countries had joined and the United States had become by far the largest contributor of aid under its auspices. Nevertheless Indian criticism of American policy continued unabated, and although the action of Communist China in invading Tibet in October 1950 called forth strong criticism from New Delhi, it did not deflect India from non-alignment. On 29 April 1954 Nehru and Chou En-lai signed the famous *Panch Sheela* statement proclaiming the mutual friendship of India and China, non-aggression, and non-interference in each other's affairs.

Meanwhile in Indo–China, the strategic hinge between the American-dominated western Pacific sphere and the formerly British-dominated Indian Ocean region, events moved to a climax with the fall of Dienbienphu on 7 May 1954.

Under the terms of the Geneva Conference, hurriedly called at British initiative, Vietminh and French forces were to regroup respectively north and south of the 17th parallel as a preliminary to the neutralization of both zones, in which free elections were to be held by 1956. However, the United States, which had not been a party to the agreement and had carried the main burden in the defence of south Korea, intervened to provide an analogous geopolitical solution in Vietnam, and so prevent the rest of southeast Asia from falling 'like a row of dominoes' under Communist domination. To this end, therefore, it sponsored the SEATO treaty of 8 September 1954, which the United Kingdom, France, Australia, New Zealand, Pakistan, the Philippines and Thailand also joined. Cambodia, Laos and south Vietnam were 'designated' areas upon which an attack would be regarded as endangering the SEATO powers' security. Moreover Washington proceeded to support Ngo Dinh Diem as a replacement for Bao Dai to head a new and more vigorous administration in south Vietnam.

Although the name SEATO implied a complement to NATO and although its purpose was to provide strategic stiffening in the mainly non-aligned zone of south and southeast Asia, SEATO's commitments were much more limited than those of NATO and only two southeast Asian states belonged to it. Predictably India strongly opposed the SEATO policy but, as the first Afro–Asian Conference at Bandung in April 1955 showed, Indian influence within southeast Asia was now on the wane. For besides representing a bid by Sukarno to replace Nehru as the spokesman for the newly independent countries by widening the area to include Africa as well as Asia, the Conference also provided Chou En-lai with an opportunity to steal the limelight by representing China as a friendly, progressive and reliable neighbour.

Meanwhile the United States remained committed to containment. In 1951 NATO had been extended eastwards to include Greece and Turkey, and in February 1955 Turkey and Iraq signed the Baghdad Pact to preserve peace and security in the Middle East. After the United Kingdom, Pakistan and Iran had also joined later in the year, the Baghdad Pact in effect bridged the geopolitical gap between NATO and SEATO, for although the United States did not accede to it, American representatives became members of its economic and military committees. When, after the revolution of 1958, Iraq withdrew and Ankara replaced Baghdad as its headquarters, the organization assumed the allusive name of CENTO or Central Treaty Organization, and the United States entered into bilateral military and economic agreements with Pakistan and Iran.

Thus the principal sector of the vast Eurasian periphery of the Sino—Soviet bloc still not covered by any Western-sponsored defence agreement was India, and as if to prove the validity of the containment doctrine, the Chinese began building a military highway across what India considered to be its own territory in Ladakh in 1958. In 1959 further encroachments were made into both the northwestern and northeastern sectors of the Indian borderlands. Then, early in 1960, China concluded a generous boundary treaty with Burma, and an equally amicable agreement followed with Pakistan over the Sinkiang—Kashmir frontier, much to the annoyance of India which claimed the whole of Kashmir. But it was only after China had made major military advances in the same two border sectors in October 1962 that India, having agreed to obtain MIG fighters from the Soviet Union, finally accepted defence assistance from the United States, the United Kingdom and other Western states.

The Sino—Soviet split and the new version of Russian containment

The decline of India's position in Asia was one of the many delayed consequences of partition and of the unresolved discord with Pakistan which was to invite further foreign intervention. The action of Pakistan in joining SEATO and CENTO had apparently been motivated more by the hope of strengthening itself against India than by serious fear of China or the Soviet Union, but as the United States and the

United Kingdom wanted a stable subcontinent they had no inducement to disturb the precarious military balance between India and Pakistan. However, since China experienced no such inhibitions, it was able in 1965 to reach an understanding with Pakistan, notwithstanding their mutually antithetical ideologies. Thus, when renewed tension between India and Pakistan led to hostilities in Kashmir in September 1965, China strongly condemned India and made threatening gestures along the Sikkim border, while the United States and the Soviet Union strongly supported the United Nations' efforts to arrange a ceasefire.

Even more significant was the subsequent action of the Soviet Prime Minister Kosygin in inviting Prime Ministers Ayub Khan and Lal Bahadur Shastri to a conference in Tashkent, which on 10 January 1966 achieved unexpected success with the cordial concurrence of these two statesmen in a nine-point agreement. While some observers saw in this diplomatic triumph a revival of Tsarist and Stalinist aspirations to control the Indian subcontinent, a more obvious explanation lay in the Soviet desire to resolve the discords between these two neighbours so as to prevent either or both from coming under Chinese control and thus exposing its own extended southern flank. In short, the Soviet Union had itself embarked upon a policy of containing China.

The initiative of the Tashkent policy marked a new stage in the growing estrangement between the Soviet Union and China. Ever since the events which led to the Treaty of Nerchinsk in 1689, the Chinese had tended to eye the Russians suspiciously as the latest wave of predatory steppe barbarians. This was an assessment which appeared to be vindicated by the Russian seizure of the Amur and Ussuri territories in 1858–60, and their penetration of Manchuria and attempted encirclement of Peking during the 1890s.

Moreover the ambivalence, which in Tsarist times had marked the Russian attitude towards Asia in general and China in particular, had continued under the Soviet regime. Thus Lenin had claimed to be siding with the 1 250 million members of the oppressed races who were being exploited by the 250 million minority in the West, but Stalin, despite his comment to Matsuoka 'I, too, am an Asiatic', tended to despise Asians, perhaps because he belonged to a minority community within the Soviet Union. The Karakhan Declaration was never implemented, and Stalin's continuing contempt for the Chinese was reflected in both his discounting of the possibility that the Yenan regime would ever win power, and in his demands against China at Yalta which were at least partly designed to curb the power of the Nationalist regime which he presumed would remain in control.

It is, therefore, understandable that some of the Chinese Communist leaders were apparently less than enthusiastic about the Sino—Soviet Treaty of 1950, though clearly there was no alternative source of help in the great task of simultaneously rehabilitating a war-ravaged China and reshaping it along Communist lines. And although in 1953, following the further mutual suspicions arising from the Korean War, the Soviet Union agreed to extend its still relatively small-scale aid to China, it insisted in so doing that Soviet advice should be sought on the location of ninety-one new enterprises which it was planned to set up.

The sharpening of distrust into outspoken dispute came soon after the death of Stalin and his replacement by Khrushchev. This left Mao Tse-tung as the world's senior Communist leader; but the dispute focused on China's advocacy of a more revolutionary policy than that which was becoming fashionable in the Soviet Union. As Lenin had realized, after the failure of Europe to rally to the Bolsheviks' lead in 1917, Marx had not appreciated that rising living standards in the industrialized countries would defuse the forces making for revolution there; while growing population, together with the built-in weaknesses of colonial or semi-colonial systems, would meanwhile intensify the pressures in Asia and elsewhere for radical economic and political change. According to Chairman Mao this process had now reached a further stage, for the Soviet Union itself was going the way of the West, in backsliding from its revolutionary ideals. But the East at least was 'red', and the prospect for 'wars of national liberation' in Asia, the Arab world and Africa was good.

However, these were not the only factors involved. In particular, the advent of the nuclear age had had a decisive effect on the Soviet Union which, under Khrushchev, was at last beginning to recover from three consecutive decades of privation and suffering and, having developed its own nuclear capability, now had far too much to risk losing in a Third World War. But such a war might be precipitated by the wild talk emanating from China, which as yet had neither nuclear weapons nor an advanced industrial structure like that of the Soviet Union. Thus the latter considered it the height of folly to bait the United States as a 'paper tiger' and to trumpet abroad the need for revolutionary war.

Furthermore the quarrel reflected deepseated differences over the emotive question of population. In an address to a closed session of Communist and Workers' Parties on 18 November 1957, Mao, in advocating a more aggressive line for the international Communist movement, had stated:

> If fighting breaks out now, China has got only hand grenades and not atomic bombs — which the Soviet Union has though. Let us imagine, how many people will die if war should break out? Out of the world's population of 2 700 million, one-third — or, if more, half — may be lost. It is they and not we who want to fight; . . . I debated this question with a foreign statesman. He believed that if an atomic war was fought, the whole of mankind would be annihilated. I said that if the worst came to the worst and half of mankind died, the other half would remain while imperialism would be razed to the ground and the whole world would become socialist; in a number of years there would be 2 700 million people again and definitely more. We Chinese have not yet completed our construction and we desire peace. However, if imperialism insists on fighting a war, we will have no alternative but to make up our minds and fight to the finish before going ahead with our construction [9].

While this statement was much more sober than the highly coloured versions of it which subsequently gained wide credence, the fact that China with a population of over 650 million now appeared to regard such massive numbers as a kind of defence in depth against nuclear warfare was extremely disturbing to the Soviet Union which, with barely 60 million people east of the Urals, shared a common but not undisputed frontier of some 7 241 km (4 500 miles) with China. Thus when Peking, frustrated by Soviet unwillingness to brandish its nuclear might in support of China's claims to Taiwan, asked Moscow in 1959 for a sample atomic bomb so that it could quickly begin making others of its own, the request was refused, and in 1960 the Soviet technicians and advisers were suddenly withdrawn from China.

This drastic move finally convinced the West of the seriousness of the split, and neither the successful detonation of China's own first atomic bomb early in October 1964, nor the dismissal of Khrushchev a week later led to any improvement in relations between the two countries. Already in the preceding July, Mao had referred to past Soviet annexations of Chinese territory and had added: 'We have not yet presented our account for this list.' And in 1965, besides its intervention in the Indo–Pakistan conflict China apparently became deviously and dangerously involved in the confused happening of 30 September in Indonesia.

Likewise in 1965 Lin Piao, the Chinese Defence Minister, outlined the doctrine that Mao's original tactics of revolutionary war in the Chinese countryside were not only applicable to similar struggles in other countries, but also provided the basis for a global revolutionary strategy in which the 'rural areas of the world' (Asia, Africa and Latin America) would encircle its 'cities' (north America and western Europe). While this statement did not mention any active promotion by China of revolutions in other countries, there had since 1960 been a growing tendency for China to regard the ultraradical nationalism of Nkrumah in Ghana and Sukarno in Indonesia as the wave of the future in the miscalled 'developing world'. China appeared to associate herself with this both because Africa was now 'the centre of the anticolonialist struggle and the centre for East and West to fight for control of an intermediary zone' [10] and also in order to try to exclude the Soviet Union from the entire Afro–Asian area. And even after the fall of Nkrumah and all that followed from it, China continued to beat the African drum, and in 1967 signed an agreement to construct, with financial aid of £100 million, a railway 1 610 km (1 000 miles) long to link Zambia with Tanzania.

Nevertheless, during the years that had elapsed since the Bandung Conference, much had happened inside China, as well as in its foreign relations, to cause many former admirers to have second thoughts. Thus after the disturbing episode of the 'Hundred Flowers' in 1957, the 'Great Leap Forward' was initiated in 1958, probably in order to hasten national self-sufficiency in view of the deepening rift with the Soviet Union. The introduction of the People's Communes, both rural and urban, clearly designed to maximize the use of China's vast manpower in agriculture and small-scale industry, led to a frenzy of activity, much of it counter-productive. For the widespread adoption of excessively deep ploughing often had the effect of reducing instead of in-creasing yields, since it triggered off soil erosion in many areas of marginal rainfall; a situation which was undoubtedly aggravated by the dry summers of 1960—62. Further, the policy of 'walking on two legs' as exemplified by developing a mass of small backyard furnaces, like those described by von Richthofen in the nineteenth century, to supplement the large-scale industrialization already under way, led to much wastage owing to the poor quality of steel which the former often produced. Thus, it seems, if one leg is strikingly shorter than the other, 'walking on two legs' may merely result in going round in a circle. At all events such miscalculations seriously disrupted the sequence of China's Five-Year Plans, and it was only in 1966 that the third of these was launched, three years late, over the wreckage of the second.

Almost at the same time in 1966 came a different but no less significant upheaval in the form of Mao's 'Great Prole-tarian Cultural Revolution'. This represented an attempt to counter the incipient tendency which he claimed to see in China of a Soviet-style retreat from revolutionary zeal. While the bureaucratic structure of the Communist Party of the Soviet Union has certainly done much towards making Russia one of the most rigidly-minded states in the world, it does not follow that the way to avoid this danger in China is to swing to the opposite extreme by inducing a condition of permanent revolution. And it is curious that a peasant-created revolution should have led to a concern for instant social engineering rather than for carefully tended social evolution; for any peasant knows that healthy growth is produced neither by chopping the heads off blossoming flowers nor by perpetually pulling up the roots to see how the plants are growing.

Besides again disrupting the economy and interrupting the necessary training of the rising generation, the Cultural Revolution revived widespread doubts in the outside world as to whether a country so vast and so populous as China could be effectively integrated into a single state. But while these doubts recall earlier foreign contempt for the supposed political incompetence of the Chinese, and as such are welcomed by those who now — as in the past — wish to keep China in check, the situation causes no satisfaction to the many who, admiring the immense cultural contribution of China, genuinely desire to see it take its proper place in the modern world.

Retrospect and prospect

If we look back over the centuries we see that China, with its superb combination of internal geographical advantages and further aided by its isolation from other major human core areas, had emerged, before the Oceanic age had begun to knit the world together, as the largest aggregate of humanity hitherto organized into a single political entity. More unified culturally than the whole of Europe and at least its equal in material civilization, China continued to grow and to buttress its isolation by extending its suzerainty over a widening ring of satellites. Yet in expanding the area of its influence but failing to solve the problems created by a burgeoning population which had by the mid-nineteenth century far outstripped that of an industrializing Europe, it was deprived through Western action first of its isolation and then of full control of its own internal affairs. Yet when, half a century after the Opium War, it began painfully to pull itself together, the vastness and proven capacity for creative energy of its population provoked the anxiety of other nations which, partly because of their much smaller numbers, had been above to move ahead more quickly.

Although the scramble of the various European powers for spheres of influence in China at the turn of the century was not specifically motivated by such fears, it nevertheless rested on the assumption that it suited the West's interests for China to be so divided. Therafter, Japanese policy during the first four decades of the twentieth century was implicitly aimed at holding the Chinese giant back. The panic which underlay the American decision in the 1950s to extend the postwar policy of containing Russia to embrace China as well, arose at least as much from the fear of 'China's millions' as from ideology as such. Finally, while the more recent Sino—Soviet dispute has certainly expressed itself in doctrinal polemics, it is not Marxist theory nor the precise position of the mutual boundary in the vicinity of Chenpao/Damansky Island, but the harsh facts of population geography which have generated the fears which propelled the Soviet Union towards 'containment', ultimately leading it to offer at the UN General Assembly in September 1969 to participate in discussions on a collective security system in Asia.

In China, on the other hand, the population problem has been viewed from the opposite end of the telescope, and numbers have tended to be seen as one of the country's few indisputable assets. This tendency moreover has been greatly aggravated by Sun Yat-sen's extraordinary conviction (derived from unreliable statistics which showed the Chinese population as having declined during the nineteenth century) that China would one day be overtaken in numbers by the Western powers and Japan [11].

These mutually contradictory fears of China and other states have reacted upon one another in a way not unlike that of the mutual suspicions of the British and the Russians regarding each other's aims in Asia during the nineteenth century. Conceivably the curious fact that the size of the Chinese population, which in 1957 was estimated to have risen to 656.6 million, was thereafter officially stated to be 650 million until 1966, since when it has been constantly reported as 700 million, may indicate that the authorities have begun to sense the alarm created by the astronomical size of their population. For unless the 1953 and 1957 figures were grossly overestimated, which seems improbable, the present total cannot possibly be under 800 million, and may be considerably higher. But even if China is becoming aware of outside fears it is impossible to deduce from the repeated shifts of official policy over family planning and related matters whether the Chinese leadership itself still believes that so huge and increasing a population is intrinsically advantageous to the state.

No doubt it is possible within China's vast territories to provide the present population with the necessities and even, in time, with more of the luxuries of life, though to the outsider the parts of China where the great majority of the people live already seem far too crowded for comfort. It may also be that the sociopolitical as well as economic tensions produced by the continuing intensification of this already acute congestion — whether recognized as such or not — constitute the root cause of the great upheavals which during the past dozen years seem to have taken the place of more orthodox manifestations of the Malthusian climax.

These remarks are not meant to suggest either that China needs to be subjected to hostile containment by outside powers, or that it should itself attempt measures which elsewhere would be considered intolerable in order radically and rapidly to reduce its population. They are offered in the conviction that a frank and open re-examination by the Chinese of their own population question is urgently needed. In the first place it is at least arguable that any advantages to China of further increases in its population will henceforth be more than counterbalanced by the disadvantages. Hence any major advances towards a better life for the people must depend on a reassessment of this entire question. Secondly, unless some such reassessment is forthcoming, China will never allay the fears of neighbouring but less densely populated countries that, sooner or later, *whatever may be China's present intentions*, the most fundamental of human pressures, for more land for more people, will reassert itself, in one way or another, at their expense. Meanwhile Western scholars and statesmen could contribute no less usefully to mutual understanding by viewing the great Chinese people in more realistic perspective, as neither the heirs to the Tartar hordes nor as an order of humanity so superior to all others as to be incapable of either selfishness or stupidity. Common sense and a mass of accumulated evidence would suggest that they are remarkably like ourselves in both respects.

It is perhaps the supreme irony of the situation that, at a time when the outstanding need was to bring China out of the isolation engendered by geography, supplemented by tradition and compounded during the past century by a wholly understandable reaction to external aggression, the strongest power in the Western world should instead have chosen to reinforce that introversion by refusing to recognize the new China and by blocking its entry to the United Nations. For if Asia, and indeed the world, is to achieve a tolerable degree of stability, it is imperative that China, its largest state, should as quickly as possible learn to appreciate the changed realities of the world outside its borders, and hence begin to adjust its own policies to them.

Since the Second World War the most important of these changes have hitherto been thought to comprise the emergence of the two super-powers and the withdrawal of colonial rule from Asia and Africa, which *inter alia* has brought intensely prized independence to most of China's erstwhile tributaries. Yet today, as the United States, under the Guam Doctrine of 1969, comes to terms with the limitations of its own power, the scene is changing again. While China, despite its many problems, has been making itself a force to be reckoned with, Japan — almost unnoticed — has leapt ahead to become the third industrial state in the world. Thus for the first time in history there are now two suns in the Asian Pacific sky, though the bid by tropical India for a leading role in southeast Asia has faded away in the face of the greater dynamism of these two temperate rivals.

In almost every respect other than the undeniably important ones of ethnic similarity and a common ancestral civilization, no two powers could be more unlike than the small, compact, technically advanced but not as yet militarily powerful Japan, and the vast, sprawling, still overwhelmingly agrarian and eight times more populous China, which has nevertheless developed its own hydrogen bomb. This surely is an even more contrasted juxtaposition than that of Wilhelmine Germany and Tsarist Russia. It is time for all concerned to begin to appraise seriously both the problems and the opportunities which it presents.

22   The Maoist revolutionary model in Asia

'The Chinese Revolution is a key factor in the world situation and its victory is heartily anticipated by the people of every country, especially by the toiling masses of the colonial countries. When the Chinese Revolution comes into full power, the masses of many colonial countries will follow the example of China and win a similar victory of their own' [1].

Twelve years following these remarks by Mao and immediately after the triumph of the Maoist revolutionary model in China, Liu Shao-ch'i reiterated its applicability to the rest of Asia. Liu predicted that revolutions throughout Asia would succeed by following the 'path of the Chinese people'. This course, he said, required a strong Communist Party to lead the masses, the creation of a 'broad united front' dominated by the working class, and the establishment 'wherever and whenever possible of strong people's armies of liberation . . . and supporting bases for the operation of these armies'. 'Armed struggle,' Liu said, 'is the main form of struggle in the national liberation struggle in many colonies and semi-colonies.'

Liu Shao-ch'i's speech was reprinted in the *Cominform Journal* and in *Pravda* [2], and on 27 January 1950 the *Journal*, in a lead editorial, pointed up the relevancy of the Chinese experience to all Communist Parties in colonial countries. The editorial further emphasized the importance of the broadest possible 'nationwide united front' and of armed struggle as 'the main form of the national liberation movement in many colonial and dependent countries' [3]. For several years thereafter the Soviets too held out the Chinese experience as a model for the rest of Asia. Nevertheless, the question of the proper path to power for the other Asian Communist Parties was to become an important issue in the Sino–Soviet dispute, in China's relations with the Asian Communist Parties, and eventually with many national governments in Asia. Differences on this question arose as the international situation seemed to require major adjustments in Communist strategy.

Maoist and Leninist models

Mao's theoretical contributions to revolution fall into two general categories: political and military. The latter involves concepts of guerilla and strategic warfare and need not concern us here [4]. On the political side, Mao's contribution has been limited to practical advice regarding the actual seizure of power. As one scholar has put it: 'In spite of the claims made for its theoretical originality, it [the pamphlet, *On The New Democracy*] actually fails to depict Mao Tse-tung's genuinely original accomplishments, which lay in the field of active statesmanship. It is rather in the area of political action that we must seek Mao's true originality' [5].

Mao's vision of the Asia of the 1930s and the 1940s was only a slight variation of the Leninist formula of the 1920s. Like Lenin, Mao believed that Asia consisted of colonial and semi-colonial societies, and that revolutions in these areas must proceed in two stages: first, a national democratic revolution directed against the 'imperialists' and accompanied by only a minimum social programme. The socialist transformation of society – the second stage – would follow. The revolution would be undertaken by a united front which would include the national bourgeoisie, the petty bourgeoisie, the peasantry, and the proletariat, with control in the hands of the last group (i.e. the Communists). There was, however, a major distinction between the Leninist and Maoist views of the national democratic revolution in Asia, although it was one of purpose rather than theory. Lenin and Stalin envisioned these non-socialist revolutions as principally serving 'international proletarianism' – that is, as a way to weaken the imperialist power. Thus they might hasten Communist revolutions in Europe and promote the security (and ideological) interests of the Soviet Union. The road to revolution in London was said to begin with an 'anti-imperialist struggle' in the Asian colonies. Mao, however, was not interested in London. He saw the national democratic revolution against imperialism in terms of his victory in China and ultimately in the rest of the colonial world. Whatever effect the revolution might have on the Western world was, to Mao, quite secondary.

Two of Mao's differences with the Leninist revolutionary

model were in the nature of emphases which followed logically from this different order of priorities: the first was on
the achievement of Communist hegemony over the national
democratic united front and the second on the development
of an independent source of armed power by the Communist
Party. In Mao's view, to compromise these two points might
not, in any one Asian country, necessarily weaken the purely
nationalist fight against Western imperialism, but it would
certainly threaten the other objective — the Communist
seizure of power. The Soviet leaders were prepared to compromise these points and if necessary to sacrifice the interests
of the Communist Party concerned, but only so long as it
seemed to serve their own struggle with the Western powers,
the main arena of which was in Europe. A third Maoist
principle — again an innovation on the Leninist model — was
that the Leninist organization should focus *primarily* upon
the mobilization of the peasantry. These principles are what
Mao meant by the 'three magic weapons' for revolutionary
success in Asia: united front, armed struggle and Party building.

The united front

As the result of his own experience, Mao stressed that two
essential ingredients were needed to achieve an effective
national democratic united front: it must be led by the
Communist Party and there must be a critical external issue
around which to unite, i.e., imperialism. In his view, alliances
could be made with non-Communist political movements or
with national bourgeois political organs, but the Communist
Party had to be maintained as an independent force, gain the
support of the peasants and take over the leadership of the
national front as soon as possible. To be truly revolutionary,
a united front had to be Communist-dominated. In Maoist
strategy the most dangerous situation of all was Communist
participation, without an independent power base, in a
national front dominated by the national bourgeoisie [6].

Lin Piao, in his September 1965 article commemorating
the anniversary of V-J Day, described in detail the Maoist
'united front' strategy as it had been so successfully applied
in China:

He [Mao] pointed out that the Japanese imperialist attempt to reduce China to a Japanese colony heightened the contradiction between China and Japan and made it the principal contradiction; that China's internal class contradictions, such as those between the masses of the people and feudalism, between the peasantry and the landlord class, between the proletariat and the bourgeoisie . . ., still remained, but that they had all been relegated to a secondary or subordinate position as a result of the war of aggression unleashed by Japan.

The anti-Japanese national united front embraced all the anti-Japanese classes and strata. These classes and strata shared a common interest in fighting Japan. History shows that when confronted by ruthless imperialist aggression, a Communist Party must hold aloft the national banner and using the weapon of the united front, rally around itself the masses and the patriotic and anti-imperialist people who form more than 90 per cent of a country's population. . . . History shows that within the united front the Communist Party must maintain its ideological, political, and organizational independence, adhere to the principle of independence and initiative, and insist on its leading role [7].

Another essential in a Maoist-type united front is brought out in Lin's article. That is, there must exist an external threat which transcends the internal class struggle. The Leninist–Maoist model of a national democratic revolution or a 'war of national liberation' is designed exclusively for a situation in which foreign oppression exists or can be made to seem to exist. A domestic situation in which there is an oppressive, reactionary or a feudal ruling class is not sufficient; the model's very essence, its *raison d'être*, is the overriding threat of imperialism.

Violent and non-violent armed struggle

Another major element in the Maoist revolutionary model is 'armed struggle'. In their polemics with the Soviets, the Chinese insist that 'violent revolution is a universal law of proletarian revolution' [8], and according to the Maoist model, to carry out a revolution it is essential to have 'a revolutionary proletarian Party, established in accordance with the revolutionary theory and style of Marxism—Leninism' [9]. In practice, however, the Maoist model is flexible on the question of violence. Armed struggle for the Asian Communist Parties, as seen by the Maoists, does not necessarily mean violence, but it definitely means the preparation for violence, for 'whoever wants to seize state power and to keep it must have a strong army' [10]. Lin Piao also emphasized this point in his article: 'Without a people's army the people have nothing. This is the conclusion drawn by Comrade Mao Tse-tung from the Chinese people's experience in their long years of revolutionary struggle, experience that was bought in blood. This is a universal truth of Marxism—Leninism' [11].

A Communist Party therefore must, in the Maoist model, always be prepared to use 'revolutionary violence against counter-revolutionary violence'. And, in the final analysis, 'the seizure of power by armed force, the settlement of the issue by war is the central task and the highest form of revolution' [12]. But upon whom the violence will be wreaked, at what time and in what manner will depend upon the objective circumstances in each case. Where the advocacy of violence appears locally feasible as well as beneficial to the national interests of Peking (as for example in Thailand, Malaysia, and the Philippines) the PRC will tend to encourage it. On the other hand, if Peking's political interests might suffer from espousing insurrection (as in Pakistan and Nepal), or if objective circumstances are not ripe (as in most of Africa), the Maoist model does not insist that the Marxist—Leninist forces engage in actual violence. Where an effective national democratic united front is being developed with the governing group (as it was in Indonesia under Sukarno), Mao urges concentration upon a 'united front from above' struggle against the 'imperialist' enemy, with concurrent development by the Communists of an autonomous source of armed power.

The Maoist model, therefore, attempts to take into account the contrasting situations existing in different countries. In application, choices must be made between

China's national and 'great power' interests, and even when world goals are paramount there may be alternate paths to their achievement. The model can thus be shaped to emphasize state-to-state relations or to stress the revolutionary movement. At its core, however, is the inviolable principle that Communist Parties may engage in united fronts or coalitions with the national bourgeoisie and even engage in legal and parliamentary struggle. However, they must never give up their independent source of armed power if they possess one, and if they do not, they must give high priority to its achievement. This is what Mao means by 'armed struggle'. It is not, as many people believe, a commandment to start shooting regardless of the situation. In the Chinese view:

> Until the time arrives for seizing state power, the fundamental and most important task for the proletarian Party is to concentrate on the painstaking work of accumulating revolutionary strength. The active leadership given in day-to-day struggle must have as its central aim the building up of revolutionary strength and the preparations for seizing victory in the revolution when the conditions are ripe [13].

Li Wei-han, a leading Chinese Communist theoretician described the 'armed struggle' principle in these words:

> The working-class Party must arm itself to the teeth ... with all the means and methods of struggle so as to be able to make timely changes in the form of the struggle to suit changes in the situation. The forms of the struggle can be divided into main or secondary, and which should be the main and which should be the secondary differs under different historical conditions in different countries [14].

Mao's insistence on the development of an armed capability, and indeed his whole model, is a reflection of the history and the experience of the Chinese Communist Party, most notably the failure in 1927 of the First United Front with the KMT and the marked Communist success with the Second United Front between 1937 and 1945. The failure of the First Front, according to Li Wei-han, was due to the fact that the Chinese Communist Party was 'in its infancy and did not understand the extreme importance of armed struggle . . . and of controlling the army, and it neglected the work of winning over the army while placing one-sided emphasis on mass movement' [15].

With Mao firmly in control of the Party by the time of the Second United Front with the KMT, this error was not repeated.

> Chiang Kai-shek often made this proposition to the Chinese Communists: 'You hand over your army, and I will give you democracy and let you join the organs of political power.' The Right opportunists lent a willing ear to these words from Chiang Kai-shek and showed much interest in them. Comrade Mao Tse-tung on the contrary always reminded us that we must not fall into this trap laid by Chiang Kai-shek. In circumstances where the Chiang Kai-shek reactionaries continuously strengthened their counter-revolutionary State machine, would it have been possible to win democracy peacefully? Would it have been possible to win political power peacefully? Obviously not [16].

The 'armed struggle' principle also holds that a bourgeois government's army is the 'most ossified instrument for supporting the old regime, the most hardened bulwark of bourgeois discipline', and that no revolution can succeed 'without the disorganization of the army'. This, according to Peking's *People's Daily*, has been confirmed by 'the revolutionary experience of a whole series of countries in Europe and Asia' [17]. This comment, published in November 1960, probably referred to military takeovers in Thailand, Laos and Burma, and most importantly to the situation then existing in Indonesia.

In summary, Mao's revolutionary model emphasizes the crucial nature of armed power but, at the same time, calls for the selective employment of violence; as the path to power, it stresses the exploitation of a national struggle against foreign (not domestic) oppression and Communist leadership over the united front engaged in this struggle. So far as we know, no Chinese Communist leader ever quarrelled with these concepts as the proper abstract formula for the seizure of

413

power. But after the success of the Chinese revolution, changing circumstances outside China required revisions in the model to reconcile it with existing realities, one of which was the Communists' responsibility for China's national interests. Thus began at an early stage in the Chinese leadership a policy split, at first invisible to outsiders, on foreign policy. The 'revisionists' were prepared to follow through with a non-revolutionary policy, but the 'purists', led by Mao Tse-tung, came more and more to oppose them.

Adjustments to model

The 'united front' approach, in which the Communist Party attempts to seize the leadership of the national struggle against a foreign oppressor, was effective in China and later in north Vietnam as the path to power. Indeed Mao has recognized that the Second United Front period was the time of the Chinese Communist Party's most significant growth in power and influence [18]. But in the rest of southeast Asia during the Second World War, the Communist international line, calling for a united front against the Japanese and cooperation with the Western 'imperialists', in most cases took little account of the needs of local nationalist movements. As a result, other Asian Communist Parties were denied the opportunities and flexibility enjoyed by the Chinese and the Indo—Chinese Communist Parties.

The failure to adjust the Leninist—Maoist model to changing circumstances in southeast Asia continued into the late 1940s and early 1950s. During this time, nationalist revolutionary movements in southeast Asia were in most cases solidly in the hands of the national bourgeoisie (that is, the non-Communist forces) who had succeeded generally without Communist assistance in expelling the 'imperialists' — a development which neither Moscow nor Peking either recognized or thought important. The basic reason for this phenomenon lay in the dynamics of the various southeast Asian nationalist movements and in their particular reactions to the Japanese ouster of the Western powers in the war's earlier years.

In both Indonesia and Burma the indigenous social and

political élites had little or no personal stake in their respective colonial regimes and therefore became in their countries the core of the revolutionary nationalists. Consequently, the anti-Dutch Indonesian and anti-British Burmese nationalist leaders were not attracted to the Communist international line calling for a united front against the Japanese. On the contrary, they were inclined to cooperate with the Japanese to defeat the colonial powers, and, hopefully, to achieve independence for their countries. Anti-Japanese resistance movements in Indonesia and Burma did not, therefore, really get off the ground until near the end of the war — when defeat seemed certain for Japan.

In what was then called Malaya, anti-Japanese nationalism could be aroused among the Chinese population; but the Malayan élite was more worried about potential Chinese dominance than either British or Japanese imperialism. In the Philippines, on the other hand, nationalism had been deliberately fostered by the United States and there was considerable residual loyalty to the Americans. Although the Philippine Communist Party came out of the war with an experienced armed force (Huks), as well as with important social issues to exploit, there was little chance that it could capture the nationalist movement from the middle-class pro-American Filipinos. In Vietnam a unique situation existed in which local Western colonialists — the Vichy French — collaborated with the Japanese. Thus the anti-Western and the anti-Japanese movements in Vietnam could be one and the same, and the Communist Party, with its tight organization and dedicated leadership and its reliance upon clandestine operations and guerrilla warfare, was able to seize the leadership of the national revolution.

During the militant postwar period of Cominform policies (1947 to about 1952) Moscow and Peking seemed to attach little or no significance to the achievements of the national bourgeoisie in the new states of Asia. Instead they sought to apply to the new conditions the prewar Leninist—Maoist revolutionary formula. By 1951 most of the Communist Parties of southeast Asia had sought to copy the model by creating front groups against the newly independent but non-Communist governments, who perforce were dubbed 'imperialist lackeys'. This strategy was doomed to failure because in most countries the national bourgeoisie had effectively cloaked itself with the mantle of nationalism. Communist efforts in Asia in the 1940s to organize popular fronts failed everywhere but in Vietnam, for many reasons, but principally because there was no overriding credible issues which called for a violent solution and which could both unite the non-revolutionary groups and make them willing to accept Communist leadership. In addition, the insurgent Communist Parties of southeast Asia had, in most cases, been defeated before Peking could pay attention to their needs.

By the mid-1950s, Peking and Moscow were faced with the problem of amending the Leninist–Maoist revolutionary model of Asia as well as their own international strategies to take into account both the independence of the new states and the general failure of violent socio-political revolutions in Asia. An additional new factor was the major strategic objective of preventing the consolidation of anti-Communist defence communities both in Europe and in Asia.

Under Moscow and Peking's new formula, such national bourgeois leaders as Nehru, U Nu, and Sukarno were recategorized as partially or potentially anti-imperialist. And although it was agreed that the countries which these men led had won nominal independence, the main contradiction or threat which they feared was still said to be the problem of imperialism or neocolonialism – how to break away completely from the West. Thus it was possible to have a 'united front from above' with these new governments on both the national and the international level. Communist governments would cultivate the national bourgeois regimes in Asia with diplomacy, aid and trade, while the Communist Party in each new country would concentrate on political activity and on seeking a common front with the ruling national bourgeoisie.

At Bandung in 1955, Chou En-lai offered peace and friendship on the basis of the 'Five Principles of Peaceful Coexistence' to most of the independent national bourgeois governments of Asia, including the Philippines and Thailand (but excluding, of course, south Vietnam and south Korea). The same offer was made to Malaya when it became independent in 1957. And in 1955 Peking also extended to the United States a proposal for *détente*. China would consider a mutual renunciation of 'the threat or use of force' provided the

United States agreed to a Foreign Ministers' conference to settle the question of relaxing and eliminating the tension in the Taiwan area [19].

At the same time most Communist Parties in the area began to emphasize a 'peace and unity' line toward their respective governments. The Malayan Communist Party offered and obtained negotiations in 1955 and proposed a national unity programme which even enjoined 'respect for the position of the Sultans' [20]. In September 1956, the Communist Party of Thailand called for the formation of a 'national united front' and, in January 1957, proclaimed that 'mutual suppression and thoughts of overthrowing the government must stop' [21]. Agreement on a Laotian coalition government of national unity including the Pathet Lao was concluded in November 1956. In 1955 the Burmese Communist Party resumed its call for negotiations, and the Philippine Communists once more announced that they wanted to enter the field of legal struggle. Lastly, the Indonesian Communist Party, unlike most of its fraternal Parties in southeast Asia, no longer possessed an armed force of its own, and by 1955 was well on the road of legal struggle and 'united front from above'.

The Communist camp turned to this strategy in an effort to create a political climate in southeast Asia in which; (1) the need for a US-centred defence alliance would seem no longer to exist; (2) the allied countries of the area could be reoriented to neutralism, away from the Western countries and to acceptance of China's national interests; (3) the Communist forces, by operating legally or with above-ground front groups, could gain new strength, influence, and legitimacy; and (4) the neutral governments could gradually be won to a close identity of interests with the Communist camp and particularly with China. This strategy, however, required another serious adjustment in the revolutionary model. Attempts by insurgent Communist Parties in southeast Asia to negotiate an end to their rebellions and to win recognition as legal parties, or to form united fronts with the ruling national bourgeoisie, implied acceptance of the possibility that the Marxist—Leninist forces could come to power through a non-violent or even a parliamentary transition. The peaceful coexistence line pursued by Moscow and Peking toward these new Asian governments also implied that the two Communist powers believed that violent seizures of power by Marxist—Leninist forces in Asia were unlikely and that attempts at such were, therefore, undesirable.

The Soviet leadership came to grips with this problem, and Nikita Khrushchev, in his 1956 address to the Twentieth Congress of the Communist Party of the Soviet Union (CPSU), confirmed the possibility of peaceful transition. This important ideological breakthrough was formalized in the 1957 Moscow Declaration of Communist Parties. But Moscow and Peking disagreed from the start as to whether the concept of peaceful transition was to be strategic or tactical. This difference in interpretation of the new foreign policy line would eventually also mark the division in Peking between revisionists and purists.

The Chinese delegation in Moscow, headed by Mao Tse-tung, signed the 1957 Declaration. However, in a memorandum to the other delegates, it privately disagreed with the section dealing with peaceful transition. The Chinese memorandum, probably written by Mao, maintained that it was tactically desirable to refer to the possibility of peaceful transition because 'it enables the Communist Parties of the capitalist countries to sidestep attacks on them on this issue, and it is politically advantageous — advantageous for winning over the masses and also for depriving the bourgeoisie of its pretext for such attacks and isolating it' [22]. But Mao's main thrust concerned the central point in his formula for the Communist Parties of Asia: the establishment of autonomous sources of power *with or without* concurrent legal and peaceful struggle.

> The parliamentary form of struggle must be fully utilized, but its role is limited. What is most important is to proceed with the hard work of accumulating revolutionary strength; peaceful transition should not be interpreted in such a way as solely to mean transition through a parliamentary majority. The main question is that of the State machinery, namely the smashing of the old State machinery [chiefly the armed forces] and the establishment of the new State machinery [chiefly the armed forces] [23].

Successes and failures of the new line

The international Communist strategy of peaceful coexistence and the 'united front from above' approach adopted by many Asian Communist Parties at first seemed to promise success. There was a trend toward neutralism in Thailand and Cambodia, and hints of it even in Malaya. The Indonesian Communist Party proved itself the strongest single Party in the 1957 elections in central Java; the Communist-dominated National United Front in Burma won 30 per cent of the vote in an election in 1958; and a 'Socialist Front' was formed in Thailand in 1957. In Singapore, the People's Action Party (PAP), in which there were many members of the Malayan Communist Party, won a landslide victory in the May 1958 elections. In addition, the capture by the Communist Party of India of political control in Kerala in 1957 seemed further to attest to the efficacy of this general strategy, as did the accession to power of the neutralist and Leftist Bandaranaike government in Ceylon in the spring of 1956 [24]. By 1960, however, these developments had led to mixed results. To Communist strategists, the most dramatic success was probably the beginning of the reorientation of the Sukarno government in Djakarta to a community of interests with Peking and a concurrent strengthening of the local Communist Party, the PKI. Developments in Cambodia were also pleasing since the government there seemed to have taken a neutralist course and to have gone a long way toward accommodation with China's 'great power' interests. In Laos, the Communist Pathet Lao improved their position through a combination of political and military manoeuvring, and the same could be said of the National Liberation Front in south Vietnam.

Nevertheless, there were also failures which presented Moscow and Peking with another ideological and policy dilemma. The United States had clearly rejected rapprochement with the PRC and had chosen a policy of isolating, and when possible, weakening her. Peking had also failed to reorient any of the Western allied nations of southeast Asia toward neutralism, or even toward some accommodation with China's national interests. The Sarit coup of October 1958 eliminated the possibility of neutralism in Thailand,

and by 1959 the faint hope in the case of Malaya had dissipated. A neutralist course had never seemed a real possibility
in the Philippines. The cooperation of Thailand and the
Philippines with American efforts in Indo—China and the
muted sympathy of both Malaya and Singapore in this regard
were all clear confirmation of Communist failures. In addition, the neutral state of Burma (like India), while accommodating to China's national interests, had not moved
significantly toward an acceptance of China's 'great power'
interests.

On the ideological front, the Communist Parties in Burma,
Thailand, Malaya—Singapore, and the Philippines were not
benefiting from the 'united front from above' policy. In
Burma, the assumption of power by General Ne Win closed
off the political road to the Communists as well as to other
Parties. In Singapore, the PAP leader of the government, Lee
Kuan-yew, effectively isolated the extreme Leftists in his
Party. And, in Malaya, as in Burma, the 'national bourgeois'
government refused to discuss legalization of the Communist
Party unless the armed guerrilla bands surrendered.

Disagreement on the national democratic state

Moscow and Peking were thus faced with the need to adjust
their revolutionary model once again. This time the problem
was how to treat neutralist national bourgeois governments in
which there was little or no place for local Communist groups
and which in many cases used the military to suppress the
'proletarian forces'. In Burma, for example, successive
governments relentlessly pursued the Communist bands [25].

The revisionist answer was the promulgation of the concept of the national democratic state — one which implied
that a non-Communist government, which followed a non-
capitalist economic path and an anti-imperialist foreign
policy, could actually lead its country into a socialist revolution. In other words, not only was peaceful transition to
socialism possible, but it could be accomplished by
non-Marxist—Leninist leadership. This doctrine was espoused
in the 1960 Moscow Declaration.

Soviet articles in 1963 made explicit the theory that even
non-Marxist Socialist Parties might become 'mass Parties of

the Marxist–Leninist type' through the growing working class within them [26]. And *Pravda*, in December 1963, amended the 1960 criteria for a national democratic state by eliminating the requirement that it must permit legalization of the Communist Party. Revolutionary democracy or non-capitalist development, *Pravda* said, could occur without the existence of a Communist Party but under 'the influence of the world socialist system' (i.e. the Soviet Union) [27].

The Chinese delegation to the 1960 Moscow Conference signed the Moscow Declaration, but only after it had privately protested the concept of the national democratic state and circulated copies of Mao's 1957 memorandum on peaceful transition. The senior Chinese delegate was Liu Shao-ch'i, later to be labelled China's leading revisionist. Was Liu only going through a formality in distributing Mao's memorandum? Perhaps, for it seems evident in the case of Burma that Liu, in practice, accepted the theory of a national democratic state and its implications for the Communist Parties concerned.

In 1964, Peking, in the course of its polemics with Moscow, publicly renounced any allegiance to the Soviet concept of peaceful transition and, by implication, to the concept of a national democratic state. The theory of a national democratic revolution or a national democratic front remained acceptable to the Maoists. The difference between peaceful transition and the existence or non-existence of national democratic states were largely theoretical. Nonetheless, these differences were to have important consequences for Peking in its relations with the governments and the Communist Parties of Asia.

Soviet leaders and the Chinese revisionists maintained that in many cases a parliamentary path to the socialist revolution — and thus presumably to an identity of interests with the Soviet Union and China — was possible. Accordingly, the revisionists held that the Communist Parties of the national democratic states could downplay the role of 'armed struggle', and that their leadership of the united front was no longer a prerequisite. While they expected a national democratic state to maintain a friendly posture toward the socialist camp and an anti-imperialist position, it was not necessary that such a state became actively anti-American. To the

Maoists, however, the creation of 'people's democratic dictatorships' in Asia remained a feasible as well as the desirable objective. Mao feared the potential consequences of revisionist policy, external as well as internal, on the achievements of both the Communist Party and his own historic mission. Such policies, he foresaw, would compromise the long range goals of his revolution. Thus, Maoism continued to require that the Communists must assert hegemony of any 'anti-imperialist' united front. Accordingly, the potential for armed struggle had to be retained; and, the immediate objective of any united front had to remain the exacerbation of the anti-US struggle.

The divergent model

There were several major developments in the late 1950s and early 1960s which prompted Peking, and in particular the Maoist leadership, to reassert the original Maoist formula and, in effect, to abandon the Bandung policy. These included: (1) the evolving Sino—Soviet split; (2) the conflict with India; (3) the success of the Maoist strategy in Indonesia prior to 30 September 1965; and (4) the intensification of the war in Indo—China.

The Sino—Soviet dispute brought into sharp focus the ideological issues at stake as well as what the Maoists saw to be the consequences of revisionist policies. As the question of the proper path to power became an issue with which Mao and his erstwhile Soviet comrades berated one another, Mao insisted more and more on applying his formula in China's sphere of influence. In addition, Peking found it increasingly difficult to turn down demands for militant support from such Maoist-lining groups as the Burmese Communist Party.

The Sino—Soviet dispute also involved differing national interests in a strategy of peaceful coexistence as applied to the United States and to Western-associated nations in Asia. The Communist failure to associate the neutralist nations with the socialist camp, to amend the China policies of the pro-Western states, or to improve the positions of the local Communist Parties represented a more fundamental defeat for Chinese than for Soviet interests. For Moscow, a neutral and non-aligned Asia, even if achieved only gradually, was a satisfactory objective for the foreseeable future. In addition, the limited Soviet–US *détente* continued, although subject to occasional, and sometimes notable, reverses as in Berlin, the Congo, Cuba and Laos.

At this point the Chinese leadership, probably including even the revisionists, began to see that Soviet policy tended to freeze the international *status quo* with China's major objectives unrealized. Such cases as the 1958 Quemoy crisis and the border war with India must have made it clear to Peking that Moscow would not risk its own security to achieve China's national objectives. Consequently, for strategic as well as ideological reasons, Peking concluded that China should not subordinate her interests to an international movement led by the Soviet Union. Nor could China remain an autonomous subsphere within the international movement. Thus, Mao decided to opt out of the Soviet-led system and attempted, in competition with Moscow, to establish Peking as the centre of a new Party–State bloc in Asia. Even Liu Shao ch'i and those who tended to think as he did probably supported this strategy, at least in theory. Nonetheless, whenever this 'great power' goal conflicted with China's more immediate interests, the Liuists were prone to give priority to the latter, even if it meant collaborating with Moscow.

In addition to the failure of the Bandung policy, other external events contributed to the reassertion of the Maoist and the rejection of the revisionist policies. Both the growing influence of the PKI in Indonesia and the potential advantages for a Peking–Djakarta alliance stemming from the conflict over Malaysia seemed to offer positive confirmation of the Maoist approach. But an even more important development was the intensification of Communist insurrection in Indo–China beginning in the early 1960s. The increasing US involvement there provided both a justification and an incentive for the stimulation of armed struggle within the Western-oriented countries of southeast Asia. In terms of the Maoist model, the situation in Indo–China played the part of the 'imperialist threat' that the Communist Parties claimed was necessary for an effective united front. The fomenting of a 'storm of anti-US struggles' in Indo–China fit the Maoist strategy for the achievement of Peking's political goals in Asia. Consequently, Peking's objective in 'punishing' countries (such as Thailand) for their cooperation with the United States in Vietnam was strategic, while Hanoi's was more tactical.

The 'other side' (the revisionists) in the Chinese leadership may have agreed to the wisdom of such pressure on the allied countries, but, in general, it probably had a more short term, tactical approach to this issue, as it may also have had on the dispute with India. Further, the opposition group in Peking very likely agreed that, in the circumstances, China's encouragement of armed struggle in Thailand, Malaysia and the Philippines was desirable as a pressure tactic. But unlike Mao, they were probably not committed to carrying such insurrection through to the bitter end. During 1965, disputes over domestic and foreign policies, as well as over the crisis in Vietnam and the Communist disaster in Indonesia contributed to further polarization within the Chinese leadership. The divisions were between revisionism and revolution, caution and boldness, national security and ideological principle, shortrun gains and long term objectives. Mao prevailed, and the result was an attempt to apply the revolutionary formula both at home and abroad.

The model as an international strategy

The Maoists tend to view the entire world struggle in terms of their own revolutionary experience. Lin Piao, in his article of September 1965, explicitly recasts the world in the shape of China's own revolution: 'Taking the entire globe, if north America and western Europe can be called "the cities of the world", then Asia, Africa and Latin America constitute "the rural areas of the world" ' [28]. As has been pointed out, for Communist leaders the analytical categories relevant to domestic and international politics are usually identical [29]. This phenomenon is particularly strong in revolutionary leaders who, having achieved power in the face of heavy odds, tend to assume universality for their strategies. So it has been with Mao Tse-tung, who has transposed, his revolutionary formula on to the world scene, categorizing forces and events not only in Marxist–Leninist terms, but also in terms of the Chinese revolutionary experience.

Thus Mao considers that the Chinese-led Asian revolution

is at a stage similar to that faced by the CCP at the time of the Resist Japan Movement. Today, the Chinese People's Republic plays the part of the revolutionary vanguard, while the role of Japanese imperialism is played by the United States, whose alleged oppression must be made into the transcending threat which can unify Asia, and ultimately Africa and Latin America, under China's leadership. In this picture, Asia and the international Communist movement today represent China and the Chinese nationalist movement in the 1930s and 1940s. The Soviets are the contemporary Kuomintang nationalists — competitors for power within the system, but also colluders and compromisers with the 'imperialist aggressors'. Mao sees China as the 'base area' of the world revolution, as Yenan was the 'base area' of the Chinese Revolution. And, in this sense, the Cultural Revolution is to the international united front what the rectification drives within the CCP in 1941 and 1942 were to the anti-Japanese front in China: an effort to maintain purity and fervour in the revolutionary nucleus.

As in 1936, the 'imperialists' are today immeasurably stronger than the 'true revolutionary' forces (the Chinese Communist Party then; China now); so too is the contender for leadership of the 'anti-imperialist struggle' (the KMT yesterday; the USSR today). And once again the Chinese Communists have called for a broad united front to oppose the imperialists. This is the basis on which Mao hopes to defeat his Soviet competitors for leadership in the system. Lin Piao put it this way:

> Just as the Japanese imperialist policy of subjugating China made it possible for the Chinese people to form the broadest possible united front against them, so the US imperialist policy of seeking world domination makes it possible for the people throughout the world to unite all forces that can be united and form the broadest possible united front for converging attack on US imperialism [30].

As Mao eventually succeeded in making the Chinese Communist Party seem to be more anti-imperialist than the KMT, today he strives to make China seem more anti-imperialist than the Soviets. As with the KMT during the war with Japan, the present policy toward the Soviets in the international united front is a combination of struggle and cooperation, with very little of the latter. In the Vietnam crisis, Mao's colleagues felt that he was deviating from the model by excluding Soviets from the united front against the United States. But Mao continues to follow the same revolutionary opportunism today as he did during the Resist Japan campaign; his main efforts are on exploiting the war so as to strengthen his position militarily and politically and to discredit his opponents — in this case, the Soviets.

According to the dissident Communist leader, Chang Kuo-tao, Mao's policy in the war against Japan was '70 per cent expansion, 20 per cent dealing with the KMT, and 10 per cent resisting Japan' [31]. The efforts of the Chinese Communist Party were in fact balanced about evenly among these three priorities. On the world scene today, Mao's priorities seem similar: strengthening China, dealing with the Soviets, and resisting the United States, in that order.

Today's struggle against US 'imperialism', like the earlier one against the Japanese, is to Mao primarily a way to achieve his revolutionary and power objectives, both in the Afro–Asian world and in the international Communist movement. The 'imperialist' threat thus remains a vital element in the Maoist domestic and international strategy. Just as confrontation with the West over Malaysia seemed to provide an opportunity for the PKI and for China in Indonesia, so the Western presence in Thailand, the Philippines, Malaysia, Singapore, and south Korea was seen as the catalyst of a united front, anti-imperialist revolution in those countries. Even in Japan, the Maoists hoped that conflicting Japanese and American interests would fuel a revolution, and the Japanese Communist Party was denounced by Peking as too practical-minded to lead the struggle.

In 1967, the Maoists also pinned their hopes on a revolutionary course in India, despite the lack of a credible imperialist intruder. This threat was likewise missing in the Burmese Communist Party's programme. The Party was reasonably strong organizationally and militarily but lacked a national class-transcending issue with which to forge a united front. It seems possible that for this reason some of the Maoists in Peking, in 1967, may actually have hoped to frighten the Rangoon government into closer political and military ties with either the United States or Moscow. Prince Sihanouk, in 1968, prophetically warned that this was also the Communist objective in Cambodia. He charged that the Communists hoped that he would have to hand power over to someone who would call for US aid and that 'when the Americans gave Cambodia arms and money, they [the Communists] would have a pretext for having their Vietnamese and Chinese masters come and invade Cambodia' [32]. This ambivalent view of imperialism is in keeping with the dialectics of Marxism—Leninism and also with Mao's own intellectual penchant. The Chinese leader, for example, has stated that while both World Wars brought terrible destruction and suffering, without them there might not have been the victories of the socialist revolution in Russia and China. Khrushchev revisionism, according to Mao, is a heinous thing but because of it a new path to Communism has been opened up in China. So the threat of US 'imperialism', while carrying with it immediate danger, will in the long run produce a new Maoist order in Asia.

Mao sees the world drama of today as a rerun of the Chinese revolution, but with the characters drawn to a larger scale. Meanwhile, his tactics and strategies are similar to those he used against the Japanese and the KMT: a 'protracted war' and the tactics of attrition and harassment to deplete and weaken the enemy and 'gradually to change the balance of forces between the enemy and ourselves'. The main revolutionary forces – the Chinese – are only committed to defend the territorial base. Applied to the present world struggle, this policy calls for safeguarding the main force (China) and avoiding a direct clash between this force and the enemy (the United States). The guerrillas who will wear down the over-extended forces of the United States and 'destroy it piece by piece' are the peoples of Asia, Africa and Latin America. In Lin Piao's words:

> Everything is divisible and so is this colossus of US imperialism. It can be split up and defeated. The peoples of Asia, Africa, Latin America and other regions can destroy it piece by piece, some striking at its head and others at its feet. That is why the greatest fear of US

427

imperialism is that people's war will be launched in different parts of the world and particularly in Asia, Africa and Latin America and why it regards people's war as a mortal danger [33].

In Asia, Mao sees Vietnam as the major battle front in his 'protracted war' with the United States. This vision is at the heart of the occasional friction between Peking and Hanoi. The latter naturally believes that its immediate goals in the war are of primary importance, while Mao views them only as part of his more important struggle with the United States and the USSR.

Further adjustments

The Maoist revolutionary formula must either adapt to the new realities in Asia or become irrelevant. As with the Soviet Union, Peking's revolutionary policy must both serve and be consistent with China's national or power interests, for by definition, that which promotes China's security and/or the expansion of its influence *ipso facto* promotes the long-term interests of world revolution. There is, in fact, little doubt that recent developments have prompted a Chinese reassessment of the threats and opportunities in Asia, which in turn, could result in a reordering of Peking's policies.

Peking, in 1969, publicly stated that Moscow intended to apply the 'Brezhnev Doctrine' to China and warned for the first time that the possibility of a Soviet attack on China was real and immediate. The Soviet Union was thus presented by Peking as not only the ideological but the national enemy of China. In addition to the 'threat from the north', the Sato—Nixon Communique of November 1969 marked a turning point in the Chinese assessment of Japan's role in Asia. Thereafter, Peking would view Japan not as an auxiliary of the United States but as an independent threat and as China's major Asian rival. Further, both the Soviet Union and Japan were increasing their influence in south and southeast Asia through trade, aid and diplomacy; and the Soviets were establishing a naval presence in the Indian Ocean. In contrast, Peking had no direct influence on many Asian governments, having in these countries gambled on the prospects of eventual victory for the local Maoists.

By 1970 it must have been obvious to the Chinese leadership that their assessment of revolutionary prospects in Asia, particularly those made during the Cultural Revolution, had been overly optimistic. The Indian Naxalites failed to spread like a prairie fire into the Indian countryside, and the Nagas and the Mizos, also supported by Peking in their rebellion against New Delhi, were being successfully pacified. The north Koreans had not been able to foster a 'liberation struggle' in the south. Japanese student disorders had died down, the Liberal Democratic Party had won an increased majority in the 1969 elections, and the United States had agreed to restore Japanese control over Okinawa, thus neutralizing the most promising nationalistic anti-US issue in Japan. The Burmese Communist Party had fared badly since 1967, when it openly espoused the Maoist line. Victory for the Communist insurgents in Malaysia, the Philippines and Indonesia still appeared to be in the far off, uncertain future. In Thailand, what gains the Communists had made were primarily by exploiting the dissidence of minority tribes in the north and Muslim areas in the far south. In south Vietnam, the long-term consequences of the 'Vietnamization' programme remained obscure, but it was undeniably weakening the 'anti-imperialist' component in the Maoist formula. It was only in Indo—China that the revolutionary course held clear promise. Sihanouk's acceptance of the nominal leadership of a Communist-dominated revolutionary movement gave heart to the Maoist strategists.

More recent, and quite different, developments may also influence a Peking decision to further adjust the Maoist model. Perhaps most important, the Nixon Doctrine, China's nuclear achievements, US moves to improve relations with Peking, and domestic pressures, have combined to persuade governments such as Japan, Malaysia, Thailand and the Philippines to explore the possibilities of accommodation with China. Thus, for the first time, political alternatives may be opening to Peking in these countries. And in the future, as generally in the past, we may expect the Chinese leadership to shape its position on revolutionary movements to serve Peking's foreign policy interests.

23 The changing pattern of US–China relations

The year 1971 will long be remembered as a major turning point in US–China relations. For more than two decades, no two major societies have had so little significant contact with each other, and no two major powers have faced each other with such a seemingly irreconcilable clash of interests and purposes. Then, on 15 July, simultaneous announcements were made in Washington and Peking that before next May President Nixon would meet with China's top leaders in Peking 'to seek the normalization of relations' and 'to exchange views on questions of concern to the two sides'.

This simple statement was a blockbuster, and it had far-reaching and immediate worldwide repercussions. Already, it seems clear that the basic pattern of international relations, especially big power relations in Asia, and the fundamental configuration of power in the region, are in the process of significant change. The decision to hold a US–China summit meeting is not, of course, the prime cause of this change. Rather, it is a symptom of it, and a result of a variety of trends that have gradually altered the positions and policies not only of Peking and Washington but of Moscow and Tokyo as well.

The announcement of President Nixon's trip came as a total surprise to all but a very few persons in the United States and Chinese governments. What was surprising, however, was the boldness of the President's decision to make a trip to Peking, not the idea that significant changes in US policy toward China, and in US–China relations, might now be possible. It has been clear for some time that many factors have been at work that were likely to lead to some change in Sino–American relations. Unless one understands them, I think, it is extremely difficult to comprehend either the historical or contemporary context in which the Nixon— Chou meeting should be viewed.

Soviet considerations

A variety of important factors and forces have been influencing Peking, for some time, to reassess its policies. The first, and probably the most important of these, has been the Sino—Soviet split. The origins of the Sino—Soviet split can be traced back at least to the 1950s, and in some respects to earlier years. Suffice it to say that by the late 1950s, particularly during the period 1957—59, a variety of conflicts of specific national interests and policies destroyed the basis of close collaboration between the two nations. By the early 1960s relations between China and the Soviet Union were characterized by basic hostility and fear rather than cooperation. During 1968—69, Chinese fears were heightened. In 1968, after the Czechoslovakian crisis, Moscow proclaimed its so-called Brezhnev Doctrine, justifying Soviet intervention in the internal affairs of other socialist states, and the Chinese were clearly worried that Moscow might try to apply this to China. Finally, in 1969, when major Sino—Soviet border clashes erupted, the two countries came dangerously close to war. Throughout this period the Soviet Union carried out a huge build-up of military forces on China's borders, which deeply worried the Chinese.

By 1969, therefore, Peking's leaders probably regarded the possibility of a military conflict with the Russians as a greater danger and potential threat to China than the possibility of armed conflict with the United States. Nothing has happened since then to basically change the situation. It is true that since the height of the conflict in 1969 tensions between Moscow and Peking have significantly cooled, but the basic Chinese fear of Russian intentions continues — and one should add that the Russians have a similar fear of Chinese intentions. One of Peking's fundamental aims now, therefore, is to do whatever it can to try to create a counterweight, or to encourage counterbalancing influences and forces, that will somehow help to restrain and deter Moscow from initiating any military action of a major sort against China.

A second major change in the international environment, as viewed from Peking, has been the rapid emergence during the past several years of Japan into a new role in Asia. The spectacular growth of Japanese economic power has been accompanied by a steady increase and broadening of Japanese political influence. Peking has obviously watched with growing uneasiness and apprehension as Japan has reasserted its new role in Asian affairs. In recent years, in fact, Peking has self-consciously adopted a very hostile policy towards the Sato government and has deliberately emphasized its fears of Japanese remilitarization, and even ultimate nuclearization.

It is difficult to know how much Peking is deliberately exaggerating such fears in order to exert political pressure on Japan to prevent remilitarization or to try to influence and manipulate Japanese domestic political forces. Japan's current military establishment is still relatively small, and is obviously designed wholly for defence. Nevertheless, an element of genuine fear is doubtless a very real factor influencing the thinking of leaders in Peking. The memory of past Japanese aggression against China has by no means disappeared, particularly among the older generation of leaders who still hold the reins of power in Peking. In short, there is no doubt that as Japan's economic growth has soared and its international influence has grown, Peking has increasingly viewed Tokyo as a current competitor and a potential future threat.

The question that the Chinese Communist leaders have had to face is what to do about Japan. The direct leverage that China can apply upon Japan is actually very limited. In the economic field, China can hardly hope to compete seriously with Japan. There are, however, several things that the Chinese can consider trying to do. They can try to convince the Japanese that Tokyo should be much more accommodating towards China, and try to influence Japanese politics in that direction. They can try to encourage a US–Japan split, in the hope that this will greatly weaken Japan's political position. Or, they can encourage Washington to assert a restraining influence on Japan and to pursue policies that will help to minimize the possibility that Japan will remilitarize, go nuclear, or try to re-establish hegemony over areas of special Chinese concern such as Taiwan and Korea. It is by no means clear which of these alternatives, policies, and objectives China is most likely to pursue. It seems very possible, in fact, that Peking has not yet made up its mind.

US role in Asia

A third major factor that has been changing the international situation in Asia, in ways that obviously affect Peking's views and policies, has been the slow readjustment of the US position throughout Asia. Peking has watched very carefully as Washington has moved toward military withdrawal from Vietnam, has talked (in connection with the Nixon Doctrine) of a general reduction of the American military role in Asia, and has put out conciliatory feelers toward Peking. China's sense of imminent potential threat from the United States appears definitely to have declined as a result of all of this. In fact, the evidence suggests that American initiatives have definitely been a factor helping to convince leaders in Peking that a more flexible Chinese policy towards the United States might well pay some dividends from Peking's point of view. One should not jump to the conclusion, however, that Peking has suddenly decided that the improvement in Sino—American relations is such a high priority goal that to achieve it Peking should be prepared to abandon long-standing Chinese positions regarding the most basic and intractable issues that have divided the United States and China — above all the Taiwan problem.

There is ample evidence that Peking will continue to press hard to achieve its basic goals and will oppose any steps that it believes would compromise China's fundamental interests and objectives — just as, of course, the United States will. Nevertheless, by at least the beginning of 1971 Chou En-lai had obviously concluded that some degree of increased flexibility in Peking's approach to the United States was both possible and desirable from the Chinese point of view. It seems probable, however, that Peking may still be uncertain and ambivalent about what it can hope to accomplish through a more flexible approach to the United States, just as it is probably still ambivalent about what its policies towards Japan should be. Leaders in Peking may well still be asking themselves some hard questions in this respect. Should China put highest priority on the goal of getting the United States to withdraw from Asia to the maximum possible extent, try to break up the US–Japan alliance, attempt to induce Washington to abandon Taiwan, and to do everything possible to hasten the US withdrawal from Korea and southeast Asia – which for many years have been among Peking's long-term goals? Or should the Chinese operate on the assumption that improved US–China relations, and a greater Chinese tolerance towards a continuing US military presence in Asia, are now desirable because the United States can have a counterbalancing and restraining effect in relation to both the Soviet Union and Japan? We cannot be sure which of these aims Peking will pursue or emphasize, in the period immediately ahead, and it is very possible that the Chinese leaders themselves are not, at this stage, sure.

Domestic considerations

A fourth factor – or set of factors – that in the recent period has significantly influenced Chinese foreign policy (including policy towards the United States) derives from domestic trends and problems in China. The Cultural Revolution, which kept China in turmoil from 1966 to early 1969, had a tremendous impact on the country, and on balance, clearly weakened its political structure and leadership. Since 1969 the country has been on the road to recovery and has been struggling with the problems of political reconstruction, but this process has been slow, and it will obviously continue for many years.

There are continuing debates and struggles within the leadership in China, presumably over both domestic and foreign policy, as well as over the internal distribution of power, and there is uncertainty about what will happen in the country when Mao dies and China faces a difficult succession problem. In a sense, therefore, China is now in a major transitional period. This fact may well reinforce Peking's sense of vulnerability, despite the steady growth of China's nuclear and missile capabilities, and it probably reinforces the arguments within the Chinese leadership of those who work for a more flexible foreign policy, to help China to break out of its isolation, to broaden its base of international political support, and to improve China's defence capabilities, by skilful manoeuvring on the world stage. Steps to increase contacts with the United States, as well as with the United Nations, have been very logical steps for China to pursue under existing circumstances.

Today, the leadership in China is in effect a coalition or collective leadership, containing very diverse elements. In the past two years, gradually but steadily, the political balance within the leadership has shifted against the radicals and in favour of the conservatives and pragmatists. In this period, despite the purge of Lin Piao and other top military leaders, military officers have continued to occupy key power positions throughout the country. However, Premier Chou En-lai has emerged as the main architect of Chinese policies, especially its foreign policy. Clearly a very large share of the credit for the new elements of flexibility and realism in recent Chinese policy can be traced directly to him. This shift within the leadership in China has been accompanied by a major shift, under Chou's aegis, in China's overall foreign policy — not just its policy towards the United States. Major foreign policy shifts of one sort or another have occurred several times since the present government came to power, and each time they have led to wide adjustments of Chinese policies towards many different areas and problems.

The long view

It is true that certain basic elements in Peking's foreign policy, and certain fundamental goals, have remained fairly constant. From the start, Peking's leaders have been, and they still are today, determined to build China into a modern powerful state and to achieve great power status. They have also been committed, in a very real sense, to stimulate revolutionary struggles around the world, even though they have been very cautious about direct intervention in most such struggles and have confined their support largely to moral exhortation. But despite the continuities in Chinese policy, Chinese strategy and tactics have changed greatly over time, and the relative stress given at particular periods to normalized state-to-state relations, or to informal people-to-people diplomacy, or to the encouragement of subversive revolutionary struggles, has varied significantly.

In the early 1950s, during the immediate takeover period and the Korean War years, Peking was very militant, but at the same time, it was highly preoccupied with internal problems. In the mid-1950s China began to look outward much more, but at the same time Chinese leaders shifted their main emphasis to normalized state-to-state relations and adopted a quite flexible and moderate overall foreign policy stance. In the late 1950s, another shift took place, this time back to verbal militancy, and Peking put primary stress on the need to pursue the struggle against imperialism more actively. Lacking Soviet support, however, the Chinese had to mute this theme in the early 1960s. Nevertheless, they greatly stepped up their activities abroad, especially throughout the underdeveloped Third World. Then, in 1965, came a series of major foreign policy setbacks and, at home, confusion and chaos as a result of political conflict. Once the Cultural Revolution was well under way, China simply retreated into a shell. For about three years, in fact, from 1966 to late 1968 or early 1969, China for all practical purposes virtually abandoned normal foreign relations. Verbally, Peking adopted an extremely bellicose stand towards the outside world and gave moral support to 'people's wars' everywhere. In practice, however, it recalled all but one of its ambassadors abroad, and, in its almost total preoccupation with political conflict at home, went into a period of extreme isolation.

The current phase of foreign policy began, then, in late 1968 and early 1969, as the Cultural Revolution for all practical purposes drew to a close. This has been a period in which, despite continuing revolutionary rhetoric, Peking has moved steadily toward more realistic, pragmatic, flexible, moderate policies on a worldwide basis (with a few notable exceptions). The emphasis has been upon the need to adopt policies that would promote immediate concrete national interests, rather than policies motivated primarily by long-term revolutionary goals. More than ever before, Peking today now seems to be influenced by *realpolitik* and balance of power considerations. China's new initiatives toward the United States have been a part of, and to some extent a product of, this general shift.

Difficult decision

All of these trends and factors undoubtedly help to explain why Peking decided early last year that it should invite President Nixon to Peking. There seems little doubt, however, that the decision was by no means an easy one for Chinese leaders. In fact, it was probably an extremely difficult one — perhaps even more difficult than the decision made in Washington. In making such a major shift in its policy towards Washington, Peking had to abandon a position that it had held inflexibly since the 1950s: that no significant improvement in US—China relations would be possible until the Taiwan problem could be solved. It also clearly compromised and damaged its image throughout the world as the world's headquarters of extreme revolutionary radicalism and anti-imperialism. It is plausible to believe that there must have been intense debate within the Chinese leadership about the advisability of such a radical shift, with the costs that it involved, and it seems possible that the debate may well be continuing today.

What led the United States to decide to abandon a two decades old policy of 'containment and isolation' directed against China, and in particular to take such a bold step as agreeing to a summit meeting with the Chinese in Peking? First of all, it should be recognized that American official and public attitudes towards China have been slowly but steadily changing, in a very significant way, for quite a few years. By the mid-1960s, the intense passions that were the legacy of the Korean War and McCarthyism had cooled sufficiently to allow leaders in Washington a much greater flexibility than previously in considering problems of relations with China. Over time, more and more ordinary Americans, as well as political leaders in Washington, began to recognize that it was both illogical and dangerous not to have adequate communications with a nation which the United States had fought once in Korea and had nearly fought on several other occasions, as a result of crises on China's periphery, and that it would clearly be in the US interest to try to reduce the dangers of conflict and moderate the tensions that had kept the United States in a state of almost constant confrontation with the largest nation in Asia for two decades.

The process of re-evaluating US policy towards China is not something entirely new, therefore. In fact all three of the last three American presidents have favoured steps to work gradually towards normalization of relations with Peking. The first tentative moves in this direction began in the Kennedy and Johnson administrations. It is significant, though, that it was not until President Nixon was elected that a major redefinition of American goals in regard to China and concrete steps to change past policies were begun in earnest. The first moves came in 1969. Then, in 1970, in his first foreign policy message to Congress, President Nixon openly called for a 'more normal and co.1structive relationship' with China and an end to Chinese isolation. Gradually, step by step, from 1969 to the early part of last year, the US government removed all restrictions on travel to China and greatly liberalized trade restrictions, opening up direct trade for the first time since the Korean War. In a sense, these steps were relatively small ones and they did not deal with the largest issues of US–China relations, but they were extremely important nevertheless. They were symbolic of the basic change going on in Washington's thinking, and the obviously had a significant impact on Peking. Peking responded by taking its own initiatives, in its ping-pong diplomacy, early last April. Then, the interaction which resulted reached a rapid climax in the stunning decision to hold a US–China summit meeting.

New China policy

The general direction of the new China policy that President Nixon is now evolving follows lines that have long been urged by many specialists on China within the US government, as well as by a large number of academic China specialists. In essence, critics of past policy have been proposing for many years a series of initiatives on the US part that would be designed to make possible a dialogue and interaction between

438

Peking and Washington, that would help to reduce tensions between the two countries, that could provide mechanisms for increased Sino—American communications, and that would minimize the chances of overt conflict. The hope has been that gradually such steps could lay the basis for an eventual normalization of relations. President Nixon and his closest foreign policy advisor, Henry Kissinger, have accepted the logic of moving in that direction, and they now are pursuing many of the policies and goals that have long been urged by those pressing for changes in China policy.

There may well be a variety of considerations and factors that help to explain what led President Nixon and Henry Kissinger to make the bold moves they have recently made. One can only speculate about these, but there are reasons to believe that they, like China's leaders, came to the conclusion that in the context of the changing big power balance in Asia, an improvement of US—China relations would clearly be in the US interest and would strengthen the American position in relations with other powers — particularly with the Soviet Union. It also seems clear that attitudes in Washington towards the possibility of a serious China threat have changed substantially. Today, as compared with even a few years ago, there is much less apprehension about the danger of Chinese military expansionism.

There are several explanations for this change. The Sino—Soviet conflict is certainly a major one; it is now realized that Peking and Moscow, instead of collaborating for common goals in Asia, are in fact intensely competitive and tend to check and balance each other. Recognition of the growing importance in the overall situation in Asia of Japan's rising economic power is another factor. Still another is the fact that, over the years, Peking's leaders have clearly demonstrated, on numerous occasions, that they are, in a basic sense, cautious in their approach to foreign policy problems, realistic in their assessment of power relations, and not inclined to be recklessly adventuristic. Finally, there seems to be little doubt that President Nixon believes that an improvement in US—China relations may help facilitate the implementation of the new broad US policies in Asia that he is pursuing — in particular, the winding down of American involvement in Vietnam, and the gradual reduction in the US military position in Asia that is called for under the Nixon Doctrine.

All of the factors that I have discussed so far, which have influenced both Peking and Washington, help to explain, I think, how we have gotten where we are. In this new situation, however, there is a new range of questions that needs to be asked. Accepting the fact that both Peking and Washington have abandoned some old and inflexible positions, how far can one now expect either the United States or China to go in changing past policies and looking toward compromise? What, more concretely, should we expect from the President's trip to Peking? Is it realistic to anticipate that a complete normalization of US—China relations will emerge rapidly? Or is this something that will still take considerable time? Finally, even if there are obvious advantages that should result from an improved US—China relationship, are there any risks and problems involved in our new course of action that should be a cause of concern?

Nixon—Chou summit

With such questions in mind, let me say first of all that, on balance, I believe the Nixon—Chou summit meeting to be an historic event of tremendous importance. From a long-run perspective it could produce extremely significant favourable results, from the US point of view. However, we should not be unrealistic and expect too much from the Nixon—Chou meeting in the way of immediate and concrete results. Further, even though the new direction of US policy makes eminent good sense, in my opinion, and deserves to be applauded and supported, it clearly does involve some risks, and like any really important new turn in international affairs, it creates some new problems which must be a focus of concern.

The principle importance of the Nixon—Chou meeting is the simple fact that it was held. It symbolized fundamental shifts in attitudes and policies on the part of both the United States and the People's Republic of China. It indicated that after twenty-odd years of intense hostility, both nations wish to halt, and if possible reverse, past trends. It demonstrated that at a minimum, American and Chinese leaders now hope to minimize the chances of direct conflict between the two countries. From now on the United States and China doubtless can, and will, have much better channels of direct communication than in the past, at the highest level, and they doubtless can and will continue after the summit meeting to discuss a wide range of problems. For all practical purposes, the meeting implies mutual recognition, including US recognition of the Peking regime's sovereignty over the China mainland.

In agreeing to meet, both sides, moreover, have abandoned at least some of the fictions and unrealistically rigid positions that have shaped their policies for many years. Both have indicated that, at least to some extent, they are willing to accommodate to realities, rather than being moved solely by ideological predispositions, in approaching the basic problems of war and peace. Furthermore, the symbolic importance of the meeting will greatly affect — and in fact already has affected — all other relationships among all the powers in Asia, large and small. From now on, for example, the relationships among the four major powers in Asia are likely to be much more symmetrical than they were in the past, and I believe this to be a very desirable change. It is a change which may contribute to the creation ultimately of a new kind of multipolar balance of a fairly stable sort, a balance in which, although in a superficial sense there may be considerable fluidity, in a basic sense there may well be a more stable foundation for peace in the region than there was with the kind of tense bipolar balance that existed in earlier years.

However — and this needs to be emphasized now, in view of some of the sudden euphoria about US—China relations that has become evident in recent months — the Nixon—Chou meeting cannot and will not suddenly resolve many of the most intractable problems that divide the United States and China, and it will not and cannot suddenly transform the US—China relations from hostility to friendship. The United States and China will continue to have an adversary relationship; we should hope, though, that it will be less hostile than in the past. There will, in short, be no sudden entente, or even for that matter, any real detente. What we will have done is start a process, but we must expect that the process will be gradual and in many respects difficult. Nevertheless, the meeting marks the end of one era in US—China relations, and the beginning of another. It should provide real basis for hope that gradually, step by step, the United States and China will be able to establish a much more normal relationship. And it has very broad implications for the entire multipolar balance in Asia.

Notes and references

Survey

*   Ping Chia Kuo, *China: New Age and New Outlook*, Harmondsworth, Penguin, rev. edn, 1960, p. 13.

1. Naval Intelligence Division, *China Proper*, vol. I, London, The Admiralty, 1944, p. 18.
2. Yi Fu Tuan, *China*, London, Longman, 1970, p. 17.
3. Naval Intelligence Division, I, 34.
4. *Ibid.*, p. 39.
5. See Jen Hu Chang, 'The Chinese Monsoon', *Geographical Review*, 61, 1971, 370–95.
6. Tuan, p. 22.
7. George B. Cressey, *Land of the 500 Million*, New York, McGraw-Hill, 1955, p. 329.
8. See Owen Lattimore, 'Chinese colonization in Manchuria', *Geographical Review*, 22, 1932, 177–95.
9. Naval Intelligence Division, I, 296.
10. Keith Buchanan, *The Transformation of the Chinese Earth*, London, Bell, 1970, pp. 5–6.
11. Edward Schafer, *The Vermilion Bird: T'ang images of the South*, Berkeley and Los Angeles, University of California Press, 1967, p. 14 (quoted by Buchanan, p. 59).
12. T. R. Tregear, *A Geography of China*, London, University of London Press, 1965, p. 52.
13. Tuan, p. 144.
14. Ping Ti Ho, *Studies on the Population of China 1368–1953*, Cambridge, Mass., Harvard University Press, 1959, p. 153 (quoted by Buchanan, p. 24).

443

15. Solomon Adler, *The Chinese Economy*, New York, Monthly Review Press, 1957, p. 2.
16. *Ibid*, p. 3.
17. T. R. Tregear, *An Economic Geography of China*, London, Butterworth, 1970, p. 8.
18. Joseph Needham, 'Science and China's influence in the world', in R. Dawson, ed. *The Legacy of China*, London, Oxford University Press, 1964, p. 238 (quoted by Tregear, *An Economic Geography of China*, p. 8).
19. Adler, p. 9.
20. E. Backhouse and J. O. P. Bland, *Annals of the Court of Peking*, London, Heinemann, 1914, p. 326.
21. Tregear, *Economic Geography*, p. 13.
22. Tuan, p. 182.
23. R. H. Tawney, *Land and Labour in China*, London, Allen & Unwin, 1932, p. 13.
24. T. J. Hughes and D. E. T. Luard, *The Economic Development of Communist China 1949–60*, London, Oxford University Press, 1961, p. 24.
25. Kuo, p. 85.
26. Hughes and Luard, p. 28.
27. *Ibid*., pp. 37–8.
28. *Ibid*., p. 38.
29. Michael Freeberne, 'The People's Republic of China', in W. Gordon East, O. H. K. Spate and Charles A. Fisher, eds., *The Changing Map of Asia*, London, Methuen, 1971, p. 390.
30. Hughes and Luard, p. 39.
31. Tregear, *A Geography of China*, p. 171.
32. Kuo, p. 151.
33. *Ibid*., p. 154.
34. Buchanan, p. 120.
35. *Ibid*., p. 121.
36. *Ibid*., p. 121.
37. Hughes and Luard, p. 166.
38. Freeberne, p. 387.
39. Hughes and Luard, p. 166.
40. Buchanan, p. 127.
41. *Ibid*., p. 129.
42. Brian Crozier, 'China and her race for steel production', *Steel Review*, July 1959, p. 7.

43. *Ibid.*, p. 9.
44. *Ibid.*, p. 10.
45. John Philip Emerson, 'Chinese Communist Party views on labor utilization before and after 1958', *Current Scene*, 1, No. 30, 1962, p. 4.
46. Choh Ming Li, 'China's agriculture: a Great Leap in 1958?', in Edward Szczepanik, ed., *Symposium on Economic and Social Problems of the Far East*, Hong Kong, Hong Kong University Press, p. 25.
47. Crozier, p. 1.
48. Reed J. Irvine, 'Phantom food in Communist China', *Asian Survey*, 1, 1961, 25.
49. See Michael Freeberne, 'Natural calamities in China, 1949–61', *Pacific Viewpoint*, 3, 1962, 33–72.
50. Choh Ming Li, 'China's Industrial Development 1958–63', *China Quarterly*, Jan.–Mar. 1964, p. 9.
51. *People's Daily*, Peking, 12 Nov. 1960.
52. Leo Goodstadt, *Mao Tse Tung: the search for plenty*, Hong Kong, Longman, 1972, p. 177.
53. Anon, 'The seven stages of the Cultural Revolution', *Bulletin of the Atomic Scientists*, 25, 1969, 16–17.
54. Freeberne, 'The People's Republic of China', p. 430.
55. *Ibid.*, p. 431.
56. Dwight H. Perkins, 'Mao Tse Tung's goals and China's economic performance', *Current Scene*, 9, No. 1, 1971, 12.
57. Jan S. Prybyla, *The Political Economy of Communist China*, Scranton, International Textbook Co., 1970, p. 549.
58. *Ibid.*, p. 550.
59. *Ibid.*, p. 565.
60. Reuter, 4 January 1973.
61. Leo A. Orleans, 'China the population record', *Current Scene*, 10, No. 5, 1972, 14.
62. Kuo, p. 243.
63. *Ibid.*, p. 259.
64. Buchanan, p. 307.
65. Robert F. Dernberger, 'Economic realities and China's political economics', *Bulletin of the Atomic Scientists*, 25, 1969, 35.
66. *Ibid.*, p. 37.

67. See Buchanan, pp. 235–9.
68. Dernberger, p. 36.
69. Buchanan, p. 310.
70. *The Asian*, Hong Kong, 21 January 1973.
71. Goodstadt, p. 93.
72. *The Asian*, Hong Kong, 21 January 1973.

3. Population and agriculture in the Yangtse delta

1. See J. E. Orchard, 'Shanghai', *Geogr. Rev.* **20** (1936), 1–31.
2. See G. B. Cressey, *China's Geographic Foundation*, New York and London, McGraw-Hill, 1934, map, Fig. 139, p. 285.
3. H. von Heidenstam, *Report on the Hydrology of the Hangchow Bay and Chien Tang Estuary*, Shanghai Harbour Investigation Reports, ser. 1, No. 5, Whangpoo Conservancy Board, Shanghai, 1921.
4. G. B. Cressey, 'The geology of Shanghai', *China Journ.*, 8 (1928), 334–45; 9 (1928), 88–98.
5. H. von Heidenstam, 'The growth of the Yangtse delta', *Journ. North China Branch of the Royal Asiatic Soc.*, 53 (1922), 21–36; ref. on p. 26.
6. *The Fenghsien District Board Record*, 20 chapters in 6 volumes, was compiled in the twentieth year of the Emperor Ch'ien Lung, 1756, and was republished in 1878.
7. *China Industrial Handbooks:* Kiangsu, Bureau of Foreign Trade, Ministry of Industry, Shanghai, 1933. The area of agricultural land to a rural family is given as a little more than 26 mu – more than double the average for the province.
8. See J. E. Spencer, 'Salt in China', *Geogr. Rev.*, 25, 1935, 353–66.

4. Luts'un: a Yunnan village

1. For the characteristics of 'outsiders' in another area, see H. T. Fei, *Peasant Life in China*, London, Routledge, 1947, p. 23.
2. In a village with which I am familiar near Kunming,

purchase of land by immigrants is effectively prevented by special, insupportable duties for water. In the country of the Yao tribesmen in Kwangsi the earliest settlers occupied the land and constituted an organized front against those who later infiltrated into the area. The servile status forced upon the latter has been maintained by laws prohibiting ownership of land by new settlers; see Tung-wei Wang, *Social Organization of Hua Lan Yao.*

3. These data are given in *A Study of the Rural Economy of Wuhsing, Chekiang,* ed. Director of Institute, Shanghai, China Institute of Economic and Statistical Research, March 1937, p. 47.

5. China: land of famine

1. *The North China Famine 1920–1921, with special reference to the West Chihli area: being the Report of the Peking United International Famine Relief Committee,* Peking, 1922.
2. C. B. Malone and J. B. Tayler, *The Study of Chinese Rural Economy*, China Internatl. Famine Relief Comm. Publ., ser. B, No. 10, Peking 1924.
3. C. G. Dittmer, 'An estimate of the Chinese standard of living in China', *Quart. Journ. of Economics*, 33, 1918, 107–28.
4. China International Famine Relief Commission Publ. ser. B, No. 10.
5. S. D. Gamble and J. S. Burgess, *Peking: a social survey*, New York, 1921, p. 268.
6. *Chinese Econ. Monthly*, 2, No. 9. Chinese Govt. Bur. of Econ. Information, Peking.
7. *Ibid.*, 2, No. 5.
8. D. K. Lieu, Food Conservation in China, *Mid-Pacific Mag.*, Honolulu, 29, 1925, 511–19.
9. W. C. Lowdermilk, Forest destruction and slope denudation in the province of Shansi, *China Journ. of Sci. and Arts*, 4, 1926, 127–35.
10. Alexander Hosie, 'Droughts in China, AD 620 to 1643', *Journ. North China Branch of the Royal Asiatic Soc.*, 12 (n.s.), 1878, pp. 51–89.

11. Co-Ching Chu, 'Climatic pulsations during historic time in China', *Geogr. Rev.*, 16, 1926, 274–82.
12. S. Wells Williams, *The Middle Kingdom*, revised edn, 2 vols, New York, 1883, i, 467.
13. L. H. D. Buxton, *The Eastern Road*, London and New York, 1924.
14. See J. R. Freeman, 'Flood problems in China', *Trans. Amer. Soc. Civil Engineers*, 85 (1922), 1405–60.
15. Paul Vayssière, 'Le problème acridien et sa solution internationale', *Matériaux pour l'Étude des Calamités*, Geneva, 1 (1924), 122–58, 274–82.
16. Raoul Montandon, 'A propos du projet Ciraolo: une carte mondiale de distribution géographique des calamités', *Rev. Internatl de la Croix–Rouge*, Geneva, 5 (1923), 271–344.
17. Wong Wen-Hao, 'L'influence sismogénique de certaines structures géologiques de la Chine', *Comples Rendus Congrès Géol. Internatl. XIII*, Belgium, 1922, 2, Liège, 1925, pp. 1161–97.
18. For a discussion of the type of habitation see M. L. Fuller and F. G. Clapp, 'Loess and rock dwellings of Shensi, China', *Geogr. Rev.*, 14, 1924, 215–26.

6. The old industrial order

1. See the Imperial Mandate of Ch'ien Lung to George III on the occasion of Lord Macartney's mission in 1793, quoted in E. Backhouse and J. O. P. Bland, *Annals of the Court of Peking*, 1914, p. 326.
2. Occupational censuses have been taken for the provinces of Kiangsu (1919) and Shansi (1923), for Kwangtung Territory (1924), and for the cities of Nanking (1925), Tsingtao (1926), and Canton (1928). See *The Chinese Labor Year Book*, 1928, i, 2–5, and *Nankai Weekly Statistical Service*, 4, No. 2, 12 January 1931.
3. The number of places described as towns in the Post Office Statistics of 1920 was 1 910. It was estimated by the Customs authorities in 1927 that the population of fifteen cities with over 200 000 inhabitants was

8 662 300. According to the *China Year Book*, 1926, there were thirty-six cities with over 1 million inhabitants each. For a discussion of the subject, see Boris P. Torgasheff, 'Town Population in China', *The China Critic*, 3 April 1930. Using a large number of different sources, Mr Torgasheff has calculated that the population of 112 cities, with over 100 000 inhabitants, was, in 1930, 30 830 400; of 178 cities, with 50 000 to 100 000, 11 556 400; and of 177 cities, with 25 000 to 50 000 inhabitants, 8 064 700, making a total of 50 451 500 inhabitants for 467 cities. When account is taken of the remaining 1 443 towns on the official list, and of those which should probably be included in it, but are not, the total town population of China should be put, he suggests, at not far short of 100 million. There is some reason for thinking that the estimate is too high, and that a total of 75 million would be nearer the truth. In that case the urban population of China may possibly form between 16 and 20 per cent of her total population. It must be remembered, however, that many town-dwellers are engaged in agriculture.

4. Boris Torgasheff, 'Mining Labor in China', *Chinese Economic Journal*, 6, No. 4, April 1930.
5. Nyok-Ching Tsur, *Die Gewerblichen Betriebsformen der Stadt Ningpo in China*, Tübingen, 1909, pp. 17—35.
6. J. B. Tayler, *The Hopei Pottery Industry and the Problem of Modernisation*, and D. K. Lieu, *China's Industries and Finance*.
7. S. B. Gamble and J. S. Burgess, *Peking: a social survey*, 1921, ch. 8 and (for statistics) App. vi, p. 430; Burgess, *The Guilds of Peking*, 1928.
8. For Chinese guilds see Gamble and Burgess, and Burgess (as above); *China, a commerical and industrial handbook*, Washington, 1926, pp. 370—6; K. A. Wittvogel, *Wirtschaft und Gesellschaft Chinas*, Leipzig, 1931, pp. 573 *et seq.*; H. D. Fong, 'Chinese Gilds Old and New', in the *Chinese Students' Monthly*, April 1928; and for earlier information, H. B. Morse, *The Gilds of China*, 1909; F. W. Williams, 'Chinese and Mediaeval Gilds', in the *Yale Review*, November 1892; and *China Imperial Customs: decennial Reports*, 1892—1901.

7. Shanghai

1. *Foreign Trade of China*, 1927—31, *The Trade of China*, 1932—34 inclusive (continuation of *Foreign Trade*), China, The Maritime Customs (I. — Statistical Ser.: Nos. 3 to 5 and No. 1 respectively), Shanghai.
2. *Ibid.*
3. *Prices and Price Indexes in Shanghai*, National Tariff Commission, China, Shanghai, December 1934, p. 23.
4. See Professor F. W. Fetter's paper, 'China and the flow of silver', *Geogr. Rev.*, 26, 1936.
5. Richard Feetham, *Report . . . to the Shanghai Municipal Council*, vol. i, Shanghai, 1931, pp. 303—4.
6. *Ibid.*
7. Complete List of Cotton Mills in China, Chinese Mill-owners Association, Shanghai, 1933 (in Chinese).
8. *Chinese Econ. Bull.*, 25, 1934, 165—6.
9. W. H. Medhurst, 'General description of Shanghae and its environs, extracted from native authorities', *Chinese Miscellany*, No. 4, Shanghai, 1850, pp. 34—5.
10. *Ibid.*, p. 17.
11. *Decennial Reports*, 5th issue, 1922—31, *China, The Maritime Customs* (I. — Statistical Ser.: No. 6), Shanghai, vol. i, p. 3.
12. Charles Gutzlaff, 'Journal of a residence in Siam, and of a voyage along the coast of China to Mantchou Tartary', *Chinese Repository*, i, 1832—33, 16—25, 45—64, 81—99, 122—40, and 180—96; reference on pp. 124—5.
13. Medhurst, pp. 107—10; Robert Fortune, *Three Years' Wanderings in the Northern Provinces of China*, 2nd edn., London, 1847, p. 104.
14. H. H. Lindsay and Charles Gutzlaff, *Report of Proceedings on a Voyage to the Northern Ports of China, in the Ship Lord Amherst*; Extracted from *Papers by Order of the House of Commons Relating to the Trade with China*, London, 1833, p. 209.
15. There entered into the port of London, on the average, each week of the three-year period 1840—42, in foreign and coastal trade, 558 vessels averaging 158 tons each (*Tables of the Revenue, Population, Commerce, etc., of the United Kingdom and Its Dependencies, 1840—1842,*

compiled from Official Returns, presented to Both Houses of Parliament by Command of Her Majesty, London).

16. Lindsay and Gutzlaff, *op. cit.*, pp. 172 and 181.
17. *Decennial Reports*, i, 39.
18. *Ibid.*, p. 18.
19. Robert Fortune, *A Journey to the Tea Countries of China*, London, 1852, p. 12.
20. *Decennial Reports,* i, 26–7.
21. *Ibid.*, pp. 32, 45, 59, and 74.
22. Medhurst, pp. 6 and 17.
23. *Decennial Reports* (see n. 11), 1st issue, 1882–91; 4th issue, 1912–21; 5th issue, 1922–31.
24. H. Lang, *Shanghai Considered Socially*, 2nd edn, Shanghai, 1875, p. 15.
25. Lindsay and Gutzlaff, p. 188.
26. Medhurst, p. 46.
27. D. B. Robertson, 'Cotton in China', *Journ. North China Branch of the Royal Asiatic Soc.*, No. 3, 1859, pp. 302–8, see also Medhurst, pp. 52–5.
28. Medhurst, p. 65.
29. *North-China Herald*, 15 May 1935, p. 284, reprint of an article published originally in *Penny Magazine* in 1843.
30. Data obtained through the courtesy of W. S. Robertson, vice-president, American and Foreign Power Co., Inc., New York, parent company of the Shanghai Power Company.
31. *Ibid.*

8. Cities as centres of change in China

1. This is not a new idea. Other and older applications of it would include Giovanni Botero, *A Treatise Concerning the Causes of the Magnificence and Greatness of Cities*, transl. Robert Peterson (London, 1606); Georg Simmel, *Die Grosstadt und das Geistesleben* (1900); Theodore Peterman, ed., *Die Grosstadt* (1903); N. S. B. Gras, 'The development of the Metropolitan economy in Europe and America', *American Historical Review*, 27 (1921–22); Michael Rostovtzeff, 'Cities in the ancient world', in *Urban Land Economics*, ed., Richard Ely

(1922); E. W. Burgess, *et al., The City* (1925); Henri Pirenne, *Medieval Cities; Their origins and the revival of trade* (1923); Max Weber, *Wirtschaft und Gesellschaft* (1925), Part I, ch. 8; Louis Wirth, 'Urbanism as a way of life', *American Journal of Sociology,* 44 (1938); A. M. Schlesinger, 'The city in American history', *Mississippi Valley Historical Review,* 44 (1940); William Diamond, 'On the dangers of an urban interpretation of history', ch. 4 in *Historiography and Urbanization,* ed. E. F. Goldman (1941); Sylvia Thrupp, *The Merchant Class of Medieval London* (1948); Pierre George, *La Ville: le fait urbain a travers la monde* (1952).

2. Karl Marx, *Capital,* edition of 1903 (Chicago), i, 387.

3. Oxford and Cambridge, as rural universities, help to enforce this point. They were proverbially conservative, their most important job the training of students for the ministry. Spain's distinction from western Europe on this and nearly every other point raised is merely a reminder of the old aphorism 'Africa begins at the Pyrenees'.

4. Generalization on matters such as this is particularly hazardous. A recent study has cast serious doubt on these commonly accepted alignments: see D. H. Pennington and Douglas Brunton, *Members of the Long Parliament* (Harvard University Press, 1953; [repr. N.Y. Shoe String Press, 1959]).

5. Compare for instance the original development of London as two cities separated by open country, Westminster as the administrative centre, and 'the city' as the centre of business.

6. Rhoads Murphey, *Shanghai: Key to Modern China,* Harvard University Press, 1953, p. 59.

7. Robert Fortune, *A Journey to the Tea Countries of China and India* (London, 1852), Vol. I, pp. 97–8.

8. See especially K. A. Wittvogel, *Oriental Society and Oriental Depotism,* Yale University Press. For example, ancient Alexandria had a population of about 1 million in a country (Egypt) with a total population of only 7 million.

9. A. C. Moule and Paul Pelliot, *Marco Polo, the Description of the World,* London, Routledge, 1939, i, 236–7.

10. Archibald Little, *Through the Yangtze Gorges*, London, 1898, pp. 87 ff.

11. Southeast China has many fine harbours and overseas trade has been prominent there for centuries. But it is effectively isolated from the main body of China by mountains, including those which help to make its harbours, and trade there has thus made much less impact on the rest of the country. The distinctiveness of the southeast is also clear in its many regional ethnic linguistic elements.

12. K. A. Wittvogel, 'Foundations and stages of Chinese economic history', *Zeitschrift für Socialforschung*, 4 (1935), 26—58, *ibid.*, *'Die Theorie der Orientalischen Gesellschaft'*, *loc. cit.*, 7 (1938), 90—123. (This article clearly states the administrative basis of the Chinese city, and discusses the reasons and implications.) *ibid., Wirtschaft und Gesellschaft Chinas* (Leipsig, 1931). *ibid., Oriental Society and Oriental Despotism.*

13. Wittvogel in *Oriental Society and Oriental Depotism* speaks of this arrangement as based on 'the law of diminishing administrative returns'.

14. The persistent unity of China despite wide regional diversity is something of a puzzle, but may be related to China's dramatic isolation and to the unitary rather than peninsular nature of her continental base.

15. As the capital and as the seat of the largest Western-founded universities. Peking was a centre of intellectual ferment by the end of the nineteenth century since intellectual contact with the West was easiest there. Traditional imperial China had by then lost enough prestige that dissension flourished in Peking itself. While many of the intellectuals rejected China's traditional civilization in whole or in part, their struggles in this scholar's community made little impact on the nation as a whole. The Chinese Communist Party was founded in Peking in 1921, but largely deserted it for a rural base. Student and intellectual ferment in Peking was revolutionary in thought, but ineffective in action. Both the treaty ports and the countryside proved in the end to be much more effective bases for change or for rebellion.

9. Population policy

In the notes to this paper the following abbreviations are used:

CB   American Consulate General, Hong Kong, *Current Background*.
CCP   Chinese Communist Party.
CKCN   *Chung-kuo ch'ing-nien (China Youth)*.
CKCNP   *Chung-kuo ch'ing-nien pao (China Youth Daily)*, Peking.
CKFN   *Chung-kuo fu-nü (Women of China)*.
CPPCC   Chinese People's Political Consultative Conference.
ECMM   American Consulate General, Hong Kong, *Extracts from China Mainland Magazines*.
HCKFN   *Hsin Chung-kuo fu-nü (Women of New China)*.
JMJP   *Jen-min jih-pao (People's Daily)*, Peking.
KJJP   *Kung-jen jih-pao (Daily Worker)*, Peking.
KMJP   *Kuang-ming jih-pao* (usually not translated), Peking.
NCNA   New China News Agency.
NPC   National People's Congress.
PCJP   *Pei-ching jih-pao (Peking Daily)*, Peking.
PRC   People's Republic of China.
SCMM   American Consulate General, Hong Kong, *Selections from China Mainland Magazines*.
SCMP   American Consulate General, Hong Kong, *Survey of China Mainland Press*.

1. Liu-li Commune Revolutionary Committee, Ch'uan-sha *Hsien*, 'Under the guidance of Mao Tse-tung thought, do a good job to promote late marriage of young people', in 'Planning childbirth and promoting late marriage', *I-liao wei-sheng tzu-liao (Medical and Health Data)*, Shanghai, No. 5, July 1970.
2. 'Practice of planned births and late marriage is formed at state cotton mill', *Kung-jen tsao-fan pao (Workers Rebel Paper)*, Shanghai, 1 Feb. 1970; and Shanghai Municipal No. 1 Health Clinic for Women and Infants, 'Planned Birth', in 'Planning childbirth and promoting late marriage' (see n. 1).
3. Shanghai Municipal No. 1 Health Clinic for Women and Infants, *loc. cit.*; Liu-li Commune Revolutionary Committee, *loc. cit.*; and 'Practice of planned birth and late marriage is formed at state cotton mill', *loc. cit.*
4. Lui-li Commune Revolutionary Committee, *loc. cit.*
5. Peking Radio, NCNA dispatch 29 Nov. 1970.
6. Mamduh Rida, 'Days in China — an interview with the No. 3 man in China', *Al Jumhuriyah*, Cairo, 18 Nov. 1971, p. 9.

7. Hunan Provincial Radio, Changsha, 12 June 1968;
   Shanghai Radio, 27 Nov. 1969; Shanghai Radio, 6 Dec.
   1969; and Shanghai Radio, 29 Dec. 1969.
8. Shanghai Radio, 24 Feb. 1970.
9. Yüan Te-liang, 'Grasp revolution, promote production,
   and whip up a new upsurge of production', *Kuang-chou
   kung-tai-hui (Canton Workers' Congress)*, No. 31, 10
   Oct. 1969; transl. in *SCMP*, No. 4342, 21 Jan. 1969, p.
   10; and Shanghai Municipal No. 1 Health Clinic, *loc. cit.*
10. 'Wei t'i-kao fu-nü chien-k'ang shui-p'ing erh tou-cheng'
    ('Struggle to raise the health level of women'), *JMJP*, 3
    Mar. 1971.
11. 'Vigorously destroy old customs and habits and practice
    frugality in weddings', *JMJP*, 31 Aug. 1969; transl. in
    SCMP, No. 4495, 15 Sept. 1969, pp. 3–4; and 'Firmly
    destroying old habits, insisting on late marriage', *JMJP*,
    31 Aug. 1969; transl. in *SCMP*, No. 4495, 15 Sept.
    1969, p. 5.
12. 'Practice of planned birth and late marriage is formed at
    state cotton mill'.
13. 'Wei t'i-kao fu-nü chien-k'ang shui-p'ing erh tou-cheng'.
14. Ross Terrill, 'The 800,000,000', *The Atlantic Monthly*,
    November 1971, p. 110.
15. 'Vigorously destroy old customs and habits and practice
    frugality in weddings'.
16. Tung Yin-ti, 'For revolution's sake insist on late
    marriage', *Nan-fang jih-pao*, Canton Feb. 1970; and
    Liang Yu-ken, 'Business type marriages should cease',
    Nan-fang jih-pao, Canton, Feb. 1970.
17. Edgar Snow, 'A conversation with Mao Tse-tung', *Life*,
    70, No. 16, 30 Apr. 1971, 47.
18. Shanghai Municipal No. 1 Health Clinic for Women and
    Infants.
19. Edgar Snow, 'Population care and control', *The New
    Republic*, 1 May 1971, pp. 21–2.
20. *Ibid.*, p. 22.
21. Shanghai Municipal No. 1 Health Clinic for Women and
    Infants.
22. Snow, 'Population care and control'.
23. Shanghai Municipal No. 1 Health Clinic for Women and
    Infants.

24. *Ibid.*
25. Snow, 'Population care and control', p. 21. In both operations, acupuncture was used for anaesthesia.
26. 'Wei t'i-kao fu-nü chien-k'ang shui-p'ing erh tou-cheng'.
27. Shanghai Municipal No. 1 Health Clinic for Women and Infants.
28. Lui-li Commune Revolutionary Committee.
29. Lui-li Commune Revolutionary Committee.
30. Mamduh Rida, *op. cit.*
31. A. G. Ashbrook, Jr., in Joint Economic Committee, Congress of the United States, *People's Republic of China: an economic assessment*, US Govt. Printing Office, Washington, DC, 1972.
32. See John S. Aird, 'Population growth', in Alexander Eckstein, Walter Galenson, and Ta-chung Liu, eds., *Economic Trends in Communist China*, Chicago, Aldine Publishing Company, 1968, pp. 244—76.

10. Development of communications: the railways

1. Sun Yat-sen, *The International Development of China*, Ministry of Information, Chungking, 1943, pp. 10—19, 23—9, 56—80, and 94—142.
2. *Ibid.*, pp. 94—5.
3. *Ibid.*, p. 12.
4. Yuan-li Wu, *An Economic Survey of Communist China*, New York, Bookman Associates (London, Constable), 1956, pp. 351—8, which cites Ling Hung-hsun (Vice-Minister of Communications 1946—49): Chung-kuo t'ieh-lu kai-lun (General Survey of Railways in China) (T'ai-pei) [?], 1950.
5. *Current Background*, No. 262, Hong Kong, 1 Oct. 1953, p. 5.
6. *People's China*, 1955, No. 16, 16 Aug., p. 24. See also 'In the news', *ibid.*, No. 1 (1 Jan.) 45.
7. Chung Ts'ao, 'The past, present and future of China's railways', *Shih-shih shou-tse (Current Events)*, 1957, No. 2 (21 Jan.), transl. in *Extracts from China Mainland Magazines*, No. 77, Hong Kong, 9 Apr. 1957, p. 27. See also *Union Research Service*, 6, No. 20, Hong Kong, 8 Mar. 1957, 280.

8. 'Quick guide to China's expanded railways', *Peking Rev.*, 1, No. 8, 22 Apr. 1958, p. 11.

9. 'The Litang–Chanchiang Railway', *People's China [PC]*, 1955, No. 24 (16 Dec.), p. 17; New China News Agency, Kuei-yang 7 Feb. 1959, transl. in *Survey of China Mainland Press [SCMP]*, No. 1954, 16 Feb. 1959, p. 21; and *Jen-min jih-pao [People's Daily]*, Peiping, 30 Jan. 1959, p. 3.

10. New China News Agency, Chungking, 21 Nov. 1959, transl. in *SCMP*, No. 2144, 27 Nov. 1959, 42.

11. 'Paochi–Chengtu Railway', *PC*, 1956, No. 14, 16 July, 28.

12. *China News Analysis*, No. 213, Hong Kong, 24 Jan. 1958, p. 2.

13. Chung Ts'ao, p. 29.

14. *China News Analysis*, No. 213, 24 Jan. 1958, p. 2.

15. Ma Tse-ching, 'Railway construction in People's China', *PC*, 1954, No. 21 (1 Nov.), pp. 18–25.

16. *SCMP*, No. 909 (16–18 Oct. 1954), 29.

17. Ma Tse-ching.

18. 'The Lanchow–Sinkiang Railway', *Peking Rev.*, 2, No. 45, 10 Nov. 1959, 17. See also 'Railway building in New China', *PC*, 1956, No. 10 (16 May), 15–17.

19. 'Paochi–Chengtu Railway'.

20. 'The Fengtai–Shacheng Railway', *PC*, 1955, No. 16 (16 Aug.), p. 24.

21. Liao Chien, 'A new harbor for South China', *PC*, 1957, No. 10 (16 May), 25–6.

22. 'The Lanchow–Sinkiang Railway'.

23. New China News Agency, Ha-mi, 1 Jan. 1960, transl. in *SCMP*, No. 2171, 7 Jan. 1960, p. 28.

24. 'In the news', *PC*, 1956, No. 11 (1 June), 41.

25. 'Quick Guide to China's expanded railways'.

26. Chung Ho, 'The steel town beyond the Great Wall', *Ching-chi tao-pao [Economic Rept.]*, No. 624, Hong Kong, 22 June 1959, p. 11.

27. *Jen-min jih-pao [People's Daily]*, 30 Jan. 1959, p. 3; and 'Round the week', *Peking Rev.*, 1, No. 23, 5 Aug. 1958, 5.

28. *Union Research Service*, 6, No. 20, 8 Mar. 1957, 285; see also Chung Ts'ao, p. 28.

29. Liao Chien, 'Fukien's first railway', *PC*, 1957, No. 4 (16 Feb.), 19—20.
30. *China News Analysis*, No. 211 (10 Jan. 1958), 6.
31. *Ibid.*, No. 217 (21 Feb. 1958), 1.
32. *PC*, 1956, No. 4 (16 Feb.), 40.
33. Chen Shih-yin, 'Travels in the Motherland IV', *Ching-chi tao-pao [Economic Rept.]*, No. 640, 12 Oct. 1959, 11.
34. *China News Service*, Peiping, 13 Jan. 1959, transl. in *SCMP*, No. 1953, 13 Feb. 1959, 19.
35. Chung Ho.
36. *SCMP*, No. 1993 (15 Apr. 1959), 16.
37. *Honan jih-pao*, Cheng-chou (5 Mar. 1959), transl. in *SCMP*, No. 2002, 29 Apr. 1959, 21.
38. *Ibid.*
39. *Sinkiang jih-pao*, Urumchi, 11—13 Mar. and 28 Oct.—1 Nov. 1959, and *Kuang-ming jih-pao*, Peiping, 11 Mar. 1959, transl. in *SCMP*, No. 2002 (29 Apr. 1959), 21—7. See also *Extracts from China Mainland Magazines*, No. 160 (1 Jan. 1959), 35, and No. 165 (20 Feb. 1959), p. 8.
40. Li Fu-chun, 'Report on the Draft: 1960 Economic Plan', *Current Background*, No. 615, 5 Apr. 1960, p. 18.

11. Industrial expansion: coal, a case study

Notes

1. Details of the pre-1949 position are from Wang (1947; pp. 53—8), except where otherwise acknowledged.
2. The Wade—Giles system of transliteration has, where possible, been used for names throughout this paper. The older spelling has, however, been given in brackets on the first appearance of the name. An exception has been made, and conventional spelling used, for the provinces of China and for the large cities.
3. 'Kailan' is the usual abbreviated name for the mines of the former Kailan Mining Administration.
4. According to the United Nations Economic Commission for Asia and the Far East, the year 1942 marked the

peak of war-time production with 58.7 million tons (UNECAFE, 1952, p. 49). G. B. Cressey (1955, p. 137), however, gives 1944 with 62.4 million tons as the peak of production. The UNECAFE estimate for 1944 is 55.8 million tons (1952, p. 49).

5. All details of new mines in this section, unless otherwise acknowledged, are from *Financial and Economic Research* (1958, pp. 58—60).

6. Figures for 1958 production at Fu-shun, Kailan and Huai-nan from Shabad (1959, p. 94).

7. Details from anon article in *China Reconstructs* (1953, pp. 6—7).

References

1. Press Reports

The main sources of information are the *People's Daily* (Peking), the *New China News Agency* (official), published in various leading cities, the *China News Analysis* (Hong Kong) and the *Survey of the China Mainland Press*, published at the American Consulate General, Hong Kong. These have been abbreviated in the main text as *PD, NCNA, CNA,* and *SCMP.*

China News Analysis 8 Feb. 1957, No. 167.

Daily Worker (Peking) 15 June 1956 (quoted in *CNA*, 8 Feb. 1957, No. 167, p. 6).

—— 2 Sept. 1959 (*CNA*, 2 June 1961, No. 374, p. 3).

—— (Shanghai) 24 Feb. 1961 (*CNA*, 2 June 1961, No. 374, p. 6).

Liberation Daily (Shanghai) 14 Nov. 1959 (*CNA*, 2 June 1961, No. 374, p. 6).

New China News Agency (Harbin) 25 Nov. 1960 (*SCMP*, 1 Dec. 1960, No. 2338, p. 15).

—— (Peking) 27 Dec. 1959 (*SCMP*, 4 Jan. 1960, No. 2168, p. 3).

—— 27 Dec. 1959 (*SCMP*, 5 Jan. 1960, No. 2169, p. 5).

—— 26 Jan. 1960 (*SCMP*, 3 Feb. 1960, No. 2188, p. 8).

—— 21 June 1960 (*SCMP*, 28 June 1960, No. 2286, p. 23).

—— 27 July 1960 (*SCMP*, 3 Aug. 1960, No. 2309, p. 5).

—— 25 Sept. 1960 (*SCMP*, 30 Sept. 1960, No. 2349, p. 16).
—— (Shanghai) 27 April 1961 (*SCMP*, 3 May 1961, No. 2488, p. 24).
—— 27 April 1961 (*SCMP*, 3 May 1961, No. 2488, p. 24).
—— (T'ang-shan) 6 April 1960 (*SCMP*, 12 April 1960, No. 2236, p. 43).
Peking Review 17 Nov. 1961, 4, 46.
—— 8 Dec. 1961, 4, 49.
People's Daily 23 May 1951 (*CNA*, 13 Aug. 1954, No. 47, p. 5).
—— 5 Oct. 1955 (*CNA*, 8 Feb. 1957, No. 167, p. 6).
—— 8 Jan. 1956 (*CNA*, 8 Feb. 1957, No. 167, p. 6).
—— 23 June 1956 (*CNA*, 8 Feb. 1957, No. 167, p. 6).
—— 2 Nov. 1957 (*CNA*, 9 May 1958, No. 267, p. 5).
—— 3 March 1958 (*CNA*, 27 Feb. 1959, No. 266, p. 1).
—— 3 Dec. 1960 (*CNA*, 2 June 1961, No. 374, p. 7).

2. Books and articles in periodicals

Anon (1953) 'Biggest open-cut coal mine'. *China Reconstructs* 2, 6 (Nov.–Dec.).
Chandrasekhar, S. (1960) *China's Population: Census and vital statistics*, Hong Kong.
Chang Kuei-sheng (1961) 'The changing railroad pattern in mainland China', *Geogr. Rev.* 51, 4.
Chang Yang (1959) 'How we dug more coal than Britain', *China Reconstructs* 7, 3 (March).
Chang Yuan-kuang (1958) 'New China's sea transport', *Geographical Knowledge* (Peking), 14 March 1958, No. 3, Trans. in *Extracts from China Mainland Magazines*, American Consulate General, Hong Kong, 23 June 1958, No. 133, p. 27.
Chao Kuo-chun (1953) 'The government and economy of Manchuria', *Far Eastern Survey* 22, 13 (Dec.), New York.
Chin Yu-kin (1954) 'Ta-t'ung coalfield', *China Reconstructs* 3, 4 (July–Aug.).
Cressey, G. B. (1955) *Land of the 500 Million*, New York, McGraw-Hill.
Dwyer, D. J. (1961) 'The development of China's inland waterways', *Geography* 46, 2.

Dwyer, D. J. (1962) 'China's natural calamities and their consequences', *Geography* 47, 3.

Financial and Economic Research (1958) No. 5 (Shanghai) (*CNA*, 27 Feb. 1959, No. 266, pp. 2—4).

First Five-Year Plan for the Development of the National Economy of the People's Republic of China in 1953—7, Peking, 1956.

Hughes, T. J. and Luard, D. E. T. (1960) *The Economic Development of Communist China*, Oxford University Press.

Jen Pi-shao (1952) Coal mining transformed. *China Reconstructs* 1, 5 (Sept.—Oct.).

Li Fu-chun (1960) 'Report on the draft 1960 National Economic Plan', *Peking Review*, 5 April 1960, 3, 14.

Liu Hsi-ching (1960) 'New techniques push up coal output', *China Reconstructs* 9, 6 (June).

Schumpeter, E. B., ed. (1940) *The industrialization of Japan and Manchukuo*, New York.

Shabad, T. (1956) *China's Changing Map*, Methuen.

Shabad, T. (1959) 'China's year of the great leap forward', *Far Eastern Survey* 28, 6 (June), New York.

Union Research Institute (1959) *Communist China 1958*, Hong Kong.

United Nations Department of Economic Affairs (1953) *Development of Mineral Resources in Asia and the Far East*, Bangkok.

United Nations Economic Commission for Asia and the Far East (1952) *Coal and Iron Resources of Asia and the Far East*, Bangkok.

Wang, K. P. (1947) *Controlling Factors in the Future Development of the Chinese Coal Industry*, New York.

12. Sinjao: a commune near Canton

1. See for example, T. J. Hughes and D. E. T. Luard, *The Economic Development of Communist China 1949–1960*, Oxford University Press, 2nd edition, 1961.
2. One catty equals 0.6 kg (1.3 lb).
3. One yuan is the equivalent of 14p.

13. The Great Leap Forward

1. For a detailed discussion, see Choh-ming Li, *The Statistical System of Communist China*, University of California Press, 1962, ch. 7.
2. *Ching-chi yen-chiu* (Economic Research), No. 10, 1959, 21.
3. *Chi-hua yu tung-chi* (Planning and Statistics), No. 1, 1959, 31.
4. *Ibid.*, No. 11 (1959), 12.
5. *Ibid.*
6. *Jen-min jih-pao (People's Daily)*, 26 June 1962.
7. *Jen-min shou-tse (People's Handbook)*, 1962, p. 233; *Ta-kung-pao (Impartial Daily)*, 7 May 1962; and *Jen-min jih-pao*, 26 May 1961.
8. *Jen-min shou-tse*, 1961. p. 238.
9. *Chi-hua yu tung-chi*, No. 9, 1959, 17.
10. *Ibid.*
11. *Ibid.*, No. 4 (1959), 6 and *Ta-kung-pao*, 26 Feb. 1961.
12. *Jen-min shou-tse*, 1962, p. 243.
13. *Ibid.*, 1961, p. 238; *Jen-min jih-pao* 26 May 1961 and 3 May 1962; and *Ta-kung-pao*, 7 May 1962.
14. *Jen-min jih-pao*, 3 May 1962.
15. *Jen-min shou-tse*, 1960, p. 400.
16. *Hung-chi (Red Flag)*, No. 9, 1959, 18; *Ching-chi yen-chiu*, No. 6, 1959, 11; *Chi hua yu tung chi*, No. 9, 1959, 6 and No. 15, 1959, 12; and *Ta-kung-pao*, 21 Nov. 1963.
17. *Chi-hua yu tung-chi*, No. 9, 1959, 20.
18. *Kung-jen jih-pao (Worker's Daily)*, 16 July 1959.
19. *Jen-min shou-tse*, 1962, p. 250.

14. The three bitter years

Sources: Li Fu-chun, 'Report on the Draft 1960 Economic Plan', *Peking Review*, Peking, 3, No. 14, 5 April 1960; *Survey of the China Mainland Press* 1960–61, US Consulate, Hong Kong; *China News Analysis*, Hong Kong, Nos. 352, 357, 358; *Far Eastern Economic Review*, Hong Kong, 1962 *Yearbook*.

15. Developing the interior: the growth of Urumchi

1. Mildred Cable, 'Urumchi, capital of Chinese Turkestan', *Geographical Magazine* 16, No. 9, Jan. 1944, 445.
2. New China News Agency, date-lined Urumchi, 25 Oct. 1962, as reported by the US Consulate General, Hong Kong, *Survey of the China Mainland Press* (*SCMP*), No. 2849, 30 Oct. 1962, p. 17.
3. US Army Map Service No. 1301P plastic relief map, scale 1 : 1 000 000, 1954, based on the 1949 AMS 1301 edition 1 NK 45, The Bogdo Ula was reported to have a height of 5 445 metres by Han Hsien-kang in *Hsi-pei Tzu-jan Ti-li (Natural Geography of the Northwest)*, Sian, Shensi Peoples Press, 1958 (US *Joint Publications Research Service [JPRS]*, No. 10177, 18 Sept. 1961, p. 44).
4. *Hsin-chiang Sheng Ti-t'u (Provincial Atlas of Hsin-chiang)*, Tung-fang Hsueh-hui (Eastern Studies Society), 1909 (place of publication unspecified).
5. Ch'en Pu-ch'ing, 'Ko-pi-t'an Shang ti Hua-yüan, Urumchi' (Urumchi, the Garden of the Gobi Desert), *Ti-li Chih-shih (Geographical Knowledge)*, 10, No. 12, Dec. 1959, pp. 543−5.
6. These and the figures in the following paragraphs, except as otherwise noted, are based on records for varying numbers of years given in *Chung-kuo Ch'i-hou-t'u (Climatic Atlas of China)*, edited by the Climate Research Office of the Central Weather Bureau, Geographic Press, Peking, 1960. Recent records for Urumchi still are very limited. Precipitation figures, for instance, are from the periods 1907−11 and 1930−31.
7. Ch'en Pu-ch'ing
8. K. P. S. Menon, *Russian Panorama*, New York, Oxford University Press, 1962, p. 191.
9. Han Hsien-kang, *Hsi-pei Tzu-jan Ti-li*, *JPRS*, No. 10177, 18 Sept. 1961, *op. cit.*, p. 54.
10. Ch'en Pu-ch'ing.
11. Han Hsien-kang, p. 62 gives Urumchi's annual rainfall as 345 mm (13.5 in). However, this represents the record for only a particular year, that for 1930. The *Climatic Atlas of China* lists Urumchi's average precipitation, based on six years' records, as 276 mm (10.8 in).

12. Han Hsien-kang, *JPRS* No. 10177, p. 64.
13. *Ibid.*, pp. 47–9. It is not clear what 'total area' Han Hsien-kung refers to in stating that 13 per cent of the total area is occupied by forests. He does not delimit the area included, although probably he refers to the forest zone between 1 400 and 2 800 metres (4 600 and 9 200 ft).
14. Ch'en Pu-ch'ing, pp. 543–5, 557.
15. Hsü Kung-wu, *Pien-chiang Shu-wen (An Account of the Border Areas)*, Chungking, Cheng-chung Bookstore, 1944, p. 51.
16. Shih Man, 'Urumchi, an ancient city full of youth and vitality', *Kung-jen Jih-pao (Workers Daily)*, 13 April 1961 (from US Consulate General, Hong Kong, *SCMP*, No. 2493, 10 May 1961, p. 23.
17. *Ibid.*
18. Annemarie von Gabain, *Das Uigurische Königreich von Chotscho, 850–1250*, Sitzungsberichte der deutsches Akademie der Wissenschaften zu Berlin, 1961, p. 19.
19. Cable, p. 447; R. H. Mathews, *A Chinese–English Dictionary*, Shanghai: 1931, character No. 2086, indicates that these ancestors of the Uighurs were a tribe of the Hsiung-nu or Huns.
20. Von Gabain.
21. Kuang Lu, 'Hsin-chiang Li-shih' (History of Hsin-chiang) in Ling Shun-sheng's compilation, *Pien-chiang Wen-hua Lun-chi (Cultural Essays on the Frontier Region)*, vol. 3, T'ai-pei, Chung-hua Wen-hua Press, 1954, p. 317.
22. Von Gabain.
23. *Ibid.*, p. 11.
24. Ch'en Pu-ch'ing.
25. *Ibid.*, Hsü Kung-wu, *op. cit.*, pointed out that the T'ien Shan in the Urumchi region at this time were known also as the Yin Shan or Shade Mountains from the shadow of the mountains cast upon their north slopes here. Thus, there is a reference in a famous poem concerning Chang Ch'un-tzu and three armies crossing the desert to the Yin Shan. This, wrote Hsü, referred not to the Yin Shan 'outside Liaotung' (i.e., north of the Yellow River) of the Hsiung-nu volume of the Han history, but to the Urumchi area.

26. Ch'en Pu-ch'ing.
27. Wang Chin-fu, *Hsi-pei chih Ti-wen yü Jen-wen (Places and Peoples of the Northwest)*, Shanghai, Commercial Press, 1935, p. 197.
28. Kuang Lu, 'History of Hsin-chiang', pp. 320–3.
29. *Ibid.*
30. Hsü Kung-wu, pp. 51–2.
31. China News Analysis No. 238, *The Political Situation in Sinkiang*, 25 July 1958, p. 3.
32. Kuang Lu, p. 224.
33. Wang Chin-fu.
34. Ch'en Pu-ch'ing. Although Ti-hua was the official Chinese name in the pre-Communist period, the Urumchi resident Chinese spoke familiarly of Ti-hua in the 1930s as Hung-miao-tzu (Red Temple), according to Mildred Cable. This temple was 'an insignificant place a few miles from the centre of town but it has succeeded in establishing its claim to give a name to the whole locality, and Hung-miao-tzu is spoken of a hundred times where Ti-hua is mentioned only once' (see Cable, p. 447).
35. Ch'en Pu-ch'ing.
36. Wang Chin-fu.
37. Kuang Lu, p. 327.
38. Ch'en Pu-ch'ing.
39. Kuang Lu.
40. *Ibid.*
41. Ch'en Pu-ch'ing.
42. Hsü Kung-wu.
43. Ella and Percy Sykes, *Through Deserts and Oases of Central Asia*, London, Macmillan, 1920, p. 243.
44. Kuang Lu, pp. 330–3.
45. *Ibid.*, pp. 333–4.
46. *Ibid.*
47. *Ibid.*, pp. 336–8.
48. *Ibid.*
49. *Ibid.*
50. Ch'en Pu-ch'ing.
51. Wang Chin-fu.
52. See *Great Achievements in Hsin-chiang during the Past*

Decade, Urumchi, Hsin-chiang People's Press, Sept. 1959.
53. Shih Man, p. 23.
54. Ch'en Pu-ch'ing.
55. Menon, p. 192.
56. Eric Teichman, *Journey to Turkistan*, London, Hodder & Stoughton, 1937, pp. 101–2, 116.
57. Menon, p. 191.
58. Cable, pp. 447–51.
59. Ch'en Pu-ch'ing.
60. Teichman.
61. Cable.
62. Teichman.
63. Ch'en Pu-ch'ing.
64. *Ibid.*
65. Yen Kuan-yi, *Hsin-chiang Uighur Tzu-chih Chü* (Hsin-chiang Uighur Autonomous Region), Peking, 1956, pp. 23–5.
66. Shih Man.
67. Yen Kuan-yi, pp. 29–30.
68. *Ibid.*
69. Basil Davidson, 'Turkestan alive', in *New Travels in Chinese Central Asia*, London, Cape, 1957, pp. 66–7.
70. *Atlas of the Republic of China*, vol. 2, Sinkiang and Tibet, T'ai-pei, 1962).
71. 'Hsin-chiang Shih-nien-lai Chien-she ch'eng-chi t'ung-chi' ('Statistics of Achievements during Ten Years of Reconstruction in Hsin-chiang'), *Chung-kuo Pien-chiang (China's Frontiers)*, 3, Nos. 1–2, Feb. 1944, pp. 30–1.
72. New China News Agency, Urumchi, 29 Jan. 1962, US Consulate General, *SCMP*, No. 2673, 7 Feb. 1962), p. 21.
73. New China News Agency, Urumchi, 29 January 1962, 'Urumchi river transformed to irrigate arid farmland in northwest China', US Consulate General, Hong Kong, *Survey of the China Mainland Press*, No. 2673, 7 Feb. 1962, p. 21; see also Jen-min Jih-pao, Peking, 29 March 1962, 'Having regard to practical needs and responsibilities, overall harnessing work is carried out on the

Urumchi river with its irrigation capacity raised year by year', *SCMP*, No. 2716, 10 April 1962, p. 7.
74. *Ibid.*
75. China News Analysis No. 252, 'Youth Canal at Urumchi', 7 Nov. 1958, p. 5.

The Ulabai Reservoir and the Youth Canal were parts of a three-part project, the first of which was a 8 km (3.1 miles) long canal leading from the Urumchi River to the reservoir, with a sluice to filter out sand and silt. The Ulabai Reservoir formerly was the Hung-yen Ch'ih, a salt lake with no outlet. In 1948 the pre-Communist Chinese Government had completed about one-quarter of a project to convert the lake to store fresh irrigation water and was irrigating some 25 000 ha (10 000 acres). During the two years 1950–51 the succeeding Communist regime took up and completed the project, and the reservoir now has a 54-million cubic metre water storage capacity.

The third part of this project was the Ho-p'ing (Peace) Canal, extending 67.5 km (42 miles) northward from Urumchi and bringing irrigation to a reported 17 535 ha (43 333 acres) of land around Ching-ke-ta (Gingda) Lake and preventing floods. A 33 km (21 miles) stretch of the Ho-p'ing Canal is said to be built as an elevated wooden aqueduct across the desert and the Urumchi River and passes through six tunnels. The inside of the aqueduct is lined with felt to prevent leakage. This is reported to be one of ten such 'gigantic' elevated wooden aqueducts in Hsin-chiang.

Subsequent to this project, the 32 km (20 miles) Youth Canal was constructed to solve the problem of inadequate water supply for the Ulabai hydroelectric plant, as well as for Urumchi's industrial needs and for the Ho-p'ing Canal. (*Source:* Wang Wei-ping and Hu Ying-mei, Hsin-chiang Uighur Autonomous Region, Peking 1959; as translated by *JPRS*, No. 7426, 9 March 1961, pp. 69–72, 105.)
76. US Consulate General, Hong Kong, *SCMP*, No. 2622 (20 Nov. 1961), p. 23.

The Meng-chin Reservoir was completed in 1955. It is located at the centre of the irrigation zone in the lower Urumchi valley 54 km (34 miles) north of the city. It has a capacity of 60 million cubic metres and connects the Lao-lung. Hei Ho and the T'ou-t'un rivers with the Ho-p'ing. Meng-chin, and Pai-i canals. (*Source: JPRS*, No. 7426, *op cit.*, p. 72.)

77. New China News Agency, Urumchi, 10 Dec. 1962 (US Consulate General, Hong Kong, *SCMP,* No. 2880, 14 Dec. 1962).

78. Davidson, p. 158.

79. Urumchi can also count on food support from the surrounding pastoral lands, since Urumchi District in 1948 produced some 8.7 per cent of all of Hsin-chiang's livestock or 18.7 per cent of north Hsin-chiang's livestock. (*Source:* V. G. Kalmykova and I. Ovdiyenko, Severozapadnyy Kitay, Moscow, 1957, as transl. by *JPRS*, No. 1025, Part 1, 12 Dec. 1958, p. 144.)

Also a newly built refrigeration plant at Urumchi can store over 580 tons of frozen meat, eggs, and fruit. (*Source: JPRS*, No. 7426, *op. cit.,* p. 109.)

80. Yen Kuan-yi, pp. 17–18.

81. Ch'en Pu-ch'ing. Another source renders the figure as 3.24 billion rather than 32.4 billion. See US *JPRS*, No. 3784, 31 Aug. 1960, pp. 33–4, 'Fuel and power base of the Chinese People's Republic'.

82. Yen Kuan-yi.

In 1957 coal production in all Hsin-chiang was about 1 250 000 tons. Plans envisaged a 20-million ton production by 1962 and 50 million tons by 1967. During this last phase, mines with capacities of from 450 000 tons to 2 000 000 tons each were to be opened at Urumchi. Hami, and I-ning. There appear grounds to doubt that the plans came to completion. One of the problems encountered at Urumchi and elsewhere in Hsin-chiang were underground coal-mine fires resulting from carelessness or spontaneous combustion. Some of these had been burning for as many as 10 or even 100 years. At Urumchi alone as much as 150 000 tons of coal were destroyed annually in this manner. (*Source: JPRS*, No. 7426, p. 104.)

83. US *JPRS,* No. 3784, pp. 43–53.

84. Ch'en Pu-ch'ing.
85. K. P. Wang, 'Rich mineral resources spur Communist China's bid for industrial power', *Mineral Trade Notes*, US Department of Interior, Bureau of Mines, Special Supplement No. 59, Washington, DC, Mar. 1960, p. 29.
86. Ch'en Pu-ch'ing.
87. *Ibid*.
88. Yen Kuan-yi, pp. 17—18.
89. *Ibid*., pp. 20—3; see also Ch'en Pu-ch'ing.
90. US *JPRS* No. 3784, *op. cit.* in note 81 above.

There is some uncertainty as to whether this 20 000 kW represents hydroelectric power alone or the combined thermal and hydropower capacities. Wang Wei-ping and Hu Ying-mei wrote in 1959 that the 25 000-kW Wei-hu-liang thermal power plant at Urumchi was supplemented by the Ulabai hydroelectric station having 2 400 kW capacity in 1954. (*Source: JPRS*, No. 7426, p. 105.)

91. Ch'en Pu-ch'ing.
92. I. Kh. Ovdiyenko, 'The new geography of industry of China', *Soviet Geography*, April 1960, p. 73 (from *Geografiya v shkole*, 1959, No. 6, pp. 28—41).

The capacity of the August First Steel Plant in 1958 was '30 000 tons of iron and steel'. Expansion took place thereafter designed to enable it to produce by 1960 up to 800 000 tons of pig iron and 600 000 tons of steel. It is not known whether this eventuated. (*Source: JPRS*, No. 7426, p. 108.)

93. Ch'en Pu-ch'ing.
94. Yen Kuan-yi.

The annual production of white cloth, twills, and beige in 1958 was more than 500 000 pieces and the dyeing department had a daily capacity of some 2 000 pieces. Expansion during 1959 was to triple the production capacity. The plant in 1958 employed over 3 000 workers. Supplies of cotton for Urumchi mills came from as far as Kashgar, but after the completion of a 50 000 spindle plant at Kashgar in 1960, 'it will no longer be necessary to send the cotton harvested there to Urumchi or the interior of China for spinning and weaving'. (*Source: JPRS*, No. 7426, pp. 108—9.)

95. Ch'en Pu-ch'ing.
96. US Consulate General, Hong Kong, *SCMP,* No. 2566, 25 Aug. 1961, p. 14.
97. US Consulate General, Hong Kong, *SCMP,* No. 2474, 12 April 1961, p. 19, 'Sinkiang extends communications lines' (from China News Agency, Urumchi, 5 Apr. 1961).
98. Ch'en Pu-ch'ing, *op. cit.*
99. Yen Kuan-yi, pp. 26—8.
100. *Ibid.*
101. Davidson. p. 60.
102. Yen Kuan-yi.
103. US Consulate General, *SCMP*, No. 2474.
104. *Ibid.*
105. *Atlas of the Republic of China,* vol. 5, T'ai-pei, 1962, plate on Railroad Transportation net.
106. Ch'en Pu-ch'ing.
107. China News Analysis, No. 112 (9 Dec. 1955), p. 6.
108. US Consulate General, *SCMP*, No. 2474.

16. Problems of urbanization

Notes

1. Chen Ting-chung (1965), pp. 54—65.
2. Ullman (1961), pp. 35—6.
3. By September 1959 Lanchou's population reached 1 200 000; see Ku (1959). Changchun's population also reached 1 million in 1959; see Li Huai-min (1967), pp. 46—59.
4. Statistically, the urban population of the municipality in mainland China may be compared to the total population of the urbanized area in the United States cities, and the total population of the municipality to total population of the standard metropolitan statistical area in the United States. See Ullman (1961).

    However, the expansion of municipal boundaries of certain cities in China in recent years may have resulted in the fact that some large municipalities in

China include a greater number of counties and possess a larger territory under jurisdiction than an average SMSA area in the United States.

5. Rein (1960), pp. 109–30.
6. The population of the walled city of Changan was in the neighbourhood of a million, with a like number in the metropolitan area outside the walls; see Wright (1965), pp. 15–23.
7. Wright (1965), pp. 15–23. For a more detailed account of the size and dimensions of the city of Changan, see Takeo (1956), pp. 7–16. Recent archaeological excavations have disclosed much information on the design and layout of the ancient city, see Bishop (1938), pp. 569–78; Hsu Chih (1961), pp. 36–7; Hsu Ming (1963), pp. 12–16.
8. Murphey (1953), p. 20. In 1910 Shanghai registered a population of 1 185 859; see Lieu (1936), p. 423.
9. Aird (1960), pp. 93–133.
10. Chao (1966), pp. 381–96.
11. Li choh-min (1959), p. 203.
12. Reubens (1964), pp. 1191–204; see also Emerson (1961), pp. 69–84.
13. Ullman (1961), pp. 35–6.
14. In planning industrial locations of mainland China, both political and economic factors have been stressed. For the theory and practice of industrial planning and urban development, see Hu (1965), pp. 1–31; Chen yun (1956), pp. 6–8; Hsueh (1963), pp. 50–61.
15. Some useful criteria of dividing regions in China and the general coincidence of regional divisions with provinces were discussed by Spencer (1947), pp. 123–36.
16. Shih Man (1961), p. 23.
17. Ullman (1961), pp. 35–6.
18. Ho Yu (1967), pp. 47–56.
19. There were twelve cities, each accommodating eleven to twenty new above-norm projects, and six cities, each having more than twenty-one new above-norm projects; however, the names of these cities were not given; see Tsao (1957), p. 4.
20. For a discussion of the geographical divisions of

economic cooperative regions and the function of industrial centres in each region, see Ho Yo-chi (1958), pp. 30—5; Hsiao (1958), pp. 33—9.

21. For the location of iron and steel centres of each region, see Wu Yuan-li (1965), p. 219.
22. Chang Chih-kang (1959), pp. 485—9.
23. *Chung-hua jen-min kung-ho-kuo hsing-cheng ch'u-hua shou-tze* (1964), pp. 1—273.
24. Chang Sen-dou (1965), pp. 313—27.
25. Chao T'ing-chien (1958), pp. 1—16.
26. Sun (1959), *JPRS,* No. 15 388, pp. 1—253.
27. Sun (1959), *JPRS,* No. 11 438, pp. 81—91.
28. Sun (1959), *JPRS,* No. 15 388, p. 18.
29. Sun (1959), *JPRS,* No. 14 954, p. 160.
30. Sun (1959), *JPRS,* No. 15 388, p. 130.
31. Yang (1964), p. 14.
32. 'Chogoku no kikai kogyo kankei kojo bunpu-zu' (1960).
33. Wu Yuan-li (1965), Table B-13, Part II.
34. Sun (1959), *JPRS,* No. 15 388, p. 122.
35. Sun (1959), *JPRS,* No. 15 388, pp. 248—53.
36. 'Water resources of China: plans and prospects for development' (1964), pp. 60—2.
37. Fung (1957), pp. 243—7.
38. Liang (1964), pp. 42—55; Lindsay (1957), pp. 36—50.
39. The discharge rate per annum in the Yangtse River basin amounts to 10 275.30 million cu metres whereas that of the Yellow River only averages 486.68 million cu metres; see Kuo (1958), pp. 109—14.
40. Lindsay (1957), pp. 36—50.
41. Lindsay (1957), pp. 36—50.
42. Ho Chih-chao (1959), pp. 403—6.
43. Kao (1959), pp. 49—54.
44. *Chuan-kuo t'ieh-lu lu-ko lieh-che shih-ko piao* (1963), pp. 1—187.
45. Yakloblev (1962), p. 44.
46. Wu Ching-cheng (1965), pp. 19—21.
47. Shih Tien (1958), pp. 25—7.
48. *Ibid.*
49. 'Some questions on the work of exchanging houses in this municipality' (1963), pp. 656—9.
50. For the extension pattern of the city of Lanchou, see

Fung (1957), pp. 243—7; for that of Taiyuan, see Wang (1959), pp. 149—70; for that of Changchun, see Mao (1959), pp. 538—42.
51. 'To improve planning minutely and economize the use of land for capital constructions' (1961), pp. 413—14.
52. Hsu Shih-ping (1963), pp. 1—27.
53. *Ibid*.

References

Aird, John S. (1960), 'Present and prospective population of mainland China', *Population Trends in Eastern Europe, the USSR, and Mainland China,* Milbank Memorial Fund, pp. 93—133.

Bishop, Carl Whiting (1938), 'An ancient Chinese capital earthworks at Old Changan', *Annual Report of the Smithsonian Institute, 1938,* pp. 569—78.

Chang, Chih-kang (1959), 'Huei-ta Pei-ching' (The Great Peiching), *Ti-li chih-shih* (Geographical Knowledge), 10, No. 11, pp. 485—9.

Chang, Sen-dou (1965), 'Peking, the growing metropolis of Communist China', *Geogr. Rev.,* 55, No. 3, pp. 313—27.

Chao, Kang (1966), 'Industrialisation and urban housing in Communist China', *Journal of Asian Studies.,* 25, No. 3, pp. 381—96.

Chao, T'ing-chien (1958), 'The hill city of Chungching', *Ti-li chih-shih* (Geographical Knowledge), 9, No. 3, pp. 102—5; transl. in *JPRS*, No. 2093, 23 Dec. 1959, pp. 1—16.

Chen, Ting-chung (1965), 'A study of food production and consumption on the Chinese mainland', *Chinese Communist Affairs,* 2, No. 3, pp. 54—65.

Chen, Yun (1959), 'The distribution of industry in China', *Peking Review,* 2, No. 10, pp. 6—8.

Chi, Tai (1958), 'Tienching, the new capital of Hopei province', *Ti-li chih-shih* (Geographical Knowledge), 9, No. 11, pp. 494—6; transl. in *JPRS*, No. 2094, 28 Dec. 1959, pp. 1—11.

'Chogoku no kikai kogyo kankei kojo bunpu-zu' (A map of the distribution of plants of machinery industries in

China), in *Shin Chugoku no kikai kogyo* (The Machinery Industry of New China) (1960), Tokyo.

Chuan-kuo t'ieh-lu lu-ko lieh-che shih-ko piao (All China Railroad Passenger Timetable) (1963), Peiching, pp. 1–128; transl. in *JPRS*, No. 21 963, 21 Nov. 1963, pp. 1–187.

Chung-hua jen-min kung-ho-kuo hsing-cheng ch'u-hua shou-tse (Handbook on Administrative Divisions of the People's Republic of China) (1964), Ministry of Interior; transl. in *JPRS*, No. 26 706, 5 Oct. 1964, pp. 1–273.

Emerson, John Philip (1961), 'Manpower absorption in the non-agricultural branches of the economy of Communist China, 1953–58', *China Quarterly*, 7, pp. 69–84.

Fung, Hsun-wu (1957), 'Lanchou ti kuo-chu yu wei-lai' (The Past and Future of the City of Lanchou), *Ti-li chih-shih* (Geographical Knowledge), 8, No. 6, pp. 243–7.

Ho, Chih-chao (1959), 'Kan-su jen-min kai-tsao ti wei-ta cheng-chiu' (The great achievement in changing the physical environment by the people in Kansu), *Ti-li chih-shih* (Geographical Knowledge), 10, No. 9, pp. 403–6.

Ho, Yo-chi (1958), 'A view on the division of economic regions in China', *Chi-hua ching-chi* (Planned Economy), 6; transl. in *Extract of China Mainland Magazines*, 141, pp. 30–5.

Ho, Yu (1967), 'Communications and transportation on the Chinese Mainland in 1966', *Chinese Communist Affairs*, 4, No. 1, pp. 47–56.

Hsiao, Liu (1958), 'On the problem of balanced development of industrial bases and regional economy in the different cooperative regions', *Chi-hua ching-chi* (Planned Economy), 7; transl. in *Extract of China Mainland Magazines*, 142, pp. 33–9.

Hsu, Chih (1961), 'Digging down a thousand years – excavation of Changan of the Tang Dynasty', *China Pictorial*, 10, pp. 36–9.

Hsu, Ming (1963), 'The excavation of the capital of the Tang Dynasty', *Eastern Horizon*, 2, No. 9, pp. 12–16.

Hsu, Shih-ping (1963, 'The main tasks of urban construction', *Chien-chu* (Architecture), **190**, pp. 1—7; transl. in *JPRS*, No. 20 028, 3 July 1963, pp. 1—27.

Hsueh, Cheng-hsiu (1963), 'A preliminary discussion on the relationship between the socialist growth of city population and the industrial and agricultural output development', *Kuang-ming jih-pao*, 7 Oct. 1963, 4; transl. in *JPRS*, No. 22 245, 12 Dec. 1963, pp. 50—61.

Hu, Hsu-wei (1965), 'On the technical—economic appraisal of industry distribution', *Acta Geographica Sinica,* **31**, No. 3, pp. 179—91; transl. in *JPRS*, No. 35 929, 9 June 1966, pp. 1—31.

Kao Yuan (1959), 'Nan-pei ta yun-ho ti kuo-chien' (Reconstruction of the Grand Canal), *Ti-li chih-shih* (Geographical Knowledge), **10**, No. 2, pp. 49—54.

Ku, Lei (1959), 'Ts'ung ta hsiao-t'iao tao ta fan-yung' (From great desolateness to great prosperity), *Jen-min jih-pao* (People's Daily), 21 Sept.

Kuo, Ching-huei (1958), 'Chung-kuo ho-liu ti shui-wen' (The hydrology of rivers in China), *Ti-li chih-shih* (Geographical Knowledge), **9**, No. 3, pp. 109—14.

Li, Choh-min (1959), *Economic Development of Communist China,* University of California Press, p. 203.

Li, Huai-min (1967), 'Population statistics of the Chinese mainland', *Chinese Communist Affairs,* **4**, No. 2, pp. 46—59.

Liang, C. S. (1964), 'A study on water resources development in three gorges of the Yangtze river', *Chung-chi Journal,* **4**, No. 1, pp. 42—55.

Lieu, D. K. (1936), *The Growth and Industrialisation of Shanghai,* Institute of Pacific Relations.

Lindsay, T. J. (1957), 'Water conservancy and hydroelectric schemes in China', *Contemporary China,* **2**, 1956—57, pp. 36—50.

Mao, Yin-hua (1959), 'Fei-yao fa-chan chung ti Chang-chun' (Rapid development of Changchun), *Ti-li chih-shih* (Geographical Knowledge), **10**, No. 12, pp. 538—42.

Murphey, Rhoads (1953), *Shanghai, Key to Modern China,* Harvard University Press.

Rein, Selma, R. (1960), 'The world's great cities: evolution or devolution', *Population Bulletin,* **16**, No. 6, 109—30.

Reubens, Edwin, P. (1964), 'Under-employment theory and Chinese experience', *Asian Survey*, 4, No. 12, pp. 1191–204.

Shih, Man (1961), 'Urumchi, an ancient city full of youth and vitality', *Kung-jen jih-pao* (Workers Daily), 13 April 1961; transl. in *SCMP*, No. 2493, 10 May 1961.

Shih, Tien (1958), 'Kuan yu cheng-shih fa-chan kuei-mu wen-ti ti yen-chiu' (On the Problems of the Size of City Development), *Chi-hau ching-chi* (Planned Economy), 1, pp. 25–7.

Spencer, J. E. (1947), 'On regionalism in China', *Journal of Geography*, 46, No. 4, pp. 123–36.

'Some questions on the work of exchanging houses in this municipality', *Peiching Evening Post*, 10 Feb. 1963, 2; transl. in *Union Research Service*, 31, No. 12, pp. 656–9.

Sun, Ching-chih (1959), *Economic Geography of East China;* transl. in *JPRS*, No. 11 438, 7 Dec. 1961, pp. 81–91.

Sun, Ching-chih (1959), *Economic Geography of Northeast China;* transl. in *JPRS*, No. 15 388 of 21 Sept. 1962, pp. 1–253.

Sun, Ching-chih (1959), *Economic Geography of South China;* transl. in *JPRS*, No. 14 954, 24 Aug. 1962.

Takeo, Hiraoka (1956), *Choan to Rokuyo* (Changan and Loyang), Kyoto Daigaku Jimbun, Kagako Kenkyujo (Kyoto University, Humanity Research Institute).

'To improve planning minutely and economize the use of land for capital constructions', *Kung-jen jih-pao* (Workers Daily), 20 Jan. 1961, 1; transl. in *Union Research Service*, 23, No. 26, pp. 413–14.

Tsao, Yen-hsin (1957), 'Arrange city construction works in accordance with the principle of diligence and thrift', *Chi-hua ching-chi* (Planned Economy), 12, No. 4.

Ullman, Morris B. (1961), *Cities of Mainland China, 1953–1958*, US Bureau of Census, International Population Reports, Series P-95, No. 59.

Wang, Cheng-ching, *et al.* (1959), 'The economic geography of Taiyuan Basin', *Ti-li hsueh tzu-liao* (Memoirs of Geography), 4; transl. in *JPRS*, No. 38 917, 1 Dec. 1966, pp. 146–70.

'Water resources of China: plans and prospects for development', *Ajia no yume,* 2 (March 1964), pp. 1—120; transl. in *JPRS*, No. 32 681, 2 Nov. 1965.

Wright, Arthur F. (1965), 'Viewpoint on a city, Changan (583—904): Chinese capital and Asian cosmopolis', *Ventures,* 5, pp. 15—23.

Wu, Ching-cheng (1965), 'Sian — an ancient city reborn', *China Reconstructs,* 14, No. 11, pp. 19—21.

Wu, Yuan-li (1965), *The Steel Industry in Communist China,* Hoover Institute Publications.

Yakloblev, M. (1962), 'Housing construction', *Vecheruyaya Moskva,* 7 Aug.; transl. in *JPRS*, No. 15 998, 1 Nov. 1962.

Yang, Wu-yang (1964), *Seaports of China,* pp. 1—47; transl. in *JPRS*, No. 27 301, 10 Nov. 1964.

Sources of Table 16.1

1922, 1935, 1946:

Glenn T. Trewartha, 'Chinese cities: numbers and distribution', *Annals of the Association of American Geographers*, 41, No. 4 (December 1951), pp. 331—47.

1953, 1958:

Morris B. Ullman, *Cities of Mainland China: 1953 and 1958,* Bureau of Census, International Population Reports, Series P-95, No. 59 (Aug. 1961) Table 3, pp. 35—6.

After 1958:

Shanghai: *New China News Agency,* Peking, 30 April 1962.

Peking: Wu Jen-tso, 'General conditions in the North China area under the control of the Chinese Communist', *Communist China* 1960, Union Research Institute, Hong Kong, 1962 (2 vols.), ii, pp. 77—106.

Tientsin: *SCMP*, No. 2580, 18 Sept. 1961, p. 26.

Mukden: *Hua-chiao Jih-pao* (Overseas Chinese Daily), Macao, 30 Oct. 1965.

Chungking, Canton, Chingtao, Chengtu, Changchun: Li Hui-min, 'Population statistics of the Chinese mainland', *Chinese Communist Affairs,* 4, No. 2 (April 1967), pp. 46—59.

Wuhan: *China News Service,* 12 Jan. 1960.

Harbin: *SCMP*, No. 2489, 4 May 1961, p. 19.

Talien: 'Red China builds merchant fleet', *New York Times*, 22 Feb. 1960.

Nanking: *Hua-chiao Jih-pao* (Overseas Chinese Daily), Macao, 30 Oct. 1965.
Sian: Wu Ching-cheng, 'Sian, an ancient city reborn', *China Reconstructs,* 14, No. 11 (Nov. 1965), pp. 19—21.
Taiyuan: 'Population of selected towns II', *Far Eastern Economic Review,* 34, No. 5 (2 Nov. 1961), p. 260.
Fushun: Fukushima Yutaka, 'Changes in Fushun', *Ajia Keizai Jumpo* (Asian Economic Thrice Monthly), No. 474, 21 July 1961, pp. 13—19, transl. in *JPRS*, No. 10 434, 11 Oct. 1961, pp. 1—7.
Lanchou: Ku Lei, 'Ts'ung ta hsiao-t'iao tao ta fan-yung' (From great desolateness to great prosperity), *Jen-min jih-pao* (People's Daily), 21 Sept. 1959.

17. Eyewitness of the Cultural Revolution

* For obvious reasons I have refrained from naming my sources, and as an additional safeguard have not indicated whether a particular item comes from my own repertoire or was reported to me. All sources are 'unofficial', and I have not used newspapers to supplement first-hand accounts, although in fact I followed the printed word with care at the time. While thanking all those whose experiences I have used here, I should make it quite clear that I alone am responsible for the facts and opinions presented in this essay.

18. China's economy in 1970

1. *Jen-min jih-pao (People's Daily), Hung-ch'i (Red Flag), Chieh-fang-chün pao (Liberation Army Daily)* of 1 Jan., in New China News Agency [NCNA], 31 Dec. 1969.
2. Peking Radio, NCNA, 24 Apr. 1969.
3. *Ibid.*
4. These items are taken from broadcasts by stations in China and quoted in the *BBC Summary of World Broadcasts, Part III, The Far East,* during Dec. 1969.
5. Senator William Proxmire, Chairman of the US Congressional Committee on Mainland China in the World Economy, *Hearings*, Washington, 1967, p. 2.
6. Robert Michael Field, 'A note on the population of Communist China', *The China Quarterly,* No. 38, Apr.—June 1969.

7. Irene B. Taeuber and Nai-chi Wang, *Questions on Population Growth in China,* New York, Milbank Memorial Fund, 1960.
8. Leo A. Orleans, 'China's population statistics: an illusion?' *China Quarterly,* No. 21 (Jan.–Mar. 1965).
9. John S. Aird, *Population Growth and Distribution in Mainland China* in *An Economic Profile of Mainland China,* Government Printing Office, Washington, 1967; also John S. Aird, 'Population growth', in Alexander Eckstein *et al., Economic Trends in Communist China,* Edinburgh University Press, 1968.
10. Leo Orleans, 'Propheteering: the population of Communist China', *Current Scene,* Hong Kong, United States Information Service, 7, No. 24, 1969.
11. W. Klatt, 'Economic growth in China and the Cultural Revolution. Comment', *China Quarterly,* No. 31, July–Sept. 1967.
12. Leo Orleans, in *Current Scene,* 8, No. 24.
13. W. Klatt, in *China Quarterly,* No. 31.
14. Subramanian Swamy and Shahid Javed Burki, 'Foodgrains output in the People's Republic of China, 1958–1965', *China Quarterly,* No. 41, Jan.–Mar. 1970.
15. Dwight H. Perkins, 'Economic growth in China and the Cultural Revolution. Reply', *China Quarterly,* No. 31, July–Sept. 1967.
16. W. Klatt, 'How much grain does Communist China produce? Comment', *China Quarterly,* No. 35, July–Sept. 1968.
17. Subramanian Swamy and Shahid Javed Burki, in *China Quarterly,* No. 41, 1970. Unhappily the authors seem to lack the knowledge of techniques by which to check claims or alleged claims of countries that do not publish their food statistics, e.g., the authors apply erroneously a constant 20 per cent 'processing' rate on *gross* output instead of applying it to that portion of the crop which is available for human consumption and thus for 'processing'. The difference between gross output and net (processed) supply for human consumption is approximately 35 per cent; see Owen L. Dawson, *Communist China's Agriculture,* New York, Praeger, 1970.

18. W. Klatt (W. K.), 'Communist China's agricultural calamities', *China Quarterly*. No. 6, Apr.–June 1961.

19. T. H. Shen, *Agricultural Resources of China,* Cornell University Press, 1951.

20. Dwight H. Perkins, in *The China Quarterly,* No. 31, 1967.

21. W. Klatt, 'Problems of food and farming in Asia', *Asian Affairs,* **57** (new series, vol. 1), part 1, Feb. 1970.

22. Even Swamy and Burki in their projections expected no more than a 50 per cent fulfilment of the target set for the last year of the twelve-year plan.

23. US Congressional Committee on Mainland China in The World Economy, *Hearings*, Washington, 1967, p. 45.

24. Dwight H. Perkins, 'Economic growth in China and the Cultural Revolution', *China Quarterly,* No. 30, Apr.–June 1967.

25. Robert Michael Field, 'Industrial production in Communist China: 1957–1968', *China Quarterly*, No. 42, Apr.–June 1970.

26. W. Klatt, 'Economic Growth. Comment', *China Quarterly*, No. 31, July–Sept. 1967.

27. NCNA, 11 May 1969.

28. Richard K. Diao, 'The impact of the Cultural Revolution on China's economic elite', *China Quarterly,* No. 42, Apr.–June 1970.

29. For such an account see W. Klatt, 'China: economic survey', in *The Far East and Australasia,* London, Europa Publications, 1970.

30. W. Klatt, 'The economy of China', in Peter Wiles, ed., *Prediction of Communist Economic Performance,* Cambridge University Press, 1971.

19. China as a trading nation

1. H. W. Arndt, 'The Role of China in World and Australian Trade': I am grateful to Professor Arndt for letting me see this unpublished paper.

20. Mao's goals

1. No one knows just what China's population growth rate has been in the 1960s, and there is some debate about

the 1950s as well. The official estimate of the rate of growth of China's population for the 1953—57 period is 2.2 per cent, but one observer in China (Ma Yin-ch'u), felt that this was an understatement. Some analysts outside China give estimates that fall below 2 per cent for the 1950s and 1960s, but these estimates would make China's rate of population growth significantly below that of virtually all other developing countries.

2. The reasoning behind Peking's decision to import grain was, of course, complex and related to many elements besides the nationwide level of per capita consumption. Still it is unlikely that China would have long continued to import grain if per capita output had been rising by say more than 1 per cent a year. For a discussion of many of these issues see, A. Donnithorne, *China's Grain: output, procurement, transfers and trade,* Economic Research Centre, The Chinese University of Hong Kong, 1970.

3. There has been in recent years a flood of literature on the pros and cons of various outsiders' estimates of China's grain output in the 1960s. Estimates for 1965, for example, range from 180 million tons to 258 million tons. My own reasons for believing that the range of plausible estimates is considerably narrower than this can be found in my 'Economic growth in China and the Cultural Revolution', *China Quarterly,* Apr.—June 1967, pp. 33—48.

4. Some parts of light industry (e.g. bicycles, chemical fibres) could have grown and probably did grow faster than the farm sector, but these were not the dominant light industries.

5. These figures can be found in numerous sources. For my views on the subject see my, 'Economic growth in China and the Cultural Revolution'.

6. Apparently there was still some disruption in 1969, however. See, for example, the discussion in P. Bridgham, 'Mao's Cultural Revolution: the struggle to consolidate power', *China Quarterly,* Jan.—Mar. 1970, p. 22.

7. If industrial output in 1957 (in 1952 prices) was 24 billion *yuan* (T. C. Liu and K. C. Yeh, *The Economy of*

481

the Chinese Mainland, Princeton University Press, 1965, p. 66) and that of 1965 was about 37 billion *yuan* (see note 5), and if 1969 output was the same as 1966, and 1966 was say 10 per cent above 1965, then the rate of growth of industry would have been 4.4 per cent a year. Different assumptions would, of course, give one different estimates. If, for example, 1969 output was 10 per cent above 1966 or 22 per cent above 1965, then industrial output for the whole 1957–69 period would have risen at an average annual rate of 5.3 per cent .

8. Prior to 1949, the small modern industrial sector grew at a fairly rapid rate (see J. K. Chang, *Industrial Development in Pre-Communist China*, Chicago, Aldine Press, 1969), but the pace in the rest of the economy probably barely matched a population growth rate of less than 1 per cent a year (see my *Agricultural Development in China, 1368–1968*, Chicago, Aldine Press, 1969, pp. 29–32).

9. In absolute terms China's growth rate is similar to that of the United States, but in per capita terms it is lower (because China's population growth rate has been higher).

10. There is no precise growth rate of agriculture that China must achieve if she is to sustain rapid industrialization, but a rate at least 1 per cent a year above the rate of increase in population is probably necessary if grain purchases for the cities are to be reasonably voluntary and rural incentives not too badly damaged.

11. This is a sweeping statement and rests on little but the author's judgement.

12. These figures for India were taken from a paper by G. F. Papanek, 'Comparative development strategies: India and Pakistan'. The growth rate figures are for 1959/60–1968/69, and the investment figures are an average of the years 1959/60, 1964/65, and 1967/68. The latter are gross and given as a percentage of GDP. Excluding foreign aid, the Indian investment rate was 13.5 per cent.

13. The clearest statement of this proposition can be found in J. Gray, 'Mao's economic thoughts', *Far Eastern Economic Review*, 15 Jan. 1970, pp. 16–18, but Gray

is only saying explicitly what numerous others have implied, albeit a bit more cautiously.

14. See Ragnar Nurkse's *Problems of Capital Formation in Underdeveloped Countries*, 1953, and Gunnar Myrdal's *An International Economy,* 1956 (repr. Harper & Row 1969). Myrdal in *Asian Drama*, 1967, Allen Lane and Penguin Books, 1968, is considerably more circumspect about the possible gains from this source.

15. See, for example, R. Kojima, 'Formation of the Great Leap Forward policy' (in Japanese), *Ajia Keizai,* Dec. 1969, pp. 47–73.

16. There are analysts on all points of the ideological spectrum that argue that one should not only read between the lines of Mao's statements, but behind them. Although there is always a problem of interpretation, this paper is based on a belief that Mao means what he says. For further thoughts along this line see B. I. Schwartz, 'Modernization and the Maoist vision: some reflections on Chinese Communist goals', *Communism and China: ideology in flux,* Harvard University Press, 1968, pp. 162–85.

17. This passage is from the English language version, p. 310.

18. Mao Tse-tung's speech at the Lushan Conference, 23 July 1959, in *Selections from China Mainland Magazines* (Supplement) No. 21, p. 16.

19. This, at least, is my interpretation of what Mao means when he speaks of the Standing Committee being divided into two fronts. See, Speech at a Work Conference of the Central Committee, 25 Oct. 1966, in *Current Background,* No. 891. p. 75.

20. M. R. Goldman, *Literary Dissent in Communist China,* Harvard University Press, 1967, p. 149.

21. Mao Tse-tung, 'The question of agricultural cooperation', 31 July 1955, in R. Bowie and J. K. Fairbank, *Communist China 1955–1959,* Harvard University Press, 1962, p. 98.

22. Mao Tse-tung, 'On the Ten Great Relationships', April 1956, in J. Ch'En, *Mao,* New York, Prentice–Hall, 1969, p. 73.

23. *Ibid.*, pp. 68–70.

24. Mao Tse-tung's speech at the Lushan Conference, p. 14.
25. This programme was 'basically passed' in late 1957 and played an important role in the subsequent two years. See discussion of this in H. F. Schurmann, *Ideology and Organization in Communist China,* University of California Press, 1966, pp. 199–202.
26. *National Program for Agricultural Development 1956–1967,* Peking, Foreign Languages Press, 1960, pp. 11–12.
27. Mao Tse-tung's speech at the Lushan Conference, p. 16. I have reversed the sentence order to make the quote read smoothly. The context makes it clear that Mao is talking about economic policy.
28. Mao Tse-tung, speech delivered at the Supreme State Conference (excerpts), 28 Jan. 1958, in *SCMM* (Supplement), No. 21, p. 2. This speech includes references specifically endorsing the forty points of the National Programme.
29. Mao Tse-tung's speech at the Lushan Conference, p. 17.
30. *Ibid.,* pp. 16–17.
31. For a further discussion of this point, see S. Schram, *The Political Thought of Mao Tse-tung* (revised edn.), University of California Press, 1969, p. 71 and elsewhere.
32. Mao Tse-tung, speech delivered at the Supreme State Conference, p. 3.
33. Mao Tse-tung, speech at the Symposium of Group Leaders of the Enlarged Meeting of the Military Affairs Commission (excerpts), 28 June 1958, *SCMM* (Supplement), No. 21, p. 5.
34. 'The situation in the summer of 1957', July 1957, *Current Background,* No. 891, p. 25.
35. Mao Tse-tung's speech at the Lushan Conference, p. 12.
36. *Ibid.,* p. 18.
37. Speech Delivered by Mao Tse-tung at the Tenth Plenum of the Eighth CCP Central Committee, 24 Sept. 1962, in *SCMM* (Supplement), No. 21, p. 39.
38. *Ibid.,* p. 41.
39. This was reported in wall posters published in *Mainichi* (Tokyo) on 9 Mar. 1967.

40. Malraux, *Antimemoirs,* New York, Holt, Rinehart & Winston, 1968, pp. 391–2.
41. Mao Tse-tung, The Great Leap Forward of China, 1964, in *SCMM* (Supplement), No. 21, p. 43.
42. See discussion of this and subsequent points in my, 'Economic growth in China and the Cultural Revolution', pp. 43–8.
43. Malraux, p. 394.
44. For a discussion of this aspect of the Tachai brigade and its spread to other parts of the country see M. K. Whyte, 'The Tachai Brigade and Incentives for the Peasant', *Current Scene,* 15 Aug. 1969.
45. Malraux, p. 393.

21. International reactions to the new China

1. *Peking Review,* 44, 2 Nov. 1962, p. 14.
2. Sun Yat-sen, 1929 (trs. Frank W. Price, ed. L. T. Chen), *San Min Chu I.* Shanghai, 1929.
3. Francis Watson, *The Frontiers of China,* New York and Washington, 1966, Praeger.
4. *Ibid.*
5. K. M. Panikkar, *The Future of South-East Asia,* New York, Macmillan; London, Allen & Unwin, 1943.
6. Nicholas John Spykman (ed. H. R. Nicholl, Intro. F. S. Dunn), *The Geography of the Peace.* New York, Harcourt Brace, 1943; repr. Hamden, Conn., Shoe String Press, 1969.
7. Jawaharlal Nehru, 1960, *The Discovery of India* (1st edn. 1946). London, New York, Asia Publishing House.
8. K. M. Panikkar, *In Two Chinas,* London, Allen & Unwin, 1955.
9. Text first released by the Chinese Government on 1 Sept. 1963 in 'Statement by the spokesman of the Chinese Government – a comment on the Soviet Government's statement of 21 August'.
10. Charles Neuhauser, 1968, *Third World politics. China and the Afro–Asian People's Solidarity Organization 1957–67.* Harvard University Press.
11. Sun Yat-sen, *op. cit.*

22. The Maoist revolutionary model in Asia

1. Mao Tse-tung, in an interview with Edgar Snow, 23 July 1936; quoted in Stuart R. Schram, *The Political Thought of Mao Tse-tung,* London, Pall Mall Press, 1967, p. 256.
2. *For A Lasting Peace, For a People's Democracy,* 30 Dec. 1949, and *Pravda,* 4 Jan. 1950; cited in Charles B. McLane's *Soviet Strategies in Southeast Asia,* Princeton University Press, 1966, p. 366.
3. *Ibid.,* 27 Jan. 1950; cited in McLane, p. 366.
4. Schram (p. 193) describes the central concepts as the annihilation of the enemy, rather than the occupation of territory and the concentration of force overwhelmingly superior to that of the enemy in each engagement, although the enemy may be vastly superior in the overall balance of forces. Alice Langley Hsieh lists the essentials of Mao's strategic thought as: '(1) rejection of the concept of a quick, decisive war based on purely military considerations, in favour of a view of war as the totality of political, economic, psychological and military factors. (2) emphasis on the concepts of strategic withdrawal, avoidance of decisive battles and even temporary abandonment of territory in the early stage of the war, in the interest of eventual victory. (3) belief in initiation of the strategic offensive only when the balance of total strength was in the Communists' favour and their victory certain. (4) subordination of the strictly military viewpoint of the professional soldier to the political—military objectives of the revolution, of the army to the Party, of weapons to man and of short-term success to long-term victory.' (*Communist China's Strategy in the Nuclear Era.*)
5. Conrad Brandt, Benjamin Schwartz, John K. Fairbanks, *A Documentary History of Chinese Communism* (New York, Atheneum, 1966), Mao's recent 'discovery' of the need for continuation of class struggle or revolution within a socialist society after the seizure of power by the proletariat has been raised to the level of theory, and according to Peking, the Chairman has thus attained equal rank with Marx and Lenin as a theoretician.
6. John H. Kautsky, in his *Moscow and the Communist*

Party of India (M.I.T. Press, 1956), defined the essential characteristic of what he called 'the neo-Maoist strategy' as a united front which appeals to the national bourgeoisie not through the alliance with their principal parties but directly or 'from below'. This hardly seems to be a startlingly new approach to the winning over of 'non-revolutionary classes' in the national democratic stage of the Asian Revolution, nor does it seem to be the distinguishing feature of Mao's 'united front' strategy. The Leninist, the Stalinist and the Maoist models of an Asian national democratic united front have all been ready to distinguish the good and the bad bourgeoisie on political rather than economic grounds and appeals have always been made to the bourgeoisie on an individual basis (i.e. 'from below') as well as to their political organs (i.e. 'from above').

7. Lin Piao, 'Long Live the Victory of People's War', *Peking Review*, vol. 8, No. 36, 1965, pp. 9—30.
8. *The Polemic on the General Line of the International Communist Movement*, p. 369.
9. In contrast to the Chinese emphasis on the role of the Party is the Regis Debray or Castro revolutionary thesis, which proclaims the heresy that 'the vanguard [of the revolution] is not necessarily the Marxist—Leninist party'. (Debray, *Revolution in the Revolution*, New York, Monthly Review Press, 1967, p. 99.) This concept is the parallel in violent revolution to the 'national democratic state' concept in peaceful transition. It is thus equally revisionist, as it denies the necessity for hegemony by the Communist Party. For a Chinese criticism of the Debray thesis, see 'Letters from China', Mar. 1968, by Anna Louise Strong (New World Press, 3 vols., 1963—65).
10. Mao Tse-tung, 'Problems of war and strategy', *Selected Works of Mao Tse-tung*, vol. ii.
11. Lin Piao.
12. *Ibid.*
13. 'The proletarian revolution and Khrushchev's Revisionism', *Polemic on the General Line of the International Communist Movement*, p. 393; emphasis added.

14. Li Wei-han, 'The struggle for proletarian leadership in the period of the new democratic revolution in China', *Peking Review,* 2 Mar. 1962. Li was a member of the CCP Central Committee and the Director of the Party's United Front Work Department.

15. Li Wei-han, 'The United Front, a magic weapon of the Chinese people for winning victory', *Peking Review,* 9 June 1961.

16. *People's Daily,* 7 Nov. 1960.

17. *Ibid.*

18. Mao Tse-tung, 'Introductory remarks to the Communists', *Selected Works,* iii, p. 54.

19. For the text of the Chinese draft declaration presented by Ambassador Wang P'ing-nan at the Warsaw meeting with US Ambassador U. Alexis Johnson, see Kenneth T. Young's *Negotiating With the Chinese Communists,* McGraw-Hill, 1968.

20. J. H. Brimmell, *Communism in Southeast Asia,* Oxford University Press, 1959, p. 333.

21. David Wilson, 'China and Thailand', *China Quarterly,* July–Sept. 1967.

22. The Chinese released the text of this memorandum in *The Polemic on the General Line of the International Communist Movement,* p. 105.

23. 'The proletarian revolution and Khrushchev's revisionism', editorial departments of *People's Daily* and *Red Flag,* 31 Mar. 1964; text carried in *The Polemic . . .,* p. 372.

    After Khrushchev's report to the 20th Congress of the CPSU, Mao told the Second Plenary Session of the CCP Eighth Central Committee that Khrushchev now said, 'it is possible to gain political power by the parliamentary road, that is to say it is no longer necessary for all countries to learn from the October Revolution. Once this gate is opened, Leninism by and large is thrown out'. (Quoted in joint editorial 1 May 1970, of *Red Flag, People's Daily,* and *Liberation Daily.*)

24. The new Ceylon government demanded the withdrawal of British bases, and an agreement to that effect was signed in October 1957. Perhaps most encouraging to

the Chinese was the revolt in Iraq and that country's withdrawal from the Baghdad Pact in August 1958.

25. The same problem existed outside Asia. In the UAR, Communist leaders were in jail, and in India the Communist government of Kerala was dismissed in 1959 by the central government. In Guinea and Ghana the Communist Party was outlawed.

26. Mikhail Kremnyov, 'Africa in search of new paths', *World Marxist Review*, 6, No. 8 (Aug. 1963), pp. 72–6; cited in William E. Griffith's *Sino–Soviet Relations 1964–1965*, MIT Press, 1967, p. 52.

27. 'For the unity and solidarity of the international Communist movement', *Pravda*, 6 Dec. 1963; quoted from *Digest of the Soviet Press*, 15, No. 47, 18 Dec. 1963; cited by Griffith, p. 52. Griffith also cites Khrushchev's remark in 1963 that while a national democratic state (that is, one which tolerated the Communist Party) was preferable, 'other forms of development along the path of national liberation and social progress' are possible. ('Replies of N. S. Khrushchev to Questions of Editors of the *Ghanaian Times, Alger Republican, Le Peuple,* and *Botataung,*' *Pravda* and *Izvestiya,* 22 Dec. 1963.)

28. Lin Piao, p. 22. D. N. Aidit, the former leader of the PKI, employed this same imagery in a speech in May 1965. But it is even more interesting that the city–country symbolism was first developed in the programme of the Sixth Congress of the Communist International in 1928, which stated: 'Colonies and semi-colonies are also important in the transition period because they represent the world rural district in relation to the industrial countries, which represent the world city.'

29. Andrew C. Janos, 'Communist theory of state and revolution', in *Communism and Revolution*, p. 40.

30. Lin Piao, p. 24.

31. Quoted in F. E. Liu, *A Military History of Modern China, 1924–1949,* p. 206.

32. Phnom Penh Domestic Radio, 6 Mar. 1968.

33. Lin Piao (1965).

Further reading

Note: In each section the works cited are arranged in a suggested order of reading.

General introductory works

C. P. FITZGERALD, *The Chinese View of Their Place in the World*, London, Oxford University Press, 1964.

PEARL BUCK, *The Good Earth*, London, Methuen, 1931. (An outstanding novel; many subsequent editions.)

MARC RIBOUD, *The Three Banners of China*, New York, Macmillan, 1966.

F. GREENE, *The Wall Has Two Sides*, London, Jonathan Cape, 1962.

EDGAR SNOW, *The Other Side of the River*, London, Gollancz, 1963.

DICK WILSON, *A Quarter of Mankind: An Anatomy of China Today*, London, Weidenfeld & Nicolson, 1966.

NIGEL CAMERON and BRIAN BRAKE, *Peking: A Tale of Three Cities*, Tokyo, Weatherhill, 1965.

Geography

A. HERMANN, *An Historical Atlas of China*, new edn., Edinburgh, Edinburgh University Press, 1966.

HAROLD FULLARD, ed., *China in Maps*, London, Philip, 1968.

GEORGE B. CRESSEY, *Land of the 500 Million*, New York, McGraw-Hill, 1955.

YI-FU TUAN, *China*, London, Longman, 1970.

T. R. TREGEAR, *A Geography of China,* London, University of London Press, 1965.

KEITH BUCHANAN, *The Transformation of the Chinese Earth,* London, Bell, 1970.

NAVAL INTELLIGENCE DIVISION, London, The Admiralty, *China Proper*, 3 vols, London, 1945.

History

L. CARRINGTON GOODRICH, *A Short History of the Chinese People,* London, Allen & Unwin, 1972.

K. S. LATOURETTE, *A History of Modern China,* Harmondsworth, Penguin Books, 1954.

HENRY McALEAVY, *The Modern History of China,* London, Weidenfeld & Nicolson, 1967.

EDWARD SCHAFER, *The Golden Peaches of Samarkand,* Berkeley and Los Angeles, University of California Press, 1963.

EDWARD SCHAFER, *The Vermilion Bird: T'ang images of the South*, Berkely and Los Angeles, University of California Press, 1967.

NIGEL CAMERON, *Barbarians and Mandarins: thirteen centuries of western travellers in China*, New York, Weatherhill, 1970.

MAURICE COLLIS, *Foreign Mud,* London, Faber, 1946.

ARTHUR WALEY, *The Opium War Through Chinese Eyes,* London, Allen & Unwin, 1958.

EDGAR SNOW, *Red Star Over China,* New York, Grove Press, 1961.

Cultural development

C. P. FITZGERALD, *China: A Short Cultural History,* London, Cresset Press, 1950.

RENE GROUSSET, *The Rise and Splendour of the Chinese Empire*, Berkeley and Los Angeles, University of California Press, 1953.

J. NEEDHAM, *Science and Civilisation in China*, Cambridge, Cambridge University Press, vol. i, 1954 — vol. iv, pt 3, 1971, continuing.

RALPH C. CROIZIER, ed., *China's Cultural Legacy and Communism,* New York, Praeger, 1970.

Modern leadership

L. SHARMAN, *Sun Yat Sen: his life and its meaning,* New York, John Day, 1934.

EMILY HAHN, *Chiang Kai Shek, an unauthorized biography,* Garden City, Doubleday, 1955.

B. F. SCHWARTZ, *Chinese Communism and the Rise of Mao*, Cambridge, Mass., Harvard University Press, 1951.

JEROME CH'EN, *Mao and the Chinese Revolution*, London, Oxford University Press, 1965.

STUART R. SCHRAM, *The Political Thought of Mao Tse Tung,* London, Pall Mall Press, 1967.

LEO GOODSTADT, *Mao Tse Tung: the search for plenty,* Hong Kong, Longman, 1972.

MAO TSE-TUNG, *Selected Works*, vols. i–iv, Peking, Foreign Languages Press, 1967.

Economy and society

R. H. TAWNEY, *Land and Labour in China,* London, Allen & Unwin, 1932.

WALTER MALLORY, *China, Land of Famine,* New York, American Geographical Society, 1926.

HSIAO-TUNG FEI, *Peasant Life in China,* London, Routledge, 1947.

JOHN LOSSING BUCK, *Land Utilization in China,* New York, Council on Economic and Cultural Affairs, 1956.

PING-TI HO, *Studies on the Population of China 1368–1953*, Cambridge, Mass., Harvard University Press, 1959.

CHALMERS A. JOHNSON, *Peasant Nationalism and Communist Power*, Stanford, Stanford University Press, 1962.

PING-CHIA KUO, *China: New Age and New Outlook,* Harmondsworth, Penguin Books, 1960.

T. J. HUGHES and D. E. T. LUARD, *The Economic Development of Communist China 1949–56*, London, Oxford University Press, 1960.

YUAN-LI WU, *An Economic Survey of Communist China,* New York, Bookman, 1956.

JAN MYRDAL, *Report from a Chinese Village,* New York, Pantheon, 1965.

AUDREY DONNITHORNE, *China's Economic System,* London, Allen & Unwin, 1967.

JOINT ECONOMIC COMMITTEE, US Congress, *An Economic Profile of Mainland China,* Washington, Government Printing Office, 1967.

JAN S. PRYBYLA, *The Political Economy of Communist China,* Scranton, International Textbook Company, 1970.

JOHN M. H. LINDBECK (ed.), *China: Management of a Revolutionary Society,* Washington, University of Washington Press, 1971.

JOINT ECONOMIC COMMITTEE, US Congress, *People's Republic of China: an economic assessment,* Washington, Government Printing Office, 1972.

JOHN WILSON LEWIS, ed., *The City in Communist China,* Stanford, Stanford University Press, 1971.

International relations

W. G. EAST, O. H. K. SPATE and C. A. FISHER, eds., *The Changing Map of Asia,* London, Methuen, 1971.

W. A. DOUGLAS JACKSON, *Russo–Chinese Borderlands,* Princeton, Van Nostrand, 1962.

GEORGE MOSELEY, 'The frontier regions in China's international politics', in Jack Grey, ed., *Modern China's Search for a Political Form*, London, Oxford University Press, 1969.

DONALD S. ZAGORIA, *The Sino–Soviet Conflict*, London, University of London Press, 1962.

JOHN K. FAIRBANK, *The United States and China*, Cambridge, Mass., Harvard University Press, 1971.

BARBARA W. TUCHMAN, *Sand Against the Wind: Stilwell and the American experience in China 1911–45,* London, Macmillan, 1970.

Periodicals

China Quarterly, London.
Far Eastern Economic Review, Hong Kong.

Current Scene, Hong Kong.
Peking Review, Peking.
China Reconstructs, Peking.
Translations from China Mainland Press, Selections from China Mainland Magazines, Current Background, American Consulate General, Hong Kong (translations into English of material published in China).

Index

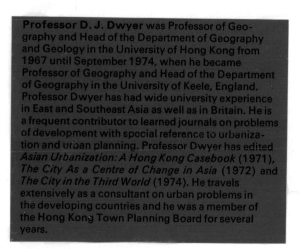

Professor D. J. Dwyer was Professor of Geography and Head of the Department of Geography and Geology in the University of Hong Kong from 1967 until September 1974, when he became Professor of Geography and Head of the Department of Geography in the University of Keele, England. Professor Dwyer has had wide university experience in East and Southeast Asia as well as in Britain. He is a frequent contributor to learned journals on problems of development with special reference to urbanization and urban planning. Professor Dwyer has edited *Asian Urbanization: A Hong Kong Casebook* (1971), *The City As a Centre of Change in Asia* (1972) and *The City in the Third World* (1974). He travels extensively as a consultant on urban problems in the developing countries and he was a member of the Hong Kong Town Planning Board for several years.

J